5991

D0915281

THE DIVIDED SELF OF WILLIAM JAMES

This book offers a powerful new interpretation of the philosophy of William James. It focuses on the multiple directions in which James's philosophy moves and the inevitable tensions that arise as a result.

The first part of the book explores a range of James's doctrines in which he refuses to privilege any particular perspective, be it that of the scientist, moral agent, artist, or mystic. The second part of the book turns to those doctrines where James favors the perspective of mystical experience. Richard Gale then attempts to reconcile the relativistic tendencies with James's account of mystical experience. An appendix considers the distorted picture of James's philosophy that has been passed down to us through the interpretations of his work by John Dewey.

Such is the range of James's philosophy that this stimulating new approach will find readers among those interested in the history of modern philosophy, especially pragmatism, as well as in the history of ideas, religion, and American studies.

Richard M. Gale is a professor of philosophy at the University of Pittsburgh.

THE DIVIDED SELF
OF WILLIAM JAMES

RICHARD M. GALE

CAMBRIDGE
UNIVERSITY PRESS

PUBLISHED BY THE PRESS SYNDICATE OF THE UNIVERSITY OF CAMBRIDGE
The Pitt Building, Trumpington Street, Cambridge, United Kingdom

CAMBRIDGE UNIVERSITY PRESS
The Edinburgh Building, Cambridge CB2 2RU, UK   http://www.cup.cam.ac.uk
40 West 20th Street, New York, NY 10011-4211, USA   http://www.cup.org
10 Stamford Road, Oakleigh, Melbourne 3166, Australia

First published 1999

Printed in the United States of America

Typeface Baskerville 10/12 pt, *System* DeskTopPro$_{/UX}$® [BV]

*A catalog record for this book is available from
the British Library.*

Library of Congress Cataloging-in-Publication Data
Gale, Richard M. (date)
The divided self of William James / Richard M. Gale.
p.   cm.
Includes bibliographical references and index.
ISBN 0-521642-69-8
1. James, William, 1842–1910.   I. Title.
B945.J24G35   1999
191 – dc21   98-30477
CIP

ISBN 0 521 64269 8 hardback

for

Mari Mori

mother-in-law extraordinaire

Contents

Acknowledgments

I thank the following persons for helping me find my way as I fumbled along trying to understand William James: Graham Bird, Deborah Boyle, Vincent Colapietro, James Conant, Paul Edwards, Eugene Fontinell, David Gauthier, Peter Hare, Henry Jackman, Edward Madden, Richard Mullin, Robert Meyers, Gerald Myers, Ram Neta, Louis Pojman, Allen Poteshman, Alexander Pruss, Ruth Anna Putnam, Nicholas Rescher, Andrew Reck, John Roberts, David Schrader, Stephen Shaw, Ignas Skrupskelis, Timothy Sprigge, Ellen Suckiel, H. S. Thayer, John Tiles, William Wainwright, and Michael Wolraich. I owe a special debt to Zelda Gale for her excellent advice on how to make my book more readable. Barbara Folsom did an excellent job of copyediting my manuscript for Cambridge University Press, whose editor Terence Moore also gave me sage advice on how to improve the style of my book. I also wish to thank the University of Pittsburgh for granting me a one-term sabbatical leave, and moreover one year in advance of its due date. I feel very fortunate to have been a member of its philosophy department since 1964, where I have received a continuing education from its outstanding faculty and students over the years.

Most of all I thank Maya – "Celeste Maya" – for teaching me what life is all about through her inspiring presence during the past forty-one years.

Works by William James and others are referred to in the body of the book by abbreviations given in the Bibliography of Works Cited at the end of the book. I will use feminine pronouns in the Introduction and odd-numbered chapters and masculine ones in the even-numbered ones.

I hope that this book will appeal to a wider audience than just professional, academic philosophers, especially as William James tried so hard throughout his career to reach this wider audience. However, there will be occasions, such as in Chapters 5 and 6, where technical issues concerning meaning and truth are discussed, that will elude nonprofessionals, and I suggest that they just skim through these sections. Doing so should not undermine their grasp of the overall thesis of this book. I regret these technical asides, but there is no way to assess the adequacy of James's accounts of meaning and truth without engaging in them. What I most hope is that my readers, be they professional philosophers or not, will have fun reading this book. If they do, I shall have succeeded in capturing the true spirit of James's philosophy.

Introduction

William James (1842–1910) was considered America's leading philosopher and psychologist during his lifetime, a distinction that many still claim for him today, though Charles Sanders Peirce and John Dewey must be recognized as serious contenders for the former title. There is no need for this book to say much about James's life, as there already are numerous excellent biographies, in particular those by Ralph Barton Perry (*TC*), F. O. Matthiessen (*WJ*), Gay Wilson Allen (*WJ*), Jacques Barzun (*SWJ*), Howard Feinstein (*BWJ*), and George Cotkin (*WJ*). After a peripatetic childhood in which his father, the theologian Henry James, Sr., hustled him and his younger siblings, among whom was the novelist Henry James, Jr., from one European nation to another in search of an adequate education, and a brief stint as a painting student of William Morris Hunt, William entered the Lawrence Scientific School at Harvard in 1861. Upon graduation in 1864 he enrolled in the Harvard Medical School, completing the M.D. degree in 1869, with a year off to participate in Louis Agassiz's research expedition to Brazil. After suffering serious ill health and depression from 1869 to 1872, William became an instructor in physiology at Harvard, where he spent his entire career until his retirement in 1907. He rapidly moved up the academic ladder, becoming instructor in anatomy and physiology in 1873, assistant professor of physiology in 1876, assistant professor of philosophy in 1880 and full professor in 1885, and a professor of psychology in 1889. Additions will be made to this bare-bones biographical sketch when it will contribute to our understanding of his philosophy, which is the primary concern of this book.

The best way to characterize the philosophy of William James is to say that it is deeply rooted in the blues. It is the soulful expression of someone who has "paid his dues," someone who, like old wagon wheels, has been through it all. Whereas its immediate aim is to keep him sane and nonsuicidal – "to help him make it through the night" – its larger one is to help him find his way to physical and spiritual health. In this respect James is very much in the Nietzschean and Wittgensteinian mold. His is not a nihilistic V.D. blues of the "I have had my fun, if I don't get well no more" variety, but rather of the "I can get well and have my fun" sort. The deep difference between James and Dewey is that Dewey couldn't sing the blues if his life depended on it.

One form the blues takes for James is "The Many Selves Blues." James is about as complex and multitalented as a man can get. Within him are numerous potential selves each crying out for full self-actualization. This poses both an *engineering* and an *ontological* problem for him. The former consists in his genius and passion being almost limitless but his time being radically restricted, thereby creating a competition between his many different selves for sufficient time for self-realization. This conflict finds expression in a letter he wrote when he was twenty-six.

Whatever we are *not* doing is pretty sure to come to us at intervals, in the midst of our toil, and fill us with pungent regrets that it is lost to us. I have felt so about zoology whenever I was not studying it, about anthropology when studying physiology, about practical medicine lately, now that I am cut off from it, etc., etc.; and I conclude that that sort of nostalgia is a necessary incident of our having imaginations, and we must expect it more or less whatever we are about. (*LWJ* 1:128)

The same sentiment is found in this humorously exaggerated, though nevertheless seriously intentioned, autobiographical aside, written twenty-two years later in *The Principles of Psychology*.

I am often confronted by the necessity of standing by one of my empirical selves and relinquishing the rest. Not that I would not, if I could, be both handsome and fat and well dressed, and a great athlete, and make a million a year, be a wit, a *bon-vivant*, and a lady-killer, as well as a philosopher; a philanthropist, statesman, warrior, and African explorer, as well as a 'tone-poet' and saint. . . . But to make any one of them actual, the rest must more or less be suppressed. (*PP* 295)

James's highly fictionalized description of the "accomplished gentleman," who "has tasted of the essence of every side of human life, being sailor, hunter, athlete, scholar, fighter, talker, dandy, man of affairs, etc., all in one," is more of the same Walter Mittyish fantasizing (*PP* 1057).

Although James did not seriously contemplate actualizing all these selves, and certainly not pursuing all of these professions, he did want to find a way of life that would maximize the realization of the full range of feelings, thoughts, and emotions that these selves experienced. For James, every type of experience is revelatory of some aspect of reality; and thus the more rich and varied our experiences, the more aspects of reality we uncover and become intimate with. If there had been a virtual-reality machine available that could simulate the experiences of all these different selves, James would have gladly plugged into it, for this would have enabled him vicariously to know what it is like to be these many different selves. The conflict that James felt so acutely did not so much concern the choice of a profession, as has been contended by many of his psychobiographers, as it concerned what existential stance to take toward the world. In particular, should it be that of the scientist, religious believer, moral agent, aesthete, or mystic? A virtual-reality machine, however, would have failed to satisfy James's most basic underlying aspiration, namely, to be a free Promethean agent in respect to his own self-realization. It would not have been enough for all of his many selves to be actualized, resulting in his having the full range of experiences open to him. He had also to bring about this self-realization through his own free, morally responsible actions. His ultimate quest was to be a Promethean agent who was the right sort of active cause of his maximizing his full range of potentialities.

James's quest for full self-realization took an especially lustful form. What was required was not only that each of his many selves got actualized, or at least got actualized in the attenuated, vicarious manner that a virtual-reality machine would afford, but did so with maximal richness and variety. He comes across as a Kierkegaardian aesthete bent on seeking ever new and exciting experiences of all the Walter Mittyish varieties. To be sure, James craved the morally strenuous life above all else, but only when the proper healthy mood was upon him, and mainly because of the thrilling tingles he derived from it, "the stinging pain inside my breast-bone," as he described it in a letter to his wife (*CWJ* 4, 571). The thought that there are genuine possibilities "is what gives the palpitating reality to our moral life and makes it tingle . . . with so strange and elaborate excitement" (*WB* 183). One ought to postulate the existence of God "as a pretext for living hard, and getting out of the game of existence its keenest possibilities of zest" (*WB* 161). James's quest for the maximal array of zest and tingles makes him the ultimate hipster, a veritable experience junkie, even when it involves so seemingly stodgy an activity as the moral life.

There is a story about another famous hipster, Charlie Parker, that could almost be true of James. When the Bird was playing at a club on Fifty-second Street, he was once found by members of his group rolling around naked in the back of a garbage truck between sets. Thinking he was juiced, they pulled him out and asked him why he was doing this, to which he soberly replied that if you go out and do something different between sets, when you get back on the stand you might have a fresh idea. That could just as well have been William James, only he would have been rolling around naked in a pile of professional journals in the stacks of the Harvard library or, more likely, experimenting with laughing gas or mescaline in the hope that he might finally understand Hegel. He claims the former did the trick, but only while he was under its influence![1] Obviously, if the war on drugs is to succeed, Hegel must be banned, for he provides too great a temptation to his reader to get

[1] See Ralph Barton Perry (*TC* 161–2).

high ("Just say no to Hegel"). Both James's and Parker's exceedingly low threshold of boredom and wild passion for everything that life had to offer continually drove them to seek out new ways of experiencing the world. James's youthful passion for painting was one way in which he pursued his pluralistic need for novelty. Arthur O. Lovejoy remarked that "William James brought . . . to human nature, and the world of ideas, the artist's freshness and purity of vision" (*TP* 94). James also availed himself of the perspective of the novelist in his attempt to understand what made the world go round, this requiring that he penetrate to the inner consciousness of things in the way in which a novelist does for each of her fictional characters.

The thesis of this book is that James's underlying quest was to find a philosophy that would enable us, as the beer commercials enjoin, to have it all, to grab for all the gusto we can. Running throughout James's writings is an obsessive use of the metaphor of leaving all doors and windows open so as not to block any experience from entering in. "Philosophy, like life, must keep the doors and windows open" (*SPP* 55). Pluralism accepts "a universe unfinished, with doors and windows open to possibilities and uncontrollable in advance" (*SPP* 73; see also *ML* 412). "The most a philosophy can hope for is not to lock out any interest forever. No matter what door it closes, it must leave other doors open for the interests which it neglects" (*PU* 19). "When one's affections keep in touch with the divinity of the world's authorship. . . . It is as if all doors were opened, and all paths freshly smoothed" (*VRE* 373; see also 381). "Because the current of thought in academic circles runs against me . . . I feel like a man who must set his back against an open door quickly if he does not wish to see it closed and locked" (*VRE* 411). Even James's taste in architecture and landscaping gave expression to his desire for open doors and openness in general. His sister, Alice, quotes him as extolling the virtues of his summer home in Chocorua by saying, "Oh, it's the most delightful house you ever saw; it has fourteen doors, all opening outwards."[2] His son, Henry, wrote that "James was an insatiable lover of landscape, and particularly of wide 'views.' His inclination at Chocorua was to 'open' the view, to cut down obstructing trees, even at the expense of the foreground" (*LWJ* 1:272).

Sometimes he used the metaphor of lowering or bursting the dam to express the same sentiment: "Man lives *by* habits, indeed, but what he lives *for* is thrills and excitements. . . . The dams of routine burst, and boundless prospects open up" (*ERM* 122). Dickinson Miller, James's student, disciple, and close friend, as well as his most outlandishly unfair critic, claimed that because James sought for the full "richness and satisfaction of human life . . . he would have us open our minds to every

---

[2] Quoted from Perry (*TC* 175).

means, even the most unexpected or unaccredited. . . . 'Open doors and windows' to any idea, mood, attitude, propensity, that might possibly aid toward the great end" (*PA* 54–5). There is another possible biographical explanation for James's open door metaphor – his need to flee his family and find his own space just after each of his children was born. Gerald E. Myers, the best of all the James expositors, has suggested that this same penchant finds expression in James's metaphor for experience as being like the successive perchings and flights of a bird, the flights being his need to depart from home after a child's birth because "any perching-place was soon uncomfortable, including his own home."[3] James's attraction to the metaphors of open doors and lowered dams is the antithesis of the preferences of the hero of August Wilson's play *Fences*, who liked fences because they blocked intrusion from outside influences. James was especially concerned not to fence out intrusion from the supernatural cosmic consciousness that envelops our ordinary finite minds. "We with our lives are like islands in the sea . . . there is a continuum of cosmic consciousness against which our individuality builds but accidental fences, and into which our several minds plunge as into a mother-sea or reservoir" (*EPR* 374). The key point is that we not fence out this surrounding mother-sea of consciousness.

James realized that every actualization carries on its back an indefinite number of negative fleas – possibilities that go unrealized. If the table is blue, then it is not red, not yellow, and so on. If James is doing anatomy, then he is not doing anthropology, not doing zoology, and so on. In this vein, James poignantly asked, "Shall he follow his fancy for Amelia, *or* for Henrietta? – both cannot be the choice of his heart" (*WB* 154). This gives rise to "The Agony of Actualization Blues." James went so far as to characterize a choice between competing desires as "deliberately driving a thorn into one's flesh" (*PP* 1141), also as a "tragic situation" because "some part of the ideal must butchered" (*WB* 154).

James's personal horror at the thought that we have only a finite future duration, that all ends with our death at some future time, is based, no doubt, on the realization that the sort of maximally rich actualization of his many selves that he craved would require an unlimited amount of time. The letter he wrote to Alice about her imminent demise expresses his feeling that our worldly life is farcical, because our innermost ideals are infinite in their demands but we have only a finite time in which to realize them.

I know you've never cared for life, and to me, now at the age of nearly fifty, life and death seem singularly close together in all of us – *and life a mere*

---

[3] Introduction to *The Correspondence of William James*, xliii.

farce of frustration in all, so far as the realization of the innermost ideals go to which we are made respectively capable of feeling an infinity and responding. (*LTR* 1:310; my italics)

His famous "farewell" letter to his dying father also expresses a feeling of regret about the brevity of one's life. "And it comes strangely over me in bidding you good-bye how a life is but a day and expresses mainly but a single note. It is so much like the act of bidding an ordinary good-night" (*LTR* 1:220). In response to those who eschewed consideration of what the indefinite or unlimited future held in store in favor of a more short-range view, James claimed that "the mind with the shortest views is simply the mind of the more shallow man" (*P* 56). Common to all religions is the faith that "Perfection is eternal" (*WB* 29), that "an ideal order . . . shall be permanently preserved" (*P* 55). In a remarkable letter he wrote when sixteen, James heartily endorses Rousseau's claim that "Life is gone in an instant. In itself it is nothing. Its value depends upon the use to which you put it. The good which you have done is lasting and that alone, – and life is valuable only by that good" (*CWJ* 4, 13). If we cannot last forever, at least we can produce something that will. Such immortality is a distant second best for James; he would have resonated to Woody Allen's remark, "I don't want to achieve immortality through my works but by living forever."

It is interesting to note that for agents intent on achieving full or unlimited actualization of all their many different selves there is an important conceptually based temporal asymmetry between their attitudes toward the past and the future: Whereas they regret that their future existence is finite they do not regret in the same way that their past existence is. The reason for this is that whereas their past finitude does not limit their possibilities for full or unlimited self-realization, their future finiteness does. For James, it is tragic that we are not temporal fatmen in the future direction, for what we need for full or unlimited self-actualization is enough time, and there never is enough. While all of a self-realizer's present first-order intentions might require only a finite future time for their realization, it is an essential part of this self-realizer's agenda to have the second-order intention always to have a new intention, always to have her projected horizon recede as she succeeds in satisfying former intentions; and, thus, death always represents a cutting off of her possibility for a fuller self-realization of her inherent potentialities.

The *engineering* problem – "The Agony of Actualization Blues" – admits only of amelioration through making the best use we can of our limited time. In contradistinction, the *ontological* problem arises from a clash between the perspectives and interests of James's many selves. Henry Adams claimed that James "was disabled by the multiplicity of his experiences, each with its shock and mystery, each implying its own world, each world different.''[4] Eugene Fontinell did not exaggerate when he wrote that ''James's 'scientific' bent, combined with his religious sensibility, gave rise to what at times appears to be almost schizophrenia'' (*SGI* 113). This creates ''The Divided Self Blues.'' Who are these different selves, and how are they to achieve unification? The underlying thesis of this book is that the primary clash was between James's Promethean and mystical selves, and the ultimate aim was to find some way in which he could unify them, or at least reconcile them with each other so that they could lie down together in peace.

I. The Promethean Pragmatist

As a result of Ralph Barton Perry's masterpiece, *The Thought and Character of William James*, the ''official'' view has become that James's ''Divided Self Blues'' involves a conflict between his scientific and religious-moral aspirations (see especially 122 and 259). Pragmatism is seen as James's way of healing this breach within his divided self by showing that there is a pragmatic method for determining both meanings and truths that these opposing selves share in common, thereby allowing him to actualize both of these selves with a clear conscience. For, if one of them is legitimate, so is the other; and, since no one wants to deny the legitimacy of science, religion and morality ride the coat tails of science to respectability, being subject to all of the rights and privileges thereunto appertaining. Pragmatism, thereby, serves as the ultimate mediator or reconciler – but, as we shall see, not the synthesizer or unifier – between his tough- and tender-minded selves.

Charles Morris rightly characterized the overall tenor of James's philosophy as the '' 'Promethean' or 'pioneer' type . . . favored by young American culture'' (*PM* 11).[5] James's preferred term for his philosophy was ''humanism,'' according to which the world is, as F. C. S. Schiller had said, ''what we make of it'' (*P* 117).[6] Metaphorically, it says that

[4] Quoted from Neil Coughlan (*YD* 112).
[5] John McDermott, in chapter 3 of *SE*, also uses the term ''Promethean'' to characterize the philosophy of James. James preferred the word ''humanism'' for his philosophy. To my knowledge, he used ''Prometheus'' only twice. In an unpublished notebook of 1903, he suggested as the motto for his planned magnum opus on metaphysics the following quote from *Moby Dick*: ''God help thee, old man, thy thoughts have created a creature in thee; and he whose intense thinking thus makes him a Prometheus; a vulture feeds upon that heart for ever; that vulture the very creature he creates'' (*MEN* xix). Another occurrence is in a letter to Thomas Davidson in 1882. ''In saying 'God exists' all I imply is that my purposes are cared for by a mind so powerful as on the whole to control the drift of the universe. This is as much polytheism as monotheism. As a matter of fact it is neither, for it is hardly a speculative position at all, but a merely practical and emotional faith which I fancy even your Promethean *Gemuth* shares'' (quoted from Edward Madden's introduction to *WB* xxix).
[6] James also used ''humanism'' to mean that, ''though one part of our experience may lean upon another part to make it what it is in any one of several aspects in which it may be considered, experience as a whole is self-containing and leans on nothing'' (*MT* 72).

"the trail of the human serpent is . . . over everything," meaning that human interests and endeavors are omnipresent, coloring not only the way in which we depict reality but even the very nature of this reality (*P* 37).[7] It will be seen that our interests, along with the actions guided by them, play a crucial role in determining the following: which world, among the many possible worlds, is the actual one; an idea's truth; the existence of value and obligation; meaning and reference; the distinction between the mental and the physical; and even our own personal identity over time. In all these cases we make things to be a certain way by freely taking them to be so. There is a sensorily given that is independent of our will and that imposes limitations on what we can create, in the way in which a marble block limits the creative possibilities of the sculptor. By taking the given in a certain way we create meaning and value, and fashion a cosmos out of a fluid and fugitive chaos.

There are several sources for James's Promethean vision of man. His depiction of man as a creator of a cosmos out of the "big, blooming, buzzing confusion" of the sensorily given, in addition to being deeply rooted in James's artistic nature, also derives from the surrounding culture of his day. On the one hand, there is the myth of the American pioneer who carves a human habitat out of a wilderness that continued to have inspiring influence in spite of the actual disappearance of the physical frontier. James had a "vision of a world to be organized, not one found in tidy completion," as Jacques Barzun aptly said (*SWJ* 199). The clearing of forest land by North Carolina mountaineers is glorified by James, although not without serious reservations, as Ellen Suckiel has pointed out to me, as "a very paean of duty, struggle, and success" (*TT* 134). He even delighted in posing for pictures at Chocorua looking every inch like a backwoodsman. According to Horace Kallen, James gave "an expression of what was noblest in the life and labor of the pioneer generation that in the nineteenth century brought into growth the arts and sciences of industrial civilization" (*ML* 55).

James failed to notice that this definition is logically distinct from the Schillerian one in that someone could be a thoroughgoing materialist and thus qualify as a humanist in the *MT* sense, and yet be an ardent scientific realist, and thus not qualify as a humanist in the Schillerian sense.

[7] An interesting question is why James chose a pejorative way of designating his beloved doctrine. Both he and his father, at various places in their writings, used the unqualified phrase "the trail of the serpent" to designate something as evil; for example, William speaks of "the trail of the serpent of rationalism" (*P* 16). So why should "the trail of the *human* serpent" represent something we should be happy about? I can think of two possible explanations, which can be used singly or together. His usage was a tongue-in-cheek ploy to disarm his rationalist or intellectualist opponents by diplomatically letting them know he is aware that they will see a form of evil in it and, furthermore, by expressing some sympathy for their point of view. Another explanation is that he himself, or at least one of his many selves, aspired to objective truth and thereby viewed his brand of humanism as a booby prize. We shall see that the mystical self of James did reach out for just such a truth about the true nature of reality.

Another source of James's Prometheanism was the technological breakthroughs that modern science made possible and which produced an unbridled optimism that there would be unlimited progress in the future. James experienced in his life the transition from trails to rails.[8] Barzun has pointed out that between 1889 and 1914 "nearly every idea of the twentieth century was hatched" (*SWJ* 182). Among the inventions were the automobile, the airplane, the movies, the X-ray, the wireless, and the use of electricity to power the factory, home, and city.

The greatest source of inspiration for the Promethean view, however, was supplied by Darwinian biological psychology, which depicted a human being as an organism whose mind was an instrument for securing a favorable adjustment with the environment. "*The pursuance of future ends and the choice of means for their attainment are thus the mark and criterion of the presence of mentality* in a phenomenon" (*PP* 21). Our biological nature determines us to be creatures continually on the make. "The current of life which runs in at our eyes or ears is meant to run out at our hands, feet, or lips . . . perception and thinking are only there for behavior's sake" (*WB* 92). The "I think" that Kant claimed to be an accompaniment of our every mental act or state is enriched by James with the "I will": "the last of presuppositions is not merely . . . that 'I think' must accompany all my representations, but also that 'I will' must dominate all my thinking" (*WB* 103). James Edie has pointed out that, for James, "There is a 'subjunctive' aspect of perceptual experience, and this is the reason why Husserl and Merleau-Ponty say that consciousness, on this primary level of experience, is more of an 'I can do' than an 'I think that,' an invitation to exploration rather than to contemplation" (*WJP* 5).

Darwinian evolutionary theory showed that when we are confronted with an object "the germinal question . . . is not the theoretic 'What is that?' but the practical 'Who goes there?' or rather . . . 'What is to be done?' " (*PP* 941). Herein James anticipated the recent movie starring Joe Louis, Ginger Rogers, and Clint Eastwood, *Duck, Dance, or Draw*. The point of the movie's title is the necessity of being prepared to act toward objects in a way that will be practically beneficial. All of our concepts, therefore, are teleological instruments that we have forged to aid us in gaining power over our environment by depicting objects in a way that tells us how we should act toward them – fight them, dance with them, make love to them, shoot them, shake hands with them, attempt to dissolve them in aqua regia, and the like. Toward this end, James's pragmatic theory of meaning reduces the meaning of a concept to a set of conditionalized predictions that connect action with experience, such a prediction being of the form "If we perform an action A,

---

[8] For a fuller account see Daniel W. Bjork (*CS* 2–5).

then we shall have some experience E." Armed with a battery of concepts that present us with these conditionalized predictions, we can act upon the objects that confront us in a way that will satisfy our needs and desires. Even metaphysical doctrines are so rendered: theism, for example, is reduced to the conditionalized prediction that if we collectively exert our best moral effort, good will win out over evil in the long run. This is the central tenet of James's beloved religion of meliorism and becomes the prime candidate for a "will-to-believe" option, in which we are morally permitted to believe upon insufficient evidence or epistemic warrant when doing so helps to bring about an overall desirable state of affairs. An idea or belief becomes true when the actions based on it produce the desired practical results of satisfying these needs and desires, and in many cases it is we who bring about these results, often as a result of our prior will-to-believe–based acceptance of some evidentially or epistemically nonwarranted proposition.

What follows is a brief overview of my book whose purpose is to supply the reader with a synoptic vision of how the different chapters hang together. Chapter 1 will show how James's Darwinian-based Prometheanism gives rise to a type of utilitarian ethical theory that holds us to be morally obligated always to act so as to maximize desire-satisfaction, that is, to act in a way that enables us, if not to have it all, to have as much of it as we can under the given circumstances. Since we are determined by our very biological nature to be always intent on satisfying some felt need or desire, it seems reasonable to make the attainment of this our moral ideal. For what other end could we have? James's naturalization of ethics resembles the attempt of natural law theorists to deduce normative conclusions from a scientifically based account of man's nature, with the exception that James did not think that the former is entailed by the latter, agreeing with Hume that *ought* does not follow logically from *is*. Rather, given the scientific account, the normative conclusion appears to be the only practically viable alternative open to us human beings. To ask whether it really is good for us to act in accordance with our nature is an idle question in just the way that a skepticism-in-general is. The challenge of the deontologist, who holds there to be intrinsically valuable states, such as justice, will figure prominently in the discussion, the outcome of which will be that James must find some way to accommodate these deontological moral intuitions within his desire-satisfaction maximizing ethical theory.

Chapter 2 will show that belief is an *action* for James in the sense that we can either believe at will (intentionally, voluntarily, on purpose) or at will do things, such as acting as if we believe, that shall self-induce belief. When this is combined with our moral obligation always to *act* so as to maximize desire-satisfaction, it follows that we are always morally obligated to believe in a manner that maximizes desire-satisfaction. This yields the following seemingly valid syllogism.

1. We are always morally obligated to act so as to maximize desire-satisfaction over the other available options to act.
2. Belief is an action.
3. Therefore, we are always morally obligated to believe in a manner that maximizes desire-satisfaction over the other available belief options.

Thus, from the moral duty to act so as to have it all, or as much of it as the circumstances permit, the moral duty to believe in a way that accomplishes this follows when it is added that belief is an action.

James, however, would not accept this syllogism unless it is added to premise 2 that belief is a *free* action, for James held that *ought* implies *can* in the full-blooded sense of *freely* can. If we have a moral duty to believe in a certain manner we must be free to do so. Chapter 3 will present James's Libertarian theory of free will and show how he applied it to belief itself. Chapter 4 will explore his famous doctrine of the will to believe that justifies our believing without adequate evidence when doing so will help to maximize desire-satisfaction. The evidentially non-warranted proposition that we are free to believe becomes a prime candidate for a will-to-believe-type option that justifies our believing that we can freely believe at will, thereby making our beliefs subject to the duty prescribed in premise 1 in the preceding syllogism.

Since the true is what we ought to believe, it follows that a proposition is true when believing it maximizes desire-satisfaction. This attempt to base epistemology on the moral duty to try to have it all is James's boldest and most original contribution to philosophy and will be the topic of Chapter 5, wherein it will be shown how James's highly revisionary analysis of truth and belief-acceptance is motivated and justified by his Promethean quest to have it all.[9] James's analysis of truth in terms of what maximizes desire-satisfaction for believers will be found to in-

[9] Several previous commentators deserve credit for seeing this unique feature of James's philosophy. Lovejoy viewed pragmatism "as essentially a practical and ethical attitude," but went on to fault "James's attempt to convert it into an epistemological theory [as] untenable and a superfluous exaggeration" (*TP* 59). H. D. Aiken very perceptively claimed that "what distinguishes James's philosophy is his tendency to view all questions of belief in essentially ethical terms. And this . . . is the primary reason why he came to identify truth as a species of good, as the good, or best within the domain of belief" (*APR* 239). Andrew Reck finds James's dedication of *Pragmatism* to John Stuart Mill apt in the light of James's "application of utilitarianism to the theory of knowledge" (*WJ* 53). Ellen Suckiel, another excellent commentator, holds that, for James, "Epistemological assessment is ultimately a practical, value-laden one. The most salient criterion of cognitive value is the fulfillment of subjective preference" (*PP* 29). Richard Rorty wrote that "James's account of truth and knowledge is a utilitarian ethics of belief" (*RF* 84, in R. A. Putnam, *RAP*).

corporate guiding principles or instrumental rules enjoining us to have beliefs that are both consistent and epistemically warranted, and to follow a conservative strategy when it becomes necessary to revise our web of belief; however, we are permitted to violate these rules when doing so on some occasion will maximize desire-satisfaction. James professes acceptance of the commonsense law of bivalence and its commitment to absolute truth but gives us a new and supposedly better way of expressing them in which this law is given a subjunctive conditional rendering in terms of what would be discovered if inquiry were to be properly pursued, with absolute truth being the ideal limit toward which properly conducted ongoing inquiry would converge. It will be shown that the subjunctive conditional version entails the categorical version, thereby capitulating to commonsense realism, and that the Peircean ideal limit theory is incompatible with James's empiricism and humanism. It will be argued that James would be well advised to abandon this attempt to placate the realist and openly admit that his morally based analysis of epistemological concepts is highly revisionary of our commonsense concepts and beliefs concerning belief-acceptance and truth.

Chapter 6 will explore James's future-oriented pragmatic theory of meaning and reference, which also is fueled by his Promethean quest to gain power to control our environment so as to realize our goals, and the theory of "truth" that falls out of it on the assumption that a theory of meaning gives truth-conditions for the proposition expressed by a sentence. This theory is at odds with the one in Chapter 5 based on maximizing desire-satisfaction. The clash will be neutralized by having James reject this assumption, thereby interpreting the pragmatic theory of meaning as giving conditions for a proposition to be epistemically warranted rather than true, thus the reason for the scare quotation marks around "truth" in the title of Chapter 6, "The Semantics of 'Truth.' "

James appeals to his Promethean ethical theory of belief formation and acceptance to legitimate letting each of his many selves take its turn at seeking self-realization, thereby enabling him to have it all. For whether we take the stance to the world of the scientist, moral agent, melioristic theist, or mystic we employ the same Promethean pragmatic theory for determining the meaning, reference, and truth of whatever we might say from these different perspectives. Unfortunately, the magical elixir of methodological univocalism does not go far enough in enabling each of his many selves to see the light of day and flourish; for there are clashes between the claims and assumptions made by these different selves from their different perspectives – and the one thing that James personally could not abide was a contradiction.

The scientific self accepts universal determinism, epiphenomenalism, and the bifurcation between man and nature, whereas the moral agent self believes that there are undetermined acts of spiritual causation in a world that has human meaning. Furthermore, whereas both use concepts as teleological instruments for gaining power to control the world of changing objects, his mystical self eschews concepts altogether in order to penetrate to the inner conscious core of a cotton-candyish reality through an act of sympathetic intuition. How are the clashes between the claims made from these different perspectives, each of which supposedly is a requirement for "having it all," to be reconciled?

Chapter 7 will explore a strategy that James had for neutralizing these seeming clashes. Let each of his many selves be directed to its own world, with no world qualifying as *the* real world absolutely or *simpliciter*. The predicate "is real" or "is the actual world" is not the monadic predicate it grammatically appears to be, but instead is the disguised three-place predicate " _____ is real for self _____ at time _____ ." When used by a person on some occasion this predicate gets filled out as "A certain world W is real for me now." This doctrine, which aptly could be called *Ontological Relativism,* allows us, as our interests and purposes change, successively to take different worlds to be the real or actual world without inconsistency.

The seeming inconsistencies between the claims made by our different selves are neutralized by restricting them to a certain perspective or world. Qua the tough-minded scientist, James affirms determinism and that there is no psychosis without neurosis, but qua the tender-minded moral agent, he rejects both and instead accepts the reality of undetermined acts of spiritual causation. Qua Promethean man of action, he carves reality up into a plurality of discrete individuals in terms of pragmatically based classificatory systems; but, qua mystic, he eschews concepts altogether so as to achieve a deep unification between himself and a surrounding mother sea of consciousness. And so on, and so on. What is real depends upon the purposes and interests that are freely selected by a self. The doctrine of Ontological Relativism turns out to be an instrument forged by James's Promethean self that aids his endeavor to have it all.

James's highly influential theory of "pure experience," often called "neutral monism," held that no individual is intrinsically physical or mental but becomes one or the other when we *take* it in a certain way by placing it in some temporal sequence of events. Whether a sequence is physical or mental depends on the manner in which its members function in relation to each other, in particular whether or not they stand in nomically based causal relations with each other in the manner described by Kant in his Second Analogy of Experience. I will argue that the theory of pure experience was implicitly restricted to the world of sensible realities and had the reconciling function of neutralizing clashes that arose between the claims of realists and idealists as to the true nature of these realities and the manner in which "inner" states of consciousness are hooked up with "outer" physical states. Through the dissolution of this pseudo-problem our intelligence is freed from the coils of traditional epistemology so that it can more effectively perform its Promethean function.

II. The Anti-Promethean Mystic

Prometheanism, however, is not the whole story about James's philosophy, as many commentators would have it. For coexisting with his Promethean self was a mystical self, and ultimately it was the mystical self that had its way, or at least the final word – quite literally, as mysticism is the dominant theme of his final two books, *A Pluralistic Universe* and *Some Problems of Philosophy*. Whereas his Promethean self wants to ride herd on objects so as to control them for his own ends, his mystical self wants to become intimate with them by entering into their inner conscious life so as to become unified with them, though not in a way that involves complete numerical identity, for James always favored pluralistic mysticism, such as is found within the Western theistic tradition, over its monistic Eastern version. But what James most craved was not unification with others but unification among his many selves that continually threatened to render him schizophrenic through disintegration into the sort of split personality that so fascinated him in the research of Janet.

This quest for intimacy, and ultimately union, between himself and others, as well as among his many selves, begins with his giving pride of place to introspection over objective causal analyses. Chapter 8 will show how James's analysis of personal identity over time is based exclusively on what is introspectively vouchsafed to each individual. Chapter 9 explores James's attempt to "I–Thou" other persons by projecting onto them what he finds when he introspects his own mind. By an act of empathetic intuition he enters into the inner conscious life of these Thous. By discovering this inner life, which is what bestows significance on their lives, they cease to be an *It* to be used by his Promethean self and become something to be cherished and respected because each has its own special way of experiencing the world and finding some meaning in it. Whereas his Promethean self accepts the ethical rule of maximizing desire-satisfaction, his mystical self enriches this with a democratic deontological principle that persons must, in virtue of their possessing a unique inner life that renders their life significant, be left free to flourish in the manner that they deem best, provided that they do not interfere with the right of others to do likewise. This entails that they cannot be used as mere means to realize the maximization of desire-satisfaction. Thus, there is a clash between the maximizing ethics of Prometheanism and the mystically based deontological ethics of reverence and respect for the autonomy of others. The I–Thou experiences between man and man get extended to I–Thou experiences between man and nature at large and, finally, to supernatural spirits, including God, also called the *More* and the *surrounding mother-sea of consciousness.*

But James's quest for intimacy and union does not stop with I–Thouing other *persons*, both natural and supernatural. He wants to accomplish this for reality at large. To accomplish this, as Chapter 10 will show, he must learn to jettison all concepts so that he can have a pure intuition of the inner life of all these others. He is aided in this endeavor by a string of a priori arguments that show the impossibility of concepts being true of reality. These arguments play the same role in James's quest for intimacy and union as do koans in Zen Buddhism: in both cases the subject is shocked into a new form of consciousness through the dialectical activity of immersing herself in the paradoxes or koans. The mystical James must dispense with all concepts because they are the agents of his active, Promethean self through their presenting this self with recipes for using objects. In order to have a pure intuition of the essence of things, he must no longer view reality as a *Duck, Dance, or Draw* movie.

To discover the true nature or essence of things he must begin by introspecting what goes on in his own consciousness and then project what he finds onto the world at large, as was the case with I–Thou-ing other persons. As Craig Eisendrath rightly pointed out, there was a reassertion of romanticism in James in which he "attributed to all existence the motions he felt in himself" (*UM* 233). What he finds through introspection of what goes on when he endures over time and acts intentionally so as to bring something about is a fusing or melting together of neighboring conscious stages; and he then assumes that there is a similar sort of mushing together between all spatial and temporal neighbors, the result of which is panpsychism, since only in consciousness can such mushing together occur. James's quest for intimacy with the universe through projecting what is introspectively vouchsafed onto external reality, thus, is also a quest for unification between both the subject and objects, as well as between the objects themselves. Thus, the quest for intimacy and unification that begins with the sort of I–Thou experiences depicted in Chapter 9 reaches its full zenith in the mystical experiences of unification between man and nature that are the subject of Chapter 10. It is not only the full-blooded mystical experiences of absorption into a surrounding mother-sea of consciousness that are salvific but also the conceptless Bergsonian intuitions of the flowing into each other of spatial and temporal neighbors.

At the root of the clash between his Promethean and mystical self is James's ambiguous attitude toward evil, his both wanting and not wanting to believe that we have absolute assurance that we are safe because all evils are only illusory or ultimately conquered. When James was in his healthy Promethean frame of mind he tingled all over at the thought that we are engaged in a Texas Death Match with evil, without any assurance of eventual victory, only the possibility of victory. This possibility forms the basis of his religion of meliorism. But there is a morbid side to James's nature, a *really* morbid side, that "can't get no satisfaction" from the sort of religion that his Promethean pragmatism legitimates. In order to "help him make it through the night" he needs a mystically based religion, which gives him a sense of absolute safety and peace that comes through union with an encompassing spiritual reality. The assurance that all is well comes not from philosophical theodicies, for James always charged them with being intellectually dishonest, but from what is vouchsafed by mystical experiences of unification.

The best way to bring out his ambivalent attitude toward evil is through an account of the two different attitudes James took toward his famous experience of existential angst in 1868 when he came upon a hideous epileptic youth in an insane asylum. He gave the following description of this experience.

That shape am I, I felt, potentially. Nothing that I possess can defend me against that fate, if the hour for it should strike for me as it struck for him. There was such a horror of him, and such a perception of my own merely momentary discrepancy from him, that it was as if something hitherto solid within my breast gave way entirely, and I became a mass of quivering fear. (VRE 134)

William Barrett has suggested that this experience of angst resulted from James's worry that he did not possess free will because all of his actions were predetermined by past causes: "That idiot will be me, and there is nothing I can do, if the particles are already irreversibly spinning in that direction. The imagination cowered before this prospect like a Calvinist shivering at the conviction of eternal damnation" (*IT* 263). This can't be the right explanation, for James must have realized that even if he possessed free will it did not assure him that horrible things would not befall him, regardless of what efforts he might make to the contrary. Free will does not give us omnipotence. Rather, the sight of the idiot made James aware of the radical contingency of existence, that everything hangs by a very delicate thread which can snap at any moment, no matter what we might do, freely or otherwise.[10]

[10] Jacques Barzun suggested that "in the figure of the idiot on his bench, he [James] had, like a painter, objectified Huxley's automaton, giving visual equivalents for the horror,

In his 1884 introduction to *The Literary Remains of the Late Henry James*, James alludes impersonally to the existential angst experience when he says: "we are all potentially sick men. The sanest and best of us are of one clay with the lunatics and prison inmates" (*ERM* 62).[11] Unlike his father, who must escape the existential angst that evil occasions by postulating some absolute being or God who gives assurance of salvation and safety, James's response is to "turn a deaf ear to the thought of being" and instead to suck it up and courageously follow the melioristic route of living the morally strenuous life without any assurance of success. He concludes his introduction with one of the most tender and diplomatic, yet cutting, sentences ever written, in which he contrasts himself with his beloved father.

Meanwhile, the battle is about us, and we are its combatants, steadfast or vacillating, as the case may be. It will be a hot fight indeed if the friends of philosophic moralism should bring to the service of their ideal, so different from that of my father, a spirit even remotely resembling the life-long devotion of his faithful heart. (*ERM* 63)

But, surprise of surprises, eighteen years later in *The Varieties of Religious Experience* (45–6), immediately upon his anonymous description of his experience of existential angst, James draws an opposite conclusion from it. The message now is that our salvation must be found, not in living the morally strenuous life, but rather in finding an abiding sense of safety and peace through absorption into a higher surrounding spiritual reality. It is as if he is treading the same path as his former Promethean self but now goes in a diametrically opposed direction when he reaches the crucial fork in the road at which sits the epileptic youth.

The theme of the insufficiency of meliorism and the healthy-minded outlook in general is repeated over and over again in this book. We are told that "the breath of the sepulchre surrounds" our natural happiness (*VRE* 118), that the advice to the morbid-minded person upon whom there falls "the joy-destroying chill" of "Cheer up, old fellow, you'll be all right erelong, if you will only drop your morbidness!" is "the very consecration of forgetfulness and superficiality" (*VRE* 118–19). What we need is a "life not correlated with death, a health not

vacancy, and desolation that the conception implied" (*SWJ* 18). Like Barrett's interpretation, this fails to realize that the source of James's angst is his awareness of the radical contingency of existence, not the fear that we are not free, be it due to our actions being predetermined or our being automata.

[11] Dickenson Miller, reflecting on his days as a student of James, reported: "Once when we were returning from two insane asylums which he had arranged for the class to visit, and at one of which we had seen a dangerous, almost naked maniac, I remember his saying, 'President Eliot might not like to admit that there is no sharp line between himself and the men we have just seen, but it is true' " (*PA* 50).

liable to illness, a kind of good that will not perish, a good in fact that flies beyond the Goods of nature" (*VRE* 119).[12] By experiencing absorption in a supernatural power, the "More" that surrounds our ordinary finite consciousness, we gain "an assurance of safety and a temper of peace, and, in relations to others, a preponderance of loving affection" that cannot "fail to steady the nerves, to cool the fever, and appease the fret, if one be conscious that, no matter what one's difficulties for the moment may appear to be, one's life as a whole is in the keeping of a power whom one can absolutely trust" (*VRE* 383 and 230). Armed with such mystically based assurance, James might now be able to view the epileptic youth without having one of his father's Swedenborgian vastation experiences, but I wouldn't bet on it, because he never completely shook off his morbid-minded self. The clashes between James's Promethean and mystical selves are synchronic rather than diachronic, for he never succeeded in becoming a unified self.

So far it has been seen that James's mystical self, unlike his Promethean pragmatic self, dispenses with all concepts so that it can assume a passive stance for the purpose of becoming unified, at least partially, with the inner consciousness of whatever it experiences. As a consequence of these unifying experiences, the mystical self adopts a deontological ethical stance toward others, in contrast to the desire-satisfaction maximizing project of the active self, and furthermore views evils as only illusory or sure to be overcome, which assurance is denied to his Promethean melioristic self. There are, however, even deeper clashes between these two selves over meaning and truth.

Whereas the Promethean self, in virtue of always running ahead of itself into the future for the purpose of satisfying desires, adopts an exclusively future-oriented theory of meaning that identifies a concept with a set of conditionalized predictions, the mystical self interprets the meaning of mystical claims in terms of the present content of mystical experiences. The pragmatic James reduced the whole meaning of claims about God and the absolute to our being licensed to take a moral holiday or feel safe and secure because all is well, but the mystical James finds their meaning in experiences of a unifying presence; the star performer finally gets into the act. Furthermore, since the meaningful content of the mystic's assertion that there exists a unification is based on the content of the mystical experience itself, the truth of the assertion will depend primarily on whether the experience is objective or cognitive. And among the most important tests for this is the immediate luminosity, the feeling of reality, supplied by the experience.

The most important clash between James's pragmatic and mystical

---

[12] For a good account of James's rejection of meliorism, see John Smith's splendid introduction to *VRE*, especially pp. xxvi, xxx, and xxlv.

selves, however, will not emerge until Chapter 11. Herein the "Big Aporia" in James's philosophy will be brought out, this consisting in a clash between his pragmatic self's metadoctrine of Ontological Relativism – that all reality claims must be relativized to a person at a time – and the absolute, nonrelativized reality claims he based on mystical experiences. An attempt will be made on his behalf to find a one-world interpretation that will succeed in neutralizing this clash. If James is to succeed in having it all, some way must be found to unify his many selves so that they all inhabit one and the same world, rather than schizophrenically occupying different worlds successively. Only through a unification of the many worlds will James's many selves become unified; for James's intellectual scruples preclude a *personal* unification of his many selves that is not anchored in a *metaphysical* unification of the many worlds toward which their interests are directed. The latter task requires no less than a synthesizing of the outlooks of the West and the East, the masculine and the feminine, even that of time and eternity. Needless to say, there is a very good chance that this attempt will fail miserably, as things probably have been rigged so that we cannot have it all. Chapter 11 has the daunting task of attempting the well-nigh impossible task.

III. The Problem of Interpreting James

Before getting down to the business of putting flesh on the preceding outline of "my William James," I need to address some thorny issues in how to read and interpret him. Because James's philosophy is an attempt to have it all, to let all of his many selves fully realize themselves, it presents the interpreter with a dazzling array of seemingly incompatible positions, and thereby the temptation to attempt to neutralize these clashes by focusing in on one of them to the exclusion of the others. Because he had such a wide diversity of selves, nothing that pertained to human nature was alien to James, and thus he was able to be the great appreciator of both persons and ideas. According to Lovejoy,

James's capacity for admiration of the intellectual performances of others was astonishing in its range and in its heartiness; not only his old pupils, but utter strangers, neglected Spinozas of the ghetto or Hegels budding unobserved in provincial newspapers, were likely at any moment to receive a letter, or one of his characteristic post cards, with a few, or sometimes many, words of heartening applause – applause often too liberal, but not undiscriminating – evoked by the reading of some piece of work that seemed to him to have in it something of freshness or individuality. (*TP* 94–5)

Justice Learned Hand lauded James because "his mind and his nature were so rich and varied that he was apparently able to harbor harmoniously what others with less gifts of conciliation found mutually rebellious. It always seems to me that the angels must have visited his cradle and bestowed on him whatever was charming and understanding and helpful and beautiful" (quoted from Townsend *MH* 164).

So great was James's appreciation of philosophical ideas that it bordered on philosophical satyrism. It seemed that he never met a philosophy to whose charms he did not succumb, at least for the time, short though it might have been, that the appropriate mood was upon him, for this philosophy, no matter what its content, was bound to appeal to at least one of his many selves. It was this quality, coupled with his literary genius, that enabled him to write the most mouth-watering sketches of the full range of alternative philosophical doctrines, even those that he was officially sworn to oppose, such as monism and determinism. These sketches captured with passion and eloquence the essence of whatever philosophy he was expounding, often making the philosophy look more attractive than did the accounts given by its defenders. In this respect James ranks as one of the great historians of philosophy, in spite of his scholarly limitations, for no one resonated more to philosophical ideas than he did.

Because James was such a great appreciator, his philosophical writings are very rich and suggestive, so much so that every major subsequent movement in philosophy can find its roots in them. But the price that James had to pay for lighting so many fires was to be the brunt of numerous self-serving anachronistic interpretations by the devotees of these different movements, anxious to further their own cause by welcoming him aboard their bandwagon. Phenomenologists portray James as one of their own heroes, a mere stone's throw from Husserl. Whiteheadians view him as a process philosopher, who unfortunately lacked the technical sophistication and systematicity of the master. Existentialists bill James as America's Existentialist, or at least as the closest thing to an existentialist that America was capable of producing. Numerous analytic philosophers have made James out to be a tough-minded verificationist who wanted to clean out the stables of traditional philosophy. Materialists of a functionalist bent claim that their approach is adumbrated in James's *The Principles of Psychology*. James has even been made out to be a deconstructionist who wanted to do away with business as usual in philosophy.

These usurping expositions, with the exception of the deconstructionist one, are of value insofar as they capture some part of James's philosophy. Unfortunately, some of them leave us with a basketcase James, because they ultimately fail to recognize the broad sweep and unity of his philosophy, such as I have just sketched. It will turn out that the existential and process interpretations are the closest to the mark, for James was an exceedingly tender-minded philosopher who wanted a universe that provides us with a cozy human habitat. None of the interpreters, however, have fully appreciated the extent of the coziness – that it winds up in mysticism. The reason why they all overlook the centrality of mysticism to James's philosophy is probably due to the fact that mysticism is not one of the fashionable movements in the professional circles within which they move. The most distorted interpretations, except for the deconstructionist ones, are those which portray James as a good naturalist who advocated the tough-minded ways of thinking of the scientist, a sort of John Dewey who was cursed with a felicitous writing style. Because this scientistic interpretation of James has gained widespread currency, in large part because of Dewey's own career-long account of James's philosophy, a special appendix will be devoted to exposing this sad chapter in the history of philosophy.

The way to avoid anachronistic interpretations, so that William James can be William James rather than an extension of the interpreter's own ego, is to make James's published writings the star performer. By doing so we respect James's autonomy, according him the dignity of his own free choices as to what writings he wanted to be publicly committed to and ultimately to be judged by. Furthermore, greater weight should be accorded to the later publications, as they represent his more mature, all-things-considered view. His numerous unpublished writings, including his diary, letters, manuscript lectures and notes, and course lecture notes, can be used to supplement his published views, but they alone can never be the basis for either attributing or denying a view to James, unless there is good evidence that he wanted them to be published.

But even if we make the published texts the *fons et origo* of our interpretation, there still is wide leeway, especially since they abound in apparent inconsistencies as a result of the philosophical satyrism, due to his many selves. To the casual reader, James's writings resemble a spotlight that aimlessly roves over a wall on which is written every possible philosophical doctrine, successively illuminating in a most brilliant manner one after the other. Certain doctrines achieve star billing because they spend more time in the spotlight or are returned to more often than others. There is a strong temptation to try and do James a favor by freezing the spotlight on one of these positions, thereby ignoring the other things he said or dismissing them out of hand as being the result of a bad day at the office. To do so is a violation of James's personhood that comes close to negating his very existence, since, as Plato said, to exist is to be a causal agent, and a philosopher achieves this mainly through publication.

If my quest-to-have-it-all thesis is correct, these inconsistencies arose from James's attempts to develop a philosophy that would satisfy the seemingly conflicting ideals and aspirations of his many different selves. The explanations that have been given for the plethora of apparent inconsistencies in his philosophy are shallow because they have not appreciated this deep source of his inconsistencies. Many claim that he did not have the patience to work out the details and thus published things without subjecting them to sufficient critical reflection. Dewey attributed the inconsistencies to James's "willingness to make concessions to his opponents in the hope of finding common ground beneath and to his large-minded indifference to minor details of his own former writings" (*MW* 6:101). Lovejoy, on the other hand, sees their source in James's being misled by his "enthusiasm . . . and . . . an instinct for the effective and emphatic way of putting things," which led him to overstate a position, omitting the needed qualifications (*TP* 59). While James's magnanimity and love of forceful, dramatic prose are part of the explanation, they are a small part.

It is up to the expositor to attempt to resolve these inconsistencies or aporias, but it must be made clear where James's writings end and the expositor's own contributions begin. I shall take my own turn at trying to neutralize these inconsistencies, but I shall be careful to follow my own advice. There are, of course, numerous ways of reworking James's texts, so I cannot claim that my interpretation is *the* right one, especially as how they get reworked will depend on what the interpreter takes to be the underlying spirit of James's philosophy, as well as what makes for the most attractive philosophy in its own right – issues about which there can be considerable disagreement. I cannot stress strongly enough that "my William James" is only one way of interpreting James. What I do contend is that the mystical aspects of James's texts that I shall bring to light are far more prevalent and important than any expositor has realized, and that any acceptable interpretation must provide an important place for them.

Although pride of place must be accorded to the published writings, our understanding of them can be enhanced by seeing how they grew out of and reflected James's life experience. James's philosophy is a paradigm case of his own sentiment of rationality doctrine, according to which one's basic philosophical commitments are rooted in psychological predilections and life experiences. Biographical excursions, in addition to being interesting in their own right because of the fascination of the man himself, one of the greatest and most enticingly complex geniuses of all time, can also serve to fill in and fill out his published writings. But, as is the case with his unpublished writings, these biographical excursions alone can never be the basis for attributing or denying a position to James.

The Promethean Pragmatist

1

The Ethics of Prometheanism

James's Promethean pragmatism attempts to show us a way to have it all, or at least as much of it as we mortals can realistically hope to have. Having it all requires that all of our many selves have their desires satisfied. The underlying assumption of this grand Promethean quest is that the ultimate good is to have one's desires satisfied. Not surprisingly, James developed an ethical theory whose ultimate normative principle is that:

1. We are always morally obligated to act so as to maximize desire-satisfaction over desire-dissatisfaction.

This chapter will give an in-depth exposition of how James arrived at and defended this maximizing ethical principle. Chapter 2 will show that the upshot of James's analysis of belief is the highly Promethean doctrine that

2. Belief is an action

in the sense of something that is done intentionally or at will. Chapter 3 will present James's analysis of freedom of action and therefore belief, given that belief is an action; and Chapter 4 will give his will-to-believe justification for believing that we have this sort of freedom of action, thereby rendering belief fair game for moral permissions and prohibitions.

From propositions 1 and 2 it follows that

3. We are always morally obligated to believe in a manner that maximizes desire-satisfaction over desire-dissatisfaction.

This attempt to give an ethical criterion for the acceptance of belief challenges the intellectualist tradition of Western philosophy from Parmenides to the logical positivists. Chapters 5 and 6 will show that it was not just belief acceptance but also meaning, reference, and truth that James attempted to ground in ethics. This attempt to base epistemology in general on ethical principles, even if it should not ultimately prove to be fully defensible, is one of the boldest and most original contributions to philosophy of all time and secures a permanent place for James in the Philosophical Hall of Fame.

James's only published effort to develop an ethical theory is his 1891 essay on "The Moral Philosopher and the Moral Life," which was re-printed six years later in *The Will to Believe and Other Essays in Popular Philosophy*. That James never felt the need to publish anything further on ethical *theory*, either before or after 1891, is strong evidence that he accepted its position throughout, especially as there is nothing in his unpublished writings indicating any doubts or reservations, only further corroboration of the 1891 essay. The word *theory* is italicized so as to emphasize the contrast with the moralizing espousal of normative prop-ositions, something that James did in profusion throughout his career. John Dewey failed to make this distinction when he said that "William James did not need to write a separate treatise on ethics, because in its larger sense he was everywhere and always the moralist" (*MW* 6, 92). It will be seen that some of his moralizing had a distinctively deontologi-cal tone that clashed with his maximizing ethical theory.

James's essay addresses in turn three different questions concerning the origin of our ethical intuitions, the meaning and status of ethical terms, and the casuistic rule for determining our moral duty in specific cases. His answer to the first question is that our moral intuitions, along with our aesthetic ones, are determined by innate structures of our brain that have resulted from chance mutations in the distant past that proved beneficial and took hold. This evolutionary account is identical with the one he gave in the final chapter of *The Principles of Psychology* of the origin of our stock of necessary truths. The moral intuitionists, therefore, were right in claiming that moral intuitions and sentiments were innate, but were wrong, as will be seen, for holding them to be a reading of objective moral truths in some Platonic heaven.

James gives as an example of a brain-born moral intuition our gut feeling that it is morally wrong to use one person as a mere means to promote the pleasure or happiness of the majority, which intuition underlies the typical counterexamples to utilitarianism.

If the hypothesis were offered to us of a world in which . . . millions [are] kept permanently happy on the one simple condition that a certain lost soul on the far-off edge of things should lead a life of lonely torture, what except a specifical and independent sort of emotion can it be which would make us immediately feel, even though an impulse arose within us to clutch at the happiness offered, how hideous a thing would be its enjoyment when deliberately accepted as the fruit of such a bargain. (*WB* 144)

This "lost soul" example will come back to haunt James's own ethical theory.

The second question is called the "metaphysical" one because it has to do with the being and meaning of ethical terms. The meaning part of the question seems to fall outside metaphysics, since it concerns what we mean by various ethical predicates, a study that was later to be called "metaethics." James tries to determine the ontological status of ethical states by analyzing the meaning of ethical terms, and this he does through an analysis of our experiential reasons for predicating them. This is in accordance with James's general empirical practice of determining both what we mean by "X," as well as what it is to be X, from a genetic account of the experiences that lead us to say of something that it is X. Later it will be seen how he does this for the concepts of actuality, negation, truth, and self-identity. Among the experiential reasons that lead us to say something is X can be the way in which our idea that it is X works in our subsequent experience. The outcome of his genetic analysis is that we mean by "good" whatever satisfies a desire, demand, or claim, for we take something to be good only when it does so. His unannounced shifting around among these three terms will be considered at the end of the chapter, and for the time being I will follow James in swinging back and forth between them. Given that the good is what satisfies a desire, and so on, and that we have an obligation to promote goodness, it follows that we have an obligation to see to it that any desire gets satisfied, unless doing so would result in the denial of a greater quantity of other desires. The obligation is a prima facie one that can be canceled only if the satisfaction of this one desire requires that a greater quantity of other desires go unsatisfied. This is what James means by his remark that "all demands as such are *prima facie* respectable" (*WB* 153). It is important to note that the obligation-creating power of a desire is completely independent of whose desire it is. When we factor in desires so as to determine what our moral duty is, we must do so behind a veil of ignorance as a result of which we do not know, or at least disregard, whose desires they are.

From this definition of "good" he draws the anti-Platonic conclusion that prior to the desiring or demanding by sentient beings nothing is good or obligatory. No conscious beings, no normative situations, for "betterness is not a physical relation."

Goodness, badness, and obligation must be *realized* somewhere in order really to exist; and the first step in ethical philosophy is to see that no merely inorganic "nature of things" can realize them. Neither moral relations nor the moral law can swing *in vacuo*. Their only habitat can be a mind which feels them; and no world composed of merely physical facts can possibly be a world to which ethical propositions apply. (*WB* 145)

There is no "abstract moral 'nature of things' existing antecedently to the concrete thinkers themselves with their ideals" (*WB* 147).

To better understand James's intuition that there is no moral goodness or obligation and, in general, no normative state of affairs, in a world devoid of conscious beings, it is helpful to contrast it with the rival intuition of a G. E. Moore. Given two worlds, both devoid of conscious beings, one consisting of a motel room that looks as if a heavy-

metal rock band and their groupies had just finished a night of de-
bauchery in it, and the other of elegant formal gardens, the latter,
according to Moore's intuitions, is the better world because it is, in
itself, more beautiful. James claims that someone who has such moral
and aesthetic intuitions is not faithfully performing the thought experiment because she is illicitly smuggling in an observer, namely herself,
whose aesthetic sensibilities are offended by the trashed room and
pleased by the gardens. But if we properly perform the thought experiment, making sure to exclude *all* observers, it becomes plain that there
is no more value or beauty in the one world than in the other. To be
sure, a tree falling in a forest unobserved makes a loud noise, unless it
falls in a snowbank or a pile of leaves, for it is just a physical fact; but
its falling cannot possess any normative feature, such as being desirable
or beautiful, unless there are conscious beings around who have appropriate desires.

This way of dismissing objective moral truths – moral truths that exist
independently of the desires and demands of conscious being – is too
quick, for it fails to make the crucial distinction between concrete states
of goodness and obligation, on the one hand, and general moral truths,
on the other. What James's thought experiment shows is that, at best,
there are no *concrete instances* of value and obligation in the world devoid of conscious beings, but this does not establish that there are no
general moral truths that hold in this world, such as the hypothetical
proposition that if there were to exist a conscious being who had a
desire, then there would be the prima facie obligation to see to it that
it gets satisfied. Plato's metaphorical description of the idea of the good
floating about in a non-spatio-temporal realm like a bigger-than-life
balloon in a Thanksgiving Day parade really amounts to the claim that
there are such objective moral truths.

We know from James's remark that "the moral law [cannot] swing *in
vacuo*" that he rejected these sorts of abstract moral truths. But why?
For there to be such an abstract moral truth there must be something
that serves as the bearer or subject of this truth, and traditionally that
has been an abstract proposition. But, in this essay, as well as in his
writings on truth, James rejects abstract propositions as absurd.[1] An
abstract proposition is a nonempirical entity, because it is not locatable
in space or time. The reason for this is that it is the denotatum of a
noun "that"-clause, such as "that Mary is baking pies," and it makes
no sense to ask where or when is that Mary is baking pies. Abstract
propositions are theoretical entities introduced for the purpose of ex-

---

[1] Dewey also dismissed abstract propositions without even giving them a hearing. For
example, in his 1909 essay, "The Dilemma of the Intellectualist Theory of Truth," he
presents a dilemma that is easily escaped by an appeal to abstract propositions, but Dewey
never even considers this way out (*MW*, vol. 4).

plaining how one can believe falsely, disbelieve what was formerly believed, believe the same as does someone else, as well as how two sentences can mean the same thing. Furthermore, the adage that there are many things better left unsaid seems committed to there being language- and mind-independent propositions to serve as the bearers of truth-values. James's nominalistic inclinations prevented him from taking seriously abstract propositions as the meanings of sentences, intentional accusatives, and truth-value bearers.[2] But he should have; for even though they are not themselves empirical entities, they might help to explain these empirical phenomena. James's empiricism, as will be seen in his treatment of the self, was sufficiently liberal as to permit the countenancing of nonempirical entities, provided they played a useful explanatory role.

James's "arguments" against abstract propositions consisted in nothing more than the heaping of rhetorical scorn on them, which is surprising, as he knew the works of some able defenders of the theory of abstract propositions, among them Bolzano, Brentano (see *PP* 916–7), the early Moore and Russell, but not Frege, who was the leading proponent of the theory. In language that prefigured Wittgenstein's mocking account of propositions as queer "shadows of a fact," James says that they are "a sort of spiritual double or ghost of them [the facts]" (*MT* 156). When we believe falsely we believe something, but it cannot be a fact and thus must be a shadow of a fact. Wittgenstein mockingly paraphrases this claim as being like the assertion that it isn't Mr. Smith who hangs in the gallery but only his picture (*BBB* 31). In each case it is implied that there is a relation between numerically distinct independent entities. These "ghosts" are so outré as to be beneath contempt. The problem of propositions will figure prominently in the discussion of truth in Chapters 5 and 6.

James makes the surprising claim that there would be concrete values and obligations, understood in the concrete sense, if there were a single, isolated desirer, which sets him apart from his fellow pragmatists Mead and Dewey, who gave a socialized account of everything that pertained to the normative. This is one among many instances of James's Robinson Crusoe approach to philosophical topics; it will be seen that he thinks an isolated individual can even have her own private concepts and language. That he so committed himself finds partial textual support in his speaking of the world of the single desirer as "a *moral solitude*" and of a world containing two desirers as having "twice as much of the ethical qualities in it as our moral solitude" (*WB* 146). The two-desirer world cannot have twice as much of the ethical qualities of the

[2] His demand that "the truth-relation [have] a definite content, and that everything in it is experienceable," precludes an abstract proposition from being the bearer of truth (*MT* 7).

moral-solitude world unless the latter has ethical qualities. The follow-ing quotation, however, really settles the matter: "Ethical relations . . . exist even in what we called a moral solitude if the thinker had various ideals which took hold of him in turn" (*WB* 159).

Before considering James's answer to the casuistic question, it is nec-essary to address a question concerning the status of James's claim that "*the essence of good is simply to satisfy demand*" (*WB* 153). Is this intended as a definition of what we ordinarily mean by "good"? If so, it falls victim to G. E. Moore's open-question challenge, as do all naturalistic definitions of ethical terms in terms of sensible properties. For it does not seem redundantly pointless to ask, "Yes, action A satisfies demand, but is it good?"; and for this reason it is not contradictory to say, "Ac-tion A satisfies demand but it isn't good." But if "good" meant satisfies demand, it would be contradictory. Plainly, if James's definition or anal-ysis is intended to be description of ordinary language, it is a miserable failure.

James is not going to be crushed by this departure from ordinary usage or common sense. In general, he has no compunctions about challenging them when there is good reason to do so. As will emerge in subsequent chapters, he knowingly gives revisionary analyses of truth, reference, the self, and material substances that challenge common sense. Whereas there is good textual evidence that he intended the latter to be revisionary analyses (and on this you must, as my late col-league Wilfrid Sellars would say, accept a promissory note, only this one will actually get cashed!), it is thin in the case of his analysis of good. He never comes out and explicitly says that he is revising ordinary us-age, but there are several good reasons for taking him to being doing just this. That many of his analyses are admittedly revisionary gives us some reason to think that he might be doing so here. And if there should be, as will now be shown, good reasons of both philosophical and internal consistency sort for this analysis to be taken as revisionary, that gives the interpreter good reason so to take it.

The first reason is based on internal consistency. If James's definition of "good" is a description of ordinary usage, he would be committed to holding that a normative proposition is entailed by a purely descrip-tive one, one that describes only the empirical properties of an act, in this case that it satisfies a desire or demand. He would be required to say that the proposition that act A satisfies a demand or desire *logically entails* that act A is so far morally good. But we know that James would not accept this entailment. In his "Notes for Philosophy 4: Ethics – Recent English Contributions to Theistic Ethics (1888–1889)," he says in effect that no normative proposition is entailed by purely descriptive ones. "Things are either immediately admitted to be good, without discussion, or there is discussion. To prove a thing good, we must conceive it as belonging to a genus already admitted good. Every ethical proof therefore involves as its major premise an ethical proposition; every argument must end in some such proposition, admitted without proof" (*ML* 182). "The scientific and the Ethical judgment are logi cally distinct in nature" (*MEN* 301). That A satisfies a demand would entail that A is good only if we were to add the additional *normative* premise that whatever satisfies a demand is so far good.

Even though James's definition of "good" is not a description of ordinary usage, it nevertheless recognizes as an ultimate objective moral truth that whatever satisfies a desire or demand is so far good. This clashes with his earlier attack on Platonism, for it would seem that there is, for him, at least this one abstract moral truth. This is the first in-stance of the making–discovering aporia, which will run throughout his philosophy. Initially, he strikes the Promethean making theme: We make things good by desiring them, yet that it is good that desires get satisfied seems to be something that is not made true by us but instead discovered. I am at a loss to extricate James from this aporia, about which a great deal more will be said in later chapters.

Because James's revisionary analysis of "good" is prescriptive rather than descriptive, it does not follow that it cannot be motivated and justified. Various doctrines of James can be marshaled to support its acceptance. All of his admittedly revisionary analyses are motivated, at least in part, by his career-long commitment to empiricism. He will be found to object to our commonsense concepts of truth, knowledge, and reference because they involve a mysterious, non-empirical saltatory re-lation, and he will replace them with concepts based on a genetic anal-ysis of the experiential conditions under which we apply these concepts. By replacing nonempirical concepts with empirically based ones, we put our conceptual house in order so that we can make more effective use of our intelligence in gaining mastery over our world.

Something similar justifies his revisionary analysis of good. In our attempts to analyze the meaning of good or the ground of obligation

> there is an inevitable tendency to slip into an assumption which *ordinary* men follow when they are disputing with one another about questions of good and bad. They imagine an abstract moral order in which the objective truth resides; and each tries to prove that this pre-existing order is more accurately reflected in his own ideas than in those of his adversary. It is because one disputant is backed by this over-arching order that we think the other should submit. (*WB* 148; my italics)

The evils occasioned by these intuitive appeals to what is written down in the Platonic heaven, in addition to being based on a mistaken view of the ontological status of moral truths and obligations, lead to point-less, intractable disputes, which are a waste of time. This is the poverty of intuitionism.

This appeal to empiricism, however, is hardly sufficient to justify James's particular empirical account of good over numerous rival empirical accounts, such as utilitarianism. James's chief reason for preferring his particular empirical account to these rivals is based on a Darwinian view of human beings as determined by their biological nature to be always intent on satisfying some felt need or desire, even if the need or desire is not itself directly determined by biological states or processes. Since this is our nature, it seems reasonable to make the attainment of this our moral ideal; for what other end could we have? Given the scientific account, the normative conclusion appears to be the only practically viable alternative open to us human beings. Unlike natural law theorists, James would not claim that the scientific account of man's nature logically entails any normative proposition. Nevertheless, to ask whether it really is good for us to act in accordance with our nature is to raise an idle question.

I believe that there was another motivation for James's revisionary account of good in terms of desire-satisfaction based on his inveterate hipsterism, which was discussed in the Introduction. He was an experience junkie intent on having as many tingles and thrills as possible. This is the object of his quest to have it all. Because we have these tingles and thrills when our desires are satisfied, his absolute normative principle should be to satisfy desire – the more the better. James recognized that there is wide diversity among people in their psychological makeups, for example, in what their sense of rationality is. No doubt, he would acknowledge wide diversity regarding what they take the good life to be. Nevertheless, he assumed that most people, like himself, were out to have it all.

The answer that James will give to the casuistic question should be obvious by now: We are morally obligated "to satisfy at all times *as many demands as we can*. That act must be the best act, accordingly, which makes for the *best whole*, in the sense of awakening the least sum of dissatisfactions" (*WB* 155). It should be noted that James shifts from a maximizing of desire-satisfaction to a minimizing of desire-dissatisfaction formulation. Maybe he thought they came to the same thing. There are, however, possible cases in which they require different acts. Imagine a deity who has a choice between creating desirers who will have some but not all of their desires satisfied or creating no desirers at all. The former choice is required by the desire-satisfaction maximizing rule and the latter by the desire-dissatisfaction minimizing rule. Probably what James had in mind was a net principle like that of the utilitarians, to the effect that

1' We are always morally obligated to act in a manner that maximizes desire-satisfaction over desire-dissatisfaction among the actions available to us.

For the sake of brevity, in the future the "over desire-dissatisfaction" qualification will be dropped, but it must be understood as applying. In the 1881 "Reflex Action and Theism," James wrote that "The only possible duty there can be in the matter is the duty of getting the richest results that the material given will allow" – hints of his hipsterism (*WB* 103). The "richest result" would seem to be one in which the maximum number of desires get satisfied. Something akin to this casuistic rule is given expression in a letter James wrote at the age of sixteen: "It is then the duty of everyone to do as much good as possible" (*CWJ* 12). It is amazing how much of James's philosophy is there from the very beginning, almost as if it were innate in him in the manner envisioned by his brain-born theory.

It is an empirical question, and a very difficult one at that, what course of action will maximize desire-satisfaction in any given situation. The sciences, especially the social sciences, will have to serve as our guide in determining which action, among those open to us, will best maximize desire-satisfaction. This union of ethics with science, not surprisingly, brought strong praise from John Dewey in a letter he wrote to James just after the appearance of "The Moral Philosopher and the Moral Life" in 1891. "The article rejoiced me greatly," Dewey wrote (quoted from the introduction to *WB* xxxii). James deserves great credit for being the first to try to make ethics into an empirical or experiential science.

A number of questions about James's maximizing casuistic rule must be addressed. How similar is it to the different versions of utilitarianism? To begin with, there is the distinction between act and rule utilitarianism: the former holding that on every occasion we should act so as to maximize utility; the latter, that we should choose general rules of conduct on the basis of maximizing utility but that once the rules are in place we must follow them, even if doing so on some occasion does not maximize utility.

James clearly recognizes the value of having general rules of conduct when there is good inductive evidence that following them for the most part maximizes desire-satisfaction, a matter about which science must guide us. "The presumption in cases of conflict must always be in favor of the conventionally recognized good. The philosopher must be a conservative, and in the construction of his casuistic scale must put the things most in accordance with the customs of the community on top" (*WB* 156). Supposedly, "the customs of the community" are to be accorded this pride of place because of their established track record in maximizing desire-satisfaction in the past. But in spite of this conservative endorsement of following conventional rules of conduct, James is not a rule desire-satisfaction maximizer, since he permits us to make exceptions to an established rule when we have good evidence that doing so on some occasion will maximize desire-satisfaction, which was another ground of Dewey's lavish praise. Quoting T. H. Green's claim that "Rules are made for man, not man for rules," he urges us to experiment with new rules and procedures for maximizing good (*WB* 156–7). Because James assigns such an important instrumental role to conventional rules but does not give them the exceptionless status that modern-day rule utilitarians do, his theory of desire-satisfaction maximization is of the *rule-instrumental* sort; rules have only an instrumental status as guiding principles and are subject to exceptions. It will be seen in Chapter 5 that James's criterion for belief-acceptance based on maximizing desire-satisfaction also is complemented with a type of rule-instrumentalism; past experience teaches us that we are well advised, for the most part, to give pride of place to the conventional rule of basing one's beliefs upon the best available empirical evidence.

Obviously, James's maximizing rule differs from Bentham's in regard to what is to be maximized, it being pleasure over pain for Bentham and desire-satisfaction for James. This is important because James thought that we desired things other than pleasure and the avoidance of pain, such as heroically struggling for our ideals. Some desires are manifestations of instinct and emotional expression that have absolutely nothing to do with pleasure and pain. "Who smiles for the pleasure of the smiling, or frowns for the pleasure of the frown?" (*PP* 1156). In a funny footnote, he takes Bain to task for his attempt to explain our sociability and parental love by the desire for pleasure, in particular that of touch. He concludes, that for most of us, it cannot possibly "be that all our social virtue springs from an appetite for the sensual pleasure of having our hand shaken, or being slapped on the back" (*PP* 1158). Bain is unable to explain why we would not derive just as much pleasure from touching "a satin cushion kept at about 98 degrees F" as we do from touching a baby's face. As Ellen Suckiel has stressed to me in correspondence, "desire-satisfaction," for James, must not be understood, as it typically is, in terms of the satisfaction of the individual's physical and psychological wants and needs.

The most striking counterexamples to the principle that the only things we desire are pleasure and the avoidance of pain are found in James's own deontological desire to do his moral duty as a free agent. It was the worry that he was not a free, morally responsible agent which triggered his emotional crisis of 1870. James did not desire just that certain desirable states of affairs be realized but that they be realized, as a result of his own free agency. Herein James recognizes an intrinsic, deontological value to being a free agent who causes in the right way the realization of desirable ends. There is a serious question whether James can be committed consistently to both his casuistic rule and his deontological values. This is exactly the same problem faced by the utilitarian who says both that we always must choose that alternative which maximizes utility and that we always must act from considerations of virtue. This attributes to us inconsistent motivations, as the latter recognizes an intrinsic, deontological value to acting from considerations of virtue that the former does not. If James is to follow his casuistic rule consistently, he must factor in deontological desires on the same level with every other sort of desire.

Although James's casuistic rule differs from classical utilitarianism in regard to what we are to maximize, does it resemble the latter in being purely quantitative? The text speaks unambiguously in favor of the quantitative interpretation,[3] as his formulation of the rule clearly shows: "There is but one unconditional commandment, which is that we should seek incessantly . . . so to vote and to act as to bring about the very *largest total* universe of good which we can see" (*WB* 158; my italics). The 1888–9 "Notes for Philosophy 4 . . ." formulates a precursor to the casuistic rule of the 1891 essay that clearly is quantitative. "Consider *every* good as a real good, and *keep as many as we can*. That act is the best act, which makes for the best whole, the best whole being that which prevails at least cost, in which vanquished goods are least completely annulled" (*ML* 185). Herein we see James seeming to side with a desire-dissatisfaction minimizing version of the casuistic rule, though it still is a quantitative rule.

To say that James's casuistic rule is quantitative does not go far enough, for there are three different ways in which it can be quantitative. Our duty could be to satisfy the desires of the greatest *number of people*, the greatest *number of desires*, or the greatest *quantity of desires* in which the amount or intensity of a desire is factored in. The same ambiguity attaches to a net version of the casuistic rule that requires us to maximize desire-satisfaction over desire-dissatisfaction. Edward Madden interprets James as saying that "Our moral obligation is to maxi-

---

[3] Ellen Suckiel, an extremely accurate and insightful interpreter of James, argues that his casuistic rule incorporates some qualitative considerations. While she recognizes that these quotations support an exclusively quantitative interpretation, she finds his occasional remarks about the desirability of seeking "inclusivity" and "balanced (equilibrium)" in desire-satisfaction an indication that he included deontological or qualitative considerations in his casuistic rule. She even goes so far as to say that, for James, "Given that some demands inevitably will be more fully satisfied than others, the optimal state of affairs will embody the most *just* distribution of satisfactions" (PP 64; my italics). No quotations are given from the text to support her attributing a concern for justice to James's casuistic rule, nor can any be given. One unattractive feature of her qualitative interpretation is that it makes James out to be inconsistent, as there are passages where he clearly espouses an exclusively quantitative version of his casuistic rule. To attribute a contradiction to James is an interpretation of last resort. Fortunately, there is no need to do so, since "exclusivity" and "balance" admit of a quantitative interpretation. The inclusivity relation between sets, for example, is a purely quantitative notion. The equilibrium that is realized by a balance beam also admits of a quantitative construal in terms of the trays having equal quantities of weight on them. That James's casuistic rule is purely quantitative but in need of qualitative supplementation is argued by John K. Roth in *EJ*.

mize the satisfaction of needs for as many people as possible" (introduction to *WB* xxxi). Andrew Reck, on the other hand, seems to side
with the second interpretation: "On James's account the moral universe is inveterately democratic. Each demand has an equal claim with
every other demand for satisfaction" (*WJ* 81).

Both interpretations are wrong, for the text of "The Moral Philosopher and Moral Life" clearly favors the third sense. To begin with he
says that "Any desire is imperative to the extent of its *amount*" (*WB*
149; my italics). What really nails down the case for this interpretation
is the manner in which he brings in God's desires and demands. God's
demands "carry the most obligation simply because they are the *greatest
in amount*" (*WB* 149; my italics). God is the biggest kid on the block,
and although he is not infinite for James, his desires and demands are
of such a magnitude as to outweigh the collective desires of men, and
thus should be obeyed. Imagine in this connection an incredibly huge
man: When he desires to eat he *really desires* to eat, and when he desires
to breathe he *really desires* to breathe. Thus, although all people count
equally, not all desires do. In other of his writings, James conceives of
God as a supremely good being and thus the one entity whose judgment of us we should care about most, but in "The Moral Philosopher
and the Moral Life" he does not make use of the deontological goodness of God but only the immensity of his desires.

Herein James runs smack into the question of Plato's *Euthyphro*: Is an
act pious (morally obligatory) because it is loved (demanded) by the
gods, or is it loved (demanded by) the gods because it is pious (morally
obligatory). Suppose that not God but Descartes's evil demon exists.
Would James still hold that the demands of the de facto biggest kid on
the block are to carry the day? Obviously James, being one of the nicest
human beings of all time, would not continue to adhere to his greatest-
in-amount version of the casuistic rule, but then he would be smuggling
in deontological considerations to the effect that the reason why we
should obey God but not the evil demon is because God is morally
good and the demon is not.

We do not have to bring in infinite or near infinite beings to find
counterexamples to the greatest-in-amount version. Suppose six units
of food are available and that our incredibly huge man desires, *really
desires,* to eat six units of food and there are five other persons who have
the mild desire to eat one unit of food. If the fat man's desire outweighs
the sum of the latter five mild desires, it follows that we have a moral
obligation to see to it that the former desire is satisfied to the exclusion
of the latter five. But this violates our democratic sensibilities. It is not
fair that one person should get to eat and five be denied. One should
not get more than his fair share because he is unusually lustful. Glut-
tony should not serve as a mark of distinction. This result would not

follow if the casuistic rule was interpreted as requiring that we act so as to minimize desire-dissatisfaction.

Although James actually went with the maximizing of the quantity of desires that are to be satisfied, maybe he could have escaped this objection of unfairness if he had instead opted for one of the other two senses of "quantity" – the greatest *number of people* or the greatest *number of desires* that are to be satisfied? Unfortunately, both interpretations are vulnerable to the same objection. A good counterexample to both versions is James's own example of the "lost soul" who is endlessly tortured so that millions can have all of their desires satisfied. Here, it is both the greatest number of people and the greatest number of desires that get satisfied. James, of course, believed that we would not allow the torture of one person so as to satisfy the desires of the multitude because he thought we had brain-born moral intuitions of a Kantian sort. But if we were not to have such a deontological desire, then we would be required to use the lost soul as a mere means to promote the maximization of desire-satisfaction over desire-dissatisfaction.

How might James meet this counterexample and a slew of similar ones? His initial response was that we have a brain-born moral intuition that would not allow us to use one person as a mere means to promote the happiness of others. In other words, we have a Kantian-type desire that one person not be used as a mere means to promoting the interests of others. But this intuition or desire is a deontological one that is incompatible, for the reason just given, with maximizing ethical theories, whether of a utilitarian or desire-satisfaction maximizing sort.

Maybe James should bite the bullet, as would an ardent act utilitarian, and say that the lost-soul counterexample is not a counterexample because we should accept the offer to have millions be happy at the cost of one lost soul who is tortured endlessly. The manner in which James defends vivisection in an 1875 article in the *Nation* would seem to commit him to this response.

A dog strapped on a board and howling at his executioners, or, still worse, poisoned by curara [*sic*], which leaves him paralyzed but sentient, is, to his own consciousness, literally in a sort of hell. He sees no redeeming ray in the whole business. Nevertheless, in a world beyond the ken of his poor, benighted brain, his sufferings are having their effect – truth, and perhaps future human ease, are being brought by them. He is performing a function infinitely superior to any which prosperous canine life admits of, and, if his dark mind could be enlightened, and if he were a heroic dog, he would religiously acquiesce in his own sacrifice. (*ECR* 11–12)

Why shouldn't what is true for this dog also be true for the lost soul? Plainly, James cannot say that we are not morally permitted to do to the lost soul what we are permitted to a dog, because the former is a *person* because of being a rational free agent, and thus entitled to certain rights, such as the Kantian one never to be used as a mere means, whereas the dog is not. For this appeals to deontological considerations that are incompatible with his exclusive maximizing of desire-satisfaction ethical theory. That a dog's pain might not be as intense as a human's does not justify using it as a mere means to promote human interests. James says that the dog would willingly sacrifice itself "if he were a heroic dog," and thus could also say that the lost soul would willingly sacrifice himself if were a heroic individual. This way out confronts the objection that not all dogs or individuals are in fact willing to be heroic martyrs, and that in cases in which they do not voluntarily step forward to sacrifice themselves we have a moral duty to see to it that they are sacrificed so as to maximize desire-satisfaction, be it in any one of the three senses of quantity. James's maximizing ethical theory, like utilitarianism, requires us to martyr ourselves heroically when this will maximize desire-satisfaction or utility, but we *ordinarily* take such an act to be supererogatory, not morally obligatory. Although James, as has just been argued, is not a slave to our ordinary or commonsense moral intuitions, he does accept our ordinary intuition that it would be wrong to use one individual as a means and in fact says that it is brain-born.

Does James have some way around this and a host of similar counter-examples? One option for him is to appeal to his rule-instrumentalism. He could say that we would do a better job in the long run of maximizing desire-satisfaction if we adopted the rule, subject to exceptions of course, that each of us be willing to sacrifice ourselves for the benefit of others, provided that the selection process is random. (Think of an organ lottery in which all of us are voluntary participants, agreeing to give up our life if our number comes up so that our organs can be used for transplants.) The problem is that if someone does not accept this rule voluntarily, she is still fair game for being the sacrificial lost soul. One is going to be a heroic martyr, like it or not. And this seems wrong, not only to the vast majority of people but to James as well, at least at those times when he was not intent on developing an ethical theory.

Another strategy open to James is to state that his revisionary analysis of good and obligation, like all of his other revisionary analyses, is not intended to hold for every possible world but only for the actual world, and thus counterexamples based on merely possible cases cut no ice. James criticized absolute idealism's attempt to give an analysis of truth that would hold "in all conceivable worlds, worlds of an empirical constitution entirely different from ours," for being "too thin, "as if the actual peculiarities of the world . . . were entirely irrelevant. . . . But they cannot be irrelevant" (*PU* 149). No doubt he would want to say the same about analyses of other concepts.

Supposedly, lost-soul-type counterexamples are too counterfactual.

James, no doubt, would have found the challenge posed by the immoralist, based on how we would act if we were to be rendered retribution-proof, say through possessing the ring of Gyges, to be too counterfactual to be taken seriously. James, along with many of his contemporaries, believed in the essential goodness of humans, that if the circumstances required, they would dutifully accept being the lost soul.

The problem with this response is that James's revisionary analysis does not even hold for the actual world. That it does not is dramatically illustrated by the doctor who says to his patient, "Mister Jones, I have good new and bad news for you. The bad news is that you will die within a month from an untreatable cancer. And the good news is that I won one million dollars in the lottery." If James were right in his estimation of human nature, the statement should not occasion a laugh. But it does, and thus James's revisionary analysis does not hold even for the actual world.

John Stuart Mill faced the same problem with his own version of utilitarianism. It took the form of explaining why we should adopt a disinterested perspective, so that the patient would take the "good news" to be good news, being able to say to the doctor in all sincerity, "It really doesn't matter whether it is you or I who is the lucky guy; all that matters is that someone is." Mill tried to convince us to adopt this disinterested standpoint by producing one of the all-time philosophical howlers. He reasoned that, since each man desires his own happiness, each man desires everyone's happiness too, which is like reasoning that because each person blows his own nose, each person blows everyone's nose.

James was not worried about how to make the transition from the self-interested to the disinterested point of view. He swept the problem under the rug because his genetic analysis loaded the dice in favor of our having the unselfish point of view. The upshot of his genetic analysis is that we take something to be good when it satisfies a desire, which gives the false impression that we are indifferent as to *whose* desire gets satisfied, it making no difference whether it is ours or someone else's. Pace James, the upshot of the genetic analysis should have been that each person takes something to be good when it satisfies *her* desire; and thus the problem of how to go from the self-interested to the disinterested point of view is still with us.

One commentator has given an interpretation of James that renders him invulnerable to lost-soul-type counterexamples, but at the great cost of making him appear to be a complete muddlehead. According to John Wild's interpretation, James was not serious in his espousal of a maximizing ethical theory in the early sections of "The Moral Philosopher and the Moral Life" and gave it up in the final Section V in favor of an existential ethics based on the paramount value of freely leading the morally strenuous life. "The strenuous ethics comes after, and supersedes the utilitarian ethics" (*RE* 282). Wild fails to give a single quotation from the text to justify his interpretation, and, fortunately, none can be given. If Wild is right that James first argued for a position and then relinquished it later in the very same essay without even announcing that he had, then James not only fails to qualify as a great philosopher, he fails even to qualify for tenure. Furthermore, Wild's contrast between "the strenuous ethics" and "utilitarian ethics" is uninformed, for one of the major problems for utilitarianism, as well as James's variation on it, is that it is too demanding because it makes supererogatory acts obligatory. Andrew Reck has suggested in correspondence that one might interpret James as holding that the sort of desires which the strenuous mood presses us to satisfy are of a qualitatively higher sort – the desires that we would have if we were to become our ideal selves.[4] If this is the right interpretation, and it might well be, then James is guilty of inconsistently smuggling in deontological considerations.

What, then, is James up to when he makes a contrast between "the easy-going and the strenuous mood" in Section V of "The Moral Philosopher and the Moral Life"? James's concern here is with the existential, as opposed to the cognitive, dimension of the ethical life. It is one thing to believe or accept an ethical proposition or rule and quite another to get oneself to follow or live up to this proposition or rule. One can know the rules of the ethical language-game but not actively participate in it. In the easygoing mood we do not sufficiently exert ourselves in following the casuistic rule, often because we fail to adopt the required disinterested perspective. A person lazily follows the course of least resistance because she considers only her present desires and not the ones that she and others will have in the future. "When in the easygoing mood the shrinking from present ill is our ruling consideration. The strenuous mood, on the contrary, makes us quite indifferent to present ill, if only the greater ideal be attained" (*WB* 159–60).

In order to satisfy the future desires of ourselves and others, we often have to make painful sacrifices in the present, consisting of our forgoing the satisfaction of short-term desires for the sake of longer-term ones that take into account the desires of our future self, as well as those of future persons who do not yet exist. There is no cognitive difference, therefore, between the easygoing and the strenuous person; both accept the casuistic rule enjoining them to act so as to maximize desire-satisfaction, in which all persons count equally, including future

---

[4] James Conant has made out a persuasive case that James accepted Emerson's doctrine of moral perfectionism, replete with its ideal self (*JR*). Ellen Suckiel also finds this doctrine informing James's philosophy of religion (*HC* 13, 24, 111).

persons, with the exception that intensity of desire must be factored in. The difference between them is that the easygoing person is lax in living up to this requirement, taking the easy route of producing short-term satisfactions through satisfying her present desires. The strenuous person does a better job of fulfilling the requirements of the casuistic rule because she factors in the long-term desires of herself and others, including those of future persons, and thus is ready, willing, and able to make the requisite sacrifices to satisfy this more inclusive set of desires. She does the better job of following the casuistic rule than does the easygoing person.

The cognitive-existential distinction not only finds textual support in Section V of "The Moral Philosopher and the Moral Life" but also accords with the "faith-ladder" formulation of James's will-to-believe doctrine at the very close of each of his final two books, *A Pluralistic Universe* and *Some Problems of Philosophy*.

The following steps may be called the "faith-ladder":

1. There is nothing absurd in a certain view of the world being true, nothing self-contradictory.
2. It *might* have been true under certain conditions;
3. It *may* be true, even now;
4. It is *fit* to be true;
5. It *ought* to be true;
6. It *must* be true;
7. It *shall* be true, at any rate true for *me*. (*SPP* 113 and *PU* 148)

Each of the steps up until 7 is cognitive in that it involves *believing* of some proposition either that it is possible or that it is desirable. It is at Step 7 that the existential or conative dimension enters in, for in saying that this proposition, which one's intellect has already assessed as both possible and desirable, *shall* be true, one is forming the effective intention or will to act so as to help make it true. This is of a piece with the distinction between our believing or accepting the casuistic rule and our psyching ourselves up so that we can form an effective intention to act in accordance with what it requires.

The major problem that James addresses in Section V is how to motivate ourselves to muster the courage to do what we intellectually recognize to be our duty. Not surprisingly, it contains an impassioned sermon; and the sermon, as you would expect, brings in God, first in the capacity of someone who knows the answer to the casuistic question, and second as our ideal social self whom we should do our best to please. A person's social self, for James, is the recognition she receives from others. "*A man has as many social selves as there are individuals who recognize him* and carry an image of him in their mind" (*PP* 281). But a person does not care equally about each person's opinion of her. She gives greater weight to the opinions of her peers and those whom she respects and loves. For most people, God would be their ideal social self, as he is the person they most respect and admire.

It has been pointed out that it is very difficult for us to determine the answer to the casuistic question, because our ability to predict the future is so radically limited. The dauntingness of the task of determining which course of action among those open to us will best maximize desire-satisfaction in the long run can easily demoralize us so that we take the easy way out and follow the line of least resistance. Given God's omniscience, or near omniscience for James, if God were to exist, the right answer to the casuistic question would exist in his mind, even though we are not able to access his mind. By postulating the existence of God and thus the existence of the right answer to the casuistic question, we gain inspiration faithfully to pursue finding the right answer. Thus, the idea of God and his knowledge is an inspiring ideal of reason that energizes us to find the answer to the casuistic question. According to James if God existed,

> his way of subordinating the demands to one another would be the finally valid casuistic scale; his claims would be the most appealing; his ideal universe would be the most inclusive realizable whole. If he now exists, then actualized in his thought already must be that ethical philosophy which we seek as the pattern which our own must evermore approach. In the interests of our own idea of systematically unified moral truth, therefore, we as would-be philosophers, must postulate a divine thinker, and pray for the victory of the religious cause. Meanwhile, exactly what the thought of the infinite thinker may be is hidden from us even were we sure of his existence; so that our postulation of him after all serves only to let loose in us the strenuous mood. (*WB* 161)

The invocation of God as an ideal of reason that benevolently energizes us is of a piece with James's occasional Peircean postulation of a future scientific millennium in which some theory is accepted by all competent scientists. "The 'absolutely' true, meaning what no farther experience will ever alter, is that ideal vanishing-point towards which we imagine that all our temporary truths will some day converge. It runs on all fours with the perfectly wise man, and with the absolutely complete experience" (*P* 106–7 and *MT* 143–4). Herein God is brought in not as the *biggest* but the *knowingest* kid on the block. We have seen that James waffles on the question of moral realism, initially denying the existence of timeless moral truths and then seemingly committing himself to the existence of at least one such truth – that it is good that a desire be satisfied and therefore we have a moral obligation to maximize desire-satisfaction. The postulation of a God in whose mind there exists the answer to the ultimate casuistic question seems to be a version of scholastic conceptualism that finds a middle ground between James's nominalism and his realism. Thus, James winds up coming down on all three sides of the nominalism-conceptualism-realism issue as it pertains to moral truths. At the end of this chapter an attempt will be made to extricate James from this apparent inconsistency and also to find some way for him to accommodate the deontological moral intuitions that underlie lost-soul-type counterexamples.

The manner in which James uses God as our ideal social self is not made sufficiently clear in Section V and needs expansion from what he said one year earlier in *The Principles of Psychology*. The key quotations from Section V are:

In a merely human world without God, the appeal to our moral energy falls short of its maximal stimulating power. Life, to be sure, is even in such a world a genuinely ethical symphony; but it is played in the compass of a couple of octaves, and the infinite scale of values fails to open up. . . . When, however, we believe that a God is there, and that he is one of the claimants, the infinite perspective opens out. The scale of the symphony is incalculably prolonged. The more imperative ideals now begin to speak with an altogether new objectivity and significance, and to utter the penetrating, shattering, tragically challenging note of appeal. (*WB* 160)

This dark passage cries out for clarification. Why should a belief in God inspire one to lead the morally strenuous life? Is it only a psychological connection? If so, James can be accused of making a hasty generalization from his own case, just as he did when he said in his 1881 "Reflex Action and Theism":

God, whether existent or not, is at all events the kind of being which, if he did exist, would form *the most adequate possible object* for minds framed like our own to conceive as lying at the root of the universe. My thesis, in other words, is this: that *some* outward reality of a nature defined as God's nature must be defined, is the only ultimate object that is at the same time rational and possible for the human mind's contemplation. (*WB* 93)

People's psychology varies greatly in these matters. Notoriously, there are those whose faith lulls them into quietism and passivity, since they think that God is big enough to take care of both himself and the universe at large without their help. Like the absolute idealist they can be lulled into taking occasional moral holidays.

To understand what James is after it is necessary to look at what he says about God as our ideal social self. Each of us is in "pursuit of an ideal social self, of a self that is at least *worthy* of approving recognition by the highest *possible* judging companion, if such a companion there be. This self is the true, the intimate, the ultimate, the permanent Me which I seek. This judge is God, the Absolute Mind, the 'Great Companion'" (*PP* 301). Again, James might be guilty of a generalization from his own case. Not all of us have as our paramount concern being judged favorably by God or even, as was the case with James, our own father.

Why does James think that it matters so much to a person to have God judge her favorably? The obvious answer, suggested by the quotation, is that it is because God is an eminently good being. Herein James is invoking God not qua biggest or *knowingest* kid on the block but qua the *morally best* person there is, or even could be. This is making a deontological use of our idea of God. Our prayerful contemplation of God inspires us to lead the morally strenuous life in virtue of our conceiving of him as unsurpassably *good*. This supplies James with an adequate answer to the underlying question of the *Euthyphro*, something that his desire-satisfaction maximizing ethics was impotent to give. The reason why we should comply with what God desires or demands is not that God is the biggest but that he is the best desirer or demander. Thus, it is because God's demands and desires are good that we are obligated to comply with them; but, as we have seen, this deontological intuition, which James accepted in some writings (*PP* 301), clashes with the official position of "The Moral Philosopher and the Moral Life," which invokes God only as the biggest kid on the block.

It is now time to tackle the thorny problem of why James used "desire," "demand," and "claim" interchangeably, using "desire" and "demand" each eleven times and "claim" five; he even speaks occasionally of "likes," "preferences," and what "feels good." It is surprising that none of the many commentators on him have been disturbed by this, since it is obvious that, although "demand" and "claim" are roughly synonymous, "desire," being a psychological term, differs significantly from each of these quasi-legalistic terms. Because "demand" and "claim" are roughly synonymous, I will not consider "claim" in what follows.

Certainly, we are more inclined to lend someone ten dollars who *desires* that we do than someone who *demands* that we do so, assuming no threat is being made. Furthermore, we desire many things that we never would demand. Every person has many desires that they would be ashamed to demand be satisfied, nor would they even want to see them satisfied. It might be thought that an easy solution to James's vacillating back and forth between "desire" and "demand" would be to have him use "desire" for what goes on in his moral solitude and restrict "demand" to the "ethical republic." But the text does not permit this interpretation, as James holds that demands occur in the world of moral solitude if the lone person's present self makes demands on her future self or vice versa. The text does not give us any easy way to explain James's apparent confounding of desires with demands, and it is up to the commentator to follow through on his behalf, which is just what I now will do.

The first step in my reconstruction of James is to point out that, although desire and demand are quite different, there still is an important connection between them, consisting in the fact that what a person demands usually is something that she also desires. The converse, as just indicated, is not true. The next step is to argue that we would do a better job of maximizing desire-satisfaction if we adopted as an instrumental rule that we should always act so as to maximize *demand-statisfaction*.

Why is this the case? First, people have many desires that ought not to be satisfied because doing so would deny satisfaction to many other desires they and others have. By adopting the instrumental rule always to act so as to maximize demand-satisfaction, we are requiring that we in effect play the rational critic to our own desires, as is argued by John Dewey in "Theory of Valuation." The immediately given urges, drives, propensities, and inclinations are reconstructed by an inquiry into their causes and consequences that converts what is desired into what is desirable. And it is what each person deems desirable after this inquiry that is fed into the casuistic equation as a demand. A demand is what a person publicly requests after such an inquiry. Thus, by adopting as an instrumental rule that we should always act so as to maximize demand-satisfaction, *subject to deontological exceptions*, we do a better job in the long run of realizing the summum bonum of maximizing desire-satisfaction.

What are the exceptions? There seem to be at least two – desirers who are either not around to make demands or who are too weak to do so. The text makes clear that James wanted us to factor into the casuistic equation the desires of yet-to-be-born persons, as well as our future selves, even though they are not around now to make demands. "There can be," he says, "no final truth in ethics any more than in physics, until the last man has had experience and said his say" (*WB* 141). In the strenuous mood, we are "awakened . . . by those claims of *remote posterity* which constitute the last appeal of the religion of humanity" (*WB* 160; my italics). There are also people who are not around to make demands because they are spatially remote and cannot get to the "polls." If they will be affected by our decisions, then their desires also must be factored in; we shall have to speak up on their behalf.

All of this clearly agrees with the letter and spirit of the text. However, it is less clear what James would want to say about those desirers who fail to make demands because of weakness and timidity, or even an inability to communicate. Many, maybe even most, persons would say that their desires should be factored equally into the casuistic equation, especially when they held by those who have not yet come of age or are infirm. James, however, says that "Some desires, truly enough, are small desires; they are put forward by *insignificant persons*, and we customarily make light of the obligation which they bring" (*WB*; my italics). These desires get factored in all right, but in a significantly discounted manner. This has an elitist ring to it implying that nice guys do finish last. People deserve respect and consideration, for example to have their desires taken seriously, only when they have the courage to demand that they be accorded this status. Only "significant" persons count, and to achieve significant personhood a person must pass the courage test by demanding that others accord her this status. An exception to this might have to be made for those who have not yet come of age, as well as for sentient animals, a topic that never enters into James's discussion. It is not clear from the text just what James meant by "insignificant persons."

Even if the desire-demand aporia has been neutralized by these considerations, there remain outstanding aporias concerning the ontological status of moral truths and the maximizing-deontological tension. Again, it is up to the commentator to follow through and do the best she can on James's behalf.

James's waffling on the realism-nominalism question as it pertains to moral truths is only a special instance of his general waffling about the ontological status of Platonic abstracta, as will be seen when an exposition is given in Chapter 11 of his account of percepts and concepts. It will emerge that his account of the latter seems to face the same aporia as a result of its apparent commitment to both realism and nominalism. Immediately after giving his nominalistic, concept-empiricist analysis, which holds that concepts are both abstracted from and dependent upon percepts, he goes on to balance the books by adding that "physical realities are constituted by the various concept-stuffs of which they 'partake' " (*SPP* 58). That James was happy to accept the realist commitment of this talk about participation in the forms is clear from his claim that the

absolute determinability of our mind by abstractions is one of the cardinal facts in our human constitution. Polarizing and magnetizing us as they do, we turn towards them and from them, we seek them, hold them, hate them, bless them, just as if they were so many concrete beings. *And beings they are, beings as real in the realm which they inhabit as the changing things of sense are in the realm of space.* (*VRE* 54; my italics)

James gives us a hint as to how to resolve the aporia when he says that

The map which the mind frames out of them [concepts] is an object which possesses, *when once it has been framed,* an independent existence. It suffices all by itself for purposes of study. The 'eternal' truths it contains would have to be acknowledged even were the world of sense annihilated. (*SPP* 43; my italics)

At first glance it looks like the latter passage commits James to a Platonic realism about concepts that clashes with his nominalism; however, the qualification "when once it has been framed" gives him a way of reconciling the two. His nominalism denies that concepts actually exist independently of empirical particulars, such as our acts of conceiving them. But, if we are to have thoughts about concepts, we must think of them as having a world-independent existence and standing in certain eternal relations to each other. In the specific case of moral truths, they do not have an eternal existence independent of our desirings, but once we frame thoughts of them we must conceive of them as having such an existence. Another way of putting this is that it is a rule of the moral language-game that moral truths be accorded a Platonic status by the players, but there are no actual moral truths or laws that obtain or are in effect until we choose to play the game.

James's oft-used potentiality–actuality distinction can be utilized here. There is the possibility of there being Platonic moral truths (or concepts) before we actually play the moral language-game (or conceive of them), but these possibilities become actualized only when we actually play the game (or conceive of them). This way of finding a compromise between nominalism and realism, as will be seen in later chapters, accords with the manner in which he deployed the potentiality–actuality distinction to truth and self-identity over time. Before a person actually judges or remembers that she is identical with some past self, she is only possibly identical with this self, and before a proposition is actually verified it is only possibly true. The categorical version of the law of bivalence, which holds that every proposition is true or false, accordingly is conditionalized by James so that it holds instead that every proposition is possibly true or possibly false. Once the proper verification or judgment of self-identity has occurred, the potentiality in question is actualized and we say retrospectively that the proposition was true all along and the person was identical with this past self. Present truth casts its shadow backward, but without the present truth there is no shadow to be cast over the past. Similarly, the things that we are required to say about the prior existence of moral truths by our present playing of the moral language-game or making obligation-creating demands cast their shadows backward. Thus, the Platonic heaven resembles a cheap boardinghouse in which there is a lot of coming and going.[5]

This way of deploying the potentiality–actuality distinction is highly Promethean. It gives us the Promethean role of being the creators of *actual* truth, moral or otherwise, as well as concepts and our own self-identity over time, through our different actions. Our verificatory and judgmental acts, however, do not create the potentialities for there be-

---

[5] Robert Meyers has suggested to me another way of resolving the nominalism-realism aporia in James's text. The ethical proposition for which James seems to give a realist account consists in necessary truths; but necessary truths, as is argued at length in the final chapter of *The Principles of Psychology*, are based on inherent structures of our brains that have resulted from past mutations that took hold and survived. Thus, what we human beings take to be necessary truths, moral or otherwise, need not be abstract denizens of a Platonic heaven.

ing these actualities. Thus, it is not Promethean all the way down. The realist is right, therefore, to insist on the need for some sort of given, which James often compared with the block of marble presented to the sculptor. A critical evaluation of this doctrine will come later, when detailed expositions are given of James's analyses of truth and self-identity.

The maximizing-deontological aporia is the more difficult of the two to neutralize. I know of no way to reconcile James's deontological intuitions, such as those that he appealed to in condemning using the lost soul (but not the dog) as a means for maximizing desire-dissatisfaction, with his casuistic rule that we are always to act so as to maximize desire-satisfaction. His writings abound in deontological sermonettes that extol the intrinsic value of freely leading the morally strenuous life, of being the right sort of cause of the realization of one's desires. He often writes like a good Kantian who sees our highest moral duty to be that of obeying objective moral truths or duties. Echoing Carlyle, he says that we must have

> the vision of certain works to be done, of certain outward changes to be wrought or resisted. . . . No matter how we succeed in doing these outward duties, whether gladly and spontaneously, or heavily and unwillingly, do them we some-how must; for the leaving of them undone is perdition. No matter how we feel; if we are only faithful in the outward act and refuse to do wrong, the world will in so far be safe, and we quit of our debt towards it . . . be willing to live and die in its service – and, at a stroke, we have passed from the subjective into the objective philosophy of things. (*WB* 134)

He also believed that there are desires, such as sadistic ones, that ought not to be satisfied, even if doing so maximizes desire-satisfaction.

We have already considered the attempt to reconcile the casuistic rule with these deontological intuitions by recognizing that among the desires people actually have, and which therefore must enter into the casuistic equation, are to see that justice is done and that people are never used as mere means. In addition to the consistency problem, this places too much weight on the contingent desires of people. If, as seems actually to be the case, the deontological desires of persons are outweighed by their purely self-interested ones, then we would be morally obligated to see to it that the latter desires are the ones that get fulfilled, to the disadvantage of the "lost souls" of the world. Furthermore, this attempted reconciliation gives the wrong answer to a variant on the question of the *Euthyphro*: Are we prima facie obligated to see to it that a desire for what is deontologically good gets satisfied because it is desired or because what is desired is good? James's casuistic rule requires us to give the former answer, but the latter is required by our and James's deontological intuitions.

I believe that the only viable way for James to resolve this aporia is to reject his claim that "*the essence of good is simply to satisfy demand,*" along with the desire-satisfaction maximizing casuistic rule based on it. He should recognize that there are a plurality of goods, of which desire-satisfaction is only one along with various deontological goods. A consequence of this is that the defeaters or overriders of our prima facie obligation to see to it that a desire gets satisfied will no longer be just an outweighing set of conflicting desires, but deontological principles that get violated as well. James's writings abound with expressions of deontological intuitions, especially concerning the intrinsic value of being a morally responsible agent who is the right sort of free cause of her own self-realization.

This expanded concept of the good requires that his casuistic rule

(1) We are always morally obligated to act so as to maximize *desire-satisfaction* over the other options available to us.

be replaced by

(1") We are always morally obligated to act so as to maximize *good* over the other options available to us.

This rule is too general to provide guidance in making real-life nitty-gritty ethical choices when there is a conflict between what is deontologically right and what will maximize desire-satisfaction (pleasure, happiness). Unfortunately, there is no more specific version of it that ensures that there will not be undecidable cases. For Rule 1, undecidability always results from incomplete knowledge, due to not all of the ballots being in or our not being able to predict the future consequences of different courses of action; but for Rule 1" the undecidability is due to the rule not being specific enough. It is a sad, even tragic, feature of our moral life that there is no acceptable casuistic rule that provides us with a clear-cut decisional procedure for weighing different goods, and thus we must muddle along with great trepidation when making moral choices.

In the remainder of this book, I will, for the sake of simplicity and closeness to James's text, work with version 1 of the casuistic rule, remembering that it is to be understood in terms of the net idea of maximizing desire-satisfaction *over desire-dissatisfaction*. It is my contention that *almost* everything that James accomplished by appeal to Rule 1 could be accomplished equally well by the use of Rule 1" instead. The reason for the "almost" qualification is that by incorporating deontological values into his casuistic rule he might somewhat have undercut the Promethean force of his philosophy, because each self now is subject to deontological constraints that might cramp her quest for full self-realization. Whether my contention is merited will have to be decided in the light of the full range of James's philosophy, and therefore I must, at this time, issue a promissory note.

2

The Willfulness of Belief

As seen in the previous chapter, it is James's contention that

2. Belief is an action.

which, it will be recalled, was the second premise of his syllogistic argument for the conclusion that

3. We are always morally obligated to believe in a manner that maximizes desire-satisfaction over the other available belief options.

For the argument to work, however, the second premise must be beefed up to assert that

2'. Belief is a free action.

the reason being that premise 3 morally obligates us to believe in a certain manner but we can have a moral obligation to act in a certain way only if we are free to do so. This chapter will concentrate on James's argument for belief being an action, leaving its freedom for Chapter 3 and our justification for believing in its freedom to Chapter 4. His overall argument for belief being an action is based on his identification of belief with the will, and the will, at least in one of its senses, with effortful attention to an idea. Since effortful attention is something that we can do intentionally or voluntarily, it follows, by Leibniz's law of the indiscernibility of identicals, that belief also is an intentional action, and thereby, provided it is free, subject to the casuistic rule

1. We are always morally obligated to act so as to maximize desire-satisfaction over the other options available to us.

It is via our acts of effortful attention that we are able to play the Promethean role of *co*creators of actuality, truth, value, meaning, personal identity, as well as the course taken by future history: The "co-" qualification is inserted because James always recognized the demand of the realist for some kind of a given. However, to be truly Promethean beings our acts of attending, willing, and believing also must be free in the radical Libertarian sense that involves a creation ex nihilo; but

All references in this chapter are to *The Principles of Psychology*, unless otherwise indicated.

again, as Chapter 3 will bring out, there is a concession to realism, since they are limited by a given situation, thereby failing to be a total *causa sui.*

That James identified attention, will, and belief, taken in a purely psychological sense, with each other is clear from the following quotations. He begins by claiming that "volition [will] is nothing but attention" and then completes the trilogy of identifications by stating that *"Will and Belief, in short, meaning a certain relation between objects and the Self, are two names for one and the same* PSYCHOLOGICAL *phenomenon"* (424 and 948). Although "attention," "will," and "belief" are coreferential, they have different senses or meanings and thus require separate treatment. That they are coreferential is a very bold and original thesis and will be found to be subject to many serious challenges. For the purpose of James's syllogistic argument for

3. We are always morally obligated to believe in a manner that maximizes desire-satisfaction over the other available belief options.

the thesis need not be true. All that is needed is that belief can be induced, either directly or indirectly, by willful attention, not that belief is identical with attention and the will. This is all that is needed for James's syllogistic argument for 3.

James's psychology employs two different ways of understanding a psychic state. "First, the way of analysis: What does it consist in? What is its inner nature? Of what sort of mind-stuff is it composed? Second, the way of history: What are its conditions of production, and its connection with other facts?" (913) The way of "analysis" involves introspecting our own mind so as to discover what goes on when we are conscious in the concerned manner. This will be called the method of "phenomenological or introspective analysis." The "way of history" is an objective inquiry into the causes and consequences of the psychic state and thus will be called a "causal analysis." Throughout *The Principles of Psychology* James tries to strike a proper balance between the two, but, as will be seen in the second part of this book, "The Anti-Promethean Mystic," he ultimately gives pride of place to the method of phenomenological analysis or introspection.

Although each of us can know what attention, will, and belief are from introspecting our own minds, we cannot define them in terms of any more basic conscious states. Each is a simple, sui generis state, similar to a sensation of green in this respect. For each of them we can phenomenologically distinguish between a simple and a complex case. In the simple case, our consciousness is filled with an idea of an act sans any other competing idea. By some preestablished neurological mechanism, this state of consciousness triggers the envisioned act. In the complex cases, we are aware of conflicting ideas competing for the sole occupation of our consciousness, and herein there is room for an intentional action of making an effort to attend or consent to one of these ideas to the exclusion of the others. This effort or fiat also is phenomenologically vouchsafed. Thus, in both the simple and the complex cases, the final conscious state is the same, some idea filling the mind without any competition; but in the complex case, there is an initial competition between conflicting ideas that is resolved by an effort to attend or consent. Another way to say this is that in the complex but not the simple case the final state of consciousness is brought about by an intentional action.

The reader is urged always to bear in mind James's distinction between the simple and complex cases of attention, will, and belief; for he sometimes makes seemingly general claims that he carelessly fails to restrict to one of the two cases. For example, he says that attention is "reactive spontaneity" and a "taking possession by the mind," which makes attention look like it is intentionally brought about in every case (380 and 381). Similarly, he says without any restriction that will involves a "consent to the idea's undivided presence" and that belief is an "acquiescence" or "consent" to an idea's presence in the mind, both of which again speak for the final state of consciousness being brought about intentionally (1169 and 913). His claim that "*Effort of attention is thus the essential phenomenon of will*" is also misleading (1167). Probably what he means by "essential" is that effortful attention is the *important* kind of attention.

Another example of such carelessness is James's account of the relation between will and desire. "If with the desire there goes a sense that attainment is possible, we simply *wish*; but if we believe that the end is in our power, we *will* that the desired feeling, having, or doing shall be real" (1098). James must have realized that if this claim is not suitably restricted it is false, since there are things that we both desire and believe to be attainable but do not will to be realized because of conflicting moral or aesthetic considerations. Judging by other things he subsequently says, it becomes clear that his claim must be restricted to desires that take place in the simple case in which there are no conflicting desires, for he later says that "What checks our impulses is the mere thinking of reasons to the contrary" (1164). Thus, if a desire clashes with a moral scruple, the subject might not will its satisfaction. That James was just being careless in failing to add the needed restriction to complex cases is clear from his repeated claims that it is only in some but not all cases that there is an effort, consent, or fiat: "The immense majority of human decisions are decisions without effort" and "There is no express fiat needed when the conditions are simple" (1141 and 1134). With these preliminaries out of the way, a separate exposition can now be given, in turn, of James's specific accounts of attention, will, and belief.

I. Attention

James begins with the newborn baby's awareness of the big, blooming, buzzing confusion, charmingly called "baby's first sensation," as if it were a toy by Mattel. This is a sheer chaos, a cotton-candyish mush, because the subject does not apply concepts or categories that relate one part of it to another. "All of the 'categories of the understanding' are contained," however, in this pure sensation, but there is not yet any attending activity on the part of the babe, and thus no part of the sensory field stands out from its background (657). As Charlene Haddock Seigfried has correctly pointed out, "The chaos is a result of an overabundance of relations, which are too numerous to be grasped, rather than an absence of relations" (CC 28).[1] There are not yet, for example, any indexically based accents of now and then, here and there, this and that, and I and you (PP 381). No *perception* has yet occurred, since, for James, a *sensation* becomes a perception only when there is an application of a concept to its sensory content. The babe *sees* all of the sensory contents and the relations between them but does not *see that* these contents stand in relations, because no concepts are applied. Because the application of a concept involves judgment or belief, the babe does not yet have any beliefs about what is sensorily given. James is not consistent on this point, for he says that if the baby's first sensation is "of a lighted candle against a dark background, and nothing else," the existence of the candle will "be believed in," will be "known to the mind in question" (917). As one cannot believe or know without using concepts, this imputes to the babe the possession of concepts. This is yet another example of James's proclivity to engage in Robinson Crusoe mythologizing, of a piece with his notion of a "moral solitude" in Chapter 1.

The babe cannot attend to any part of the originally given chaos until it has acquired concepts and the ability to wield them in judgments. "*The only things which we commonly see [perceive] are those which we preperceive,* and the only things which we preperceive are those which have been labelled for us, and the labels stamped into our mind. If we lost our stock of labels we should be intellectually lost in the midst of the world" (420). A preperception is "nothing but the anticipatory imagination of what the impressions or the reactions are to be" (415). For

---

[1] I regret that I am unable to do justice in my book to her two excellent books on James. Sad to say, I am not sufficiently knowledgeable in the contemporary Continental movements within which she situates James.

James, concepts are acquired through abstraction from past sensations, which is to be a topic for Chapter 11. The babe has not yet had a sufficiently rich fund of past sensations from which to derive the concepts that are needed to label things.

It is unclear whether baby's first sensation counts as an *experience* at all. James first makes the Kantian claim that "Millions of items of the outward order are present to my senses which never properly enter into my *experience*" because "My *experience* is what I agree to attend to" (380; my italics). This has the consequence that baby's first sensation is not an experience at all. But James immediately adds that "without selective interest, *experience* is an utter chaos," which seems to allow for an unattentive experience of the baby's-first-sensation sort (381). The best way for James to resolve this terminological confusion is to reserve "experience" for attended consciousness and call baby's first sensation a mere case of consciousness. This squares with James's claim that without attention "the *consciousness* of every creature would be a gray chaotic indiscriminateness, impossible for us even to conceive" (381; my italics).

Again, it is important to stress that James recognized a distinction between simple and complex cases of attention. In the simple case, "Attention to an object is what takes place whenever that object most completely occupies the mind" (*TT* 69), there being no need for the subject to be an active agent in bringing about this state of consciousness. You could just find yourself attending to one part of the sensorily given to the exclusion of others; your idea of it just happens to stand out from the pack. Similar remarks are made about will and belief. "Volition . . . is absolutely completed when the stable state of the idea is there" and "Belief means only a peculiar sort of occupancy of the mind" (*PP* 1165 and 1166). But he also says that attention is "reactive spontaneity" (380), a "taking possession by the mind" (381), which points to it being an intentional action. Again, the reader must make the suitable restriction to complex cases on James's behalf.

It might be urged that *all* cases of attention involve an intentional action on the grounds that, since attention requires the application of a concept, it involves the intentional action of *making* a judgment or *forming* a belief. The problem with this is that although we can at will join concepts together in our imagination into a propositional complex, we cannot in most cases believe at will. James asks rhetorically: "If belief consists in an emotional reaction of the entire man on an object, how *can* we believe at will? We cannot control our emotions" (948). How James deals with the problem of self-inducing beliefs is to figure prominently in his account of the will to believe and thus will be considered later.

So far we have been considering only James's phenomenological analysis of attention. His causal analysis of attention in terms of interest contains an apparent inconsistency. He says, on the one hand, "The things to which we attend are said to *interest* us. Our interest in them is supposed to be the *cause* of our attending" (393). Yet he also says that "what-we-attend-to and what-interests-us are synonymous terms" (1164). But since the terms designating respectively a cause and an effect are not synonymous, it follows that interest is not the cause of our attending, pace what James has just said on page 393. I believe that the account that makes interest the cause of attention squares better overall with the text and thus is the one that will be employed. No doubt whatever we attend to is of interest to us, either directly or through its association with things that have direct interest (you attend to a relative in whom you have no direct interest because you are interested in obeying the maxim that one should take care of one's relatives); however, this is not because attention and interest are one and the same but rather because attention, whether simple or complex, always is caused by interest, and thus they go together.

That attention always is caused by interest raises an active-passive, creating–discovering aporia, which will be found to run throughout James's Promethean philosophy. In Chapter 1 it involved a clash between our *creating* value and obligation through our desirings or demandings and our *discovering* an objective moral truth, the casuistic rule, by appeal to our moral intuition. In the simple case, we do not intentionally bring it about that we are in the attending state, as we make no previous effort to be in this state. It is only in regard to the complex cases that James speaks of our choosing to attend as we do. "Each of us literally *chooses*, by his ways of attending to things, what sort of a universe he shall appear to himself to inhabit" (401). This is the height of his Prometheanism, according to which each of us chooses which one of the many possible worlds is to be the actual world, thereby usurping the Deity's prerogative of doing this.

The problem is that our choice to attend to one universe or object over its competitors is caused by our interest, but our interest, in turn, being an emotional state, is not subject to our wills. We can no more control at will what interests us than we can control what we love. James seems to agree: "The accommodation and the resultant feeling *are* the attention. We don't bestow it, the object draws it from us. The object has the initiative, not the mind" (425). This clashes with his activistic claim that attending in the complex case involves a "taking possession by the mind," a "reactive spontaneity." The best expression of the aporia comes from James's own pen. In both the simple and the complex cases, the mind "turns to it [the object that is to be attended to] . . . in the *interested active emotional way*" (948; my italics). The agent discovers rather than creates its emotionally based interest. An attempt will be made on James's behalf to resolve this aporia in the next chapter.

II. Will

Everything that has been said about attention has a parallel with respect to the will, since "attention" and "will" refer to one and the same psychological phenomenon for James, although they differ in sense. As he did in his account of attention, James will again distinguish between an active and a passive case, though at times he writes carelessly as if all cases of will involved an intentional effort or fiat. His exposition begins with the simple or passive case of willing, called "ideomotor action," which has no fiat or effort to attend. He then goes on to consider the complex case of a conflict between ideas that requires for its resolution a fiat or effort.

All human behavior initially is involuntary. Incoming sensations are followed by bodily behavior either through instinct, reflex, or accident. That sensations will lead to a motor discharge is due to the fact "that consciousness is *in its very nature impulsive.... Movement is the natural immediate effect of feeling, irrespective of what the quality of the feeling may be*" (1134–5). The organic material of the human brain is highly plastic, permitting new neural pathways to be formed in it. "An acquired habit, from the physiological point of view, is nothing but a new pathway of discharge formed in the brain, by which certain incoming currents ever after tend to escape" (9). When there is a constant conjunction between a sensory input and a motor discharge, this causes a new habit to be formed, consisting in a new pathway from that part of the brain in which the incoming sensory input is registered to some motor response (11).

The bodily behavior, say the moving of your arm, caused by the incoming sensation has experiential accompaniments consisting in kinaesthetic and visual sensations of your arm moving and some of its effects. Thus, there will result another constant conjunction, this one between your sensory ideas of your arm moving and its moving. By a complex physiological law, which I will not formulate here (see 1183–8 for details), your having the idea of your arm moving can take the place of the original incoming sensation as the triggering event of your arm's moving. Thus a new habit is formed that enables your having kinesthetic and visual ideas of your arm moving and its effects to discharge into the motor organs that move your arm. Notice that there is no mysterious sort of backward causation going on here. Initially, these ideas came after or while your arm moved, but now, after the formation of this secondary habit, they come before the movement and thus cause it in an ordinary forward-directed manner.

Once the secondary habit has been formed, the subject can voluntarily or willfully move his arm. He does so by activating his memories of what it felt like when his arm moved, thereby consciously ideating in a my-arm-is-moving manner. If there is no conflicting idea in his mind to that of his arm moving, such as the thought that he must not move his arm because it is broken, his arm will move in virtue of the secondary habit. "*A supply of ideas of the various movements that are possible, left in the memory by experiences of their involuntary performance, is thus the first prerequisite of the voluntary life,*" the other prerequisite, in the simple case of ideomotor action, being the lack of any competing idea (1099–1100).

That the mere thought of the sensations you have when your arm moves is sufficient to cause your arm to move challenges Wundt's innervation theory, which holds that *in every case* there must be a fiat or volitional mandate that comes *after* the having of the thought of the action in question. James advances both introspectively and a priori-based objections to this theory. In the case of an ideomotor action, "*An anticipatory image . . . of the sensorial consequence of a movement . . . is the only psychic state which introspection lets us discern as the forerunner of our voluntary acts.* There is no introspective evidence whatever of any still later or concomitant feeling attached to the efferent discharge" (111–12). The innervationists confound the feelings of effort that are sometimes caused by the movement with the fiat that triggers the movement, thereby reversing cause and effect.

The a priori objection is that the innervation theory violates the logical principle of parsimony. "*There is a certain a priori reason why the kinaesthetic images* OUGHT *to be the last psychic antecedents of the outgoing currents, and why we should expect these currents to be insentient; why, in short, the soi-disant feelings of innervation should* NOT *exist*" (1107). Once the subject has acquired the secondary habit that enables his idea of a movement to replace the original sensory input as the cause of the movement, there is nothing left for any additional conscious state, such as a fiat, to do. "It is a general principle in Psychology that consciousness deserts all processes where it can no longer be of use. . . . by virtue of this principle of parsimony in consciousness the motor discharge *ought* to be devoid of sentience" (1107–8). The innervationist could accept the principle of parsimony but challenge James's *empirical* claim that the mere conscious thought of the movement alone, even when there is no competition, is causally sufficient for the movement to ensue. In the absence of hard empirical evidence for the theory of ideomotor action, an appeal to the principle of parsimony is premature.

James holds that it is a brute contingent fact that our will is efficacious only over our own body, that we can cause our arm but not the table to move by thinking of it as moving (947–8 and 1165). As an avid psychical investigator, he took seriously the possibility of telekinesis, though he did not find the evidence for it very strong. James adds the rather startling claim that he is able to will or exert a volition that a table should move and is surprised that others report themselves unable to do so. He speculates that the reason why they think they cannot do so is that they know it is not in their power to move the table, and this "sense of impotence inhibits the volition" (1165). If they were to have a desire for the table to move, it would be a mere wish, not a want, since the desire is a conflicted one.

I very much doubt that this is the right account of why these people, and James ought to be among them, are unable to will that the table move. The crucial idea of a movement in the case of ideomotor action is of the resident kinesthetic sensations that accompany the movement, rather than just the idea of the visual sensations occasioned by the movement or its effects, such as one could have of the table moving. Obviously, we have no idea of the kinesthetic sensations that are resident in a table's moving and thus have no idea of what it is like for a table to move voluntarily. And as a result we have no idea of the manner in which we should ideate so as to cause the table to move. We just do not know, in general, what it is like to be a table and do tablely things, like stoically remaining immobile when someone thumps on us to emphasize the point that it is this very table which he refers to when he makes counterfactual claims about it.

In a complex case of will there is a competition among warring ideas to be the sole, steadfast occupant of the mind and thereby to attain satisfaction. In such a case our idea of each action is inhibited from discharging into the appropriate motor response by its competitor. This produces in us a state of indecision. James wrongly says that "As long as it lasts, with the various objects before the attention, we are said to deliberate," for to deliberate requires that, in addition to being conflicted, we examine each of the conflicting ideas in regard to its suitability for realization (1136). While deliberating, we oscillate between the different futures portrayed by the ideas. We are in a state of tense unrest and thus desire to decide the issue so that we can take repose in action. But this desire is countered by the "dread of the irrevocable" (1137).

James outlines five ways in which a decision finally is made. First, there is the "reasonable type" of decision that comes after rational deliberation in which one of the alternatives emerges as the one best supported by the facts. In the next two types of decision, the final fiat occurs before the completion of a rational inquiry. We let ourselves indifferently drift in one of the directions on the basis of either an external or an internal accident. In the fourth, some outward experience causes us suddenly to undergo a radical change of mood, say from the easygoing to the strenuous mood. It is in the fifth type that an express volition or effort decides the matter. We feel a "heave of the will" that succeeds in inclining the beam in one of the directions. Even after we have settled on one of the possible courses of action, the thought of the rejected possibilities tortures us. Herein we motivelessly make one of the competing motives emerge as the decisive one through our effort to attend to it. What this portends for the freedom of the will is to be the topic of Chapter 3.

Some of the very best commentators have found James's theory of the will wanting. T. L. S. Sprigge finds James's account too loose, because it gives "the impression that . . . we have a case of ideomotor action wherever an idea causes a movement through having been associated with it in the past" (*JB* 99). Thus, if the ideas of going to bed and Latin words, respectively, have become associated with drinking a cup of tea and yawning, it would seem that James is committed to saying that the former ideas respectively will the latter occurrences; but this is wrong because the ideas are not even of them, though they are a cause of them. It is only a conditioned ideational reflex. To get around this difficulty, James must explicitly restrict his theory of ideomotor action to conscious states that not only cause a subsequent action but also are *of* them. "The idea must in some genuine sense envisage either the movement or its likely results. . . . Some distinction is required, then, between ideas which produce behaviour which actualises their content and those which produce behaviour with which they have no direct intentional connection" (*JB* 100). There could be a case in which the willer, remembering that his tea drinking always is followed by his retiring, wills that he retire by thinking of his drinking tea, but this requires a conscious intent to bring about his retiring by intending that he drink tea. Sprigge also points out that James must enrich his theory so as to allow the ideational state to consist of words as well as images, for we often form intentions in terms of sentences rather the sensory ideas.

Both of Sprigge's points are good ones; however, James has developed elsewhere the resources to enrich his theory so as to meet them. He has a theory of the of-ness relation between an idea and its referent, which will be considered in Chapter 6, and an account of how we associate images with words so that the words are able to replace images in our thinking.

Gerald Myers objects to James's general linking of attention and will:

But the connection between the attending, the willing, and the acting is much too loose for the theory of ideo-motor action to be built upon. There is no basis for James's contention that the action of will upon behavior is always through the intermediary of ideas. We are less likely to cause an act by first fixing attention on an idea of it than we are by deciding to do it without being aware that any act of attention or crucial idea is involved. (*WJ* 209)

There is no doubt that James is a suitable target for this objection, for he explicitly says that "*the terminus of the psychological process in volition, the point to which the will is directly applied, is always an idea*" (1171).

Myer's objection aptly could be called the "Just do it" objection. The issue, I take it, is not whether the willer has a prior idea or thought of his intended action, though Myers is skeptical about this; it concerns, rather, what he does intentionally. According to Myers, he typically intends to perform the action rather than have this idea. The easiest way to move your arm is just to move it rather than intentionally bringing it about that your consciousness is steadfastly occupied by the image of your arm moving. Furthermore, you could bring about the latter but still not move your arm. For example, you might know that your arm will move if you get into this state of consciousness but be unable to ideate in this my-arm-is-moving manner, so you hire a brain surgeon to bring about this ideating by exciting your brain with a probe. You bring it about that your arm moves but you do not move your arm. A lawyer once sent me a document to sign, and instead of saying, "Sign your name at the bottom," as would some ordinary riffraff off the street, requested that I bring it about that my signature appear at the bottom; so I thought of hiring a hypnotist to put me in a trance and give me the posthypnotic suggestion to write my name at the bottom.

Certainly, Myers is right. But all is not lost for James. Although his theory is not true in general, it does apply to some cases that are among the most important ones in our lives, because we in effect decide what kind of persons we will become. As Ruth Anna Putnam aptly put it, these cases require "not only the ability to picture to oneself vividly what one is about to do and its immediate consequences for oneself and others, but also the ability to visualize the kind of person one will be . . . if one pursues this path rather than that, commits oneself to this ideal and not that one" (*LI* 288). These are complex cases in which we are not able to "just do it" but instead must first work on our own minds so that we become vividly conscious in a certain manner. In the important character-determining cases, we need to dramatically envision our performing the competing alternative actions and the consequences of doing so. Not only can this be the key factor in determining us to pursue one of the alternatives, it also can greatly increase the chances of our successfully pursuing it.

We are like actors to whom many scripts are presented from which we must choose one in which to star. We reject some scripts immediately because we cannot seriously entertain playing that role. Getting ourselves eventually to accept one of the scripts over its serious competitors consists in vividly playing over one of the roles in our imagination until it dominates, this amounting to the that's-me feeling, and thereby the decision to play that role.

The same sort of aesthetic ideating is crucial, at least for many persons, in selecting the character they will play in real life. Consider James's marvelous case of the reformed alcoholic who is offered a drink by his host.

His moral triumph or failure literally consists in his finding the right *name* for the case. If he says that it is a case of not wasting good liquor already poured out, or a case of not being churlish and unsociable when in the midst of friends, or a case of learning something at last about a brand of whiskey which he never met before, or a case of celebrating a public holiday, or a case of stimulating himself to a more energetic resolve in favor of abstinence than any he has ever yet made, then he is lost; his choice of the wrong name seals his doom. But if in spite of all the plausible good names with which his thirsty fancy so copiously furnishes him, he unwaveringly clings to the truer bad name, and apperceives the case as that of "being a drunkard, being a drunkard, being a drunkard," his feet are planted on the road to salvation; he saves himself by thinking rightly. (*TT* 110)

More than just finding the right name is involved. There also is the dramatic envisionment of his futures as a sober man or as a drunkard. On the one hand, he could form comforting pictures of himself being the carefree, hard-drinking bon vivant, or even the sullen, self-destructive alcoholic so irresistible to women and novelists, maybe even one of the delightful characters in O'Neill's *The Ice Man Cometh*, who says, "What have you done to the booze, Hickey? It's lost its life." On the other hand, he could vividly ideate about his future life as a drunkard in a way that would deter him from electing to play this role. He could imagine the deleterious physical effects of drinking, being an object of derision and contempt, letting down his loved ones. Or, even better for James, he could form positive images of his future sober life in which he would experience "the blessings of having an organism kept in lifelong possession of its full youthful elasticity by a sweet, sound, blood, to which stimulants and narcotics are unknown, and to which the morning sun and air and dew daily come as sufficiently powerful intoxicants" (*TT* 114). It is clear that the man does not reject the offer of a drink in this case by "just doing it," but rather by the complicated, circuitous process of dramatic projection into alternative future roles that will determine what sort of a person he will become.

Many of our important moral decisions are made through aesthetic ideational projection into different roles. This could be called the theory of "Hollywood Ethics." A person might not steal, for example, not because he feels constrained by the moral law, but rather because he cannot see himself playing the role of someone who cares that much about material possessions. Unlike other ethical theories, Hollywood Ethics does not purport to tell us what is the ethically good or right thing to do, but when practiced seriously and honestly, it can help us to find our authentic selves and a way of life that is right for us. According to the "ideal observer theory" of ethics, the morally right or good thing to do is what the ideal observer, who is completely rational and possessed of all the relevant facts, would choose to do. The fully dedicated and honest performer of the thought experiment required by my Hollywood Ethics is not the "ideal observer," but he is the closest that we mortals can come to achieving this status. That James's theory of complex cases of will neatly fit in with Hollywood Ethics is, I take it, a point in its favor.

III. Belief

Finally, we come to the major concern of this chapter, belief, and in particular whether it is inducible at will, thereby making it subject to James's casuistic rule, provided it is also free. Belief, like will, is nothing but the attending to an idea sans competitors and admits of the same distinction between simple and complex cases, depending on whether or not the attending state results from an effort. There is, of course, a difference between belief and will in that we can have beliefs about things, such as a table moving, that we do not or, some would say, cannot will, because our will directly controls only our own body. This, however, is only a physiological, not a psychological, difference. The reader of the chapter on "The Perception of Reality" in *The Principles of Psychology* must be especially alert to the distinction between the two senses in which James uses "belief": (i) the stable occupancy of an idea in consciousness sans competitors; and (ii) a propositional attitude of consent or acceptance taken to an idea, resulting in a state of type (i). Whereas it is made clear that every case of belief must involve a type (i) state, he fluctuated on whether *every* act of believing also requires a type (ii) consensual act. If it does, belief hardly is the same as the will, since, as several quotations have attested, there can be a case of will that is only of type (i).

The following quotation brings to a head James's waffling over whether there can be a belief state without an act of consent that brings this state about.

In its inner nature belief, or the sense of reality, is a sort of feeling more allied to the emotions than to anything else. Mr. Bagehot distinctly calls it the 'emotion' of conviction. Consent is recognized by all to be a manifestation of our active nature. I just now spoke of it as acquiescence. It would naturally be described by such terms as 'willingness' or the 'turning of our disposition.' What characterizes both consent and belief is the cessation of theoretic agitation through the advent of an idea which is inwardly stable, and fills the mind solidly to the exclusion of contradictory ideas. (*PP* 913)

The first two sentences clearly speak for the possibility of there being a type (i) belief state without any type (ii) act of consent. Notice that he uses the term "conviction" to characterize the belief state. A conviction or being convinced, unlike acquiescence and consent, is not an action, it being absurd to say that you became convinced, as opposed to consented or acquiesced, intentionally, on purpose, voluntarily, carefully, and so on for all the other intentional action modifiers. The charitable way to interpret this passage is to say that when James switches in the third and fourth sentences to speaking respectively about acquiescence and consent, he shifts from talking about the passive type (i) beliefs to the active type (ii) beliefs. Unfortunately for this interpretation, the third sentence, "I just now spoke of it as acquiescence," through its use of the anaphoric "it," refers back to the type (i) beliefs of the previous two sentences. James certainly did not mean to require that every belief state result from an act of consent. Other passages of a similar ilk could be quoted.

There *are* passages, however, in which James clearly allows for an exclusively type (i) belief, for example his highly mythologized "baby's first sensation" of the lighted candle that is believed (!) by the babe to be existent because "*Any object which remains uncontradicted is ipso facto believed and posited as absolute reality*" (918). James's attempt to make this sound plausible appeals to a false dichotomy between believing and disbelieving – since the babe doesn't disbelieve the reality of the candle, it must believe in its reality – which overlooks the third possibility of having no belief at all. James might have been misled into accepting this false disjunction because he confounded it with his other thesis that "The sense that anything we think of is unreal can only come, then, when that thing is contradicted by some other thing of which we think" and "We never disbelieve anything except for the reason that we believe something else which contradicts the first thing" (914 and 918).

James asks us to "compare this psychological fact with the corresponding logical truth that all negation rests on covert assertion of something else than the thing denied" (*PP* 914). Herein we see James's penchant to semanticize and ontologize a genetic analysis of the psychological cause of our taking something to be the case, just as he did in Chapter 1, with his genetic analysis of the conditions under which we take something to be good or obligatory. Since we are led to deny the existence of something when we discover or believe that there is some positive reality that logically excludes it, what we mean by, for example, "The table is not red" is "There is some positive property of the table, F-ness, that is incompatible with redness," and, furthermore, the very being of a negative state of affairs – a lack, absence, want, or privation – is logically dependent upon there being some positive reality whose properties are incompatible with its properties.[2]

Not only does the incompatibility theory seem false in general, since I might believe that some man lacks an odor without believing that he has some positive property that logically excludes his having an odor,

[2] For a full account of this and related matters, see my book *Problems of Negation and Non-Being, The American Philosophical Quarterly,* Monograph no. 7 (1975), chapter 1.

and even be right about this, it is also inconsistent with James's prized and oft-repeated doctrine of the mystery of existence. James was intent on showing that, pace absolute idealism, there must be some fact that defies explanation, namely that there is something rather than nothing (See primarily *EPH* 58–64 and *WB* 107–8, as well as *PP*1 269, *SPP* 27, and *ML* 412.) As Bergson showed in his *Creative Evolution*, the incompatibility theory of negation, when interpreted ontologically, entails, pace the doctrine of the mystery of existence, that it is necessary that there exist some positive reality, and thus that there is something rather than nothing, as something can fail to exist only if there exists in its place some positive reality that logically excludes it. This constitutes an ontological argument for the existence of positive entities.[3] James read this book in 1907 and heaped lavish praise upon it, but he still adhered to the mystery of existence in *Some Problems of Philosophy*, which he began to write two years later. I believe that the best way for James to resolve this inconsistency between the mystery of existence and the incompatibility theory of negation would have been to give up the latter, for not only does it seem false, it goes too far in the direction of rationalism, being only a stone's throw from the principle of sufficient reason in demanding an explanation for every negative fact in terms of positive facts alone.

James makes use of Brentano's theory of judgment to account for the active, type (ii) beliefs. There are various propositional attitudes, called "psychic attitudes" by James, that the mind can adopt to a proposition, understood as a "combination of 'ideas' by a 'copula' " (917 and 916). There is that completely neutral attitude of merely entertaining or thinking of the proposition, which can then give way to a believing, denying, or questioning of the proposition. James's remark that "All that the mind does is in both cases [will and belief] the same; it looks at the object and consents to its existence, espouses it, says 'it shall be my reality' " seems to equate the belief and will psychic attitudes (948).[4]

It is crucial that a proposition can retain its identity from one manner

---

[3] For a full discussion, see my "Bergson's Analysis of the Concept of Nothing," *The Modern Schoolman* 51 (1974): 269–300.

[4] The alert reader will wonder how this commitment to propositions as the intentional accusatives of psychic attitudes can be squared with James's general dismissal of abstract propositions, as was brought out in Chapter 1. James cannot escape commitment to them by breaking up the unity of the believed proposition, as did Bertrand Russell in his Multiple Relation theory of belief, into a mere laundry list of unrelated items, each of which the believer is separately acquainted with. For James stresses the internal unity of the propositional accusative by hyphenating its components, as in "Columbus-discovered-America-in-1492" (*PP* 916). James has a nominalistic response available to this challenge. Given that he made a complex of ideas in someone's mind the bearer of a truth-value, he could say that this mental proposition also functions as the accusative of psychic attitudes.

of being attended to by a psychic act to another, for otherwise certain valid argument forms would not be valid. Consider the valid argument form of *modus ponens*: If p then q. p. Therefore, q. The proposition p is not asserted or consented to in the hypothetical premise, but it is in the second premise. Unless p is the very same proposition in both of its appearances, the argument fails to be valid through equivocation.

James is quite explicit that the Brentano theory applies only to complex cases of type (ii). "Often we first suppose and then believe. . . . But these cases are none of them *primitive* [simple] cases. They only occur in minds long schooled to doubt by the contradictions of experience" (946). It is when there is a conflict between two or more ideas competing for sole occupancy of our mind that there is a need for a psychic attitude or act of belief, in the form of a consent, acceptance, or acquiescence to one of the competing ideas.

Once the act of consent has succeeded in bringing about a type (i) state of consciousness, neurophysiology will take over and lead to a motor response. When the state consists in thinking of one of our own actions, the action will follow in just the same way as if we had willed it, but if it consists instead in a thought of some object other than our own body behaving in a certain way, the behavior will not follow.

That action is the normal outgrowth of belief can help to explain James's startling remark that "We would believe everything if we only could" (*PP* 928). This preference cannot be explained in terms of the belief state's peace of mind vis à vis that of indecision – our "proneness to act or decide merely because action and decision are, as such, agreeable, and relieve the tension of doubt and hesitancy" (1137). This explains only why we want to be in a belief state, not why we want to believe *everything*. Nor is the explanation to be had in terms of our having a *National Inquirer*–type mentality that delights in believing "everything" about everybody. I believe an explanation can be found in terms of James's Promethean quest to actualize all of his many selves. To actualize all these selves, an incredible diversity of acts must be performed. Since belief leads to action, the more beliefs we have, the more actions we perform, and thus the more headway we make on this grand Promethean quest. There also is an appeal to James's hipsterism, as each action occasions its own special tingle or thrill.

One gets the feeling that James's reasons for insisting that a belief lead to action were not based exclusively on neurophysiological facts, which were exceedingly sparse at that time, but on normative considerations as well. At the heart of the pragmatism of both Peirce and James is Bain's claim that a belief is what a man is willing to act on. For James this was not a purely descriptive claim based on conceptual analysis or neurophysiology but in part normative. A man *ought* to act on his beliefs.

James had an intense disdain for the idle dreamer and aesthete. "There is no more contemptible type of human character than that of the nerveless sentimentalist and dreamer, who spends his life in a weltering sea of sensibility and emotion, but who never does a manly concrete deed" (129).[5]

> The habit of excessive novel-reading and theatre-going will produce true monsters in the line. The weeping of a Russian lady over the fictitious personages in the play, while her coachman is freezing to death on his seat outside, is the sort of thing that everywhere happens on a less glaring scale. Even the habit of excessive indulgence in music, for those who are neither performers themselves nor musically gifted enough to take it in a purely intellectual way, has probably a relaxing effect upon the character. One becomes filled with emotions which habitually pass without prompting to any deed, and so the inertly sentimental condition is kept up. The remedy would be, never to suffer one's self to have an emotion at a concert, without expressing it afterwards in some active way. (129)[6]

By identifying the type (i) belief state, which is an emotional state, with the will state, James assured that belief would find its proper hookup with "concrete manly deeds." No sniveling, effeminate beliefs need apply!

James's causal analysis of belief deals with its causes as well as its effects, which are or, better, ought to be, overt actions of a "manly" sort. His analysis of the causes of belief also parallels that of the causes of the will. Any uncontested thought constitutes a belief, as well as a will. There are two different ways, one active and the other inactive, in which one can have an uncontested thought, whether or not it is preceded by a conflict between rival thoughts. It can be caused in a nonactive way by the thought having emotional sting based on its "coerciveness over attention, or the mere power to possess consciousness"; "liveliness, or sensible pungency"; "stimulating effect upon the will"; "emotional interest, as object of love, dread, admiration, desire"; "con-

---

[5] This moralistic penchant might account for the criticisms he made in some of his letters to his younger brother, Henry, that his stories wallowed too much in subtle sensitivities and lacked a morally uplifting plot. In one letter he wrote: "But why won't you, just to please Brother, sit down and write a new book, with no twilight or mustiness in the plot, with great vigor and decisiveness in the action, no fencing in the dialogue, no psychological commentaries, and absolute straightness in the style? Publish it in my name, I will acknowledge it, and give you half the proceeds" (*CWJ* 3:301). Henry's marvelous response was, "I mean . . . to try to produce some uncanny form of thing, in fiction, that will gratify you, as Brother – but let me say, dear William, that I shall greatly be humiliated if you *do* like it, & thereby lump it, in your affection with things, of the current age, that I have heard you express admiration for & that I would sooner descend to a dishonoured grave than have written" (*CWJ*, 3: xlii).

[6] A paradigm case of someone who availed himself of this remedy is the Italian army officer who leapt from a balcony, damn near killing a few people in the orchestra, at the premier of Verdi's *La Battaglia de Legnano*, in emulation of the daring leap of the opera's hero, Arrigo, out of a high turret window and across a moat so that he could join his regiment for the battle.

gruity with certain favorite forms of contemplation''; or ''independence of other causes'' (*PP* 928–9). Plainly, none of these causes involve intentional agency. The believer does not control them at will. James's claim that ''the more a conceived object *excites* us, the more reality it has [for us]'' also makes the cause a nonaction, since we cannot control at will what excites us (935). This is the first leg of the creating-discovering aporia.

There is, however, an active way in which a belief state can be caused, and that is through the effort to attend to an idea. The *acts* of consent, acceptance, or acquiescence are things that an agent does intentionally. In the conflicted cases, the act of consent often comes as a result of effort, and this raises the question of what causes this effort. This will be discussed in the next chapter, since it gets to the root of James's theory of freedom.

In some cases, try as we may to attend to an idea, we are unable to establish its steadfast, uncontested presence in our mind. As James puts it, ''a man cannot believe at will abruptly'' (948). Fortunately, there is an indirect way of willfully inducing such recalcitrant beliefs, namely by *acting as if* we believed, which is just what Pascal enjoined nonbelievers who want to acquire real faith to do. ''*We need only in cold blood* ACT *as if the thing in question were real, and it will infallibly end by growing into such a connection with our life that it will become real*'' (949). This acting-as-if-you-believe recipe for self-inducing a belief is given in a letter written eighteen years earlier, in 1872, to his brother Bob: ''Have faith and wait, and resolve whatever happens to be faithful 'in the outward act' (as a philosopher says) that is *do* as if the good were the law of being, even if one can't for the moment really believe it. The belief will come in its time'' (*CWJ* 4:432). In ''The Gospel of Relaxation'' James says that ''Action seems to follow feeling, but really action and feeling go together and by regulating the action, which is under the more direct control of the will, we can indirectly regulate the feeling, which is not'' (*TT* 118). Given that belief is a feeling of conviction for James, this recipe applies also to belief. For this chapter's purpose of establishing that James held belief to be an action, this is all that is needed. Although belief is not always a ''basic action'' in the sense of something that we just do without first intentionally doing anything else, it is self-inducible by basic actions and thereby becomes subject to our will. Accordingly, the second premise of James's master syllogism must be understood as asserting that

2'. Belief is a free action or inducible by free actions.

but for the sake of brevity the final disjunct will be omitted. The conclusion is:

3. We are always morally obligated to believe or get ourselves to believe in a manner that maximizes desire-satisfaction over the other available belief options.

There is a curious anomaly in James's text that has escaped all of his commentators. Seven years after he wrote this, in "The Will to Believe," James raised the objection that we cannot believe at will.

Does it not seem preposterous on the very face of it to talk of our opinions being modifiable at will? Can our will either help or hinder our intellect in its perceptions of truth? Can we, by just willing it, believe that Abraham Lincoln's existence is a myth, and that the portraits of him in *McClure's Magazine* are all of someone else? . . . We can *say* any of these things, but we are absolutely impotent to believe them. (*WB* 15–6)

James responded to this objection by arguing that *all* of our beliefs, even scientific ones, are passionally or emotionally caused. "Our non-intellectual nature does influence our convictions. There are passional tendencies and volitions which run before and others which come after belief, and it is only the latter that are too late for the fair; and they are not too late when the previous passional work has been already in their own direction" (*WB* 19–20).

This is a disastrous response that leads right into the creating-discovering aporia. We are supposed to be able to create some of our beliefs by making the effort to attend, but now we are told that the cause of all beliefs is passional, and since we cannot control our passions at will neither can we control at will our beliefs. This makes us into passive registerers or discoverers of our beliefs.

Why, for heaven's sake, did James not avail himself of his earlier causal recipe for indirectly inducing belief by acting as if we believe? This would have sufficed to blunt the force of the belief-is-not-an-action objection to his will-to-believe doctrine, for the doctrine need not require that we can believe at will, only that we can at will do things that shall self-induce belief. I am not sure what the answer is. Certainly, it is not attributable to his not remembering what he wrote seven years earlier. Probably, it was due to the fact that "The Will to Believe" was presented as a popular lecture, and for this occasion he was satisfied to win a debater's victory over scientisitic objectors, the Cliffords and Huxleys, by the *tu quo que* response that their scientific beliefs are just as emotionally based as are those of the theist.

Before considering James's account of freedom of the will, and thereby of attention and belief as well, I shall raise some objections that are intended to show: first, that there are no type (ii) or exclusively type (i) beliefs; and, second, that every belief involves a psychic or propositional attitude different from that involved in a case of willing, which should not come as a surprise as we knew all along, pace James, that belief and will are different.

That there are no type (ii) beliefs in the sense of a *consenting* to, *acquiescing* in, or *accepting* of a proposition is due to the fact that none of the italicized terms are the same as believing. That they are not is because they are intentional acts but believing is not. The evidence for this is that, whereas it makes sense to say that someone voluntarily consents, acquiesces, or consents, it makes no sense to say that he voluntarily believes. It is for this reason that there is an Austinian performatory use as illocutionary force indicator for "consent," "acquiesce," and "accept" but not for "believe," "I hereby believe" being out of order. By publicly saying the former in the proper *social conventional* circumstances, one brings it about that one consents to or accepts a proposition, but by saying the latter one does not bring it about in virtue of a *social convention* that one believes the proposition. The social convention qualification is needed to ward off certain counterexamples, such as the following one that I owe to Alexander Pruss in conversation. A person has had a serious accident and is worried that he has lost the power of speech. To test the ability, he tries to utter the sentence, "I believe that I can speak." If he succeeds, the uttering of the sentence brings about the belief described in it, but not in virtue of a *social convention*. Furthermore, one can consent to or accept a proposition that he does not believe, as might happen in the course of a debate in which one consents to or accepts a proposition just for the sake of argument. Thus, James is wrong to identify belief with consent; and this holds even for internal acts of consenting in which one commits oneself to treating a certain proposition as if it were true, for one can do this without believing the proposition.

That there are no beliefs that are exclusively of type (i), that is, an uncontested ideational state sans any psychic attitude, is due to the fact that without the attitude there is no way to distinguish between believing and willing, which we already know to be different. That they are different can be established by showing the possibility of a person believing without willing or vice versa, when what is in question is the movement of the person's own body. A person could have an uncontested idea of his arm moving and believe but not will that his arm will move, because he knows that he cannot move it and the physical therapist shortly will move it for him (Remember my verbose lawyer in this connection.) Or, contrariwise, he could be ideating in exactly the same way but now will that his arm move but not believe that it will; he has just recovered from surgery to restore the use of his arm and thus tries to move it without having sufficient assurance that he will succeed, and thus does not believe that his arm will move.

The only thing in favor of James's identification of belief and will is that it, in conjunction with Berkeley's idealism, gives us a good theodicy, according to which all the evils of our world are attributable to an innocent mistake on God's part. It will be recalled that Berkeley's God created the heavens and earth by simply ideating in a heavenly and earthly way. Unfortunately, he was not apprised of the truth of James's theory, a minor chink in his omniscience (which is understandable, as James's theory is false) and thus did not realize that by simply ideating in this manner, as he might have done while daydreaming or envisioning different possible worlds that he might actualize, he was in effect willing, and thereby creating, given the absolute efficacy of his will, this heaven and earth with all the evils therein contained. He mistakenly thought that to create he must add a fiat to the ideas he entertained. In fact, right after he finished ideating in this heaven and earth manner, he said, "Damned if I can't do better than that!" which was followed by a horrified "Oops! Sorry about that."

Attractive as this theodicy is, it is not enough to save James's identification of belief and will. Fortunately, James's theory can easily be patched up. The best way to do it is to require that every belief involve a unique belief-type psychic attitude directed toward a proposition that is different from the sort of psychic attitude which occurs in a case of will. All cases of believing and willing are of type (ii), differing in their operant psychic or propositional attitude. That a unique sort of fiat or willing attitude is required for a case of will goes a long way in the direction of the innervation theory. The difference between the case in which I believe but do not will that some proposition be true and the one in which I will but do not believe that this proposition will be true is that, in the former, I adopt a believing but not a willing attitude toward the proposition, whereas in the case in which I will but do not believe this proposition the reverse is the case.

James himself, at times, seemed to recognize a difference between the believing and willing psychic attitudes.

We stand here [in the case of the will] exactly where we did in the case of belief. When an idea *stings* us in a certain way, makes as it were a certain electric connection with our Self, we believe that it *is* a reality. When it stings us in another way, makes another connection with our Self, we say, *let it be* a reality. To the word 'is' and to the words 'let it be' there correspond peculiar attitudes of consciousness which it is vain to seek to explain. The indicative and the imperative moods are as much ultimate categories of thinking as they are of grammar. (*PP* 1172–3)

This seems, by its use of the plural "attitudes of consciousness," to make the believing attitude different from the willing or "let it be" attitude, even when directed toward one and the same proposition.

This passage, however, conflicts with others in which James identifies both the believing and willing attitude with the act of consent.

My slightly amended version of James's theory is a three-tiered affair. On the first level is the entertaining of a proposition in a manner that is neutral between different psychic or propositional attitudes. The second tier involves a psychic or propositional attitude toward this proposition of believing, willing, questioning, doubting, hoping, and the like, each of which is unique. On the third level is the effort to adopt one of these psychic attitudes toward the proposition, which might consist in an effort to attend in a certain manner, as for example to ideate in the manner required by my Hollywood Ethics. It will be shown in the next chapter that for James freedom enters on the third level, it being the amount of effort expended that is subject to the free will of the person. As a result of this third-tier freedom, a person has the freedom to control what he believes, sometimes just by making an extra effort either to attend to an idea to the exclusion of its competitors or to adopt a believing psychic attitude toward it, and, at others, by making an extra effort to will to do things that will indirectly induce belief.

For the purpose of James's master syllogism, it is necessary that belief is not just an action but also a free action, or inducible by free actions. Since the conclusion of the syllogism

3. We are always morally obligated to believe in a manner that maximizes desire-satisfaction over the other available belief options.

obliges us to believe in a certain manner, it is required that we are free to believe in this manner. For *ought* implies *can* in its most full-blooded sense of being free to do what is morally required. The major burden of the next chapter is to show how James analyzes freedom and establishes through his will-to-believe doctrine our right to believe that we have freedom of belief.

3

The Freedom Of Belief

The previous chapter presented James's reasons for thinking that belief is an intentional action, or inducible by intentional actions. The purpose of this chapter is to explore his reasons for claiming that belief also is a free action in his Libertarian sense. The next chapter will lay bare his doctrine of the will to believe and how it justifies believing that the will and belief are free in this sense. This chapter will be subdivided into four parts. The first presents James's theory of freedom. The second gives his reasons why it cannot be decided on epistemic or evidential grounds through empirical inquiry that we are or that we are not free in this sense. The third expounds his reasons for thinking that it is desirable in terms of maximizing desire-satisfaction to believe that we are free. The fourth presents some objections to his theory of freedom and how James could respond to them; herein some of the finer points in his analysis will emerge. It will be found in Chapter 4 that among the several necessary conditions for having a will-to-believe option are that the proposition to be believed cannot have its truth or falsity determined on epistemic or evidential grounds and that believing it has desirable consequences. Thus, if one or more of the objections to James's theory should prove fatal, his theory would not qualify as a candidate for a will-to-believe option, because its *falsity* can be epistemically determined.

I. What Freedom Is

Throughout his adult life, James ardently believed in the Libertarian doctrine of free will, replete with its contracausal spiritual acts of will. It was this belief that helped him make it through the night, for the most intense form the blues took for James was the "I Aint Got No Contracausal Free Will Blues." His near life-ending emotional crisis of 1870 was occasioned by his doubt that he was "free" in this sense, and therefore that he was able to function as a morally responsible agent. By a Promethean act of will, he self-induced this belief by following his formula of acting as if he believed, part of which involved publicly declaring that he was free; thus the point of his claim that "our first act of freedom, if we are free, ought in all inward propriety to be to affirm that we are free" (*WB* 115; see also *PP* 1177). Through this public avowal he commits himself in the eyes of his fellow persons to acting as if he were free and thereby assuming full moral responsibility for his actions. Because this belief in free will was foundational to his existence as a man, he was unable to resist his own strictures in *The Principles of Psychology* against metaphysical digressions when he got to the subject of freedom in the chapters on "Attention" and "Will." He not only waxed metaphysical but did so in the manner of an itinerant New England preacher out to save our souls, which is what he really was. It is quite amazing in the middle of a psychology textbook suddenly to find oneself in a locker-room at halftime being given a pep talk by the author.

James, for reasons that shortly will be considered, was a committed incompatibilist, believing that a free act must, among other things, not have a prior sufficient cause. A free act must be at least a *chance* occurrence in that it is not determined in any way by prior states of the universe. For James, no free acts are to found on the first tier in my reconstructed version of his theory of will and belief outlined at the end of the last chapter, since it is causally determined by the workings of the brain which ideas enter consciousness and thus are entertained in the neutral sense. It also is causally determined whether an effort is made on tier three to bring about a willing or believing on tier two of one of these ideas from tier one. The only place that free will can get into the act is in regard to the *amount* of effort that is made to will or believe one of these ideas via attending to certain ideas, such as in my Hollywood Ethics. It is only to "the *effort to attend*, not to the mere attending, that we are seriously tempted to ascribe spontaneous power. We think we can make more of it *if we will*; and the amount which we make does not seem a fixed function of the ideas themselves, as it would necessarily have to be if our effort were an effect and not a spiritual force." (*PP* 426–7).

James characterizes this spiritual force as an "original force" and the "star performer" (*PP* 428). Its free efforts "originate ex nihilo, or come from a fourth dimension" (*PP* 1178). To be an original force, for James, it must be an irreducibly conscious event that is not causally determined. After giving a very fair and forceful exposition of the epiphenomenalistic "effect theory" of the amount of the effort to attend, according to which it is only a causally determined effect of physiological events, he expresses his personal preference for the "cause-theory." "The reader will please observe that I am saying all that can *possibly* be said in favor of the effect-theory, since, inclining as I do myself to the cause-theory, I do not want to undervalue the enemy" (*PP* 424–5).

This cause-theory gives James a way of dissolving the creating-discovering aporia. We do not "create" in his prime mover or ex nihilo first-cause sense the fact that we are conscious of or attend to certain ideas or that we make an effort to adopt a certain psychic attitude toward them: All of these facts are causally determined by our interests, which, in turn, are causally explained in terms of physiological facts pertaining to the activity of the brain. Thus we merely discover but do not create these facts. We are the free cause and sole creator only of the *amount* of effort that we make to adopt a certain psychic attitude toward one of these ideas. It will be seen that although the area within which our free will operates is very constricted, the long-range effects of this radically limited use of free will can be very extensive.

II. The Epistemic Undecidability of Freedom

That the amount of these efforts to attend against the course of least resistance, such as in a case of moral temptation, do not have a prior sufficient cause in the physiological workings of the brain cannot be epistemically determined, since we cannot make sufficiently fine-grained measurements of brain events so as to discover whether the effect-theory is true. "The feeling of effort certainly *may* be an inert accompaniment and not the active element which it seems. No measurements are as yet performed (it is safe to say none ever will be performed) which can show that it contributes energy to the result" (*PP* 428). Thus, "The last word of psychology here is ignorance, for the 'forces' engaged are certainly too delicate and numerous to be followed in detail" (*PP* 429). This gets repeated in the later chapter on "Will," when he says that such measurements "will surely be forever beyond human reach" (*PP* 1176).

This account of why it is not epistemically decidable whether or not we have free will is different from and far superior to the one James gave six years earlier in his 1884 "The Dilemma of Determinism." His strategy then was to argue that the issue gets down to the truth of certain counterfactual conditionals, but there is no truth of the matter with respect to them, a position that Peirce defended in his 1878 "How to Make Our Ideas Clear," which James first became aware of when it was presented to the Metaphysical Club in the early 1870s. The counterfactuals enter in because determinism entails that if the same state of the universe *were* to recur, though it doesn't, it would be followed by the very same state it formerly was, whereas indeterminism denies this entailment, allowing for history to take a different course the second time around than it in fact did the first time. But the universe or history happens only once, thus rendering the determinist's claim about what would happen if some state of the history of the universe were to recur counterfactual.

But why do counterfactuals lack truth-value for James? The reason is that

Science professes to draw no conclusions but such as are based on matters of fact, things that have actually happened; but how can any amount of assurance that something actually happened give us the least grain of information as to whether another thing might or might not have happened in its place? Only facts can be proved by other facts. With things that are possibilities and not facts, facts have no concern. If we have no other evidence than the evidence of existing facts, the possibility-question must remain a mystery never to be cleared up. (*WB* 119)

Something has gone radically wrong here. To be sure, scientific inductive arguments appeal only to matters of fact concerning what has "actually happened." But from this it does not follow that science cannot give good inductive arguments from such bagged facts to what would happen in a counterfactual situation. The very same inductive argument for the prediction that when I leap from the top of the Chrysler Building one hour from now I will fall to earth can be given for the counterfactual proposition that if I were to leap from this building one hour from now (though I will not) I would fall to earth. James, along with Peirce, gave up this misbegotten view that counterfactuals lack a truth-value, but for some reason that I cannot fathom he did not bother to tell the reader of *The Principles of Psychology* that he had given up his earlier account in "The Dilemma of Determinism" for the epistemic undecidability of determinism. It is well that he gave up his implausible view of counterfactuals; for, if they were to lack a truth-value, they could not be an object for a will-to-believe option, in which they are believed upon insufficient evidence. There would be no truth of the matter concerning indeterminism, as it entails counterfactuals, and thus indeterminism could not be believed, as we can only believe something that has a truth-value or wherein there is a fact of the matter.

III. The Desirability of Believing in Freedom

James makes it clear that his reasons for believing that the amount of effort we make to attend are contracausal are "ethical." His so believing has great benefits for him, enabling him to satisfy his most important desires, namely to function as a morally responsible agent. "The whole feeling of reality, the whole sting and excitement of our voluntary life, depends on our sense that in it things are *really being decided* from one moment to another, and that it is not the dull rattling off of a chain that was forged innumerable ages ago" (*PP* 429).

Our very sense of our own self-worth as persons depends on this belief, since "the effort seems to belong to an altogether different realm, as if it were the substantive thing which we *are*, and those ["our strength and our intelligence, our wealth and even our good luck"] were but externals which we *carry*" (*PP* 1181). James extols the stoical

hero who, regardless of external deterrents, can still find life meaningful "by pure inward willingness to take the world with those deterrent
objects there" (*PP* 1181). "The world thus finds in the heroic man its
worthy match and mate; and the effort which he is able to put forth to
hold himself erect and keep his heart unshaken is the direct measure
of his worth and function in the game of human life" (*PP* 1181). This
sets the stage for the eloquent concluding paragraph of the section on
free will.

Thus not only our morality but our religion, so far as the latter is deliberate,
depend on the effort which we can make. "*Will you or won't you have it so?*" is
the most probing question we are ever asked; we are asked it every hour of the
day, and about the largest as well as the smallest, the most theoretical as well as
the most practical, things. We answer by *consents or non-consents* and not by
words. What wonder that these dumb responses should seem our deepest organ
of communication with the nature of things! What wonder if the effort demanded by them be the measure of our worth as men! What wonder if the
amount which we accord of it be the one strictly underived and original contribution which we make to the world! (*PP* 1182)

We are essentially a "spiritual force," for that is the "substantive thing
which we *are*" (*PP* 1181). A lot more will be said in Chapters 8 and 9
about the nature of this immaterial, nonnatural self, which is not a
denizen of the natural spatio-temporal order that science describes and
explains, but instead a transcendental being or force from James's
"fourth dimension" that brings about effects in this order.

James sometimes found it convenient to overlook the nonnaturalistic
commitments of his theory of free will, as for example when he made
this disclaimer in his 1904 "The Experience of Activity":

I have found myself more than once accused in print of being the assertor of a
metaphysical principle of activity. Since literary misunderstandings retard the
settlement of problems, I should like to say that such an interpretation of the
pages I have published on effort and on will is absolutely foreign to what I
meant to express. . . . Single clauses in my writing, or sentences read out of their
connexion, may possibly have been compatible with a transphenomenal principle of energy; but I defy anyone to show a single sentence which, taken with its
context, should be naturally held to advocate such a view. (*ERE* 93)

The sentences that have just been quoted from *The Principles of Psychology* on effort as an "original spiritual force, as originating *ex nihilo* [as]
. . . from a fourth dimension," more than meet James's challenge.
James is not alone in overlooking his nonnaturalistic account of the will
in this work. So eminent an historian of American philosophy as Herbert Schneider could write that "There is a coherent exposition in
Chapters I–VI, XI–XIV, and XXII–XXVI [in *PP*] of his biological account of mental *acts*, culminating in his naturalistic treatment of the
will" (*AP* 498). And to make matters even worse, Elizabeth Flower,
another highly respected authority on American philosophy, echoed

this: "Clearly, James is attempting to deal with voluntary behavior without resorting to a faculty of will and certainly not to a supernatural agency" (*PA* 2:660). It is almost as if there were a conspiracy among naturalistically inclined historians of American philosophy to remake James in their own image no matter how much of his writings they must overlook.

It might be conjectured that the reason for James going back on his earlier "metaphysical" account of the will is that the 1904 paper was his presidential address to the American Psychological Association, and he wanted to impress the "brethren" that he was as tough-minded as they. James was not above playing to his audience like a barnstorming politician. He knew that they thought he was too tender-minded and gullible because of his interest in the paranormal and made a ritual throughout his career of allaying their suspicions by taking an outwardly hardheaded stance to the field.[1] A similar sort of misleading tough-minded posturing is found in his 1898 "Human Immortality: Two Supposed Objections to the Doctrine." He begins by saying that he cannot understand why the Ingersoll Committee chose him to give this lecture, as he is no friend of the doctrine of human immortality and has little personal concern for it. He then goes on to neutralize the two major objections to it, to mount an inference to the best explanation argument in support of it, about which more will be said in Chapter 10, and to end with a will-to-believe justification for believing in it! With opponents like this, a doctrine does not need any defenders.

James's greatest fear was that he might wind up like his father, who was perceived as a genius, but a very eccentric one whose writings therefore could safely be ignored. There are poignant remarks in letters to his brother Henry after the publication of *The Literary Remains of the Late Henry James* in 1884, of which William was the editor and contributor of a lengthy introduction. In a 1885 letter he writes: "Houghton's July semi annual account shows only six copies sold in six months, and me in their debt for bindings. Alas! poor Father. It is sad" (*ERM* 217). And in a letter of 1887 there is more of the same: "I got Ticknor's account last week – poor Father's literary remains has sold only one copy in the past six months! It is pitiful, but there's nothing to be done about it" (*ERM* 217. (I bet that sole buyer mistakenly thought it was by his son, Henry – was he disappointed!) In his farewell letter to his father he patronizes him by telling him about some prominent persons who praised his books, knowing that this would elate his father on his deathbed because he had agonized all his

[1] Martin Gardner, in his carefully researched paper JP, makes a convincing case that James's extensive investigations of medium Adrian Piper, whom he concluded had paranormal powers, fell far short of the standards for scientific inquiry, overlooking some fairly obvious ways in which she could have cheated.

life over the total neglect of his publications: "At Paris I heard that Milsand, whose name you remember in the 'Revue des Deux Mondes' and elsewhere, was an admirer of the 'Secret of Swedenborg,' and Hodgson told me your last book had deeply impressed him" (*ERM* 214. This is almost like one of Willie Loman's sons trying to cheer him up by informing him that when he was in Macy's the week before the buyer asked after his father, saying, "No one could sell women's underwear like Willie." James was going to avoid his father's fate no matter what it took, even if he had to play both sides of the street and tell each audience what they wanted to hear. He was determined that everyone was going to love him and read his publications assiduously, both of which they did in abundance.

It is in his famous article on "The Dilemma of Determinism" that James gives his fullest and most compelling reasons for thinking that it is desirable for most people to believe that they are one of these immaterial selves possessed of his sort of contracausal free will. We have already seen that James assumed that most other people were like him in this respect; their whole sense of their own self-worth and the meaningfulness of life depended on their believing that they had such freedom, for without it they could not function as morally responsible agents. He now develops an ingenious argument to show the disastrous consequences for the believer in determinism, consequences that are avoided by the believer in his contracausal free will. This is the dilemma of determinism argument, from which the article took its title.

The key assumption underlying the argument is that determinism is incompatible with free will because it entails fatalism, namely, that whatever happens is the only thing that could have happened, that possibilities are not in excess of actualities, that nothing that happens could have been avoided or prevented. In order to show that determinism entails fatalism, an acceptable definition of *determinism* must first be given. James is well aware of the danger of begging the question at the outset by giving an emotively charged definition. Whereas the words *freedom* and *chance* have associations that are respectively eulogistic and approbrious, fortunately "no ambiguities hang about this word [*determinism*] or about its opposite, *indeterminism*. Both designate an outward way in which things may happen, and their cold and mathematical sound has no sentimental associations that can bribe our partiality either way in advance" (*WB* 117; my italics).

James, however, immediately forgets his admonition against using emotive and rhetorical language, for in the very next paragraph he gives about as question-begging a rhetorical definition of *determinism* as one could imagine. Determinism, we are told, "professes that those parts of the universe already laid down absolutely appoint and decree what the other parts shall be" (*WB* 117). This is repeated in *The Princi-ples of Psychology* when he writes that if determinism is true then what-ever efforts of will we make were "*required* and *exacted*," that "whatever object at any time fills our consciousness was from eternity bound to fill it then and there, and *compel* from us the exact effort, neither more nor less, which we bestow upon it" (*PP* 1175; my italics). Plainly, James's use of legalistic language confounds positive with scientific laws because it makes the unnoticed slide from an event happening in accordance with a scientific law to its being coerced or compelled to occur by some positive law of the state or decree of a sovereign. It is as if the law of *f* = *ma* were to threaten all the material particles in the world that they sure as hell better obey it or else.

But this is not the end of James's question-begging rhetorical defini-tion of *determinism*. He also avails himself of ball-and-chain–type meta-phors in his description of causation. Determinism holds that "The whole is in each and every part, and *welds it* with the rest into an abso-lute unity, an *iron block*, in which there can be no equivocation or shadow of turning" (*WB* 118; my italics). This is followed by talk about "one unbending unit of fact" if determinism is true. And, again, if determinism is true, then the whole of our voluntary life is "the dull rattling off of a *chain* that was forged innumerable ages ago," and "the world must be one *unbroken* fact" (*PP* 429 and 1177; my italics). Plainly, it is unfair to burden the determinist with accepting a view of causation that makes an effect a link in a chain or inexorably welded to its cause in one big iron block, for this makes the effect look like an unfortunate member of a chain gang, completely destitute of any freedom.

Yet another rhetorical device that James employs to make determin-ism appear to have fatalistic consequences is the use of metaphors that spatialize the time of a deterministic universe so that future events are always there, our mind coming upon them one after the other in its journey up its world-line, to paraphrase the accounts given by Weyl and Eddington of the Minkowskian world of relativity theory. For determin-ism, "There is nothing inchoate . . . about this universe of ours, all that was or is or shall be actual in it having been from eternity virtually there," and "The future has no ambiguous possibilities hidden in its womb" (*WB* 118 and 117). Indeterminism, on the other hand, holds that "actualities . . . float in a wider sea of possibilities from out of which they are chosen; and, *somewhere*, indeterminism says, such possi-bilities exist, and form a part of truth" (*WB* 118). This spatialization of time in the deterministic universe suggests that as our minds "travel" up their world-lines into the future they come upon preexistent events and thereby play no active or creative role in bringing them about, and, furthermore, when they make a choice there is only one choosable object hanging from the rafters in the Hall of Future Possibilities. Time presents them with no branching tributaries that they might choose to journey along.[2]

While James's "arguments" for determinism entailing fatalism amount to nothing but a skein of question-begging rhetorical definitions, his incompatibilist intuitions still might be right. If determinism is true, then whatever we do is the only thing that it was causally possible for us to do. But if we causally could not have done otherwise, then could we have done otherwise? Could we have avoided or prevented doing what we did? My intuitions, along with those of many other philosophers, not to mention the vast majority of laypersons, require a negative answer to these questions. If James were alive today, he would look with favor on some recent arguments to prove that determinism entails fatalism, such as the unpreventability argument. If determinism is true, there is a deductive-nomological explanation for every event. Take any future event E that we think we are able to prevent. There is a deductive nomological explanation of E in terms of a conjunction of a set of causal laws and a description of the state of the universe before we were even born. Since we can prevent neither the universe from having been in this state nor these causal laws from holding true, we cannot prevent anything that is entailed by their conjunction, such as the future occurrence of E.

Having explored James's reasons, or lack thereof, for believing in incompatibilism, we are in a position to consider his dilemma of determinism argument, which, it must be emphasized, is directed against, not the truth of determinism, but only the desirability of believing it to be true. Since the determinism issue is not epistemically decidable, he thinks that we are justified in choosing what to believe in this matter on the basis of the consequences for good and ill of believing one way or the other.

The argument begins with the fact that we express judgments of regret about some evil or ought-not-to-be, in which the world abounds. Assuming both determinism and incompatibilism, it follows that these evils could not have been prevented or avoided. And this is pessimism. But "our deterministic pessimism may become a deterministic optimism at the price of extinguishing judgments of regret" (*WB* 127). This requires saying that our judgments of regret are false. A false judgment, however, is itself an evil or ought-not-to-be, and thus we still face the same pessimistic consequence.[3] In fact, one cannot believe falsely

---

[2] I owe these criticisms of James to Paul Edwards, who presented them to his graduate seminar, of which I was a member, in 1957.

[3] Assuming that false belief or assertion is an evil, the sentence, "There is evil," is pragmatically self-verifying in that it is necessary that any use of it expresses a true proposition, but only a contingently true proposition.

that there is evil; for if their belief is true there is evil, and if it is false there again is evil, namely, their own false belief.

The theoretic and the active life thus play a kind of see-saw with each other on the ground of evil. The rise of either sends the other down. Murder and treachery cannot be good without regret being bad; regret cannot be good without treachery and murder being bad. Both, however, are supposed to have been foredoomed; so something must be fatally unreasonable, absurd, and wrong in the world. It must be a place of which either sin or error forms a necessary part. From this dilemma there seems at first no escape. (*WB* 127)

For the purpose of critically evaluating this dilemma argument, it is necessary that it be given an explicit mounting. The argument is formulated in the form of a conditional proof, in which pessimism is deduced from the assumption that determinism is true, along with certain other truths.

1. Determinism is true. [assumption for conditional proof]
2. If determinism is true, then whatever happens could not have been avoided or prevented. [the incompatibilist premise]
3. There is a judgment of regret, J, that there are events that ought not to be. [an empirical premise]
4. J is either true or false. [an instance of the law of bivalence]
5. If J is true, then there are events that ought not to be but could not have been avoided or prevented. [first horn of the dilemma and follows from (1), (2), (3)]
6. That there are events that ought not to be but could not have been avoided or prevented is pessimism. [true by definition]
7. If J is true, pessimism is true. [from (5) (6)]
8. A false judgment is an ought-not-to-be. [premise]
9. If J is false, there are events (namely, false judgments) that ought not to be but could not have been avoided or prevented. [second horn of dilemma and follows from (1), (2), and (8)]
10. If J is false, then pessimism is true. [from (6) and (9)]
11. Pessimism is true. [from (4)–(10) by dilemma argument]
12. If determinism true, then pessimism is true. [from (1)–(11) by conditional proof]

Supposedly, it is quite undesirable to believe in pessimism, for then we would have no reason to take life seriously and try to make the world a better place (you know, by putting our shoulder to the wheel). But pessimism is a logical consequence of determinism. Does this argument show that anyone who believes in determinism will also believe in pessimism? Of course not. Belief is not closed under deduction, a person not having to believe everything that is entailed by what she believes. It only shows that someone who is rational enough to be aware of the deductive consequences of her belief in determinism, coupled with the

controversial assumption of incompatibilism, will believe that pessimism is true. The irrational types are beyond redemption by this argument. Thus, James's argument must be restricted to those who are sufficiently rational as to be among the saving remnant. This is not much
of a concession on James's part, as he supposes that his readers want to
think logically and thus would welcome help in doing so. Nor does the
argument even show that every sufficiently rational person who accepts
determinism will take a seat on the sideline in life's struggles against
evil; for the psychology of some persons would allow them both to
accept pessimism and to lead the morally strenuous life. James just
happens not to be among them.

There is a way out of the dilemma that consists in challenging its
second horn,

(9) If J is false, there are events (namely, false judgments) that ought
    not to be but could not have been avoided or prevented.

by denying premise

(8) A false judgment is an ought-not-to-be.

The gnostic or subjectivist denies that false judgment is an evil and is
prepared to give a theodicy of sorts for false beliefs based on their
promoting the outweighing good of deepening our awareness and understanding of evil. James gives a most eloquent and convincing presentation of this view that results from not only his passion for fairness
but also, I suspect, his philosophical nymphomania; however, he soon
thereafter pulls the plug on it. To find our highest good in our subjective appreciation of the world's evils belittles the morally strenuous life,
sapping our incentive to take seriously our moral duties to perform
certain overt actions. James tells us that it "violates my sense of moral
reality through and through" (WB 136). Subjectivism, at least in those
whose psychology resembles James's, thereby engenders an undesirable
passivism and ethical indifference.

> Once consecrate the . . . notion that our performances and our violations of
> duty are for a common purpose, the attainment of subjective knowledge and
> feeling, and that the deepening of these is the chief end of our lives – and at
> what point on the downward slope are we to stop? . . . And in practical life it is
> either a nerveless sentimentality or a sensualism without bounds. Everywhere it
> fosters the fatalistic mood of mind. It makes those who are already too inert
> more passive still; it renders wholly reckless those whose energy is already in
> excess. All through history we find how subjectivism, as soon as it has a free
> career, exhausts itself in every sort of spiritual, moral, and practical license. (WB
> 132)

Indeterminism alone makes of the world a suitable arena for our
deepest moral concerns and aspirations. "It says conduct, and not sensibility, is the ultimate fact for our recognition. With the vision of cer-

tain works to be done, of certain outward changes to be wrought or resisted, it says our intellectual horizon terminates" (*WB* 134). One senses James's Promethean proclivities lurking in the background, for what matters is changing the world through our overt actions. James admits that not everyone shares his sentiment of rationality in this matter, and he attempts to win them over through his impassioned prose in his halftime pep talks.

James fails to note that subjectivism or gnosticism is not the only basis for justifying or constructing a theodicy for false belief. There is, for example, the free will theodicy for false belief, such as was given by Descartes in his fourth *Meditation*, according to which false belief results from our misuse of our free will, but that is no reason for indicting the Deity, since there is in general such great value to our having free will. This theodicy is not available to the determinist if free will is incompatible with determinism, as James was convinced it was.

The worry is that James's dilemma of determinism argument proves too much, precluding any theodicy for any type of evil. James made a careless remark that had the effect of ruling out the possibility of any theodicy succeeding: "The *ideally* perfect whole is certainly that whole of which the parts also are perfect – if we can depend on logic for anything, we can depend on it for that definition" (*PU* 60). Far from logic requiring this, James's reasoning commits the fallacy of division by assuming that the parts must have the same properties as does the whole. But this is not James's considered opinion, for when he was in a healthy mood he extolled the value of the traditional soul-building theodicy, favored by all the great medieval theists. But take any evil, *E*, and any theodicy that attempts to show that *E* has overall beneficial consequence in that *E* is necessary for either the realization of an outweighing good or the prevention of an even greater evil. *E*, being an evil, is an ought not to be, but, James would go on to argue, if the theodicy works, then *E* is not after all an ought not to be, and thus *E* both is and is not an ought-not-to-be. Because our initial intuition is to take *E* to be an ought-not-to-be, we feel a moral duty to try to prevent and eliminate *E*-type events. But when we accept the theodicy for God's allowing *E*, we no longer view *E* as an ought-not-to-be and thereby do not feel morally obligated to try to prevent and eliminate *E*-type events.[4]

---

[4] Somewhat similar considerations hold for a defense of God in the face of evil *E*, in which a defense is a description of a *possible* world in which God has a morally exonerating excuse for allowing *E*. (A theodicy goes on to argue that this possible world also is the actual world.) If we give a defense for *E*, we put ourselves in the position of having to say both that *E* is an ought-not-to-be and it is possible that *E* is not an ought-not-to-be (because God could have a justification for permitting *E*). While there is no contradiction in asserting *p* and possibly not-*p*, to believe that what we take to be an ought-not-to-be might not be an ought-not-to-be saps our incentive to fight to eliminate and prevent such events.

There is a failure in this argument against the viability of any theodicy to relativize an ought-not-to-be, either to us finite creatures or to God. Thus, when a theodicy shows that some evil, E, is justified, it means that God is morally justified in bringing about or permitting E, not that we are. E, therefore, is not an ought-not-to-be relative to God, the planner and creator of the entire universe, with the possible exception of our free acts and their consequences. This does not entail that E is not an ought-not-to-be relative to us finite creatures, for our position and role in the scheme of things are quite different from God's. We are thrown into the world at a later time with the moral duty to prevent and eliminate every evil we can. God, as the planner and creator of the universe has a different role to play and therefore is not subject to the same duty that we are. Thus, it would be unfair to challenge the soul-building theodicy's attempt morally to exonerate God for creating natural evils, such as physical impediments, as a means to our developing higher character traits, by an analogy with a finite father who purposely breaks his son's legs so that the boy will have an opportunity to engage in soul building, certainly a wicked thing to do. For this overlooks the radical difference in the perspective and role of God and those of finite creatures. A broken limb is an ought-not-to-be relative to us but not to God.

IV. Some Objections

If there is a telling objection to James's theory of free will, it will stand as epistemically discredited and thus not be a suitable target for a will-to-believe option. The standard objections to Libertarian theories will be considered. First, there is the perennial objection that a Libertarian-type freedom, in virtue of postulating a nonphysical cause, be it a Cartesian soul substance or some type of spiritual act of effort or will, of some change in the physical world, violates the law of the conservation of angular momentum. Herein some spiritual event that is not itself possessed of any physical energy, and thus cannot get plugged in for the f in the $f = ma$ law, causes an acceleration of a physical object, thereby violating the law of the conservation of angular momentum.

James never explicitly addressed this objection, but the manner in which he developed and defended his theory indicates that he was concerned with finding a way around it. James's version of Libertarianism is far superior to that of others, from Aristotle down through Sartre and Chisholm, in giving hope of escaping this objection. For in his version a free act of effort operates directly on consciousness, having as its immediate effect the sustaining of attention to some idea or the adoption of a psychic attitude rather than a bodily movement, as is the case with other versions of Libertarians. For example, in Aristotle's famous example of the stick moving the stone, the hand moving the stick, and the man moving his hand, something that is not an event in the physical world, the man, directly causes an acceleration. By making the immediate effect of an effort of will the strengthening of an idea in consciousness rather than the acceleration of a physical object, James's theory does not seem to violate the conservation law.

James gives some hints that he was worried about his theory violating a conservation law, for he wrote that "The world . . . is just as *continuous with itself* for the believers in free will as for the rigorous determinists, only the latter are unable to believe in points of bifurcation as spots of really indifferent equilibrium or as containing shunts which there . . . *direct existing motions without altering their amount*" (*MT* 303; my italics; see also *PP* 144 and *ERM* 87). This is a variant on Descartes's pineal gland theory and, unfortunately, involves the same violation of the conservation of angular momentum. The shunts – acts of free will – do alter, pace James, the *amount* of existing motions, not by changing the speed of any object but instead its direction and thereby its velocity, resulting in a change in the angular momentum of the entire system. Obviously, a lot more work would have to be done to rework James's theory so that it does not violate this conservation law, but James would not be in agony if it did, since he believed that this law was only an empirical generalization that permitted occasional exceptions. Moreover, as will be seen in Chapter 7, he thought that we are free to adopt the perspective of the moral agent rather than that of the scientist and thus to reject the law of the conservation of angular momentum in its universal form. "Science . . . must be constantly reminded that her purposes are not the only purposes, and that the uniform causation which she has use for, and is therefore right in postulating, may be enveloped in a wider order, on which she has no claims at all" (*PP* 1179). "When we make theories about the world and discuss them with one another, we do so in order to attain a conception of things which shall give us subjective satisfactions" (*WB* 115). This involves an application of his casuistic rule from Chapter 1 to the formation of theoretical beliefs.

Another objection to Libertarianism of the Aristotelian variety that is escaped by James's version is that there is a commitment to a troublesome sort of backward causation, for when Aristotle's man freely moves his hand, he brings about *earlier* events along the efferent nerves linking his brain with his hand (By clenching my fist I ripple my forearm muscles.) James's theory, in virtue of making the immediate effect of a free act of will the strengthening or sustaining of an idea in consciousness, avoids this problem.

An even more prevalent objection than the conservation law one is the charge that the Libertarian's concept of a causally undetermined free act is conceptually absurd. There are two versions of this objection. The first, and less formidable, version is that an undetermined action is a purely random or chance occurrence and therefore is not attributable to a person in a way that makes her morally responsible for it. The second version holds that the absurdity is due to the fact that the undetermined free acts are without reason or motive and therefore not intentional actions at all.

James opens himself up to the first version of the objection by his popularizing penchant for giving nutshell definitions of complex ideas, not realizing that the only thing that should be put in a nutshell is a nut. He falsely makes it appear as if a free act is *merely* a causally undetermined one when he says that " 'free will' . . . is the character of novelty in fresh activity-situations" (*ERE* 93; see also *SPP* 72 and *ML* 412). The same message is sent by his other nutshell definition of *freedom* as "meaning a better promise as to this world's outcome" (*P* 63; see also *MT* 6). There could be *promise* of a better future independently of what we might freely do. A *novel* action could be a purely capricious or chance occurrence, such as a causally undetermined twitch of a person's nostrils that never occurred before. Furthermore, qualitatively novel states can occur in a deterministic system, such as a collection of billiard balls moving according to Newton's laws, and an action can be free even though it is qualitatively identical to earlier actions. Yet another one of James's nutshell definitions is " 'Freedom' means 'no feeling of sensible restraint' " (*SPP* 38). This certainly does not give a sufficient condition, as I could act without feeling any sensible restraint yet be doing so under posthypnotic suggestion and thereby not be doing so freely.

Fortunately, James has much more to say about freedom than is supplied by these misbegotten nutshell definitions. He has an extended response to the objection of reducing freedom to mere capriciousness in "The Dilemma of Determinism" (*WB* 121–4), the chapters on "Attention" and "Will" (*PP* 428–30 and 1175–82), and "Abstractionism and 'Relativismus.' " (*MT* 136–8). He charges this objection with vicious abstractionism that consists in taking just one part of what a word means to the exclusion of everything else. Because the indeterminist's past is *causally* disconnected from the future when a free act occurs, it is assumed that the past is *totally* disconnected from the future, thereby overlooking all the other ways in which the past and future are connected in this case. "If any spot of indifference is found upon the broad highway between the past and the future, then no connexion of any sort whatever" is to be found (*MT* 137).

To understand what these other connexions are, in virtue of which a free act can rightly be attributed to an agent as something for which she is morally responsible, it is necessary to take the insider's approach by introspecting what goes on when one makes a free choice. Recall that for James there are two ways to investigate a phenomenon, either by an introspective (phenomenological) or a causal analysis. A free act, being undetermined, eludes a causal analysis, since it cannot be subsumed under a covering law, as it must be in a deductive-nomological explanation. But it would be for James a scientistic prejudice of the worst sort to infer from this that such an act is unintelligible, for there still is the phenomenological way of understanding it through a description of what it is like from the inside to live through the exerting of an effort to attend to an idea in a case of conflict, such as in a case of moral temptation.

> I am . . . entirely willing to call it, so far as your choices go, a world of chance for me. To *yourselves*, it is true, those very acts of choice, which to me are so blind, opaque, and external, are the opposites of this, for you are within them and effect them. To you they appear as decisions; and decisions, for him who makes them, are altogether peculiar psychic facts. Self-luminous and self-justifying at the living moment at which they occur, they appeal to no outside moment to put its stamp upon them or make them continuous with the rest of nature. Themselves it is rather who seem to make nature continuous; and in their strange and intense function of granting consent to one possibility and withholding it from another, to transform an equivocal and double future into an inalterable and simple past. (*WB* 123)

James produces brilliant introspectively based descriptions in the mentioned sources of a free choice. A central theme of Chapters 8, 9, and 10 is that reality in general – in particular, change, causation, and the self – can be properly understood for James only through introspective analysis. He makes a far stronger claim than that the insider and outsider approaches are equally valid, each having its own special advantage relative to some human interest and purpose. Rather, he will argue that the externalized approach of the scientist that breaks reality up into a succession of numerically discrete states and coexistent objects renders reality unintelligble, a breeding ground for all of the a priori paradoxes from those of Zeno against change down through those of Bradley against relations.

According to the second version of the objection, the Libertarian's free choice is without any motive or reason. The deep objection in the *Euthyphro* to saying that something is good because God chose it to be, rather than vice versa, is that it renders God's choice reasonless. But a choice must have a reason consisting in some good that the chooser thereby hopes to realize. If the choice creates what is good, there is nothing that is good when the choice is being made that could be appealed to as a reason for the choice. And thus God's choice is reasonless and thereby absurd.

The same objection applies to James's free choice. Consider his beloved case of moral conflict or temptation in which two conflicting ideas are racing around in a person's mind, one being the idea of the action in the course of least resistance, the other being of the action that is dictated by conscience or duty. Finally, the chooser makes an effort to attend to one of the ideas to the exclusion of the other so that it will dominate her consciousness and, as a result, lead her to perform the envisioned action. It is causally determined for James that the two ideas are entertained by her, and even that she makes an effort to attend to one of them, but what is not determined is that she makes the *amount* of effort she does, and it is the amount of the effort that ultimately determines whether the idea in question wins out over its competitor. She can give no reason for exerting the amount of effort that she does other than the unhelpful one of "Because that's the sort of person I want to become, namely, someone who chooses from the moral point of view rather than that of self-interest." But she has no reason for that, for wanting to become that sort of person. She is a naked self, devoid of any character that could supply her with reasons for her choice. What she does is to choose her character ab initio, as if it were a cold cut laid out in a delicatessen's glass case. But this is absurd, because it requires her to make a reasonless choice.

Although James never explicitly considered this objection, I am quite certain that he would challenge the charge of absurdity, since his truly Promethean person must be a *causa sui* with respect to her own character, and thus she must perform some acts, such as exerting just the amount of effort she does in resolving a moral conflict, that will create her character ex nihilo. Through this ultimate Promethean act she makes one of the two competing reasons or motives out to be the dominant one, but she has no reason for doing this. My own intuitions are not clear on this matter, and as I do not know what to do in resolving the issue, I shall leave the dispute between James and the objector hanging.

Another objection to Libertarianism is that it give us no basis for determining forensic responsibility. A legal system is not pragmatically viable unless there are fairly straightforward ways of determining empirically when a person is responsible for violating one of its laws and is thereby fit to be punished in the prescribed manner. James's account of freedom is useless in this regard, since, admittedly, it is not epistemically determinable when the amount of a person's effort to attend is causally undetermined. The great advantage of Soft Determinism over Libertarianism is that it supplies us with empirically workable criteria for a person acting freely, namely that the action was not externally or internally coerced.

James must grant that, for pragmatic or utilitarian reasons, our forensic criteria for responsibility cannot be based on his criteria for a free act but instead on the verifiable criteria supplied by Soft Determinism. But it is clear from the overall tenor of James's discussion that he is not concerned with the forensic use of "free" and "responsible" but rather with how we *should* think about our freedom in personal contexts in which we take stock of ourselves, our worth as persons, as well as that of our intimates – our friends and lovers, even our enemies. I advisedly use the word "should" because his analysis, as is typical of his analyses, is in part revisionary, being concerned with how we should conceive of things so as to promote the good life consisting in our full self-realization. It is not an ordinary language analysis that purports to describe how we actually use language. In these personal contexts we are not concerned with the way in which blame, shame, responsibility, and punishment are affixed in the public arena, but how to judge ourselves, and thereby our intimates, in our hearts. James's contention really is that it is in these moments of solitude that we should think of ourselves as an original spiritual force that can mold our own character ex nihilo. And, James would add, by so thinking of ourselves we persuade ourselves to make greater efforts to mold our own characters, thereby satisfying the desirable-consequences-for-the-believer necessary condition for having a will-to-believe option to believe.

A closely related objection to the preceding one is that James's Libertarianism radically restricts the range of our free actions, confining them to the rather infrequent cases in which we exert a certain amount of effort to attend to a difficult idea in a case of moral conflict, and thereby trivializes our free will. For example, we do say, pace James, that people act freely, even in nonconflicted cases, provided there is no coercion. Thus, it is correct to say of the person of charitable character who donates to charity without coercion or conflict that she did it freely, of her own free will.

Again, James's response must be that he is not giving an ordinary language-type analysis of such *public* uses of "free," but rather a partially revisionary and normative analysis of the private cases in which we are alone with ourselves and ask who we are, what worth we have, and decide how we want to be judged and in turn to judge our intimates. It is this existential dimension of freedom that James wants to capture.

James also has a good response to the charge of triviality. Although the *number* of our free acts is far less than it ordinarily is taken to be, the *importance* of these acts is anything but trivial, since in them we define our characters and thus how we will behave in the most important matters of life, which, in turn, can have the most important, far-ranging impact on the future history of the world. "Our acts of voluntary attention, brief and fitful as they are, are nevertheless momentous and critical, determining us, as they do, to higher or lower destinies" (*TT* 111). Their remote effects "are too incalculable to be recorded"; however, "the practical and theoretical life of whole species, as well as of individual beings, results from" them (*PP* 401). The acts they occasion "may seal our doom." Think of James's example of the reformed alcoholic and the "fatal glass of beer." Thus, these sporadic efforts to attend are anything but trivial in their importance.

James is making use of a primitive type of Chaos Theory, similar to the parable of the war that was lost for the want of a nail that kept one horse from being shod and thus unavailable for the battle that was lost but would have been won had it participated, this lack eventuating in the loss of the war. The nail part of the story begins with whether or not we freely make enough of an effort to attend to the right idea in a case of moral conflict. The amount of effort we make will determine what action we perform, for good or ill. The impulse to do the ideal or right thing, I, might alone be insufficient to overcome the propensity, P, to do what is in the course of least resistance. It might be, in other terms, that "I $per\ se$ < P"; but when sufficient effort to attend to I, E, is added to the equation, it could result in "I + E > P" (PP 1155). The next part of James's parable concerns how acting in accordance with I factors into the big equation of history, this being the counterpart to the outcome of the battle, and eventually the war. Let M represent the entire world minus the reaction of the thinker upon it, and x be what we contribute by way of action, which result in crucial, character-defining cases, from the amount of effort we freely make to attend. M alone could make for a quite dismal future, whereas $M + x$ makes for a radically different future in which we realize the good life. "Let it not be said that x is too infinitesimal a component to change the immense whole in which it lies embedded. . . . The moral definition of the world may depend on our contributed x factor, miniscule though it is in terms of quantity: Many a long phrase may have its sense reversed by the addition of three letters, n-o-t; many a monstrous mass have its unstable equilibrium discharge one way or the other by a feather weight that falls" (WB 81; see also EPH 333–4).

This is as Promethean as it can get. As a result of our relatively few acts of free will, the entire fate of the world can be sealed for good or ill. This is anything but a trivializing of free will. In fact, it makes our free will so momentous that some will crack under the strain, wanting assurance that forces beyond our control will assure that the ultimate outcome or denouement of history is a good one, that eventually good wins out over evil. James was among these in his sick, morbid-minded moods during which he was racked with existential angst at the thought of the hideous epileptic youth, who represented in general the evils that might befall us. James could turn in an instant from the healthy Promethean mood, in which every fiber and cell in his body tingled at the thought of engaging in an all-out struggle with evil without any assurance of success, to the morbid one of existential angst.

"The Dilemma of Determinism" is an all-out expression of James's Prometheanism up until the final section, wherein he trivializes our freedom by invoking a God who will assure an ultimately good outcome of history no matter what we do with our free will. He draws an analogy between God's relation to us and that of a chess master to a journeyman opponent. It is assumed that both we and the journeyman have free will and that our actions thereby are not predictable by God or the chess master. No matter what unforeseen move the journeyman might freely make, the chess master can make use of it to bring about the ultimate checkmate of the journeyman. Similarly, no matter what unforeseen acts we freely perform, God will have the power and knowledge to bring it about that history ultimately has a good denouement in which good wins out over evil.

> The belief in free-will is not in the least incompatible with the belief in Providence, provided you do not restrict Providence to fulminating nothing but *fatal* decrees. If you allow him to provide possibilities as well as actualities to the universe, and to carry on his own thinking in those two categories just as we do ours, chances may be there, uncontrolled even by him, and the course of the universe be really ambiguous; and yet the end of all things may be just what he intended it to be from all eternity. (*WB* 138)

We can be assured that our "world was safe, and that no matter how much it might zigzag he [God] could surely bring it home at last" (*WB* 140).

This 180-degree turnaround on the status of evil and the importance of our free acts in combating it is an example of the sort of thing Santayana, no doubt, had in mind when he wrote that James "was really far from free, held back by old instincts, subject to old delusions, restless, spasmodic, self-interrupted: as if some impetuous bird kept flying aloft but always stopped in mid-air, pulled back with a jerk by an invisible wire tethering him to a peg in the ground" (*PP* 401). And he adds, in his characteristic overinflated and unkind manner, that James, as a result, "got nowhere." This is quite unfair. That James, in certain moods, recanted his Promethean philosophy, does not show that he got nowhere, for the manner in which he developed and defended this philosophy is one of the great contributions to the history of philosophy, despite his occasional loss of nerve, as in the final section of "The Dilemma Determinism." And the same can be said about James's anti-Promethean mystical philosophy, which is to be the topic of the second part of this book. It, too, is great in its own way.[5] I believe that James was led to use his anxiety-allaying chess analogy because he wanted to

[5] Kim Townsend has given an opposite interpretation of Santayana's characterization of James's aborted flight than to one I offer, which is sure to please those who are devoted to political correctness. "He wanted to fly 'aloft,' but he was held back by the masculinity he perfected, in the environment that was encouraging him and learning from his example" (*MH* 194). If I am right, it was not his "masculinity," the Prometheanism of his philosophy, that jerked him back to earth, but his "femininity," that is, his mysticism.

please the theists in the audience by showing how his view of free will could be reconciled with their creedal doctrine of Providence. We have freedom but not significant freedom, because the free contribution we make to the cosmic equation cannot affect its outcome. It is as if our freedom were limited to ordering the chocolate or the strawberry sundae. It's just another case of working the audience, making sure that he would get everyone's vote when he ran for the presidency. As the book progresses, other examples of James's philosophical politicking will be unearthed, especially his attempts to placate the realist, which is to be a topic of Chapter 5.

4

The Will to Believe

This is rightly considered James's most distinctive and influential doctrine. Had James looked as goofy as Kierkegaard and the street boys in Cambridge been as mean-spirited as those in Copenhagen who followed Kierkegaard around, taunting him with the shouts of "Either or, Either or!" James would have been hounded by shouts of "Will to believe, Will to believe!" He wouldn't have minded, because at least he would have known that, unlike his father, someone was reading his books. He expounded this idea with religious fervor throughout his career whenever there was the slightest pretext for doing so. It seemed to be innate in him, as were so many of his important doctrines. He defended it in his first major philosophical publication in 1878, at the end of each of his final two books, and in every major publication in between. When he was only twenty-four years old, he gave expression to a protoversion of it in a letter to Oliver Wendell Holmes, Jr.: "But as man's happiness depends on his feeling, I think materialism inconsistent with a high degree thereof, and in this sense maintained that a materialist should not be an optimist, using the latter word to signify one whose philosophy authenticates, by guaranteeing the objective significance of, his most pleasurable feelings" (*CWJ* 4, 147). The budding idea is that one can be justified in believing some metaphysical world-hypothesis because of the beneficial consequences of so believing.

This doctrine, which allows us to believe, or get ourselves to believe, a proposition upon insufficient evidence when doing so will have desirable consequences, works hand and glove with his foregoing accounts of will and belief discussed in Chapter 2 and the conditions supplied in Chapter 3 under which they are free. In what follows, the qualification "or get ourselves to believe" will be dropped for the sake of brevity, and to simplify the discussion we can imagine that each person is able to self-induce a belief in any proposition, p, by ingesting a belief-in-p-inducing pill. This is a surefire way of self-inducing belief, unlike that of acting as if you believe, which can be messy and chancy. (Because there are an infinite number of propositions, each person's medicine cabinet will be quite crowded and require that each pill, other than the one on the extreme left, be half the size of its immediate left-side neighbor, which is the spatial analogue to a "supertask.") Although belief is not identical with will, because they involve different psychic attitudes in my amended version of James, it resembles the willing state in having behavioral consequences as a result of established neural pathways from the concerned part of the brain to the motor organs. We are supposed to have the power, and the free power at that, to get ourselves, directly or indirectly, into various belief states and thereby bring it about that we act overtly in certain ways. Our free efforts to self-induce belief are part of the crucial x factor we contribute to the cosmic equation and which, like the want or presence of the nail in the parable, can make a crucial difference to the future course of history for good or ill. At a minimum, how we believe can have the most important consequences for *our* future flourishing as human beings.

It is at this point that the doctrine of the will to believe enters the story. We have the power to control what we believe, be it directly or, so to speak, through popping a pill, and what we believe can make a decisive difference to whether or not we find the good life of self-realization. Now it often is the case that there is some proposition for which there is little evidence one way or the other but which it would be beneficial for us to believe. James's most important example of such a proposition is that we have a contracausal free will. It seems only reasonable that we should have every right to believe this proposition, in spite of W. K. Clifford's universal admonition that "It is wrong always, everywhere, and for anyone, to believe anything upon insufficient evidence" (*LE* 186). Given that the title of his essay was "The Ethics of Belief," it is clear that by "wrong" he means morally wrong. Had he meant epistemically wrong, he would have been uttering the empty tautology that it is epistemically wrong to believe anything upon insufficient evidence, that is, that it is epistemically wrong to believe.

According to Clifford and his scientistic cohorts, there is only one type of justification for a belief, that being an epistemic one based on evidence unearthed through an empirical inquiry, or a proof if the belief is a mathematical one. To believe on any other grounds is a violation of our moral duty to measure up to our essence of rationality.[1] James, *when he is espousing his will-to-believe doctrine,* challenges Clifford's univocalist account of belief justification. At these times, he claims that there are *two* different ways to justify believing a proposition: the *epistemic* way, based on empirical evidence and proofs; and the *pragmatic* way based on the desirable consequences that accrue to the believer of the

[1] While there are some deontological-sounding pronouncements in Clifford's essay, for the most part he argues from the perspective of a crazed act utilitarian. His "Just Say No to Epistemically Nonwarranted Belief!" crusade is based on the implausible empirical claim that if we ever allow ourselves a single epistemically nonwarranted belief, however trivial, it will cause a radical deterioration in our character, resulting in our turning into "the liar and the cheat," which, in turn, will create a plague that will cause humanity eventually to sink back into barbarism. For a discussion of this, see chapter 9 of my *The Nature and Existence of God* (Cambridge: Cambridge University Press, 1991).

proposition. The former is directed toward establishing the truth of the proposition; the latter, to establishing the desirability of believing that the proposition is true, quite a different matter.

I added the qualification "when he is espousing his will-to-believe doctrine" because I will argue in the next chapter that James, like Clifford, has a univocalist account of belief justification, only it is the reverse of Clifford's, holding that the only justification for believing is pragmatic, based on maximizing desire-satisfaction, with epistemic considerations entering in only in a rule-instrumental manner as useful guiding principles. This should not surprise the reader, as it already has been established that James is firmly committed to both of these propositions.

1. We are always morally obligated to act so as to maximize desire-satisfaction over the other options available to us.
2'. Belief is a free action.

Thus, we are not only *morally justified* in believing a proposition on pragmatic grounds, we are *morally obligated* to do so.

This immediately raises the question, if James was so firmly committed to a univocalist theory of belief justification why, *when he was espousing his will-to-believe doctrine*, did he accept the dualistic account of justification, and moreover, as will be seen, in a form that gives pride of place to epistemic over pragmatic reasons? The answer is that James was wisely following the principle of Minimal Ordinance enjoining us to use the weakest, least controversial premises that are required to establish the desired conclusion, since thereby we cut down on the risk of one of our premises being false or rejected by our opponent. James is sweating with conviction that if he only can get his audience to agree that they are morally permitted to believe certain propositions upon insufficient evidence, especially that God and free will exist, great benefits will accrue to them and their society. To win them over he did not need to use the very strong, controversial premise that the only justification for a belief is pragmatic, which almost everyone would reject out of hand on either Cliffordian or mutivocalist grounds. All he needed was the weaker and therefore less challengeable premise that there are both epistemic and pragmatic modes of justification of belief, with the former taking precedence over the latter, thereby allowing pragmatic reasons to be appealed to only when epistemic ones are of no avail. For the time being, James is willing to work with a hierarchical dualism of justifications for belief that gives a dominant position to epistemic reasons, namely,

4. We are always morally obligated to believe in a manner that is epistemically warranted, except when epistemic reasons are not available.

The "except when epistemic reasons are not available" qualification permits believing on the basis of the will-to-believe doctrine so as to maximize desire-satisfaction when epistemic reasons cannot be had. This goes a long way toward placating those of Cliffordian leanings in his audience.

James even argues for the weaker conclusion that we are *morally permitted* to believe upon insufficient evidence when doing so will have desirable consequences rather than the stronger one that we are *morally obligated* to do so, as is required by his casuistic rule.[2] He must have realized that many in his audience would not grant him his casuistic rule. At any rate, they should not have, because of the many powerful objections that were advanced in Chapter 1. This one-problem-at-a-time approach fits the spirit of James's claim that "sufficient to that day will be the evil thereof" (*PP* 286).

Before we get down to the details of his account, two different sorts of counterexamples to Clifford's universal prohibition will be presented so that they can be set aside as not relevant to James's concerns. First, there is the trust case, in which a person is required to believe certain things about another person in virtue of having a special relation to that person, even when they lack adequate evidence for these beliefs. For example, spouses are morally required to believe in the faithfulness of the other person, even when they lack adequate evidence for this belief. Were they even to inquire into the matter, say by hiring a private detective, it would place them outside the trust relation and thus destroy the relationship. They have a duty not even to inquire into the matter. Of course, they might get to a certain point at which they could not help but harbor suspicions; as Big Joe Turner used to sing, "You

---

[2] James Wernham, alone among the commentators, has seen that James's casuistic rule commits him to the stronger conclusion (*EB* 291). James's first published presentation, in the *Nation* for 1875, originally was going to have the strong moral obligation conclusion but retreated to the weaker moral right or permission one as a result of Chauncey Wright's criticisms of a rough draft of the paper. Wernham interprets James as moving "not from a stronger to a weaker *moral* claim. It is from a moral to a *prudential* claim. The claim is still about what *ought* to be done. What, if anything, has happened is that the moral 'ought' has been replaced by the prudential one" (*WB* 15). There is nothing in James's text to support this admittedly heretical interpretation, which is surprising if James was saying what Wernham imputes to him. Furthermore, Wernham seems to forget that James's casuistic rule morally, not just prudentially, obligates us to believe, when doing so maximizes desire-satisfaction. He also overlooks the fact that James's will-to-believe doctrine was advanced as a counter to Clifford's essay, titled "The Ethics of Belief," not "The Prudence of Belief." Since there is no textual support for Wernham's interpretation and this is a book on James's philosophy, it will not receive further consideration. In addition, the view he attributes to James, in my opinion, has little philosophical interest or merit in its own right. Another off-the-wall interpretation of James's conclusion is given by Stephen Davis. James sometimes used "lawfully may" in place of "are morally permitted" in stating his conclusion. According to Davis, by "lawfully may" James means "with full epistemological justification." Again, there is absolutely no textual basis for this interpretation, and much in the text that weighs against it (*WT* 232).

came home in the wee hours of the morning and your clothes didn't fit you right." It is then that the trust relation ends. James did not discuss the trust case, but there is no doubt he would agree that it is a counterexample to Clifford; however, it is not a very telling one, because Clifford can easily protect his universal prohibition against it by building in an ad hoc restriction that excludes trust cases. Thus, trust cases are not telling counterexamples, because they are too easily localized.

Much of the recent discussion of the will to believe has concentrated on extreme cases in which there is an overwhelming utilitarian justification for acquiring an epistemically nonwarranted belief, because doing so either prevents a horrendous outcome or brings about some exceedingly beneficial one. For example, an eccentric billionaire might publicly promise to donate a billion dollars to charity if Jones were to acquire the epistemically nonwarranted belief that Cleopatra weighed 109 pounds when she died, or if some overwhelmingly powerful alien invader were to threaten to destroy the planet unless Jones acquired this belief. Again, James would readily grant that a counterexample has been unearthed but would find it of little interest for his purpose in formulating a will-to-believe doctrine. In the first place, "extreme cases" are, with very rare exceptions, counterfactual, and James in general has little concern with merely possible cases in his analyses, being satisfied if his analysis fits the way things actually are. More important is the point that in extreme cases the realization of good consequences or the prevention of bad ones is completely external to the believer, being connected with his belief only via the intercession of a third person, the billionaire or alien in the examples. James's version of the will to believe is concerned with the personal or existential dimension of belief, the manner in which it changes a person's character and thereby his readiness to act in certain ways. There is a causal theory of value underlying James's will-to-believe doctrine according to which the value of an outcome depends, at least in part, on how it is brought about. For this reason, extreme cases can be left out of the discussion of James's doctrine.

James's intent was not just to produce some counterexamples to Clifford's prohibition. If it had been, he could have availed himself of the rather obvious trust and extreme-case counterexamples and been done with it. Rather, his aim was to spell out the conditions under which *in general* we are morally permitted to believe upon insufficient evidence. His dislike of doing philosophy in a formalistic, by-the-numbers manner kept him from explicitly listing all these conditions in a neat package of numbered indented sentences, informing us which of them are necessary and which combination of them are sufficient for being morally permitted to believe without epistemic warrant. It will be argued that things go best for James if he is taken as giving a set of sufficient but not necessary conditions, although some individual members of the set are necessary. A great deal of work is left to the expositor in extracting these conditions and determining their sufficiency and/or necessity. Thus there is considerable room for alternative interpretations, though there are some conditions that plainly are intended to be necessary.

James begins his essay "The Will to Believe," his most complete and forceful exposition of the doctrine, by explicitly listing three conditions that together comprise what he calls a "genuine option" to believe. A person's option to believe a proposition at a certain time is a *genuine option* just in case it is *live, momentous,* and *forced.* Because a genuine option is dependent on variable psychological factors, it must be relativized to a person at a time. What is live and momentous can vary across persons as well as across different times in a single person's life.

For a proposition to be *live* for a person at a time, it must then be a real possibility for that person to believe it, as well as to believe its contradictory. His mind must not be made up one way or the other. Thus, the proposition, along with its contradictory, can be seriously entertained even if it cannot win at that time uncontested occupancy of the believer's mind and thereby qualify as a belief for James. To achieve this status will require some work on the part of the believer in the way of making efforts to attend or acting as if he believes (or popping the pill). James parries the capriciousness objection to his account of free will, according to which a person is just as likely to act out of as in character, given that our free choices are undetermined, by pointing out that the range of one's free will is limited to living options. Because a person of benevolent character cannot seriously entertain the thought of committing some sadistic act, it is not a live option for him.

A proposition is *momentous* for a person at a time when the consequences of his believing or not believing it will have very important consequences, relative to his personal scheme of values, supposedly at the time of his decision to believe rather than at some future time. That an option to believe is unique, pace what James says, does not alone qualify it as momentous. My one and only chance to see Barry Manilow live is his farewell concert tonight, but that alone hardly makes my option to see it momentous. Again, there can be widespread divergences among persons and a single person at different times in respect to the momentousness of a given option.

An option to believe is *forced* when the person will not wind up believing the proposition in question unless he decides to believe it. No one, such as a crazed brain surgeon or a mad cyberneticist, is going to compel him to have this belief regardless of what he might do. It is completely up to him whether or not he acquires the belief. We might call the alternative in a forced option that the chooser winds up with if no decision is made the "negative alternative." Dated options, such as to accept a proposal of marriage by midnight tomorrow or never to see the man again, are good examples of forced options. A forced option, like a unique one, need not be momentous, which would be the case if this proposal were offered to a lesbian.

Several supposedly astute and fair commentators have interpreted James as holding that the three conditions for having a genuine option to believe are together sufficient for having a moral right to believe upon insufficient evidence. This will be shown to be a terrible distortion of the text. Once this perverse strawman version is given, they have an easy time denigrating it as the will to gullibility or wishful thinking. It licenses me to believe the propositions that I am the sultan of Wisconsin, the inventor of the sandwich, and the author of *The Critique of Pure Reason*, if my psychology is such that they are live and momentous for me and my option to believe them is forced. James would be the last person to agree that the pleasure I derive from believing them justifies my doing so.

The original culprit was Dickinson Miller: "The particular class of cases [for James] in which we have 'a right to believe' was that in which the option before our mind was (1) 'living,' (2) 'forced,' and (3) 'momentous' "[3] (*PA* 286). A. J. Ayer, in a similar vein, wrote, "To claim [as did James] the freedom to believe whatever one chooses may be emotionally satisfying, but I should hardly call it rational"[4] (*OP* 191). Marcus Peter Ford, a very sensitive and imaginative interpreter, wrote: "The 'right to believe' only pertains when a decision is 'forced' and 'momentous' and when it concerns 'live options' " (*WJ* 32). What is overlooked by these interpretations are the further restrictions that James places upon a will-to-believe option. They not only are stated explicitly but also inform all of his examples, making it hard to understand how any attentive reader could miss them.

Of these additional conditions, the one that is most important for

---

[3] It is especially bizarre that Miller, who professed to be a friend and disciple of James, would have written this. With a friend and disciple like Miller, James didn't need any enemies. James knew what he was talking about when he called Miller "my most penetrating critic and intimate enemy" (*LWJ* 2:48). Miller's distortion of James's doctrine results not from of a lack of keenness but probably from his abhorrence of it and thus a desire, possibly unconscious, to present it in a strawman fashion. Only by basing our beliefs on empirical facts, he believed, could we make ourselves better and accomplish our ideals for humanity. If you have a bit of a sadistic streak and enjoy seeing a philosopher suffer total humiliation and defeat, the exchange of letters between Miller and C. J. Ducasse (in Hare and Madden *CPB*) is required reading. Ducasse mops the floor with him and then hangs him out to dry.

[4] Arthur Murphy also presents James's will to believe as requiring only that the belief option be genuine and, accordingly, attacks James along the same lines that Miller did (*PCR* 337). Giles Gunn, a nonphilosopher, in his introduction to *CWJ*, vol. 4 wrote: "One has the right to believe [for James] in whatever presents itself as a live, forced, and momentous option" (xxxiii).

responding to the wishful-thinking objection is the requirement that the chooser cannot determine at the time of his decision the truth-value of the proposition in question on epistemic grounds. "Our passional nature not only lawfully may [is morally permitted to], but must decide an option between propositions, whenever it is a genuine option that cannot by its nature be decided on intellectual [epistemic] grounds," and, "*In concreto*, the freedom [moral permission] to believe can only cover living options which the intellect of the individual cannot by itself resolve" (*WB* 20 and 32). Sometimes James presents the epistemic requirement in a weaker way that would license believing even in the face of significant evidence against the belief. He speaks of "the right to believe in things for the truth of which *complete objective proof* is yet lacking" and of voluntary choice being permitted when "*objective proof* is not to be had" (*MT* 138–9 and PP 1177; my italics). Herein the available evidence need not be neutral between the truth or falsity of the proposition. Given that James wants to win over his audience by giving the Cliffordian types as much rope as possible, he ought to go with the stronger version, especially as it is satisfied by his most cherished examples – belief in free will and the good destiny of the world. For these reasons, it is the one that will be operative in what follows. It should be borne in mind, however, that James's real position, the one he keeps in the closet when he is trying to win over the Cliffordians, is that if the option is of overwhelming momentousness to the believer, such as Kierkegaard's option to believe in Christianity, the weaker version is operative: One is permitted to believe in the teeth of quite powerful contrary evidence.

When James says that the intellect of the person *cannot* settle the matter, the "cannot" can be of either the *in principle* or the weaker *in practice* sort. In practice, human neurophysiologists cannot verify that our efforts to attend are not causally determined by brain events due to limits in their powers of mensuration, but it is in principle possible that they do so, for they, along with their instruments, could suddenly make like the incredible shrinking man.[5] It is important to realize that the epistemic undecidability concerns the chooser alone, not other observers. It is conceptually impossible that the chooser, at the time he is

---

[5] John Dewey held James to have implicitly restricted his will to believe to philosophical world hypotheses, not applying it to "conclusions which fall within the scope of matters of fact" (*LW* 15:7; see also *MW* 4:113). Not only does Dewey overlook James's application of his doctrine to straightforward factual propositions, such as in the confidence-building cases, he fails to note that there is for James a fact of the matter even with respect to a belief in a metaphysical proposition or world hypothesis, the doctrine of Libertarian free will being a good case in point. I have no idea how Dewey could have so blatantly distorted James's doctrine. O'Connell follows Dewey's misinterpretation: "The thesis of 'The Will to Believe' legitimately applies only to what James called over-beliefs, or propositions of weltanschaulich dimensions" (*WJ* 4). Maybe these commentators are confounding being the most important case with being the only case.

deliberating, verify what choice he will make and thereby the occurrence of any event for which his choice is a necessary cause, since he
can deliberate only if he is in ignorance of what he shall choose; someone else, however, could verify at that time what his choice will be by
appeal to a well-founded inductive argument based on his past track
record.

It must be stressed that James's epistemically undecidable-by-the-
chooser-before-the-choice-is-made requirement is not the weak requirement that at the time of the choice the chooser, as a matter of fact,
lacks adequate epistemic grounds or evidence for determining the
truth-value of the proposition, which could be realized if the chooser
made a point not to investigate the matter, like Clifford's dishonest
shipowner who makes a point of not investigating whether his ship is
safe to send to sea. Rather, it is the strong requirement that the chooser
lacks adequate evidence one way or the other after discharging his
epistemic duty to perform all of the relevant inquiries. Laziness, especially self-interested laziness, will not enable the chooser to satisfy the
epistemic-undecidability requirement.

Another question concerning epistemic undecidability that must be
resolved concerns whether there is a single method or criterion for
determining when a proposition is epistemically warranted that is common to all propositions, regardless of their subject matter. There are
contemporary language-game fideists who would contend that each language-game or doxastic practice – normative rule-governed human
practice for warranting beliefs – such as a specific organized religion or
one of the branches of science, has its own unique ontology, along with
its own criteria of rationality and epistemic warrant for a belief. The
criteria that inform the different practices are incommensurable in the
sense that each practice is a self-contained normatively rule-governed
activity that is immune from criticism from without. Whether or not
James agrees with these Wittgensteinian language-game fideists does
not admit of a simple yes or no answer. Chapter 7 will show that in
regard to the ontology part of their thesis he is in agreement, for what
is real for James is relative to the assumptions of a given practice or
perspective, but in regard to the epistemic part he is not with them.
The ontological assumptions of different doxastic practices differ, but
not their epistemic procedures for warranting belief. Since a choice
cannot be made between them by use of their shared epistemic procedures, we are morally permitted to make one in the will-to-believe manner. Not only is there no indication in the text that James believed that
criteria for epistemic warrant vary across practices, there is good evidence that he believed that these criteria were the same for all practices, based on his attempt to show that existential claims based on
mystical experiences are subject to the same checks and tests as are

those based on ordinary sense experience, which is a subject for Chapter 10. He even said that "Science, metaphysics and religion . . . form a single body of wisdom, and lend each other mutual support" (*SPP* 20). Also, in regard to the seeming opposition between common sense, science, and philosophy, James said, "There is no simple test available for adjudicating offhand between the[se] divers types of thought" (*P* 93). He did not say that each has its own unique epistemic procedures for warranting belief.

James not only explicitly states the requirement for epistemic undecidability for a will-to-believe option, all of his many examples satisfy it, thus making it all the more amazing that it could have been missed by so many commentators. The stranded mountaineer who must jump across a chasm to reach safety and can increase his chances of succeeding if he believes that he has the capacity to do so, is not able, *at that time*, epistemically to determine whether he has the capacity, though he can do so after he has attempted the leap, though, if he misses, he'll have to do it very quickly. The person who psychs himself up to lead the morally strenuous life by believing the proposition that good will win out over evil in the long run cannot epistemically determine its truth-value, since, in addition to it being beyond our capacity to predict the direction history will take in the long run,[6] the choices that he *shall* make, which is the crucial *x* factor that he contributes to the cosmic equation, are not knowable by him in advance of his choices. In contrast to these Jamesian cases, my epistemically nonwarranted beliefs about being the sultan of Wisconsin and the like are, both in principle and in practice, epistemically determinable by me now; and, furthermore, I have violated my epistemic duty by not performing adequate inquiries – to which my response is that since I *am* the sultan of Wisconsin, I have lackeys to do the drudge work.

Four conditions for a will-to-believe option have been unearthed so far from the text. A person, *A*, is morally permitted to believe a proposition, *p*, at a time *T* without adequate epistemic warrant if *A*'s option to believe is (1) live, (2) momentous, (3) forced, and (4) *A* cannot epistemically determine at *T* the truth-value of *p*. The text gives some but not decisive reasons to think that James required, in addition to (1)–(4), that *A*'s believing *p* helps to make *p* become true: "There are, then, cases where a fact cannot come at all unless a preliminary faith

---

[6] James once naively said that this sort of proposition, like those dealing with universal order, "may remain subjects of doubt for many centuries to come" (*EPH* 337). But why only many centuries?. That's hardly the long run. The long run seems to have no cut-off date, which renders the truth-value of this proposition perennially impossible to verify or falsify. Suppose a good order comes to prevail, how do we know that it will continue to do so throughout the indefinite or infinite future? And, how ever many years we might toil without success to make good win out over evil in the long run, how can we know that at some more future time we won't succeed?

exists in its coming. And where faith in a fact can help create the fact, that would be an insane logic which should say that faith running ahead of scientific evidence is the 'lowest kind of immorality' into which a thinking being can fall," and "In truths dependent on our personal action, the faith based on desire is certainly a lawful and possibly indispensable thing" (*WB* 29 and 29). In the 1878 "Some Considerations of the Subjective Method," James wrote that the subjective method, the name he then used for the will-to-believe doctrine, "can only be harmful, one might even say 'immoral' if applied to cases where the facts to be stated do not include the subjective R as a factor," in which R is the contribution that we make through the actions caused by our belief (*EPH* 335).

What is not completely clear from these quotations is whether the belief-helping-to-make-true condition is intended to be necessary for any will-to-believe option or is a feature of only some cases of this option. If the latter interpretation is given, as it is by Elizabeth Flower (*AP* 1:686), Robert O'Connell (*WJ* 72), and James Wernham (*WB* 14), a person would be morally permitted to believe a proposition if (1)–(4) were satisfied, even though his believing made no difference to whether or not it was true, as would be the case with his belief that there are Platonic forms or that the God of traditional Western theism exists. If his belief gives him pleasure, why deny him this, even if his pleasurable belief state is completely disconnected from activities in the workaday world?

I favor the former interpretation. First, two of the quotations that were given seem to support it. Furthermore, every example that James gave throughout his career of a will-to-believe option involved a belief that played a causal role in helping to make the believed proposition become true or, as will be shortly seen, some other desirable proposition. The Alpine and the good-will-win out cases clearly satisfy the causal condition, as do all of his confidence-building cases – the Alpine leaper, the ardent but somewhat unconfident suitor, the person who wants to be liked, et al. The reason James became so preachy whenever he discussed free will is that he thought that if we believed we had free will we would make the sort of all-out effort to attend to an idea in difficult cases of conflict that would help to bring it about that we do have free will. "If . . . free acts be possible, a faith in their possibility, by augmenting the moral energy which gives them birth, will increase their frequency in a given individual" (*WB* 84). It is very much in the spirit of James's Promethean pragmatism to have a causal requirement, since the significance and value of belief in general are the worldly deeds to which it leads, a thesis for which, as we saw, James gave both physiological and normative reasons. Remember how he railed against sentimentalists and aesthetes, including his own brother. Merely to be in a pleasurable belief or aesthetic state is not its own justification. There must be some behaviorally rooted reason for choosing to get oneself into such a state. Thus, it would violate the Promethean spirit of James's pragmatism to justify an epistemically nonwarranted belief solely in terms of its being a pleasurable belief state. Furthermore, by having a causal requirement James found yet another way, in addition to having the epistemic undecidability requirement, to protect his doctrine against the wishful-thinking objection. My ill-founded pleasurable delusions of grandeur were ones that my believing could not help to make true.

Assuming that James required that causal condition, there are some questions that need to be answered. First, must P's belief be causally sufficient, necessary, or both for making p true? The answer is none of the above. James's examples, especially the good-will-win-out one, involve only the very weak requirement that P's belief can help to make p true.[7] The Alpine leaper's belief, obviously, does not have to be either causally sufficient or necessary for his leaping successfully; for him to be permitted to acquire the belief, it is enough that his believing increases the probability of success. This is all that common sense, as well as James, requires. Furthermore, this weak interpretation dovetails with James's insistence that a very minor difference in the initial conditions can make the crucial difference in the final outcome, as in the parable of the nail. For these reasons I will include the weak version of the causal condition as a fifth requirement for a will-to-believe option.

Adopting this requirement requires, in turn, adopting yet another condition, namely, that it is desirable that the believed proposition become true. This requirement is assumed throughout his discussion, for James's will-to-believe justification is a substitution of this argument form:

Doing x helps to bring it about that p.
It is desirable that p.

Therefore,

It is morally permissible to do x,

in which "believing p" is substituted for "x" throughout. Notice that the moral permission in the conclusion is not qualified as prima facie, which would make it subject to defeaters or overriders. If we knew only

---

[7] Ellen Suckiel seems both to support and not support this weak interpretation of the causal requirement. "Perhaps in cases of uncertainty the reasonable individual would adopt a policy prescribing that when the consequences are so important that for the sake of *increasing the probability of achieving them*, one is justified in assuming himself to be in a situation where faith is *necessary for the fact* (*PP* 90; my italics). The "increasing the probability of achieving them" supports the weak interpretation, but the "necessary for the fact" supports the stronger, causally necessary interpretation.

that p's being true would satisfy some desires but not that it would maximize desire-satisfaction, then, if we accept James's casuistic rule, we would have to make this prima facie qualification. Since James's casuistic rule was rejected at the end of Chapter 1 in favor of a vague, mixed-bag rule that included deontological factors along with desire-satisfaction, we will interpret "desirable" according to the latter criterion, as we had agreed to do. Thus, even if p's being true were to maximize desire-satisfaction over its being false, this alone would render it only prima facie morally permissible to believe p. Given James's strong commitment to deontological ethical principles in many of his writings, though not in "The Moral Philosopher and the Moral Life," James would agree to this and thus would accept my deontological revision of his casuistic rule.

To illustrate this, consider the case in which I promise to give Jones a revolver, but in the interim he turns into a homicidal maniac and vows to kill Smith.

My giving Jones a revolver helps to bring it about that I keep my promise.
That I keep my promise is desirable.

Therefore,

I am morally permitted to give Jones a revolver.

Obviously, the permission must be qualified as only prima facie, for were I to keep my promise and give Jones a revolver it would result in the death of an innocent person, Smith. This deontological defeater is not overruled if it would maximize desire-satisfaction to give Jones the gun: Smith could be a widely disliked person whose death would maximize desire-satisfaction over his continuing to live.

At this point it will help the reader to pause for a recap of the six conditions that have so far been unearthed from the text for a will-to-believe option. Person A is morally permitted to believe proposition p without adequate epistemic warrant at a time, T, *if* (only a sufficient condition is being given) the option to believe p is: (1) live; (2) momentous; and (3) forced for A at T; (4) A cannot epistemically determine p's truth-value; (5) A's believing p helps to bring it about that p; and (6) it is, all things considered, desirable that p become true.

In fairness to those commentators who have not included the causal requirement for any will-to-believe option, it must be pointed out that sometimes James stated his doctrine in a way that did not justify *believing* an epistemically undecidable proposition but only *adopting it as a working hypothesis,* as we do in science when we select some untested hypothesis as a working hypothesis for the purpose of setting up experiments, or in everyday life when we simply act as if the proposition were true. It will be shown that the causal requirement is not applicable to some working-hypothesis cases.

The following quotations clearly speak for the working-hypothesis version. Some of them simply identify belief or faith with the adoption of a working hypothesis: "Faith is synonymous with working hypothesis," and "To sum up, faith and *working hypothesis* are here one and the same" (*WB* 79 and *EPH* 337). Clifford's prohibition is now interpreted as prohibiting adopting as a working hypothesis (acting as if you believed) an epistemically nonwarranted proposition rather than believing it. "Suppose that, having just read the 'Ethics of Belief,' I feel it would be sinful to act upon an assumption unverified by previous experience . . ." (*WB* 80). At the beginning of "The Dilemma of Determinism," James states his intention "to induce some of you to follow my own example in assuming it [the doctrine of Libertarian free will] true, and acting as if it were true" (*WB* 115). Among the actions to be performed is publicly declaring that it is true, even though you do not believe what you are saying. His presentation of the "faith ladder" in the 1905 "Reason and Faith," which is the final form taken by his will-to-believe doctrine, says that we are to treat the proposition we desire to be true "as if it *were* true so far as my advocacy and actions are concerned" (*ERM* 125). This very same faith ladder gets repeated at the end of each of his final two books (*PU* 148 and *SPP* 113).

James's examples also reflect his vacillating back and forth between the belief and working-hypothesis versions of his doctrine. In "Some Considerations of the Subjective Method" he uses the example of the Alpine climber who must leap across a chasm to get to safety (*EPH* 332). What is required here to increase his chance of success is good old-fashioned sweating with a convicted belief that he has the capacity to succeed, not just the adoption as a working hypothesis that he has it. But in the final paragraph of "The Will to Believe" James has an Alpine example of a climber who is confronted with alternative paths and has to pick one of them if he is to save himself from freezing to death and has no reason to prefer one of them over the others. Obviously, he must pick one of them and journey along it, for to make no choice assures his death. In this circumstance, he chances of his success are in no way increased by his believing that the chosen path is the right one. He has only to adopt it as a working hypothesis and thereby act as if it is the right one by following it.

The working-hypothesis version of the will to believe does not in general require a causal requirement. James himself recognized this when he wrote, "And your acting thus [as if you believed] may *in certain special cases* be a means of making it securely true in the end" (*PU* 148; my italics). The "in certain special cases" qualification implies that in some cases adoption of a proposition as a working hypothesis does not help to make it true. By adopting a proposition as a working hypothesis a scientist does not help to *make* it true but only helps to *discover* that it is true. But "in certain special cases," such as adoption of the hypothesis of Libertarian freedom, it does help to make it true, since by acting as if we were free in this sense we help to bring it about that we are. James recognized cases in which believing, in the full-blooded sense, can help in discovering that a proposition is true. By believing that God exists, we increase the chances that we shall have apparent direct nonsensory perceptions of God, such experiences, as Chapter 10 will bring out, counting as evidence for God's existence.[8]

It is plain that James operated with two quite different versions of the will to believe. They are different because believing is not the same as acting as if you believe or adopting a proposition as a working hypothesis. James recognized this when he gave us the act-as-if-you-believe causal recipe for self-inducing a belief, as a cause cannot be identical with its effect. But why did he keep two sets of books? It cannot be explained in terms of an evolution in his thinking, the belief version being his earlier formulation and the working-hypothesis version supplanting it from 1905 on, for he ran them in tandem throughout his career. For example, "The Will to Believe," which gives prominence to the believing version because of its heavy reliance on confidence- and courage-building cases that require real, sweating-with-conviction–type belief, also endorses the working-hypothesis version.[9]

The most likely explanation may be found in terms of James's attempt to win over his audience by being as accommodating as possible; but his weak, working-hypothesis version goes too far in that direction – so far, that it trivializes his dispute with Clifford. Clifford, being a man of science, was the last person who would want to issue a prohibition against using working hypotheses, for he must have been aware of their fruitfulness in furthering the progress of science. James abused the principle of Minimal Ordinance that enjoins us to use the weakest premises possible to support the desired conclusion, not to replace the desired conclusion with one that trivializes what is at issue. Fortunately, there was no need for James to engage in the trivial exercise of running through open doors, for his exciting, belief version, when strengthened so as to meet certain objections, which shall now be considered, is quite formidable.

---

[8] G. L. Dore, in an otherwise admirable essay, misses this feature of James's account (*EB* 355).

[9] The interpretation of the will to believe by John Roth (*EJ* 75) and James Muyskens (JD 45) in terms of hope or justified hope, like that in terms of adoption as a working hypothesis, is too weak to handle the confidence-building cases. In most cases, the leaper who only hopes that he has what it takes will have far less chance of succeeding than will the one who firmly believes that he does.

I. Objections

The first objection comes from that tireless critic of the will to believe, Dickinson Miller. The chooser is supposed to get himself to believe a proposition that he himself takes to be evidentially nonwarranted, but this is impossible. "You cannot believe and yet in the heart of that very belief be heroically facing the uncertainty of your whole position. Your state of mind would not be belief, which is regarding something as fact, not as uncertain" (*PA* 288). Miller is right that to believe a proposition is to believe it is a fact, for a fact is a true proposition and one cannot believe a proposition without believing that it is true; but, pace Miller, that does not require that it is believed to be certain in the sense of supported by overwhelming evidence. That there are so many antirationalistic theists of the Kierkegaardian variety shows Miller's inference from *take to be true* (or a fact) to *take to be certain* to be bogus. Miller is not alone in his mischaracterization of belief. Many contemporary philosophers, such as Richard Swinburne in *Faith and Reason*, wrongly claim that to believe a proposition is to believe that its probability is greater than one-half relative to the available evidence.

There is a close cousin to Miller's objection that might fare better. The point is not that one cannot believe without believing to be certain, but rather that if one believes what he takes to be evidentially unfounded, he will not, pace James, have his confidence and courage boosted so that he can act more effectively in making the believed proposition true. The wrong response to this objection is to find some procedure for making the believer forget that he acquired his belief on the basis of a will-to-believe option; there could be a second set of pills, neatly arranged in descending order of size from left to right on the second shelf of the medicine cabinet, such that after one has popped a belief-inducing pill he pops the appropriate one from the second shelf that makes him forget the nonrational means by which he acquired this belief and instead implants in his mind the false apparent memory of having acquired it after a successful empirical inquiry. The problem with this way around the objection is not only that the believer must deceive himself, which is bad enough, but that in the process he destroys his own integral unity and winds up as a divided, schizophrenic self. James's Promethean quest to have it all will be found in Chapter 11 to have this deleterious consequence, and ways will be devised to attempt to escape it. The ideal of an integrated, rational self is a powerful one that deserves more respect than is accorded it by this drastic solution.[10]

[10] This does not mean that a person is never permitted to self-induce a belief by nonrational means. To use an example suggested to me by Nancy Davis, imagine a diamond cutter who has very good inductive evidence based on his past successes that he is capable of successfully cutting some valuable diamond, but because he suffers from an

A better response is that human psychology is far more variable than this objection envisions. Although it is true that there are some people who are so constituted psychologically that they cannot realize the confidence-building benefits of a belief that they take to be evidentially nonwarranted, there are many people whose psychology permits them to do so, such as our nonrationalist theists. It has already been seen that a will-to-believe option is relative to a person at a time because human psychology is variable in regard to which propositions a person takes to be live and momentous belief options. All this objection shows is that there is another psychological reason for relativizing a will-to-believe option to a person at a time. A seventh condition could be added requiring that

(7) *A*'s psychology at *T* is such that he can realize the confidence- and courage-boosting benefits of a belief that *p*, even if he takes *p* to be evidentally nonwarranted.

James's will to believe is acquiring more and more epicycles, but I will not pause at this point to give an explicit mounting of them, since even more are to come in response to yet other objections. This next objection comes from James himself. Why, he asks, cannot someone act so as to help make some desirable proposition become true without actually believing it? His response:

> Since belief is measured by action, he who forbids us to believe religion to be true, necessarily also forbids us to act as we should if we did believe it to be true. The whole defence of religious faith hinges upon action. If the action required or inspired by the religious hypothesis is in no way different from that dictated by the naturalistic hypothesis, then religious faith is a pure superfluity, better pruned away, and controversy about its legitimacy is a piece of idle trifling, unworthy of serious minds. (*WB* 32)

James even goes so far as to claim that there is no behavioral difference between suspending belief in *R* and actually disbelieving it. "We cannot escape the issue by remaining sceptical and waiting for more light, because, although we do avoid error in that way *if religion be untrue*, we lose the good, *if it be true*, just as certainly as if we positively disbelieve" (*WB* 26). The agnostic must act "meanwhile more or less as if religion were not true" (*WB* 29–30).

This is a disastrous response. By the "religious hypothesis" James here means the proposition that

R. Good will win out over evil in the long run.[11]

irrational lack of confidence cannot get himself to believe it by any ordinary means. There is no objection to his taking the belief-inducing pill, for what he winds up with is an evidentially warranted belief and thereby no need to pop a second-order pill to make him forget how he acquired this belief.

[11] James also includes a second component, namely, that "we are better off even now if [we] believe her first affirmation [*R*] to be true" (*WB* 25–6). I have dropped this component because it is not a creedal tenet of any religion but rather a proposition

He claims that because belief is measured by action, a person will act so as to help make R become true by leading the morally strenuous life if and only he first believes that R is true. Such benevolent behavior is "dictated," "required," or "inspired" by R. As an empirical generalization about human psychology, this is false, because we know of many people who do not believe R but nevertheless lead the morally strenuous life.[12]

Underlying James's response is the false assumption that for every proposition, p, there is a set of actions, B, such that a person believes p if, and only if, he performs or is disposed to perform the actions in B. This assumption fails to do justice to the psychological variability among persons in respect to how their beliefs mesh with their actions. For example, two persons can believe one and the same proposition but act in radically different ways. Both could believe R but only one of them act so as to help make it true. The person who sits on the sideline might be made overconfident by his belief in R and think that his active participation on the side of the good is not needed, or he might have devilist leanings and not want to see R become true. James's assumption of a one-to-one correlation between belief and action is not able to distinguish between believing the factual proposition that R is true and believing the normative proposition that it is good that R is true. The person who acts so as to help make R true could believe the latter but not the former.

There is an easy way around this difficulty that consists in building in yet another epicycle concerning the way in which a will-to-believe option must be relativized to a person's psychological makeup at the time of the choice, namely,

(8) A knows at T that he will act so as to help make p become true only if he first believes that p is true.

Why must A know this fact about his own psychology? The reason is that the conditions for having a will-to-believe option are supposed to justify A's believing or acquiring the belief that p. But what justifies a belief gives the believer a reason for so believing, something that he could give in response to the challenge to justify his belief. This re-

---

about the dynamics of religious faith, such as might be made by a social scientist or an apologist for religion.

[12] There is an important difference between "inspire," on the one hand, and "dictate" and "require," on the other, for the former, unlike the latter, is a purely causal notion that involves no normative social conventions. In the old vaudeville routine a man would go berserk every time he heard "Niagara Falls." The name inspires or causes him to act in this manner, but does not thereby dictate or require such actions; however, they are no part of its meaning because they are not connected with the name by any normative social conventions. It will be seen in the next chapter that James can be interpreted as giving a purely causal account of meaning that results in a term's meaning varying among individuals due to differences in their psychological makeup.

quires that he be aware of this reason or justification. This seemingly innocent point will be the basis for the next objection.

Imagine that A satisfies conditions (1)–(7) for having a will-to-believe justification for believing that p is true. Among his reasons for this belief is that only by so believing can he act in a way that will help to make this desirable proposition become true. Thus, if we ask A why he is toiling to help make p become true, among the reasons he will give is that p will in fact become true. But that's an irrational reason for trying to make p true. A relevant reason would be that it is good that p become true. Because you believe that Jones will succumb to his cancer of the liver hardly gives you a reason for acting so as to help bring this about.

Because A has such an irrational reason for acting so as to make p true, he does not do so as a rational, morally responsible agent; and, since rationality is a necessary but not sufficient condition for acting freely, he does not do so freely. This is a very serious matter, especially for the likes of James, who prizes so highly being a free, morally responsible agent. Just recall the emotional breakdown of 1870 occasioned by his doubts that he was such an agent. The problem takes an especially virulent form with a will-to-believe-based belief in R, given the very extensive nature of the actions and dispositions that are caused by this belief. Whatever good might be realized by A's irrationally acting so as to make R true is outweighed or defeated by his loss of or diminution in his freedom and moral responsibility. At least these are my deontological intuitions, and James's as well, I believe.

The irrationality objection, devastating though it is, is easily neutralized. All that is required is to separate the proposition that A must first get himself to believe from the one he thereby helps to make true. Thus, (8) must be revised as

(8') A knows at T that he will act so as to help make q become true only if he first believes that p is true, in which q is not identical with p.

By separating p from q, James can give a will-to-believe justification for believing in good old-time theism, not just his pale moral substitute for it, R. A's psychology at T could be such that he will act in the proper good-making fashion so as to help R become true only if he first believes that the God of traditional Western theism exists. Herein he would have a prudential reason for acting benevolently, since he believes that God will reward him for doing so. This may not be an admirable reason but nevertheless is a rational one. In the case in which a belief that God exists increases the believer's chance of gaining evidence that God exists for his religious experiences, the believer helps to bring about the desirable proposition that there is evidence for the existence of God by believing that God exists.

There is some textual evidence that James was aware of the need to separate the believed proposition from the one that it is desirable to make true, for he often formulated his will-to-believe option in a way that separated them. Sometimes, though not in "The Will to Believe," he did so in the confidence-building cases. The proposition that the Alpine leaper must believe in order to increase his chances of leaping successfully across the chasm is not the *categorical* proposition that he will successfully make the leap but rather that he has the capacity to do so, which is the *conditional* proposition that if he were to attempt the leap he would succeed. This is the proposition that he first must believe in order to increase his chance of bringing it about that he successfully makes the leap. When James says, "I wish to make the leap, but I am ignorant from lack of experience whether I *have the strength* for it" or the "*ability* for [this] exploit," he is making use of this conditional proposition (*EPH* 332; my italics). The leaper's belief that he has the capacity to succeed, unlike the belief that he will in fact succeed, is a rational reason for attempting to make it true that he leaps successfully. The you-will-like-me case admits of the same resolution. *A* first gets himself to believe the conditional proposition that if he acts in a friendly manner, people will end up liking him so that he can muster the necessary courage and confidence to act in a friendly manner and thereby help to bring it about that people will indeed like him. His conditional belief is a rational reason, though not the sole reason, for his acting in a friendly manner. Among the other reasons must be the desirability of being liked by people.

James flipflops in his manner of stating the common denominator of all religions. In "The Will to Believe" he gives this categorical formulation: "The best things are the more eternal things, the overlapping things, the things in the universe that throw the last stone, so to speak, and say the final word," which I paraphrased as

R. Good will win out over evil in the long run.

This is the proposition that *A* first must believe so as to act in the sort of good-making manner that will help to make *R* become true. This interpretation is nailed down by James's claiming, with respect to propositions like *R*, that "There are, then, cases where a fact cannot come at all unless a preliminary faith exists in its coming" (*WB* 29). Herein the proposition that first must be believed and the one that is to be made true via the belief are identical.

But in his other writings he gives a conditionalized formulation of religion to the effect that

R.' If we collectively exert our best moral effort, then *R* (good will win out over evil in the long run).

For instance, he writes: "Suppose that the world's author put the case to you before creation, saying: 'I am going to make a world not certain to be saved, a world the perfection of which shall be *conditional* merely, the condition being that each several agent does its own 'level best' '" (*P* 139; my italics). This conditionalized formulation of the religious hypothesis is repeated at two places in his lecture notes: "Meanwhile I ask whether a world of hypothetical perfection conditional on each part doing its duty be not as much as can fairly be demanded," and pluralism holds that "the world . . . may be saved, on condition that its parts shall do their best" (*ML* 319 and 412). What *A* does, accordingly, is to get himself to believe *R* so that he will act in the morally strenuous way that will help to make *R* become true. Similar considerations apply to a will-to-believe-based belief in a metaphysical or world-hypothesis. One believes in theism so that he can get himself to live in some desirable way.

Although (8') goes some way toward neutralizing the irrationality charge, it has to go even further. According to (8'), among *A*'s reason for helping to make the desirable proposition *q* become true is that *p* is true. But his psychological makeup at *T* could be so bizarre that his belief that *p* is true, although a *causal factor* in his acting so as to make *q* true, does not constitute a *rational reason* for so acting.[13] For example, *p* could be the proposition that Verdi wrote *Ernani* and *q* be *R*, and his psychology be such that he will act so as to help make *R* become true only if he first believes *p*. Remember the "Niagara Falls!" routine. Thus, when he is asked why he is living the morally strenuous life so as to make *R* true, he will respond that it is because Verdi wrote *Ernani*, thereby rendering his action irrational, and thereby not one for which he is morally responsible. Plainly, yet another epicycle is required, namely,

(9) *A*'s belief that *p* is a rational reason for him to act so as to help make *q* become true.

It is now time to pause and give an explicit recap of all the many conditions that together are *sufficient* for being morally permitted to believe upon insufficient evidence. *A* is morally permitted at time *T* to believe an epistemically nonwarranted proposition, *p*, for the purpose of helping to make true another proposition, *q*, *if* *A*'s option at *T* to believe *p* is:

(1) live;
(2) momentous; and
(3) forced.

---

[13]Again, the problem of undue reliance on purely external causal connections raises problems for James, as pointed out in note 12.

And furthermore:

(4) *A* cannot epistemically determine at *T* the truth-value of *p*;

(5) *A*'s believing *p* can help *A* to bring it about that *q*;

(6) It is, all things considered, desirable that proposition *q* become true;

(7) *A*'s psychology at *T* is such that he can realize the confidence- and courage-boosting benefits of a belief that *p*, even if he takes *p* to be evidentally nonwarranted;

(8') *A* knows at *T* that he will act so as to help make *q* become true only if he first believes that *p*; and

(9) *A*'s belief that *p* is a rational reason for him to act so as to help make *q* become true.

I have italicized *sufficient* and *if* to emphasize that conditions (1)–(9) together are taken to be sufficient but not necessary for a will-to-believe option. The reason for not affirming the necessity of (1)–(9) is to avoid the following universalizability objection. Imagine that *A* has a brother, *B*, whose psychology exactly resembles his except that *A* alone satisfies condition (8') requiring that the believer knows at *T* that he will act so as to help make *q* become true only if he first believe that *p*. Because *B* is sufficiently strong-willed that he does not need to have the confidence- or courage-building belief in *p* in order to do his best to make *q* become true, he is not morally permitted to believe *p* upon insufficient evidence, whereas the weaker-willed *A* is.[14] This violates the principle of universalizability – if *A* is morally permitted (or forbidden) to perform an action in a certain set of circumstances, then everyone in like circumstances is morally permitted (or forbidden) to do the same. It is implausible to respond that *B* is not in the same circumstances as *A* because he has a stronger will; for someone's being subject to a moral rule should not depend on whether he is weak-willed or cowardly. A similar problem would result if *p* were live (or momentous) for *A* but not for *B*.

Because conditions (1)–(9) purport to give *only* a sufficient condition, there is a ready response to the universalizability objection. That *B* does not satisfy these conditions does not entail that he is not permitted to believe *p*; this would follow only if the conditions together were necessary. He can be accorded the same moral right to believe *p* upon

---

[14] It is strange that James should say that it takes "courage" to believe on the basis of a will-to-believe option, for only a weak-willed person can satisfy condition (8') for having this option (*WB* 32). Maybe James had this in mind. One who exercises his right to acquire a belief under the conditions of the will-to-believe doctrine so that he can make his very best effort to bring about the truth of some desirable proposition willingly runs the risk of a dramatic and decisive failure, and it takes courage to do this. I thank David Schrader for this point.

insufficient evidence as is A, only he will not have to exercise this right because of his stronger character.

Given that a major concern of this chapter is to see how James's will-to-believe can justify an epistemically nonwarranted belief in his doctrine of Libertarian free will, it will be instructive to see how conditions (1)–(9) apply to it. There are many people for whom it is a genuine option to believe the proposition that they possess this sort of freedom. Let this be proposition p. Because of limitations in our powers of mensuration – we are too big and the brain events are too small – it cannot be epistemically determined whether p is true or p is false, thereby satisfying (4). Let q be the proposition that we exert our best moral effort to attend to the idea of the morally good or right alternative in a case of moral temptation. Certainly, it is desirable that q be true, thus satisfying (6). There are persons, William James for example, whose psychological makeup is such that they can believe that q is epistemically undecidable and yet have their confidence and courage raised by their belief in p, as (7) requires. By raising their confidence level they are able to exert themselves in a way that will help to make q become true, thus satisfying (5), and furthermore know this fact about themselves, in accordance with the demands of (8'); (9)'s conditions are met because of their belief that p is a rational reason for their acting so as to make q become true. A good reason for trying to get yourself to attend to a difficult idea in a moral conflict case is that you have the Libertarian sort of free will to do it. Believing that you have free will is both a necessary cause and a rational reason for their attempting to exert yourself to attend to the idea of the morally right alternative in a case of moral conflict.

II. Summation

I believe that James's reconstructed will-to-believe doctrine in terms of the jointly sufficient set of conditions (1)–(9) for believing upon insufficient evidence is a formidable doctrine that deserves our respect, if not our whole-hearted agreement. No doubt, if we put our minds to it, we could think up more objections, but there is reason to be optimistic that they can be met, perhaps by adding on some more epicycles. Some, including William James, might not be happy with so many epicycles. His remark that "The over-technicality and consequent dreariness of the younger disciples at our American universities is appalling" might be directed against my reconstructed version (*PU* 13). If I am charged with making a crashing bore out of his exciting doctrine, my response is that I am not to be blamed because the universe is so complex. The price James must pay for having a more defensible version of the will to believe is that he could no longer fit it neatly into his typical one-hour lecture for a general audience: No more one-night stands on the lecture circuit. He would have to stick around the visited campus for at least a few days so he could give a whole series of lectures on the will to believe.

I hope that I have adequately discharged my duty as a commentator by being both unsparingly critical and as sympathetic and constructive as possible. James's doctrine of the will to believe is one of the great contributions to the history of philosophy, and it has been my intent to show its great importance and resiliency. I also have attempted to show that a slightly revised version of it is quite plausible and moreover marshalable in support of our justification for believing that we have his sort of contracausal freedom of will. And, when this is combined with the outcome of Chapter 2 – that belief is an action – we are justified in believing that

2'. Belief is a free action.

And when 2' is combined with James's casuistic rule

1. We are always morally obligated to act so as to maximize desire-satisfaction over the other options available to us.

it follows that

3. We are always morally obligated to believe in a way that maximizes desire-satisfaction over the other belief options available to us.

The next two chapters will explore the manner in which James utilized 3 in his analysis of belief-acceptance and truth.

5

The Ethics of Truth

It has been established in the previous four chapters that James was firmly committed to each of the following propositions:

1. We are always morally obligated to act so as to maximize desire-satisfaction over the other options available to us;[1]

and

2'. Belief is a free action.

These propositions serve as the premises of a valid syllogistic argument for

3. We are always morally obligated to believe in a way that maximizes desire-satisfaction over the other belief options available to us.

Propositions 1–3 constitute *master syllogism* that underlies James's Promethean pragmatism.

James's ethical account of belief-acceptance on the basis of 3 can be extended to truth. He defines truth as "what we ought to believe" and then asks rhetorically, "Ought we ever not to believe what it is better for us to believe?" (*P* 42).[2] When this implicit claim that

4. The true is what we ought to believe.

is conjoined with 3 it makes for another valid syllogism, whose conclusion is:

5. A proposition is true when believing it maximizes desire-satisfaction.[3]

This could be called James's "truth syllogism."

Another way of deriving 5 from 3 is to conjoin James's slogan that

---

[1] This is James's casuistic rule, and, as argued in Chapter 1, things would go better for him if it was replaced by "We are always morally obligated to act so as to maximize *good* over the other options available to us," in which the *good* includes both deontological factors and desire-satisfaction.

[2] James's later claim that " '*The true*,' *to put it briefly, is only the expedient in the way of our thinking, just as 'the right' is only the expedient in the way of our behaving*" is a bit misleading, since belief is an action for him (*P* 106).

[3] This is a mere stylistic variation on James's claim "that a true proposition is one the consequences of believing which are good," given that the meaning of "good" for James is what maximizes desire-satisfaction (*MT* 146).

6. "The reasons why we call things true is the reason why they *are* true." (*P* 37)

with his claim that

7. The reasons why we call something true is that our belief in it has proven satisfactory.

Given that, for James,

8. Being satisfactory is maximizing desire-satisfaction.

It follows again that

5. A proposition is true when believing it maximizes desire-satisfaction.

Surprisingly, James never explicitly asserted the master syllogism comprising 1, 2', and 3, nor did he ever assert its conclusion, in spite of the fact that he did assert both of its premises. Furthermore, he never asserted the truth syllogism comprising of 4, 3, and 5, even though he explicitly accepted 4 and was firmly committed to 3. This is surprising, since James hardly was ignorant of syllogistic reasoning. The mystery is intensified by the fact that at one place he stated what is essentially the same argument as his master syllogism only to reject it as a mockery of his philosophy perpetrated by his critic, McTaggart.

All good desires must be fulfilled;
The desire to believe this proposition is a good desire;
Ergo, this proposition must be believed.

He [McTaggart] substitutes this abstraction for the concrete state of mind of the believer, pins the naked absurdity of it upon him, and easily proves that anyone who defends him must be the greatest fool on earth. As if any real believer ever thought in this preposterous way, or as if any defender of the legitimacy of men's concrete ways of concluding ever used the abstract and general premise 'All desires must be fulfilled'! (*MT* 140)

Why was James so skittish about owning up to what he was committed to by his promulgation of 1 and 2'? The most obvious explanation, but unfortunately one that does not work, is that the major and minor premises of the syllogism in the quotation need to be qualified, respectively, as follows:

All good desires create a prima facie obligation to be fulfilled.
The desire to believe this proposition is a good desire, all things considered.

The major premise would not require this "prima facie" qualification if it were read initially as "All desires that are good, all things considered, must be fulfilled"; for the "all things considered" qualification would mean, in accordance with James's casuistic rule, maximizing desire-satisfaction over any alternative option. But this does not seem to be how James interprets it, for he makes an unannounced shift at the end of the quotation to the completely unqualified "All desires must be fulfilled." If his reason for rejecting the syllogism is that its premises require qualification in the manner suggested, you would expect him to say so and then give the proper qualifications; but he does not do this.

The key to finding an explanation is to understand what James means here by the respectively derogatory and honorific terms "abstract" and "concrete." The argument is viciously abstract because its premises abstract from the way in which we actually decide which propositions to believe. Thus, they require further supplementation, especially as they seem to license wishful thinking and gullibility, which, it will be recalled, was the major objection to his doctrine of the will to believe.

The problem begins with the casuistic rule itself, of which the argument's major premise, properly qualified, is only a stylistic variant. It does not give sufficient guidance in making specific, concrete ethical decisions regarding which action-option will maximize desire-satisfaction. The problem is that, because of radical limitations in our predictive powers, we rarely are in a position to determine which action-option, including belief-options since belief is an action, will maximize desire-satisfaction in the long run. Therefore, proposition 3, which is the application of proposition 1 to the special case of belief-acceptance, will not give us sufficient guidance in the vast majority of cases in determining what to believe. Bertrand Russell's objection to James's desire-maximizing account of truth and belief-acceptance, that "It is far easier . . . to settle the question of fact: 'Have Popes been always infallible?' than to settle the question whether the effects of thinking them infallible are on the whole good," is based on our predictive limitations (*TT* 201). Because proposition 3 cannot give sufficient guidance in making concrete belief choices, many people will believe whatever gives them immediate comfort, thus encouraging wishful thinking and gullibility. I'm back to believing that I'm the sultan of Wisconsin ("No one eats any cheese in this state without my permission!").

The prediction problem also plagued act utilitarians and was remedied by their arming the chooser with a number of empirically well-founded generalizations to guide her, just as the navigator goes to sea supplied with empirically well-founded navigational charts. It was seen in Chapter 1 that James followed their example by supplementing his casuistic rule with the guiding principle that we should follow the dictates of traditional morality, unless we have very good epistemic reasons for believing that violating it on some occasion, or replacing it with a new code of morality, would maximize desire-satisfaction. It was the "except" qualification that distinguished James's rule-instrumentalism from rule-utilitarianism, whose utilitarian-based rules permit of no exceptions, even when doing so maximizes utility on some occasion.

A similar sort of supplementation is needed for 3 and will enable James to get around Russell's objection. The germ of it is to be found in the way in which James, in the last chapter, protected the doctrine of the will to believe against the gullibility-charge by recourse to a hierarchical dualism of reasons or justifications for belief-acceptance that made use of

9. We are always morally obligated to believe in a manner that is epistemically warranted, except when epistemic justification is not possible,

in which the "except"-clause recognized the legitimacy of deciding what to believe on the basis of maximizing desire-satisfaction when epistemic reasons cannot be had. The dualism of reasons for belief-acceptance countenanced by 9 is hierarchical because it gives pride of place to epistemic over pragmatic reasons. Thus, if there should be a clash between what you desire to be true and what the best available empirical evidence indicates is true, you are obligated to believe in accordance with what the latter dictates. For example, if you enter a room and seem to see and touch a chair but desire that there not be one in the room because you bet someone that there is none, you are obligated to believe that there is a chair in the room.

Unfortunately, James cannot consistently accept both:

9. We are always morally obligated to believe in a manner that is epistemically warranted, except when epistemic justification is not possible;

and

3. We are always morally obligated to believe in a way that maximizes desire-satisfaction over the other belief options available to us.

James has an easy way out of this impasse. There is good textual evidence, soon to be given, that James intended 9 as a guiding principle or instrumental rule that is adopted because

10. By having beliefs that are epistemically warranted, desire-satisfaction is maximized in the long run.

If this is the case, the obligation in 9 is only prima facie, since it allows us to violate it when doing so will maximize desire-satisfaction; however, such exceptions will be quite rare, because we do not have the time or the wherewithal in the vast majority of cases to figure out which of the belief-options available to us will maximize desire-satisfaction in the long run. Thus, 9 must be qualified as

9'. We are always prima facie morally obligated to believe in a manner that is epistemically warranted, except when epistemic justification is not possible.

even though it is very unlikely that there will be any defeater or over-rider to the obligation in question.

When James was trying to sell the Cliffordians in his audience on his will-to-believe doctrine he tried to go as far as he could with them and still establish his conclusion – that under the conditions (1)–(8) given at the close of the last chapter one is morally permitted to believe upon insufficient evidence – and thereby did not make the needed "prima facie" restriction in 9. By qualifying the obligation in 9 as only prima facie, the clash with 3 is eliminated, since the obligation in 3 is absolute, admitting of no exceptions.[4]

There is considerable textual support for interpreting James as an epistemological rule-instrumentalist in regard to truth and belief-acceptance. He claimed that "True ideas would never have been sin-gled out as such, would never have acquired a class-name, least of all a name suggesting value, unless they had been useful from the outset" and that "Our obligation to seek truth is part of our general obligation to do what pays. The payments true ideas bring are the sole why of our duty to follow them" (*P* 98 and 110). He says, further, that pragmatists do not deny truth but "have only sought to trace exactly why people follow it and always ought to follow it" (*P* 38). The intellectualist critics who stress truth for truth's sake should

follow the pragmatic method and ask: "What is truth *known-as*? What does its existence stand for in the way of concrete goods?" – they would see that the name of it is the *inbegriff* of almost everything valuable in our lives. The true is the opposite of whatever is instable, of whatever is practically disappointing, of whatever is useless, of whatever is lying and unreliable, of whatever is unverifi-able and unsupported, of whatever is inconsistent and contradictory, of what-ever is artificial and eccentric, of whatever is unreal in the sense of being of no practical account. Here are pragmatic reasons with a vengeance why we should turn to truth (*MT* 48).

And, for good measure, James says that he cannot conceive "that the notion [of truth] would ever have grown up, or that true ideas would

---

[4] It might be thought that by giving 3 the power to trump 8' James renders 8' otiose, since the only defeater for the prima facie obligation in 9' is maximizing desire-satisfaction, which is just what 3 absolutely obligates. Since 9' is the opposite of 3, he really is saying 3 is true and the opposite of 3 also is true, except when 3 is true. This objection overlooks the fact that 3 stands in need of supplementation and the prima facie obligation in 9', in the vast majority of cases, supplies the needed supplementation.

ever have been sorted out from false or idle ones, save for the greater sum of satisfactions" (*MT* 89).

There is an apparent clash between James's contrast between true ideas and what it pays to believe and his acceptance of:

5. A proposition is true when believing it maximizes desire-satisfaction.

This seeming clash is easily neutralized once it is seen that James means by "true ideas" and "truth" in these quotations what people *ordinarily* take to be "true." These are ideas that people take to be epistemically warranted relative to the best available evidence. On the other hand, when he speaks of a belief that "pays" (*PP* 98 and 110), he means one that maximizes desire-satisfaction – achieves "the greater sum of satisfactions." It is such a belief that will count as true belief relative to his *revisionary* analysis of truth in terms of 5. If James were to have meant by "true ideas" and "truth" in these quotations his favored 5–based sense of "true," he would have been uttering, in essence, the uninformative proposition that we seek true ideas – ideas which are such that believing them maximizes desire-satisfaction – so as to maximize desire-satisfaction, which is a special instance of "We seek X so as to obtain X."

Hints of rule-instrumentalism are found also in James's response to Bertrand Russell's objection to his seeming identification of truth with what has good consequences for the believer.

We affirm nothing as silly as Mr. Russell supposes. Good consequences are not proposed by us merely as a sure sign, or mark, or criterion, by which truth's presence is habitually ascertained, tho they may indeed serve on occasion as such a sign; they are proposed rather as the lurking *motive* inside of every truth-claim, whether the 'trower' be conscious of such motive, or whether he obey it blindly. They are proposed as the *causa existendi* of our beliefs, not as their logical cue or premise, and still less as their objective deliverance or content. (*MT* 146–7)

The cause (*causa existendi*) of our seeking true beliefs is that true beliefs, by and large, do a better job of securing "good consequences," that is, maximizing desire-satisfaction. James also is saying that it is not part of the content or meaning of the believed proposition that believing it has good consequences, a point that will become important at the end of this chapter.

The basic idea underlying James rule-instrumentalist epistemology is that our underlying moral quest to believe in a way that maximizes desire-satisfaction is furthered by our adopting the guiding principle that

9'. We are always prima facie morally obligated to believe in a manner that is epistemically warranted, except when epistemic reasons are not available.

There are other guiding principles in addition to 9' that James implicitly employs in his rule-instrumentalist account of belief-acceptance and truth. The first of these principles enjoins us to avoid an inconsistency in our web or network of beliefs, comprised of beliefs based on sense experience, theoretical consideration, and logical principles. By advocating the adoption of

11. Make sure that your web of beliefs is internally consistent.

James hopes to placate his intellectualist critics who ask, rhetorically, "Has not the knowing of truth any substantive value on its own account, apart from collateral advantages it may bring?" They are giving expression to our needs to have beliefs that are theoretically respectable, but are not these theoretical needs

all mere matters of *consistency* – and emphatically *not* of consistency between an absolute reality and the mind's copies of it, but of actually felt consistency among judgments, objects, and habits of reacting, in the mind's own experienceable world? And are not both our need of such consistency and our pleasure in it conceivable as outcomes of the natural fact that we are beings that do develop mental *habits* – habit itself proving adaptively beneficial in an environment where the same objects, or the same kinds of objects, recur and follow 'law'? If this were so, what would have come first would have been the collateral profits of habit as such, and the theoretic life would have grown up in aid of these. In point of fact, this seems to have been the probable case. (*MT* 58)

Our habit of seeking consistency within our web of belief results from past adaptive behavior that has proven beneficial in helping us to maximize desire-satisfaction, and thus we adopt as a guiding rule:

11. Make sure that your web of beliefs is internally consistent.

James's fallibilism holds that for every member of the web there is a conceivable set of circumstances under which it would be best to give it up. It would appear that, for James as well as for Quine, the law of noncontradiction is not a member of the web but a guiding principle for operating on the web. But it would be wrong, at least in James's case, to infer from this that it is an exception to his fallibilism, for there are conceivable circumstances in which we would do a better job of maximizing desire-satisfaction by not adopting 11, or at least not in its universal form. In fact, in Chapter 11, this will emerge as one possible way in which James can enable himself to have it all. That the law of noncontradiction was not an inviolable absolute for James clearly emerges from his instrumentalistic account of it in the following passage: "Our nouns and adjectives are all humanized heirlooms, and in the theories we build them into, the inner order and arrangement is wholly dictated by human considerations, *intellectual consistency being one of them*" (*P* 122; my italics).

But 11 does not go far enough, for it does not tell us how to resolve an inconsistency within our web of beliefs once it breaks out because of, for example, the addition of a new member. James has another guiding principle that enjoins us to reestablish consistency within our web of beliefs by making the minimal number of changes. A person "saves as much of it [his web of belief] as he can, for in this matter of belief we are all extreme conservatives" (*P* 35). This conservative belief-revision strategy can be formulated as:

12. Whenever a contradiction breaks out in your web of belief revise the web in a way that makes the minimum changes in it.

As was the case with 9', there is good empirical evidence that:

13. By following the rule of consistency we maximize desire-satisfaction in the long run; and
14. By following the rule of conservative belief-revision to eliminate a contradiction in our web of belief, we maximize desire-satisfaction in the long run.

It must be emphasized that 11 and 12 are only guiding principles or instrumental rules and thus admit of an exception when a better job can be done on some occasion of maximizing desire-satisfaction by rejecting 11 or 12.

There is, as Michael Wolraich has pointed out to me, an interesting internal inconsistency in the rule-instrumentalism I attribute to James. The only reasons that can be given for why we are well advised to accept his three instrumental rules:

9'. We are always prima facie morally obligated to believe in a manner that is epistemically warranted, except when epistemic reasons are not available;
11. Make sure that your web of beliefs is internally consistent; and
12. Whenever a contradiction breaks out in your web of belief revise the web in a way that makes the minimum changes in it.

are inductive arguments from past experience that show that, for the most part, we do the best job of maximizing desire-satisfaction if we base our beliefs on them. Thus, there are three propositions that are believed on exclusively epistemic grounds:

10. By having beliefs that are epistemically warranted, desire-satisfaction is maximized in the long run;
13. By following the rule of consistency we maximize desire-satisfaction in the long run; and
14. By following the rule of conservative belief-revision to eliminate a

contradiction in our web of belief, we maximize desire-satisfaction in the long run.

And, therefore, 10, 13, and 14 constitute counterexamples to

3. We are always morally obligated to believe in a way that maximizes desire-satisfaction over the other belief options available to us.

Wolraich's counterexamples to 3 must be conceded, for it would launch us on a vicious infinite regress to say that our justification for believing 10, 13, and 14 is that we thereby maximize desire-satisfaction; for, again, the only justifications for this claim are inductive arguments based on our past experience. Maybe the best that can be done on James's behalf is to make an ad hoc restriction of 3 to first-order beliefs – beliefs that are not about other beliefs or propositions. This would permit second-order beliefs, of which 9', 11, and 12 are instances, to be acquired on exclusively epistemic grounds, such as inductive arguments from past experience. One reason that I do not feel bad about making this ad hoc restriction on James's behalf is that something similar occurs in set theory and semantics. Think of attempts to escape set-theoretical paradoxes, as well as the liar and barber paradoxes, by appeal to a theory of types. An even more important reason, which is quite independent of the acceptability of a theory of types, is that even with the ad hoc restriction, 3 still is a very bold and exciting thesis.

It is now time for me to blow the whistle on my rule-instrumentalistic interpretation for ignoring parts of the text in a way that sweeps under the rug the most controversial of all of James's many controversial ideas, namely, that personal satisfactions are confirmatory of a belief. The problem arises from those passages in which James portrays his web as including, in addition to beliefs, conative and emotional states. This more inclusive web aptly could be called the "web of mentation" or "thought," which was James's generic term for any conscious state (*PP* 186). The web of mentation will include, in addition to propositional beliefs, conative states, such as desires and wants, and emotional ones consisting in feelings of satisfaction and the like.

There are many passages, the majority of them in fact, in which James portrays the web as a web of belief.[5] "The individual has a stock of old

---

[5] A passage such as "In admitting a new body of experience, we instinctively seek to disturb as little as possible our pre-existing stock of ideas" is indecisive, because "ideas" admits of a generic interpretation that would apply to any state of consciousness, as does "Thought" for James (*TT* 96). Another indecisive passage is: "*ideas . . . become true just in so far as they help us to get into satisfactory relation with other parts of our experience*," for "experience" admits of a similar type of generic interpretation. There is nothing ambiguous, however, about " 'How far am I verified?' is the question which each kind of union and each kind of separation asks us here, so as good pragmatists we have to turn our face towards experience, towards 'facts,' " since he uses "facts" to paraphrase "experience" (*P* 34).

opinions already, but he meets a new experience that puts them to a strain. . . . He saves as much of it as he can, for in this matter of *belief* we are all extreme conservatives" (*PP* 34–5; my italics). "A new *opinion* counts as 'true' just in proportion as it gratifies the individual's desire to assimilate the novel in his experience to his *beliefs* in stock" (*PP* 36; my italics). His use of "opinion" seems to be a synonym for "belief." In the following, "belief" occurs explicitly: "Experience is a process that continually gives us new material to digest. We handle this intellectually by the mass of *beliefs* of which we find ourselves already possessed, assimilating, rejecting, or rearranging in different degrees" (*MT* 42; my italics).

In other passages "knowledge" is used in place of "belief," but knowledge involves belief. "Our knowledge grows *in spots.* The spots may be large or small, but the knowledge never grows all over; some old *knowledge* always remains what it was. . . . Later, its growth may involve considerable modification of opinions which you previously held to be true. But such modifications are apt to be gradual" (*MT* 82 and 83; my italics) and "Our minds thus grow in spots; and like grease-spots, the spots spread. But we let them spread as little as possible: we keep unaltered as much of our old *knowledge,* as many of our old prejudices and beliefs, as we can" (*MT* 83). And, for good measure, there is, "The amount of accord which satisfies most men and women is merely the absence of violent clash between their usual thoughts and statements and the limited sphere of *sense-perceptions* in which their lives are cast," which, by its use of "sense-perceptions," seems to exclude conative and emotional states (*MT* 59; my italics).

These passages clearly speak for a web composed exclusively of beliefs; but, as Ram Neta and William Wainwright have shown me, there are other passages that speak for the richer web of mentation or thought. In the passage already quoted (from *PP* 34) James adds, "Somebody contradicts them [his stock of opinions]; or in a reflective moment he discovers that they contradict each other; or he hears of facts with which they are incompatible; or *desires* arise in him which they cease to satisfy" (*PP* 34–5; my italics). Up until the final disjunct the web is of beliefs exclusively, but suddenly, in the final disjunct, he injects desires into it. It appears, after all, that your desire that there not be a chair in the room (because you made a bet that there aren't any in the room) gets into your web, along with your perceptually based beliefs that a chair is present, and must be weighed in with the latter in determining whether you should believe that a chair is present. Therefore, conative states, along with beliefs, count as evidence for and are partially confirmatory of a belief. Needless to say, this is shocking to most philosophers, coming close to mortal sin in their eyes.

That this injection of desire into the web is not due to a momentary careless lapse on James's part becomes clear when it is compared with what he says about the confirmation of empirical beliefs, such as that there is a house along the cow-path. What he says gives credence to Dewey's claim that James's "real doctrine is that a belief is true when it satisfies both personal needs and the requirements of objective things" (*MW* 4, 112).[6] At one place James seems to restrict the confirmatory experiences to sense experiences alone: "Following our mental image of a house along the cow-path, we actually come to see the house; we get the image's *full* verification" (*P* 99; my italics). But, at other places, he seems to require personal satisfaction as well as confirmatory sense experiences for full verification. "The true thought is useful here because the house which is its object is useful" (*P* 98). This makes it appear as if the truth of your belief depends in part upon how pleased you are with coming upon the house, so that if it should contain a wicked witch who eats you alive, your belief would not be true!

This seems to be the implication of these further claims: "truth [is] essentially bound up with the way in which one moment in our experience may lead us towards other moments *which it will be worth while to have been led to* (*P* 98; my italics). "Agreement thus turns out to be essentially an affair of leading – leading that is useful because it is into quarters that contain objects that are *important*" (*P* 103; my italics). That the confirmatory experiences for an empirical belief are of the mixed-bag sort seems to be the implication of James's claim that "ideas [that are true] must point to or lead towards *that* reality and no other, and . . . the pointings and leadings must yield satisfaction as their result" (104). Herein, James is concerned with reference, a topic for the next chapter, and is requiring that the referent be one that we are pleased to come upon. No wicked witches allowed for true beliefs. Since the satisfactions or dissatisfactions you have upon reaching the house are confirmatory or disconfirmatory of your belief, they will become part of your future web and thereby will play a role in determining which candidates for admission to the web will be accepted. James says that, in general, we call propositions " 'true' in proportion as they facilitate our mental or physical activities and bring us outer power and inner peace" (*MT* 43).

The way in which desire-satisfaction counts as confirmatory must not be confused with the manner in which it provides a will-to-believe justification for a belief. As was seen in Chapter 4, when James is presenting his will-to-believe doctrine so as to win over his Cliffordian opponents, he does not count the desirable consequences that accrue from a belief as confirmatory of the proposition believed, but only as supplying a

---

[6] Martin Gardner agrees: "In the absence of contrary evidence, if a belief satisfies a human desire, that too is a practical consequence and therefore [for James] a legitimate basis for calling certain beliefs true" (*PS* 38).

pragmatic or will-to-believe justification for acquiring the belief. But when James is intent on developing a general account of truth, he seems, at least in certain passages, to count the desirable consequences of the belief to count as confirmatory of the proposition believed. Thus, James's making satisfactions confirmatory of a belief in no way results from his doctrine of the will to believe, as Dewey incorrectly claimed, about which more will be said in the Appendix. The root of the confusion, very likely, is due to the fact that certain members of the web, especially beliefs in scientific and philosophical theories, gain entrance, in part, on a will-to-believe basis because of the satisfactions, aesthetic and moral, that are yielded by a belief in them. James thought that all theories, be they scientific or philosophical, are accepted at least in part on a will-to-believe basis. In regard to metaphysical theories, he claimed that "When we make theories about the world . . . we do so in order to attain a conception of things which shall give us subjective satisfaction" (WB 115). The manner in which we choose between rival worldviews will be taken up in Chapter 7. In regard to scientific theories, he said that "The superiority of one of our formulas to another may not consist so much in its literal 'objectivity,' as in subjective qualities like its usefulness, its 'elegance' or its congruity with our residual beliefs" (MT 41).

James's house-along-the-cow-path belief, in contrast with these theoretical beliefs, is a straightforward empirical belief. One problem with allowing the personal satisfactions that one experiences upon arriving at the house to count as confirmatory is that it renders confirmation, and thereby truth, subjective because of the variability among persons in regard to what satisfies them. One person abhors the idea of being eaten alive by the wicked witch in the house at the end of the cow-path, but another, of a Jamesian hipster mentality who is willing to try anything once, finds the idea attractive. The person who bet against there being any chair in the room is dissatisfied upon perceiving, and thereby verifying, at least for most people, that a chair is there, but the person she bet is quite pleased with this perceptual outcome. It would be implausible in the extreme for James to try to escape this Protagorean relativistic nightmare by appealing to a general agreement among people as to what gives satisfaction because they share a common human nature. This fails to square, not only with patent facts about the widespread diversity among people in regard to what outcomes give them satisfaction, but also with James's "sentiment of rationality" doctrine, according to which people differ with respect to which philosophy they find attractive because of their psychological differences. Furthermore, allowing personal satisfaction to be confirmatory is inconsistent with James's rule-instrumental theory of belief-acceptance and truth based on the guiding principle

9'. We are always prima facie morally obligated to believe in a manner that is epistemically warranted, except when epistemic reasons are not available.

Another problem concerns the incommensurability between conative and emotional states, on the one hand, and perceptual ones, on the other, in respect to their confirmatory or evidential force. How are we to weigh the evidential value of your desire that there be no chair in the room in relation to your seeming to perceive one there? Whereas we have rough-and-ready procedures for hefting one piece of sensory evidence against another, we have no idea of how to factor in conative and emotional states. When this deleterious consequence of allowing the latter to be confirmatory is conjoined with the subjectivistic consequences of doing so, it renders our notion of truth totally inoperative, a most unfortunate outcome for a pragmatist.

What is the commentator to do when faced with this inconsistency? As the Introduction stressed, the first thing is to admit that there is an inconsistency in the text, which has been done, and then to try to resolve it by appeal to the underlying spirit and intent of James's philosophy, as well as to which of the incompatible doctrines is the more philosophically attractive in its own right. I believe that rule-instrumentalism is more in accord with the underlying spirit and intent of James's philosophy as a whole. It is in agreement with his taking the rule-instrumentalist route in other areas of his philosophy, such as ethics, and also has far more textual support. Not only does James, for the most part, describe his web as one comprised of beliefs, there are many quotations that can be garnered, as I have done, in support of his acceptance of rule-instrumentalism.[7] Furthermore, I think it will be readily granted that James's rule-instrumentalism is both far more attractive than his theory that counts satisfactions as confirmatory, for the reasons just given, and a rather attractive and defensible doctrine on its own. Like any interesting philosophical doctrine, it has problematic aspects, some of which will now be considered, along with the responses available to James. This will bring out some of the more subtle points in his account that often get overlooked and will thereby put us in a better position to evaluate it critically.

The first objection charges that James's account of truth fails to ac-

[7] For the most part, the 1909 *The Meaning of Truth* excludes conative and emotional states from the web, as is evident in: "The percept here not only *verifies* the concept, proves its function of knowing that percept to be true, but the percept's existence as the terminus of the chain of intermediaries creates the function. Whatever terminates that chain was, because it now proves itself to be, what the concept 'had in mind';" and "My idea of this pen verifies itself through my percept" (*MT* 64 and 87). But what is said in this book must not be relied on too heavily, since James was fighting a rear-guard action against his intellectualist critics and tried to placate them by radically downplaying the more controversial aspects of his earlier account of truth in *Pragmatism*.

cord with commonsense or ordinary language. The leading proponents of this objection were G. E. Moore and Bertrand Russell. Both failed to detect James's rule-instrumentalism. This is evident in Russell's objection that it is easier in most cases to find out whether a proposition is true than whether believing it maximizes desire-satisfaction, an objection that is easily deflected by James's rule-instrumentalism, as has been shown. I will recast their objections so that they take into account that rule-instrumentalism.

James's "definition" of truth based on proposition 3 was:

5. A proposition is true when believing it maximizes desire-satisfaction.

Moore, in his typical arrogantly humble fashion, goes to excruciating lengths to show that this definition fails to square with ordinary usage (PJ). He does this by showing that there are true sentences in which "is true" is used (not mentioned within quotation marks) that become false when James's alleged synonym, "is such that believing it maximizes desire-satisfaction," is substituted for "is true." It certainly is true that it is possible that believing proposition p maximizes desire-satisfaction, even though it is not the case that p is true; but, when the substitution is made, this true proposition turns into the necessarily false one that it is possible that believing proposition p maximizes desire-satisfaction, even though it is not the case that believing p maximizes desire-satisfaction. Descartes's evil genius, for example, could rig things so that our beliefs that maximize desire-satisfaction, as well propositions that are epistemically warranted, are out of correspondence with reality.

The ordinary language-based fire of Moore and Russell also is directed against another aspect of James's analysis – the requirement that a true proposition be actually verified, about which more will be said later on. Their objection applies equally well to an account, such as James's, in which what gets verified is that belief in the proposition maximizes desire-satisfaction as it does to one in which what gets verified is the proposition itself. They again play the substitution game to refute this analysis and appeal to the commonsense law of bivalence:

B. For every proposition p, either p is true or not-p is true.

This law is necessarily true but ceases to be true at all when either "is epistemically warranted" or, as James would have it, "is verified" is substituted throughout for "is true," since obviously not every proposition either is verified (epistemically warranted) or its denial is verified (epistemically warranted). The failure of the verified or epistemically warranted analysis to satisfy the requirement of substitutivity *salve veritate* shows that "is true" is not synonymous with "is verified" or "is epistemically warranted," which is checkmate for this analysis.

These two objections based on ordinary usage run through open doors. James not only grants that his analysis departs from ordinary usage but boasts that it does, for he charges the ordinary sense of truth and reference, based as it is "on a static relation of 'correspondence,' " with being an "an absolutely empty notion" (P 39).[8] "Common-sense theories [of truth] left the gap untouched, declaring our mind able to clear it by a self-transcending leap" (MT 61). The postulation of some absolute reality with which our true ideas must correspond is totally vacuous, for how can "the partisan of absolute reality know what this orders him to think?" (MT 47). In response to another one of his ordinary language critics, J. B. Pratt, James counters that Pratt's unanalyzable notion of correspondence "ought to consist in something assignable and describable, and not remain a pure mystery" (MT 93). The same tactic is employed in an exchange of letters in the *Journal of Philosophy, Psychology and Scientific Methods* for 1907 in response to another of his realist critics, John E. Russell, who also takes the truth or reference relation to be unmediated and transcendent. James charges that this permits an idea to be true of some reality although it is in principle unverifiable that it is. "There might be no empirical mediation between it [the idea] and its object, no leading either to the object, or towards it, or into its associates, and yet it might still be true as 'agreeing' with the object" (ERE 152).[9]

At the core of James's objection to the commonsense notion of an unmediated, transcendent correspondence relation is his lifelong commitment to empiricism. This notion is empirically vacuous and thus empty, mysterious, and unintelligible. "The popular and traditional position" of a true idea corresponding with "a standard beyond itself," an absolute reality, is based on the fallacious inference from the fact that "finite experiences must draw support from one another [to] the notion that experience *überhaupt* must need an absolute support" (MT 55). He calls this transcendence relation "saltatory," because it involves an idea mysteriously jumping out of its own skin and hitting some distant target. In contrast, his eliminative analysis of the truth or reference relation is based on "ambulatory relations," in which an idea leads us to a direct perception of its referent, or to one of its associates if it be an unobservable scientific entity or another person's conscious state, through a series of intermediate experiences that are constitutive of the idea's meaning (MT 245). This will be the topic of the next chapter.

[8] Among the commentators, Suckiel (PP 42) and Gardner (PS 41-4) have seen that James's analysis of truth was revisionary.
[9] This exchange of letters best brings out the exact points of opposition between James and his realist opponent but unfortunately has not received the attention it deserves, not being included in any of the many anthologies of James's writings, probably because it is badly misplaced by appearing in ERE rather than MT, as it should.

In general, James had no compunction about giving revisionary analyses of commonsense concepts when they did not measure up to his empirical standards. Commonsense concepts are not hard-wired into our brains, as are our necessary beliefs about logical and mathematical concepts, but are the result of ancient inventions by past geniuses that caught on and have stood the test of time. But they are challengeable and have been challenged with some success by science and critical philosophy, and therefore James tells us that "We have seen reason to suspect it [common sense]" (*P* 94). One of the reasons that James felt common sense to be fair game for philosophical criticism, and ultimately for revision, is that he saw it as incorporating a "popular philosophy" that really was a repository for past metaphysical theories, as is seen in his comment that "noumenal substances as matter, nature, power, are admitted alike by metaphysics and by popular philosophy *or* common sense" (*ECR* 323; my italics). He once quipped that "Every philosopher pretends that all the others are metaphysicians against whom he is simply defending the rights of common sense" (*LWJ* 2: 232–3).

James himself challenges our commonsense concepts of the soul, material substances, the mental–physical dualism, and essences as lacking proper empirical credentials: "Scholastic psychology and common-sense have always believed in a simple immaterial soul substance" (*PP* 181; see also 15 and 314). In basic accord with Locke, James claims that "the substantial Soul explains nothing and guarantees nothing [and has] only proved its superfluity for scientific purposes" (*PP* 331–2). It will be seen in Chapter 8 how James replaced common sense's soul substance with a psychologically connected succession of states of consciousness in the manner of the bundle theory of traditional British empiricism: "Scholasticism has taken the notion of [material] substance from common sense and made it very technical and articulate," and it "has tried to eternalize the common-sense categories by treating them very technically and articulately" (*P* 46 and 90). But "vainly did scholasticism, common-sense's college-trained younger sister, seek to stereotype the forms the human family had always talked with, to make them definite and fix them for eternity" (*P* 92). Berkeley succeeded in showing on pragmatic grounds the meaninglessness of "the scholastic notion of a material substance unapproachable by us, behind the external world, deeper and more real than it, and needed to support it" (*P* 47; see also 111). James follows the phenomenalistic strain in Berkeley's philosophy by attempting to reduce a material object to a set of actual and possible percepts.

"Common sense and popular philosophy," James tells us, "are as dualistic as it is possible to be" (*ERE* 69). But James, as will be seen when his doctrine of pure experience is expounded, goes on to challenge this dualism on phenomenological grounds, for he is unable, when he introspects his own mind, to separate a mental component of a percept from its physical one. Our commonsense concepts of the nature or essences of things are "prejudices, so petrified intellectually, that to our vulgarest names, with their suggestions, we ascribe an eternal and exclusive worth" (*PP* 961). There could be good empirical reason, such as science supplies, to reconstruct our classificatory systems of concepts.

But to show that the commonsense notion of truth as a saltatory correspondence relation is empirically vacuous is not alone sufficient to justify James's revisionary analysis of truth in terms of maximizing desire-satisfaction for believers. After all, there are many other ways to reconstruct the concept of truth. Some positive justification is needed, and for James it seems to be the moral one that by getting us to think about truth, the most honorific of honorific terms, in his new way we shall be better motivated to believe in a way that will maximize desire-satisfaction, his summum bonum. His revisionary analysis resembles in some ways one of Charles Stevenson's "persuasive definitions," except that it does not purport to be a report of ordinary usage, that changes the ordinary meaning of "true" so as to redirect our attitudes of approval and ultimately our conduct. The things that counted as true under the old definition will no longer be esteemed as highly, this being reserved for the denotata of James's persuasive definition of "true" in terms of maximizing desire-satisfaction for the believers. By getting ourselves to speak in his new way about truth, we are given an incentive to follow the path of his Promethean pragmatism so as to promote maximal human flourishing.

An obvious but unfounded objection is that there are possible worlds in which Descartes's evil genius brings it about that the beliefs that maximize desire satisfaction arc out of whack with what is true in the ordinary sense, or at least with what is warranted by the best evidence that it is possible for us to acquire under those circumstances. As was indicated in Chapter 1, James's analyses are not meant to hold for every conceivable world, but only for the actual world. Not only is there no reason to think that the actual world is an evil-genius world or one in which we are brains in vats and the like, but the very intelligibility of such worlds is suspect for James's empiricistic philosophy, since they are empirically indiscernible from worlds devoid of the evil genius or the horrible Doctor Input. This is James's reason for refusing to take skepticism-in-general seriously. Against those who think that the actual world holds counterexamples to James's revisionary analysis, he is ready to reply that a "true" belief "is what works best in the way of leading us, what fits *every* part of life best and combines with the *collectivity* of experience's demands, *nothing being omitted*" (*P* 44; my italics). "The true is what works well, even though the qualification 'on the whole' may always have to be added" (*VRE* 361). These quotations are typical of James's repeated insistence on taking the broadest possible view of the effects of a belief. Beliefs that are, *in the actual world*, epistemically *un*warranted, not just *non*warranted, are notoriously unsatisfactory, all things considered, in the long run.

Although my interpretation of James as giving a revisionary analysis that holds for the actual world but need not hold for merely possible worlds deflects the ordinary language-based objections of Moore and Russell, it still faces an axiologically based objection from Russell that applies to the Promethean assumption that motivated James's revisionary analysis – namely, that our highest good is to be a desire-satisfaction maximizer, our quest for "truth" in the sense of what is epistemically warranted having only an instrumental value in helping us to realize this. It is this ultrahumanistic or Promethean orientation that is the target of Russell's fundamental objection to pragmatism.

This objection is made to Dewey's instrumentalism in the following quotation, but it applies with equal force against James's account of truth.

There is a profound instinct in me which is repelled by instrumentalism: the instinct of contemplation, and of escape from one's own personality. Escape from one's own personality is something which has been desired by the mystics of all ages, and in one way or another by all in whom ardent imagination has been a dominant force. It is, of course, a matter of degree: complete escape is impossible, but some degree of escape is possible, and knowledge is one of the gateways into the world of freedom. Instrumentalism does its best to shut this gateway. The world which it allows us to know is man-made, like the scenery on the Underground: there are bricks and platforms and trains and lights and advertisements, but the sun and stars, the rain and the dew and the sea, are no longer there – sometimes we seem to catch a glimpse of them, but that is a mistake, we only see a picture made by some human being as an advertisement. It is a safe and comfortable world: we know how the trains will move, since we laid down the rails for them. If you find it a little dull, you are suffering from the 'genteel tradition,' you belong to an 'upper' class given to a detached and parasitic life. I have now expressed my bias as regards the view that we are not free to know anything but what our own hands have fashioned. (PD 20)

Plato's cave has been brought up-to-date as the subway.

There is a deep intellectual mystical strain in Russell that sees man's highest good in becoming a detached, objective knower who tries to be the observer of all time and eternity, thereby overcoming his all-too-human situation due to possessing a body tethered to a certain place and time, with its attendant wants, needs, and desires. This is movingly expressed in his "Mysticism and Logic" essay of 1914.

There is some sense – easier to feel than to state – in which time is an unimportant and superficial characteristic of reality. Past and future must be acknowledged to be as real as the present, and a certain emancipation from slavery to time is essential to philosophical thought. . . . The felt difference of quality between past and future . . . is not an intrinsic difference, but only a difference in relation to us: to impartial contemplation, it ceases to exist. And impartiality of contemplation is, in the intellectual sphere, that very same virtue of disinterestedness which, in the sphere of action, appears as justice and unselfishness. Whoever wishes to see the world truly, to rise in thought above the tyranny of practical desires, must learn to overcome the difference of attitude towards past and future, and to survey the whole stream of time in one comprehensive vision. (ML 20–1)

As was argued in the Introduction, it is of the very essence of a Jamesian Promethean moral agent to have attitudes that are asymmetric between the past and the future, giving greater importance to denouements and outcomes over inceptions and outsets – "All's well that ends well" and "Count no man fortunate until after he is dead" – and to regret her future finitude in a way that she does not regret her past finitude.

Russell's way of intellectually transcending our radical finitude, along with the pernicious temporally asymmetric attitudes it gives rise to, is primarily through the study of theoretical physics, for herein we succeed in totally abstracting ourselves from our human situation by finding a way of describing reality that holds true for all possible observers, however different from us in their biological makeup and position in space and time. The study of mathematics and logic does an even better job, as it holds true not only for all possible observers in the actual world but for every possible world. Even if it should turn out that the saltatory truth relation is without meaning, still, for Russell, we ought to exert every effort to view the world as a whole in impersonal terms on the basis of the best epistemic evidence. This is our calling, our summum bonum, and through it we find the only type of salvation that is possible for us.

Russell's objection to the radical Prometheanism of pragmatism, of both the Deweyan and Jamesian varieties, for placing us in a Platonic subway cave is extremely honest and heartfelt. He is not trying to be clever at their expense, as was his wont, but is letting it all hang out. His ultimate parting of the ways with the humanistic pragmatists is not over whether their accounts of truth square with ordinary language, but rather whether we ought to use that soul-stirring word "truth" in their humanistic manner, so that our moral obligation is to believe in a way that maximizes desire-satisfaction or, as Russell would have it, on exclusively epistemic grounds when they can be had. Because of James's guiding principle 9' that holds us to have a prima facie duty to believe on epistemic grounds, there will be little difference between the *outward* behavior of the Jamesian and the Russellian truth seekers; but there will be a great difference in the inner spirit with which they seek the truth. James does so with the motive of promoting the fulfillment of human desires; Russell, of discovering truth or what is epistemically warranted for its own sake. One is placing man in the spotlight on center stage, the other hiding him on the other side of the footlights as a mere spectator. Although the Jamesian and Russellian truth seekers, like the Kantians and utilitarians, outwardly act in similar manners, the inner spirit and motivation with which they seek is quite dissimilar. When James was promoting his Promethean pragmatism, he radically downplayed these inner accompaniments of our outward actions, it being outward action alone that mattered; but for the more mystically inclined James, as will be seen in Chapters 9 and 10, it is the inner accompaniments which are the most important thing about a person. We shall find James desperately trying to penetrate to the inner conscious life of everything, objects as well as persons.

What response could James or Dewey make to Russell's axiological objection? It would be wrong to try and neutralize the objection by making Russell's anti-Promethean noetic quest to seek truth for truth's sake one desire among others that get factored into James's casuistic equation; for this would require that Russell be inconsistently motivated – that he seek truth both for its own sake, regardless of whether or not this would maximize desire-satisfaction, and also for the sake of maximizing desire-satisfaction. In other words, Russell could not consistently hold to both his mystical noetic quest for truth and James's definition of *truth*:

5. A proposition is true when believing it maximizes desire-satisfaction.

The honest response is that, unlike Russell, James and Dewey enjoy hanging out in the subway. To each his own. This is squarely in the letter and spirit of James's sentiment of rationality doctrine, according to which the ultimate differences among philosophers are due to differences in their psychological predilections. James would go on to heap moral scorn on those possessed of Russellian type motivations, but this implicit appeal to his own Promethean ethics ultimately rests on nothing more than his own psychological predilections, so his doctrine of the sentiment of rationality would have it. No doubt, James would want to say more in opposition to Russell's view of what truth is and why we should seek it. He would see Russell's psychological predilections as strikingly similar to those of the "gnostic" or "subjectivist" of "The Dilemma of Determinism," who hold our ultimate purpose to be that of understanding rather than controlling our world. He would then point out that such a stance toward the world encourages a morally objectionable sort of quietism and passivism. If he were to make this response to Russell, he could again be charged with making a hasty generalization from his own psychological makeup, with Russell himself representing a counterexample to his generalization; for Russell actually showed great courage in taking stands and making great sacrifices to promote his moral ideals, for example, going to jail during World War I because he was a conscientious objector.

James's moral struggles, in contrast, were not on the social but the personal level. Although he did support his pet social and political causes, such as his opposition to Yankee imperialism and the pernicious defensiveness of the medical establishment, by writing letters to the editor, his real moral struggles were with his own personal demons, who were imprisoning him and preventing him from realizing his true greatness as a psychologist-philosopher. Only someone possessed of considerable courage could have displayed the kind of continual emotional, spiritual, and intellectual growth that James did throughout his life. His body gave out but his spirit did not. Russell, in contrast, enjoyed great health and longevity but ceased to grow as a philosopher after he was thirty and, in general, was not willing to take the kind of risks as a philosopher that James was. In fact, he hardly advanced beyond his British empiricist predecessors. His strength and courage were displayed in his struggles with overt evils; James's, with the evils within.

I wish that my interpretation of James as a revisionary, rule-instrumental theorist about truth and belief-acceptance were the whole story, because I think that this view is not only consistent but also bold and original, well deserving of respect and serious consideration, if not acceptance. Unfortunately, James compromised his revisionary analysis by making two concessions to his intellectualist or realist opponent that have the effect of undoing his entire theory. It is James at his political worst, working his audience so as to win everyone over. In doing so he winds up like Santayana's bird that soars mightily on the wings of some exciting idea only to be jerked back to earth by a wire tethering it to the ground. Maybe he suffered from vertigo when he soared so high, knowing that a sizable portion of his philosophical audience would think ill of him for undermining their revered concept of truth as the great mirror of nature.

This realist view of an absolute truth is part of what James calls "popular philosophy or common sense." In Michael Dummett's view, it amounts to an acceptance of the law of bivalence:

B. For every proposition p, either p is true or not-p is true.

Our knowledge is radically constricted, omitting most of the past, almost all of the future, as well as what is spatially remote in the present. But reality is not so restricted. These unknown objects and events have a reality of their own independent of our epistemic activities, and, for every one of them, there is a true proposition reporting its existence or occurrence as well as a false one that denies it. Consider some possible event of which we are now ignorant, say Aristotle's famous sea-fight tomorrow. Either it is true that the sea-fight will occur tomorrow or it is true it will not. *B* is the cash value of the metaphor of truth as the great mirror of nature, an absolute that is independent of our relation to reality.

James cannot grant the commonsense realist this *categorical* version of *B*. In the first place, it quantifies over abstract propositions when it says "for every proposition *p*," and we know from Chapter 1 that James's gut nominalistic intuitions precluded him from countenancing them. After being chided in a letter of 1909 from Dewey for occasional lapses in applying truth to the facts rather than, as is proper, to our ideas and beliefs about the facts, James was careful to reserve truth for the latter (Perry, *TC* 310).[10] It must be borne in mind that, for both James and Dewey, as well as most of their contemporaries, facts are concrete events locatable in space and time, being the referent of a participial nominalization, such as "Mary's baking pies," as opposed to the abstract proposition that Mary is baking pies, it making sense to ask where and when Mary's baking pies occurs but not where and when that Mary is baking pies occurs.[11]

Of even more importance is that its truth relation is of the empirically objectionable saltatory sort. Over and over again James challenges his realist opponents to specify the nature of this relation and finds their responses to be empirically vacuous. But James, good ward-heeler philosopher that he is, is not willing to leave the realist without a piece of the action. It is at this point that he engages in Berkeley's good old practice of speaking with the vulgar but thinking with the learned, something he did when he gave his phenomenalistic (called "phenomenist" by James) analysis of material objects. Berkeley's analysis, "So far from denying the external world which we know, . . . corroborated it" (*P* 47). But "When Berkeley had explained what people meant by matter people thought that he denied matter's existence" (*P* 111). Berkeley did not intend to deny any material-object proposition that is

---

[10] Both James and Dewey used "fact" for the worldly referent of a participial nominalization – "Mary's baking pies," for example – not for a true (abstract) proposition, that Mary is baking pies. The former, unlike the latter, is spatio-temporally locatable.

[11] At one place James explicitly recognizes "that for certain logical purposes it may . . . be useful to treat propositions as absolute realities, with truth or falsehood inside of them respectively, or to make of a complex like 'that-Caesar-is-dead' a single term and call it 'truth' " (*MT* 151). He then goes on to object to this use of "proposition" because it is ambiguous, sometimes meaning an idea in someone's mind and sometimes the worldly correspondent of this idea, that being some event or "fact." Pace James, there is no such confusion in the realist's use of "proposition," since she uses it to refer to something that is neither a subjective idea nor a worldly event. It refers to an abstract entity. What is interesting, however, about the quotation from *MT* 151 is that it shows James's willingness to countenance abstract propositions as theoretical entities, in spite of their lacking empirical properties. He just thought that they were not helpful theoretical entities.

taken to be true by common sense, but only to give people a new and improved way of expressing it, this being the "thinking with the learned" part of his task. Similarly, James does not want to deny any proposition, such as *B*, that is enshrined in common sense, but merely to give us a new and better way of expressing it, and better because it will avoid ontological commitment to queer entities and nonempirical relations.

James makes it clear that he accepts the law of bivalence and the view of absolute truth that it entails: "Unquestionably common sense believes this, and so do I" (*MT* 155). All he wants to do is to give us a better way of expressing these commonsense truths that will have the therapeutic advantage of extricating us from certain perplexities and confusions that are occasioned by the use of empirically vacuous concepts. What he proposes is a conditionalized version of bivalence, coupled with the Peircean view of absolute truth as an ideal limit of inquiry. You can almost hear him saying to his realist critics, in his attempt to win them over, "Ich bin ein Realist." It now will be shown that each of these attempts to placate the commonsense realist winds up in total disaster, the former accepting the realist's categorical version of bivalence and the latter violating his own empiricistic and humanistic commitments.

James's conditionalizing of bivalence occurs most clearly in "A Dialogue." He begins by imagining a critic who presents him with the following dilemma argument. Either you accept bivalence or you do not. If you do, you reject your pragmatic account of truth; and, if you do not, you depart from common sense. Thus, you either reject pragmatism or common sense. James responds that he can escape this dilemma by showing that his pragmatism is compatible with bivalence, provided that "you let me hold consistently to my own conception of truth, and do not ask me to abandon it for something which I find impossible to comprehend" (*MT* 155). Herein James is following Berkeley's strategy of talking with the vulgar but thinking with the learned.

He then goes on to give his "learned" conditionalized revision of *B*. There cannot be *actual* truths about unthought-of events, since the bearer of truth is a thought or idea in someone's mind; however, there are *virtual* or *possible* truths about them. The truth about any such unthought-of event, however, "is thus already generically predetermined by the event's nature; and one may accordingly say with a perfectly good conscience that it virtually pre-exists. Common sense is thus right in its instinctive contention" (*MT* 155). This does not mean just that, if there were to exist someone who formed the appropriate belief in her mind about this event, her belief would actually be true. James requires more for there to be actual truth, namely, a successful act of verification consisting in a sequence of empirically vouchsafed steps that terminates in a direct perception of the event or one that goes proxy for it, as in the case of subatomic events or events in other minds. Only upon its successful completion does the virtual or possible truth become actual. "Truth *happens* to an idea. It *becomes* true, is *made* true by events. Its verity *is* in fact an event, a process: the process namely of its verifying itself, its veri-*fication*" (*P* 97). The requirement that a true idea be actually verified amounts to equating truth with knowledge. "Truth and knowledge are terms correlative and interdependent" (*MT* 158). Wherever there is the one there is the other. A lot more will be said about this in the next chapter.

This subjunctive conditional sense of "virtual truth" must be carefully distinguished from another sense in which James uses this phrase.

In our world, namely, abounding as it does in things of similar kinds and similarly associated, one verification serves for others of its kind, and one great use of knowing things is to be led not so much to them as to their associates, especially to human talk about them. The quality of truth, obtaining *ante rem*, pragmatically means . . . the fact that . . . innumerable ideas work better by their indirect or possible than by their direct and actual verification. (*P* 105)

What James is talking about here are ideas that have not been conclusively or directly verified but which are inductively supported by analogical arguments. "Just as a man may be called an heir and treated as one before the executor has divided the estate, so an idea may practically be credited with truth before the verification process has been exhaustively carried out – the existence of the mass of verifying circumstance is enough" (*MT* 91; see also *MT* 4).

This sense of "virtual truth" in terms of being inductively supported stands in sharp contrast with his possibility-of-verification sense based on what would be discovered if an idea were properly tested. Such a possible truth is not verifiable in the sense that it admits of the mere possibility of being tested or verified but in the stronger sense that if it were properly tested it would be verified in the sense of being discovered to be true.

The truth of an event, past, present, or future,[12] is for me only another name for the fact that *if* the event ever *does* get known, the nature of the knowledge is already to some degree predetermined. The truth which precedes actual knowledge of a fact means only what any possible knower of the fact will eventually find himself necessitated to believe about it. (*MT* 157)

The idea that gets actually verified and thereby discovered to be true was "virtually . . . true previously. Pragmatically, virtual and actual truth

---

[12] Herein James is carelessly backsliding into predicating truth of an event or fact and will incur the wrath of Dewey. What he says is elliptical for "The truth of idea of an event, past, present, or future."

mean the same thing: the possibility of only one answer, *when once the question is raised*" (*MT* 60). Before some human witness actually counted the number of stars in the Big Dipper constellation, "they were only implicitly or virtually" seven in number (*MT* 56). This definition of "virtually (possibly) true" implicitly appeals to the Peircean notion of an ideal limit toward which *properly* conducted inquiries converge, which will be the next issue to be considered. This is why there is "the possibility of only one answer" and why the possible knower "will eventually find himself necessitated to believe" the proposition in question. Thus, James's conditionalizing of *B* requires his Peircean account of absolute truth.

James employs this strong sense of being virtually or possibly verifiable or knowable to give a subjunctive conditional version of the realist's categorical law of bivalence. Instead of saying that every proposition is actually true or its contradictory is, he conditionalizes bivalence by holding that every proposition is possibly true or its contradictory is, meaning that if there were to be a thinker who properly tested this proposition, either it would be discovered that it is true or it would be discovered that its contradictory is. Thus, James replaces

B. For every proposition *p*, either *p* is true or not-*p* is true.

with this conditionalized version of it:

B'. For every proposition *p*, either if *p* were to be properly tested *p* would be discovered to be true or if not-*p* were to be properly tested not-*p* would be discovered to be true.

James must restrict *B'* to propositions that we can verify, so that if there should be a radical causal hiatus between the past and the future, such that there are at present no traces or effects of the past, *B'* would not apply to any proposition about the past.

James's attempt to finesse commonsense realism by substituting *B'* for *B* is an exercise in futility, for it can be shown that *B'* entails *B*; and, as a result, he does not escape commitment to the categorical version of bivalence: He need not place "Realist" within scare-quotes any more in his parting "Ich bin ein Realist" pronouncement. To show this, it must first be shown that the proposition that if *p* were to be properly tested, *p* would be discovered to be true (to be abbreviated as "*p* is verifiable") logically entails that *p* is true (to be abbreviated as "T*p*").[13] That this entailment holds becomes obvious once it is realized that a proposition cannot be verified or discovered to be true unless it is true.

---

[13] The only commentator who has realized that James's possible truth entails actual truth is Moreland Perkins: "*p* is verifiable [possibly true or knowable] if and only if If *p* *were* carefully tested over an indefinitely long period of time it *would* be verified (confirmed) to an increasingly higher degree" (*NP* 577).

What we are "necessitated to believe" at the end of a *proper* inquiry is true. Therefore, that *p* is verifiable (in James's strong sense) entails T*p*. This has the consequence that *B'* entails *B*, as the following deduction of *B* from the assumption of *B'* clearly shows.

(1) Either *p* is verifiable or not-*p* is verifiable. [assumption of *B'* for conditional proof]
(2) If *p* is verifiable, then T*p*. [true for the reason just given]
(3) If not-*p* is verifiable, then Tnot-*p*. [same as (2)'s justification]
(4) Either T*p* or Tnot-*p*. [from (1)–(3) by dilemma argument]
(5) If either *p* is verifiable or not-*p* is verifiable, then either T*p* or Tnot-*p*. [from (1)–(4) by conditional proof]

Not only does James's conditionalized version of bivalence yield the categorical version, it also commits him to countenancing the realist's abstract propositions, or at least something just as queer from a nominalistic point of view. He responds to the realist that "when you try to impale me on your second horn [in which James departs from common sense by rejecting bivalence], I think of the truth in question as a mere *abstract possibility*, so I say it does exist, and side with common sense" (*MT* 159; my italics). The abstract possibility consists in the possibility of there existing a knower who performs a proper verification. The realist's abstract truth is "only another name for a *potential* as distinguished from an actual knowledge of the reality. . . . It is knowledge anticipated, knowledge in the form of *possibility* merely. . . . truth *possible* or *virtual* might exist, for a knower might *possibly* be brought to birth" (*MT* 157–8; my italics). Unfortunately for James, the *abstract possibility* that there should exist a knower is ontologically on all fours with the realist's abstract proposition. Like the latter, it is not locatable in space or time and is devoid of any sensible properties. From a nominalistic point of view, replacing abstract propositions with these abstract possibilities is like jumping from the frying pan into the fire.

James's attempt to capture the realist's intuition that there is a reality independent of the knower and of which there are true and false propositions implicitly makes use of Peirce's definition of the absolutely true as an ideal limit of *properly* conducted inquiry, for a proposition that is virtually true is one that would be verified if the appropriate tests or inquiries were properly conducted. James, unlike Peirce, does not specify what counts as a properly conducted inquiry in terms of the normative standards accepted by reputable members of the scientific community, although at one place he speaks of "the whole environment of social communication of which they [opinions] are a part and out of which they take their rise" (*MT* 145); but James, no doubt, being a

member in good standing of that community, would agree with
Peirce.[14]

There are several places where James, in an attempt to throw a bone
to his realist opponent, gives lip service to the ideal limit account of
absolute truth (I say "lip service" because it is dubious that James was
deeply committed to it.) "The 'absolutely' true, meaning what no farther experience will ever alter, is that ideal vanishing-point towards
which we imagine that all our temporary truth will some day converge"
(*P* 106– 7). There is a convergence toward a limit with respect to both
agreement and the content of our scientific theories. This is clearly
brought out by his claim that there is "an ideal opinion in which all
men might agree, and which no man should ever wish to change" and
"Truth absolute . . . means an ideal set of formulations towards which
all opinions may in the long run of experience be expected to converge" (*MT* 142 and 143). That there is an ultimately true solution to
the casuistic rule also makes use of the ideal limit doctrine: "Actualized
in his [God's] thought already must be that ethical philosophy which
we seek as the pattern which our own must evermore approach" (*WB*
161).

Sometimes James formulates this doctrine in an unhappy manner, as
for example when he says that "The truer idea is the one that pushes
farther; so we are ever beckoned on by the ideal notion of an ultimate
completely satisfactory terminus. I, for one, obey and accept that notion. I can conceive no other objective *content* to the notion of ideally
perfect truth than that of penetration into such a terminus" (*MT* 89).
For herein James seems to follow Plato's confusion of inferring the
existence of something that is absolutely *F* or has the greatest degree of
*F*ness possible from the fact that some things are more *F* than others.
Another example of the commission of this fallacy is his claim that "To
admit, as we pragmatists do, that we are liable to correction . . . *involves*
the use on our part of an ideal standard" (*MT* 142).

Occasionally James is careless and makes it appear as if the convergence is toward agreement only rather than the content of a theory. In
applying the doctrine of absolute truth as an ideal limit to his own

[14]The germ of this theory of absolute truth as definable in terms of the ongoing inquiries
of members in good standing of the scientific community is found in a short story Peirce
wrote when he was ten. "Charles & Ben were two brothers. Ben was four years older
than Charles and when he was a little boy – he thought he would try to climb the hill of
knowledge. Now this is a very high hill & full of stones and briars – & rough places –
but at the top there is a beautiful palace where there are many good & sensible people
assembled. Ben was very successful & in a few years had reached the palace & had begun
to make quite a figure among its learned inhabitants, when Charles undertook the same.
He is now on his way there & though he has not pursued exactly the same path yet he
goes on so slow & sure that there can be no doubt of succeeding as well I hope as his
brother" (quoted from Joseph Brent, *CSP* 41–2).

theory of pragmatism, he says "that the more fully men discuss and test my account, the more they will agree that it *fits*, and the less will they desire a change," making it appear that it is convergence to a limit of complete agreement that is in question (*MT* 142). The same is true of his remark "that there is a tendency to such convergence of opinions, to such ultimate consensus," it again appearing that it is convergence toward agreement and not content that is in question (*MT* 143–4).

The reason it is so important to distinguish between these two different limits of convergence is that there could be one without the other. Let C be the corpuscular theory of light and W be the wave theory. Imagine that there is a succession of nonoverlapping time intervals, such that T_1 is one-half of a century, T_2 one-quarter of a century, T_3 one-eighth, and so on ad infinitum. During T_1 half of the people believe C and half believe W, *during* T_2 one-fourth believe C and three-fourths believe W, during T_3 seven-eighths believe C and one-eighth believe W, and so on ad infinitum. This geometric series of belief-stages is converging toward a limit of complete agreement at the end of the century, but it does not converge toward some theory as its limit. From the information given, neither C nor W can be deduced to be the one that will be accepted when complete agreement is reached after one century has elapsed. This shows the possibility of having convergence toward agreement without convergence toward any specific theory or content. A less sophisticated, or should I say less sophistical, example could have been given in which there is convergence toward agreement, as in the given example, but the content of the successive theories shows no contentful convergence, which seems actually to be the case in the history of science.

Assuming that James's ideal-limit account of absolute truth required convergence to a limit with respect to both agreement and content, it now can be asked whether it passes James's own empiricistic requirement for meaningfulness and his humanistic account of theories.[15] There is no problem with the empirical credentials of the convergence to agreement, since it could be empirically determined that there was such convergence over time, as in the example just presented. It is the contentful convergence to an ideal limit that is empirically suspect.[16] There must be some way of empirically determining either when we are at last in possession of the absolutely true theory or that the succession

---

[15] For an excellent treatment of this topic see Suckiel *PP* 110–115.

[16] The concept of a "properly" conducted inquiry, which is essential to the ideal limit of inquiry account of absolute truth, also is dubious. We are able to rank order inquiries with respect to the relative adequacy of the methods employed in them, but this does not give us any grasp of what a perfectly conducted inquiry would be like. What theory of probability and what instruments would it have to employ?!!

of theories is converging toward some specific theory as a limit. The former is very unlikely. At any rate, James could not consistently combine it with his deep-seated, career-long commitment to fallibilism, which holds that *every* proposition admits of the possibility of being revised or rejected in the light of *future* experience. The theory that is believed to be absolutely true when we reach the scientific millennium cannot be subject to this fallibilistic principle.

Maybe it is possible to determine empirically that there is a contentful convergence to a limit by the successive theories. Not only does James deny that there is, as a matter of contingent fact, such convergence, his Kuhnian account of scientific theories precludes the very possibility of it. Any given phenomenon will be equally well explainable by more than one scientific theory. In the first place, every scientific theory will contain factors that appeal to aesthetic predilections, but, notoriously, they vary among persons. "The superiority of one of our formulas to another may not consist so much in its literal 'objectivity,' as in subjective qualities like its usefulness, its 'elegance' or its congruity with our residual beliefs" (*MT* 41). Even more important is that the very idea of a scientific theory being a literal copy of reality as it is in itself has lost scientific credability in modern science. According to Mach, Ostwald, and Duhem: "no hypothesis is truer than any other in the sense of being a more literal copy of reality. They are all but ways of talking on our part, to be compared solely from the point of view of their *use*" (*P* 93). All of our theories "are instrumental, are mental modes of *adaptation* to reality, rather than revelations or gnostic answers to some divinely instituted world-enigma" (*P* 94).

Up to about 1850 almost everyone believed that sciences expressed truths that were exact copies of a definite code of non-human realities. But the enormously rapid multiplication of theories in these latter days has well-nigh upset the notion of any one of them being a more literally objective kind of thing than another. There are so many geometries, so many logics, so many physical and chemical hypotheses, so many classifications, each one of them good for so much and yet not good for everything, that the notion that even the truest formula may be a human device and not a literal transcript has dawned upon us. (*MT* 40)

Science, thus, is an all-too-human creation, an instrument that we forged to do certain jobs. This humanistic view of science seems to preclude the possibility of there being a contentful limit to which successive scientific theories converge.

Since James's humanistic and fallibilistic views of science preclude the very possibility of empirically determining either that some theory is absolutely true or that there is a contentful convergence to a limit among successive theories, it must be concluded that James's ideal-limit doctrine of absolute truth must go; for the former doctrines are much more deeply entrenched in his Promethean pragmatism than is the Peircean ideal-limit theory of truth.

Because James's attempts to placate commonsense realism by employing a conditionalized version of bivalence and the ideal limit account of absolute truth fail miserably, the former capitulating to realism by an unwitting commitment to the categorical version of bivalence and the latter violating his empiricistic and humanistic commitments, I suggest that we do James a favor and simply drop them from his philosophy. There is a price that he must pay for this – no more whistle-stop campaign speeches of the "Ich bin ein Realist" sort. He is not going to get everyone's vote, but no philosopher should have this ideal, for it can be achieved only by the devious promulgation of inconsistent theses.

Having played the role of the harsh critic, I now want to switch hats and attempt to show there are features of James's philosophy that make available to him a better way of placating the realist, one in which he will not either capitulate in toto to realism or violate his own empiricism and humanism. The basic idea is to accept the law of the excluded middle

E. For every proposition p, either p or not-p.[17]

but reject that law of bivalence

B. For every proposition p, either p is true or not-p is true.

By accepting E, James captures the realist's intuition that nature houses events and objects that are neither known nor noted. Concerning the sea fight that might occur tomorrow, either it will or it won't occur, as is required by E, but, James would add, it is neither true now that it will nor true now that it won't. Although this way of interpreting James is somewhat anachronistic, as he never spoke of the law of excluded middle distinguishing it from bivalence, it is very much in the spirit of his philosophy.

Any realist worth her salt will immediately respond that it is contradictory to accept E and reject B, since B can easily be deduced from E by the following conditional proof.

---

[17] Since E quantifies over propositions, James will have to give up his antirealist stance against them, but this will not require any significant change in his overall philosophy, because his rejection of them was based on nothing more than a mere nominalistic prejudice. As for his empirical scruples ruling them out, James was willing to countenance nonempirical concepts when they played a useful theoretical role, and the defenders of abstract problems argued, as seen in Chapter 1, that they have a useful theoretical role in explaining a wide range of empirical facts about language and meaning.

(1) Either p or not-p. [assumption of the law of excluded middle for conditional proof]

(2) If p, then Tp. [necessary truth]

(3) If not-p, then Tnot-p. [necessary truth]

(4) Either Tp or Tnot-p. [from (1)–(3) by dilemma argument]

(5) If either p or not-p, then Tp or Tnot-p. [from (1)–(4) by conditional proof.]

Thus, James could not consistently hold E and reject B, as I am having him do.

A very careful and selective reading of James's response to Bertrand Russell[18] reveals that he rejects the principle on which premises (2) and (3) rest. This principle, which could be called "the principle of truth entailment," is

T. For every proposition p, if p, then Tp.

"Beliefs have their objective 'content' or 'deliverance' as well as their truth. . . . When I call a belief true, and define its truth to mean its workings, I certainly do not mean that the belief is a belief *about* the workings" (*MT* 150). Herein James is distinguishing between a proposition – the objective content of a belief or the what-is-believed – and the truth of this proposition. They are different propositions. He then goes on to claim that one could believe a proposition without believing that it is true. "The social proposition 'other men exist' and the pragmatist proposition 'it is expedient to believe that other men exist' [meaning 'it is true that other men exist'] come from different universes of discourse. One can believe the second without being logically compelled to believe the first; one can believe the first without having ever heard of the second; or one can believe them both" (*MT* 150).

That one can believe p without believing Tp, does not *alone* show that

---

[18] I say "selective" because the well-meaning interpreter must separate the wheat from the chaff in this response. As has been seen, Russell and Moore reduce to absurdity James's definition of *truth* in terms of what it is expedient to believe in the sense of maximizing desire-satisfaction by showing that there are true sentences that cease to be true when "true" is replaced by "is expedient to believe." James claims, for reasons that are left completely obscure, that one who makes such definitionally based substitutions assumes that any individual that satisfies the definition has *only* the properties specified in the definition. "But since meaning and things meant, definitions and things defined, are equivalent and interchangeable, *and nothing extraneous to its definition can be meant when a term is used*, it follows that whoso calls an idea true, and means by that word that it works, cannot mean anything else, can believe nothing but that it does work" (*MT* 148–9; my italics). James is making Russell into a strawman opponent by needlessly shackling him with the crazy belief that an instance of a defined term has *only* the properties specified in the definition. This strawman-ing tactic is repeated in *A Pluralistic Universe*. "The treating of a name as excluding from the fact named what the name's definition fails positively to include, is what I call 'vicious intellectualism' " (*PU* 32). I doubt that any real-life philosopher accepted "vicious intellectualism." James has conveniently created a strawman opponent.

the principle of truth entailment, T, is false, for belief is not closed under entailment; one can believe a proposition without believing every proposition that it logically entails. Think of a deductive system, such as geometry, in this connection. It does show that p is not identical with Tp, a result that would upset many philosophers. However, when it is combined with the following uncontroversial proposition, it does entail that T is false, namely that if p were logically to entail Tp, it should be such a basic and obvious entailment that one conceptually could not believe a proposition without also believing it to be true. This would be analogous to one being conceptually barred from having a belief about a material object unless one also believed that the object occupies space. The entailment of the proposition that O occupies space by the proposition that O is a material object is so obvious and basic in the sense of being concept defining, that anyone who did not recognize and make use of it could not have any beliefs about material objects. Analogously, if T were true, it would be such an obvious and basic principle that anyone who did not recognize and make use of it could not have any beliefs at all.

James's reason for believing that p does not entail Tp are more straightforward than that just given, which admittedly is highly speculative and thereby dubious. Because I seem to see a chair in the room, I believe that there is a chair in the room, but I have no basis for determining whether believing that there is a chair in the room will maximize desire-satisfaction in the long run and thereby do not believe that this proposition is true, assuming that I accept James's revisionary definition of truth.

He objects to his critic's "taking the word 'true' irrelatively, whereas the pragmatist always means 'true for him who experiences the working' " (*MT* 97). Because a proposition does not become true until its good consequences are actually realized and verified, the truth of a proposition must be relativized to a time as well as a person. Truth is an event in the life of a proposition, something that happens to it when the good consequences of believing it become verified. "Truth is *made*, just as health, wealth and strength are made, in the course of experience" (*P* 104).

The verifying act, in virtue of which truth is made, has a "retroactive validating power" (*MT* 67). Once a proposition becomes true, it casts a shadow backward, making the proposition to have been true; but because *it is now true* that it was true yesterday that there would be a sea fight today, it does not follow, according to this temporally relativized theory of truth, that *it was true yesterday* that there would be a sea fight the following today. Since James accepts the law of excluded middle but not that of bivalence, he could say that from this present truth it follows that yesterday there was going to be a sea fight on the following day. Since he rejects the truth entailment principle (p entails Tp), he would deny that the latter entails that it was true yesterday that there was going to be a sea fight on the following today. In general, that it is true at a given time that p does not entail that it is (or was) true at earlier times that p. James would have looked with favor on the tensed logic of A. N. Prior and others. Embedded truth-ascriptions are not detachable, which is yet another respect in which James's analysis departs from commonsense or ordinary usage.

6

The Semantics of "Truth"

In the previous chapter James was interpreted as giving a morally based revisionary analysis of belief-acceptance and truth that held us to be morally obligated to believe in a way that maximizes desire-satisfaction, with the result that a proposition counts as true when believing it maximizes desire-satisfaction. He supplemented this account with guiding principles enjoining us to have beliefs that are both consistent and epistemically warranted, and to follow a conservative strategy when it becomes necessary to revise our web of belief, which really was a web of mentation since it included conative states and emotions along with beliefs. It was suggested that things would go best if James went with a web comprised exclusively of beliefs. Because the rationale for accepting these guiding principles is to help us maximize desire-satisfaction in the long run, they admit of exceptions when doing so on some occasion can achieve this. Thus, they are merely instrumental rules.

James professed acceptance of the commonsense law of bivalence and its commitment to absolute truth but gave us a new and supposedly better way of expressing them in which this law is given a subjunctive conditional rendering in terms of what would be discovered if inquiry were to be properly pursued, with absolute truth being the ideal limit toward which such inquiry would converge. It was shown that the subjunctive conditional version entails the categorical version, thereby capitulating to commonsense realism, and that the Peircean ideal-limit theory of truth is incompatible with James's empiricism and humanism. James would be well advised to abandon this attempt to placate the realist and openly admit that his morally based analysis of epistemological concepts is highly revisionary of our commonsense concepts and beliefs concerning belief-acceptance and truth.

James's analysis, like any revisionary analysis, stands in need of justification; for our commonsense concepts and beliefs, in virtue of having passed the test of time, must be accorded pride of place, unless good reason is given not to do so. James's reasons were seen to be a mixture of therapeutic and moral ones. By accepting his moralizing of epistemology, we avoid commitment to the empirically vacuous truth or correspondence relation, with all of the mental cramps and perplexities that this occasions, and aid our Promethean endeavor to achieve our summum bonum, that being the full self-realization for each of our many selves. The therapeutic justification really is a species of the latter, since by getting our conceptual house in order we clear the decks so that we can function more effectively in realizing our summum bonum. It was seen that not all philosophers believe that "having it all" constitutes our highest good, notably Bertrand Russell, who thought our highest good to consist in becoming a detached, objective spectator of all time and eternity; and, as a consequence, our most basic duty is to believe in a way that is epistemically warranted rather than in a way that maximizes desire-satisfaction. This clash between James and Russell in regard to their basic axiological commitments seemed irreconcilable, being a paradigm case of James's sentiment of rationality doctrine that finds a psychological basis for ultimate disagreements among philosophers. By making moral concerns central and all-consuming, James is squarely within the Hebraic tradition; Russell, within the Greek or gnostic one. For the one, our ultimate goal is to do what is morally required of us; for the other, to be a detached knower.

There is another strategy available to the opponent of an axiologically driven revisionary analysis than challenging its moral commitments, namely, to show that it requires, for the sake of consistency, further revisions within our conceptual system that are unacceptable. A revisionary analysis of an ordinary concept will require, for the sake of consistency, that extensive revisions be made in other concepts that are logically intertwined with it, and the question is whether these additional revisions are acceptable. It is not just whether our conceptual system ceases to be a recognizable analogue to its former self but, even more important, whether we are happy with the resultant system.

There is a very striking additional revision required by James's revisionary analysis of truth and belief-acceptance that escaped the notice of both James and his commentators, namely, that truth must be cut loose from semantics. Our ordinary concepts of meaning and truth are logically connected because the meaning of a sentence supplies truth conditions for the proposition it expresses, with a proposition being true when these truth-conditions are fulfilled. Think in this connection of Tarski's convention T that holds a sentence "s" to be true if and only if s. James, as this chapter will show, severs this conceptual connection between meaning and truth. It then will be determined just how harmful this consequence is to his revisionary analysis.

It now will be shown that the theory of truth entailed by James's pragmatic theory of meaning, *on the assumption that a theory of meaning supplies truth-conditions for sentences*, is at odds with his morally based theory of truth according to which

5. A proposition is true when believing it maximizes desire-satisfaction.

This, of course, is an exercise in hypothetical reasoning, because James must reject this assumption given that his commitment to 5 results from the underlying Promethean intent and spirit of his pragmatic philosophy. First, James's pragmatic theory of meaning will be presented and then it will be shown what theory of truth it entails, *if it is assumed that a theory of meaning gives truth-conditions for sentences.* According to my interpretation, which certainly is not the only one that can find some support in James's text and also is philosophically interesting, the theory of truth that is entailed by his semantics must be downgraded, so as to be consistent with his morally driven revisionary analysis of truth, to a theory of "truth" in scare quotation marks to indicate that it is not what truth really is but only the conditions under which people ordinarily take a proposition to be true, thus the point of this chapter's title, "The Semantics of 'Truth.' " This theory of meaning does not even yield a theory of the common sense concept of truth but only of when a proposition is taken to be true, that is, to be epistemically warranted. His theory, thereby, serves to clarify what is meant by "epistemically warranted" and "epistemic justification" in his instrumental rule

9'. We are always prima facie morally obligated to believe in a manner that is epistemically warranted, except when epistemic justification is not possible.

The one constant in James's philosophy, from the first to the last words he wrote, was his passionate commitment to empiricism. It was, however, a most liberal form of empiricism, which countenanced not only the sensible qualities of the external senses and the sensations of inner sense but also relations, which were excluded from Hume's empiricism, as well as the contents of religious and mystical experiences in which the subject has an apparent, direct nonsensory perception of some purely spiritual, supernatural being. Although James's empiricism was a constant, the particular form or species it took varied. We shall see him shuttling back and forth between two species of empiricism: One is the exclusively future-oriented operationalistic or pragmatic empiricism that he officially endorses as his pragmatic theory of meaning, according to which the whole meaning of an idea is a set of conditionalized predictions stating what experiences would be had in the future upon performing certain actions, and the other that of classical British empiricism, which finds the meaning of an idea in terms of the sensory or experiential contents that its analysis comprises, regardless of whether they are future or not. The latter species of empiricism will be called "content empiricism" and the former "operationalist or pragmatic empiricism."

James's shift back and forth between these two species of empiricism were unannounced and escaped both his and his critics' notice. An indication of his confounding the two species can be found in the subtitle of his book *Pragmatism: A New Name for Some Old Ways of Thinking.* The "old ways of thinking" refer to the empiricistic reductions given by Locke, Berkeley, and Hume, whom James recognized as the forerunners of pragmatism (*P* 30). These reductions were based upon content empiricism, the meaning of an idea of *X* consisting in the experiences that would be had upon experiencing *X*. But the operationalistic form of empiricism that James espouses in *Pragmatism* and officially dubs "pragmatism" is a quite different species of empiricism from that of these classical British empiricists, as it is exclusively future-oriented and concerns the actions required by the subject as well as the experiences attendant upon those actions. Thus, the subtitle of *Pragmatism* should more appropriately have been "*A New Name for a New Way of Thinking That Is a Different Species of an Old Way of Thinking*" – hardly a grabber.

Another example of James's confounding the two species is found in his famous example of the dispute over whether a man succeeds in walking around a squirrel when he circles the tree on which the squirrel is affixed but the squirrel moves in such a manner as always to keep the tree trunk between itself and the man (*P* 27–8). James attempts to resolve the dispute by deploying his pragmatic theory of meaning, but what he actually does is to apply the content empiricist theory to the rival claims to show that, in spite of their differences in language, they mean the same thing, because they describe the same experiences or experiential contents. That he is using this species of empiricism is manifest in his confining his experiential rendering of the "rival" claims to the experiences an observer would have had *at the time of the circling*, not those which would be had at some future time if certain steps were to be taken, such as subsequently checking the tree for tiny claw marks and the ground for human footprints and squirrel droppings.

Certain claims that James made about the relation between his pragmatism and radical empiricism make sense only if he countenances a distinction between the operationalist and content species of empiricism, assuming that meaning gives truth-conditions. Pragmatism is a theory of both meaning and truth. An idea's meaning is a set of conditionalized predictions, with its truth consisting in the actual fulfillment or verification of these predictions, as is required by this assumption. Pragmatism, therefore, is a conjunction of an operationalist empiricism (O for short) with a theory of truth (T for short) based on it, on the assumption that meaning gives truth-conditions.

Radical empiricism, on the other hand,

consists first of a postulate, next of a statement of fact, and finally of a generalized conclusion.

The postulate is that the only things that shall be debatable among philosophers shall be things definable in terms drawn from experience. . . .

The statement of fact is that the relations between things, conjunctive as well as disjunctive, are just as much matters of direct particular experience, neither more so nor less so, than the things themselves.

The generalized conclusion is that therefore the parts of experience hold together from next to next by relations that are themselves parts of experience. The directly apprehended universe needs, in short, no extraneous trans-empirical connective support, but possesses in its own right concatenated or continuous structure. (*MT* 6–7; my italics.)[1]

James was none too clear about the relation between radical empiricism and his pragmatism – the conjunction of O and T. At first he says, "there is no logical connexion between pragmatism, as I understand it, and a doctrine which I have recently set forth as 'radical empiricism' " (*P* 6). But later he says that the establishment of the pragmatic theory of truth "is a step of first-rate importance in making radical empiricism prevail" (*MT* 6). Both remarks are correct but need further explanation.

Some commentators have mistakenly thought that radical empiricism entails pragmatism but not vice versa. The reason for this is that they thought that radical empiricism's postulate of empiricism *is identical with* the O conjunct of pragmatism, its operationalist theory of meaning; and, since O entails T and radical empiricism entails O, radical empiricism entails the conjunction of O and T (pragmatism). Pragmatism, thus, is a logically necessary condition for radical empiricism, since one of the conjuncts in radical empiricism, its postulate of empiricism, entails pragmatism.[2] What these commentators failed to realize is that pragmatism's operationalist theory of meaning, O, is only one species of empiricism; and, since the empirical postulate refers to a generic empiricism, of which content empiricism, along with O, are different

[1] James is not saying that the universe-as-a-whole is self-subsistent, which would be inconsistent with his career-long commitment to the mystery of existence, that there is one fact that seems to defy explanation, namely, that anything at all exists, that there is something rather than nothing (*EP* 58–64, *PP* 1269, *WB* 107–8, *ML* 412, and *SPP* 27). All he means is that there is no need to invoke, as Kant did, a transcendent source of the relational features of the universe.

[2] I am embarrassed to say that I am one of the culprits. I wrote: "Since the postulate [of empiricism] is a variant on the pragmatic theory of meaning, radical empiricism entails this theory, though not conversely; and, since the latter entails the pragmatic theory of truth, radical empiricism entails pragmatism, understood as encompassing both its theory of meaning and truth" ("Pragmatism versus Mysticism: The Divided Self of William James," *Philosophical Perspectives* 5 [1991]). Charlene Haddock Seigfried claimed that "Radical Empiricism includes both the pragmatic method and the principle of pure experience," thereby equating the former's empirical postulate with the pragmatic theory of meaning, O (*WJ* 317). Eugene Taylor says that "Radical Empiricism is also pragmatic" (*WJ* 113). Andrew Reck initially endorses James's claim that his pragmatism and radical empiricism are logically distinct but then goes on claim that "the methodological postulate of radical empiricism . . . contends in effect that realities are what they are 'experienced as' " (*WJ* 58 and 60). The empirical postulate of radical empiricism contends no such thing, since it postulates a generic brand of empiricism. Graham Bird, whose book on William James is one of the very best overall accounts of James's philosophy, claimed that the empirical assumption of radical empiricism could be viewed as the pragmatic method's insistence on a decision procedure for settling disputes (*WJ* 66.) This is a valuable insight, but it must be stressed that the decision procedures given by the former and the latter are not identical.

species, this postulate does not entail O. For, whereas a species entails the genus, the converse does not hold: That something is a tiger entails that it is an animal but not vice versa.

The reason the establishment of the pragmatic theory of truth "is a step of first-rate importance in making radical empiricism prevail" is that it eliminates certain prominent counterexamples to the empirical postulate of the latter, consisting in the truth, correspondence, and reference relations. The pragmatic theory of meaning shows how these relations can be empirically analyzed in terms of a succession of experiences that terminates in a percept of the correspondent or referent in the truth or reference relation. Thus, pragmatism, although it does not entail radical empiricism, helps it to prevail by protecting its flank against some seemingly powerful counterexamples.

Some have claimed that James did not have a *theory* of meaning, or of any other important concept of traditional philosophy, such as truth, knowledge, and goodness. Richard Rorty, in particular, has portrayed James as opposing the attempts of traditional philosophers to devise theories about the essence or nature of these concepts. "As long as we see James or Dewey as having 'theories of truth' or 'theories of knowledge' or 'theories of morality' we shall get them wrong" (*CP* 160; see also 139). Instead, James had a " 'therapeutic' conception of philosophy familiar from Wittgenstein's *Philosophical Investigations*" that showed us a way of avoiding the fruitlessness of doing philosophy in the traditional manner (*ORT* 3).

There is no textual support for Rorty's deconstructionist interpretation of James, not only with respect to meaning but also to the other concepts beloved by traditional philosophers. To be sure, James does speak of "the pragmatic method" and claims that it "is primarily a method of settling metaphysical disputes that otherwise might be interminable," which has a bit of a deconstructionist ring to it; but it is clear that this method rests on a general account or theory of meaning (*P* 28).[3] It better, for the disputants would not accept James's attempt to resolve their apparent dispute by employing his pragmatic method to bring out the meaning of their respective claims unless they believed that this method for determining meaning held *in general* and thus rested on an acceptable theory of meaning. The pragmatic method for settling disputes, therefore, is no better than the theory or account of meaning that backs it.

[3] James explicitly claimed to have a theory of truth, which is a bedfellow of meaning since meaning gives truth-conditions. "Meanwhile the word pragmatism has come to be used in a still wider sense, as meaning also a certain theory of truth" (*P* 32). "Such then would be the scope of pragmatism – first, a method; and second, a genetic theory of what is meant by truth" (*P* 37). James sometimes used "account" instead of "theory." "The pivotal part of my book named *Pragmatism* is its account of the relation called 'truth'" (*MT* 3). "My account of truth is realistic" (*MT* 117). It would be bizarre if James were to have had a theory of truth but not a theory of meaning.

That James saw the dependency of the former on the latter is manifest in his entry under "Pragmatism" in Baldwin's 1902 *Dictionary of Philosophy and Psychology*. Pragmatism is

The doctrine that the *whole* 'meaning' of a conception expresses itself in practical consequences either in the shape of conduct to be recommended, or in that of experiences to be expected if the conception be true; which consequences would be different if it were untrue, and must be different from the consequences by which the meaning of other conceptions is in turn expressed. If a second conception should not appear to have other consequences, then it must really be only the first conception under a different name. In *methodology* it is certain that to trace and compare their respective consequences is an admirable way of establishing the differing meanings of different conceptions. (*EP* 94; my italics)

It is clear that his "methodology" is introduced in an ancillary manner that makes it dependent on his theory of meaning. Furthermore, in support of my interpretation of James as espousing a theory of meaning, he claims that his account gives "the whole 'meaning' of a conception," not just a part of its meaning, as some commentators would have it. According to the likes of Suckiel, Giuffrida and Madden, and Thayer, James did not have a *pragmatic theory of meaning* but a *theory of pragmatic meaning*, because he recognized cognitive and pragmatic (or operational) meaning as different species of meaning and restricted himself to giving an account of only the latter. According to my interpretation, which is very close to Suckiel's, James promulgated a pragmatic theory of meaning but inconsistently shifted at times to the nonoperationalist theory of meaning based on content empiricism, which could be viewed as the "cognitive" meaning of these interpreters. More will be said about this as we proceed.

The claim to be giving a theory of meaning in general, not just of one species of meaning, also informs James's 1898 formulation of pragmatism in "Philosophical Conceptions and Practical Results," reprinted in the *Journal of Philosophy, Psychology, and Scientific Method* for 1904 under the title "The Pragmatic Method," which, in turn, is repeated almost verbatim in his 1907 *Pragmatism*. After crediting Charles Sanders Peirce with first introducing the pragmatic theory of meaning in his 1878 "How to Make Our Ideas Clear," James goes on to characterize it as presenting the *sole* or *whole* significance or meaning of a belief.

Mr. Peirce, after pointing out that our beliefs are really rules for action, said that, to develope [*sic*] a thought's meaning we need only determine what conduct it is fitted to produce: that conduct is for us its *sole* significance. . . . To attain perfect clearness in our thoughts of an object, then, we need only consider what conceivable effects of a practical kind the object may involve – what sensations we are to expect from it, and what reactions we must prepare. Our conception of these effects, whether immediate or remote, is then for us the *whole* of our conception of the object, so far as that conception has positive significance at all. (*P* 28–9; my italics)

There is some controversy concerning how much influence Peirce actually exerted on James. There cannot be any doubt that there is some, for James first became acquainted, "about 1870" according to his own estimate (*EP* 266), with Peirce's pragmatism when he heard an early version of "How to Make Our Ideas Clear" at a meeting of the Metaphysical Club. But according to both James's wife and son, Henry James III, the influence was quite minor. In a letter to F. C. S. Schiller, his wife wrote that her husband had a habit of

confessing to obligations which he never owed. It used to puzzle me in so strictly truthful a nature. Even Charles Peirce said to me, "I never thought much less taught the views William says I did. I have very different opinions." For years poor C.S.P. had appealed to William for help until at last he acquired the habit of tugging that poor derelict through troubled waters. . . . When William was a student in the chemical laboratory, and absorbed in philosophy, he found Charles Peirce a stimulating acquaintance; so when years after William sought to give a name to the faith he had long held, he glanced backwards and said to himself, "I must have owed Pragmatism to Peirce." I protested and begged him not to handicap a cherished belief with so wanton a name. He was sorry afterwards, and preferred Humanism. (quoted from Myers, *WJ* 492)

Henry James III concurred in a note that he left in the Houghton Library in which he claimed "that his father's dedication of *Principles* [*of Psychology*] to François Pillon was gratuitous, as were most of his expressions of indebtedness to Chauncey Wright and C. S. Peirce" (quoted from Myers, *WJ* 492). James's long-standing colleague at Harvard, George Herbert Palmer, wrote in 1919 that "James's over-estimate of Charles Peirce, and too ample acknowledgment of his own debt to Peirce's thought, I believe to have sprung quite as much from pity as from admiration" (in Simon, *JR* 31). John Elof Boodin, a student and close philosophical confidant, also claimed that James's "generous feeling toward those that had in some measure contributed to his insight" caused him to overrate "the mastery other minds had possessed over him" (in Simon, *JR* 209).

There was a complex of reasons for James's penchant to overstate the influence that others had upon him. One was his affability, which led him to reach out to others by finding common ground between their respective ideas. Recognizing his views in others also bolstered his self-confidence in his own views, a good example of which was his lavishing praise on Bergson in *A Pluralistic Universe* for presenting him with a role model that gave him the courage at last to come out of hiding and go public with his own long-standing conviction that the laws of logic cannot apply to reality. He even manages to get Peirce into the act through his claim that "Peirce's 'tychism' is thus practically synonymous with Bergson's 'devenir reel' " (*PU* 153). Yet another reason was James's movement mentality. By attributing his key ideas to others, he got them aboard his bandwagon and thereby gave the public the impression of a groundswell movement within the field of philosophy. This was true not only of his theory of pragmatism[4] but also of his later panpsychistic mysticism in *A Pluralistic Universe.* There also was a political motive for his overemphasis of Peirce's influence and importance, namely, to further his continuing but unsuccessful effort to secure an academic position for Peirce, "that poor derelict," especially at Harvard, where President Eliot bitterly opposed the appointment.

The best way to determine the importance of Peirce's influence on James's development of pragmatism is to perform the following thought experiment. Ask yourself whether James's pragmatism would have evolved in pretty much the way it in fact did if Peirce were not to have existed. And don't say that in this counterfactual situation James suffered from delusions in which he credited an imaginary friend, Charles Sanders Peirce, with being the originator of pragmatism, any more than you would want to say that if Princess Grace were not to have died in that car accident, she would now be clawing at the inside of her coffin (A similar abuse of counterfactual reasoning underlies Clarence Darrow's humorous comment that he was so glad that he hated spinach; because if he were to have liked it that would have been awful.) In this counterfactual situation, James does not hear Peirce's paper in the early 1870s, does not read Peirce's first published version of pragmatism in his 1871 review of Frazer's edition of the works of Berkeley in the *North American Review,* and so on.

It seems clear to me that in this situation James's pragmatism does develop in pretty much the same way as it in fact did; for, whereas Peirce's version of pragmatism derived largely from the operationalistic habits of laboratory scientists, especially their preoccupation with finding ways to measure physical properties, and was confined to general concepts that admitted of precise operationalistic analyses, James's version applies to *all* concepts and derives from Darwinian biology's depiction of man as an organism who must use his intelligence as a practical instrument to aid him in his endeavor to survive, and survive well, in a hostile environment. It is the coming to fruition of his labors in chemistry, anatomy, and physiology during the 1860s and 1870s. The Darwinian view of man, which James recasts as the Promethean view of man, informs all of James's writings, beginning with his three initial philosophical essays of the late 1870s – "Remarks on Spencer's Definition of Mind as Correspondence," "Quelques Considerations sur la méthode subjective," and "The Sentiment of Rationality" – on through *The Principles of Psychology* and reaching its culmination in *Pragmatism*

---

[4] See especially: *EP* 103,106, and 148; *ERE* 44; P 30; *MT* 38–9, 93, and 128; *PU* 143; *LWJ,* 2:245, 267, 268, 271, 279, 282, 310, and 348. Dewey was quite right when he spoke of "the pragmatism which Mr. James urged with apostolic fervor" and claimed that he "was an apostle seeking the conversion of souls" (*MW* 6:96 and 102).

and *The Meaning of Truth*. Basically, James wants a theory of meaning that will connect a belief's meaning with the role that it plays in guiding the believer in his effort to cope successfully with his environment. It is for this reason that he makes an idea's meaning completely prospective, a matter that will concern us later.

But exactly what is *James's* pragmatic *theory* of meaning, assuming that he had a theory and that it evolved out of his own basic philosophical commitments, rather than being taken over from someone else? The origin of his theory is Bain's thesis that belief is "that upon which a man is prepared to act." Peirce's claim that "our beliefs are really rules for action," which is endorsed by James, offers a variant on this claim (*P* 29 and *VRE* 351). It is, however, a potentially misleading ellipsis, for neither the psychological belief-state, the believing, nor the what-is-believed, the content of the belief, can be identified with a rule without absurdity. Whereas the believing is temporally locatable, a rule itself is not so locatable, although its being followed or enforced is. Furthermore, what is believed when one believes that snow is white is not a rule, such as the rule to assert "Snow is white" when asked what is the color of snow; for one could believe that there is such a rule but have no disposition to follow it. What Peirce and James meant, no doubt, is that to believe that snow is white is to have the disposition to follow this rule, as well as other rules that specify how one ought to act toward snow, such as to infer that one will have white visual images when confronted with snow under standard conditions. A belief, therefore, is a habit of acting, "the establishment in our nature of a rule of action," as Peirce said (*CP* vol. 5, para. 397).

James unwittingly gives both a normative and a nonnormative account of this disposition. The former makes room for evaluating the believer's behavior, whether intentional or nonintentional, as being correct or incorrect in respect to the way in which it is connected with the original belief or thought, but the latter does not, it being confined to a mere causal account of the relation between the belief and the subsequent behavior.

James's initial definitions of pragmatism give the normative account when they speak of "conduct to be *recommended*" in the Baldwin's *Dictionary* and of "what conduct it is *fitted* to produce in *Pragmatism*" (my italics; see also *VRE* 351). There are other normative-sounding expressions that James uses to characterize the behavioral disposition of the believer. He speaks of the conduct that a belief "dictates" or "calls for" (*EP* 124). He also speaks of the "conduct that *should* be followed" by the believer or that is "*required*" by the belief (*EP* 335 and *WB* 32; my italics). When contrasting the meanings of Pluralism and Absolutism, he says that whereas a belief in either "permits" our leading the morally strenuous life, only the belief in Pluralism "demands" it (*MT* 123). A conception of God is meaningful only if it *"implies certain definite things that we can feel and do at particular moments of our lives, things which we could not feel and should not do were no God present"* (*EP* 127; my italics). "Should" seems to be a synonym for "ought" or "require" here. What a believer ought or is demanded to do is different from what he will be caused to do by his having the belief in question. The use of "recommended," "fitted," "calls for," "should," "required," "demanded," "implies," and "deduced from" makes it look as if the believer's behavioral disposition is normatively based. Before investigating the source of this normativity, it will be shown that James inconsistently gave a purely causal, nonnormative account of these dispositions, often in the very same paragraph in which he gave the normative account, thereby precluding any attempt to dispel the apparent inconsistency diachronically in terms of a development in his views of the dispositional relationship.

Usually James characterizes the behavioral disposition in purely causal terms, devoid of any type of oughtness or shouldness. He says that a belief "inspires" (*ER* 124 and *WB* 32) and "instigates" (*P* 97) certain behavior. "We know an object by means of an idea, whenever we ambulate towards the object under the *impulse* which the idea communicates" (*MT* 80; my italics). The idea of the Absolute, for example, is meaningful if it "can be shown to have *any consequences* whatever for our life" (*P* 129; my italics). "Consequences," "impulses," "inspires," and "instigates" appear to be purely causal, nonnormative terms. Sometimes James describes the relation between a belief and the attendant behavior in purely temporal terms, as when he speaks of the "conduct consequent upon" or that "follows on" a belief (*ER* 125 and *MT* 34). There is not even a hint of anything normative in these temporal and causal characterizations.

Again, we face a deep aporia in James's philosophy and we must look for some way to resolve it that best squares with the text and fits the spirit of his philosophy, as well as making for the more attractive philosophical view in its own right.[5] Before arguing that the normative interpretation of James's theory of meaning best satisfies these three de-

[5] The clash between his normative and causal accounts of belief is paralleled by a clash between his reason-based and causal accounts of the source of philosophical beliefs. In the opening pages of *Pragmatism*, he finds a psychological basis for the ultimate parting of the ways between philosophers: "The history of philosophy is to a great extent that of a certain clash of human temperaments" (*P* 11). A philosopher's temperament is the major *cause* of his acceptance of a certain philosophy. But he then converts this cause into a reason for a philosopher's belief when he says that a philosopher's temperament "gives him a stronger bias than any of his more strictly objective premises," and that "the potentest of all our premises is never mentioned" (*P* 11). A premise gives a reason, not a cause, for a belief. Later in the lecture, he switches back to the causal account when he says that "Temperaments with their cravings and refusals do *determine* men in their philosophies, and always will" (*P* 24).

siderata, the unattractiveness of his causal theory of meaning will be indicated.

The problems with James's causal theory of meaning were adumbrated in Chapter 4. They resulted from the fact that the behavior that is *caused* or *followed* by a given belief or thought is determined by features of the believer's psychological makeup, but they are notoriously variable among persons. This results in a subjectivistic Protagorean nightmare in which meanings become so person-relative that communication becomes practically although not theoretically impossible, since in principle enough could be known about a person's external behavior so that his behavior upon hearing certain words could be predicted. Recall the "Niagara Falls" comedy routine in which every time Lou Costello would innocently mention Niagara Falls it would cause Bud Abbott to go berserk and start pounding on him. There also was the odd chap who would be disposed to act so as to make

R. Good will win out over evil in the long run.

become true by the performance of good-making actions only if he first believed the irrelevant proposition that Verdi wrote *Ernani.* These examples, of course, are exaggerated, but they serve to remind us of how variable the connection between belief and action among persons is.

It was necessary in Chapter 4 to protect James's doctrine of the will to believe, which licenses a person to believe an epistemically nonwarranted proposition when doing so will help him to make some desirable proposition become true, against counterexamples based on such variability between belief and action by stipulating that

(9) *A*'s belief that p is a rational reason for him to act so as to help make q become true.

James masked the problem of relativism in meaning, due to the variability of the connection between belief and action, by espousing the empirically false doctrine that there is a one-to-one correlation between belief and action: For every proposition, p, there is a set of actions, B, such that a person believes p, if and only if, he performs or is disposed to perform the actions in B (*WB* 32). Counterexamples to this doctrine are crawling around everywhere: Jones and Smith, for example, both believe it is raining, but only Smith takes measures to protect himself from the rain when he ventures out, the reason for this behavioral difference being that Jones, unlike Smith, is a Christian Scientist. The reasons for these counterexamples is that the connection between belief and action depends on the peculiarities of the believer's psychology consisting in respect to background beliefs, desires, fears, and the like. An attempt was made to save James's doctrine of the will to believe from reliance on this false doctrine by adding the additional condition:

(8') *A* knows at *T* that he will act so as to help make *q* become true only if he first believes that *p* is true.

What condition (8') does is to relativize a will-to-believe option to the psychology of the believer at time *T*.

Fortunately, James's nonnormative causal theory of meaning is not his final word. For the most part, he advances this theory only when engaged in his perverse, nutshelling activity of giving one- or two-sentence accounts of his theory of meaning, but when he is actually working out the details of this theory, with regard to both general and singular terms, he goes with the normative account. Unlike Peirce, who found the source of the normative in the way in which the community of scientists agreed upon the use of general terms, James eschews any appeal to normatively rule-governed human practices to explain the normative. It will be seen that his account of the normative basis for the proper use of both general and singular terms is in terms of an intention to follow a "private rule," and thus he is still left with the problems of relativism and subjectivism. An account first will be given of his account of general concepts, then of singular ones.

I. General Concepts

James's account of general concepts equivocates between content empiricism and operationalism. According to his operationalistic or pragmatic theory of meaning, the meaning of your idea is determined by what "difference . . . its being true will make in some possible person's history, and we shall know, not only just what you are really claiming, but also how important an issue it is, and how to go to work to verify the claim" (*SPP* 38). But he then immediately countenances content empiricism as bringing out part of the meaning of a concept when he says that in obeying this pragmatic rule for determining meaning "we neglect the substantive content of the concept, and follow its function only." The *function* of a concept or idea – what it portends for future experience and conduct – is only a part of its meaning; it has in addition a *substantive content*. This content will be, for James, an experiential one, as is required by content empiricism.

> To understand a concept you must know what it *means*. It means always some *this*, or some abstract portion of a *this*, with which we first made acquaintance in the perceptual world, or else some grouping of such abstract portions. All conceptual content is borrowed: to know what the concept 'colour' means you must have *seen* red, or blue, or green. (*SPP* 46)

In this passage James espouses Hume's concept empiricism, which requires that all concepts be derived by a process of abstraction from sense experience. These sense experiences constitute the "substantive content" of a concept's meaning. They need not be future experiences that are attendant upon the performance of certain operations.

A similar distinction between function and content underlies James's remark that "The meaning of a concept may always be found, *if not in some sensible particular which it directly designates,* then in some particular difference in the course of human experience which its being true will make" (*SPP* 37; my italics). The sensible particular that is directly designated, supposedly, constitutes its substantive content. The distinction between a concept's pragmatic function and its substantive empirical content also is found in his account of the three forms that a concept can take. "The concept of 'man,' to take an example, is three things: 1. the word itself; 2. a vague picture of the human form which has its own value in the way of beauty or not; and 3. an instrument for symbolizing certain objects from which we may expect human treatment when occasion arrives" (*SPP* 36). Condition 3 concerns the function or pragmatic meaning of the concept, which in the case of abstract contents is the only form that the concept takes. Definition 2, on the other hand, is the substantiative content, as it involves the "vague picture" or the image part of the concept. James goes on to add that, "however beautiful or otherwise worthy of stationary contemplation the substantive part of a concept may be, the more important part of its significance may naturally be held to be the consequences to which it leads." But this countenances the substantive content as part of the meaning of certain concepts (*SPP* 37). This distinction between the substance and the function of a concept gives some support to the Suckiel-Thayer-Madden-Giuffrida interpretation that views James as having a theory of pragmatic meaning rather than a pragmatic theory of meaning because he recognized a nonpragmatic cognitive or substantive meaning in addition to a pragmatic one.

Since a singular or individual concept can also be carried by a word or image, what is it that makes a word or image general, that is, applicable to more than one individual? James's answer is that it is not any intrinsic feature of the word or image but the intention of the subject to apply it generally that makes for the difference. Whether we mean a given word or image to function as a singular or a general concept "*is an entirely peculiar element of the thought*" that accompanies it (*PP* 446). "This added consciousness is an absolutely positive sort of feeling, transforming what would otherwise be mere noise or vision into something *understood*; and determining the sequel of my thinking, the later words and images, in a perfectly definite way" (*PP* 446). It is a "vague consciousness," a fringe or halo that "surrounds the image" and "constitutes an "intention that the name or mental pictures employed should mean all the possible individuals of the class" (*PP* 451). Via this intention "we always do know which of all possible subjects we have in mind" (*PP* 454).

But exactly how does the subject's intention succeed in collecting together an extension of individuals that satisfy or are instances of his general concept? What makes it correct for him to apply it to all of them? His answer is based on

> a fundamental psychical peculiarity which may be entitled "*the principle of constancy in the mind's meanings*," and which may be thus expressed: "*The same matters can be thought of in successive portions of the mental stream, and some of these portions can know that they mean the same matters which the other portions meant.*" One might put it otherwise by saying that "the mind can always intend, and know when it intends, to think of the Same." (*PP* 434)

This principle rests on a fundamental law of psychology: "That we can at any moment think of the same thing which at any former moment we thought of is the ultimate law of our intellectual constitution" (*PP* 920).[6] This principle or law is of a subjective character, as it is the subject's "intention . . . to think of the same," about which he cannot be mistaken, that determines the extension of his general concept over time (*PP* 435). "Each thought decides, by its own authority," whether its present content is an instance of what it formerly intended to count as an instance of some concept. In other words, each subject follows an in-principle private rule in determining which individuals count as instances of a given general concept. He and he alone knows whether he is correctly following his intention to call these experiences instances of this concept.

This commitment to an in-principle private language in *The Principles of Psychology* becomes fully explicit in James's last publication, *Some Problems of Philosophy*.[7] A general word for a sensible quality, say, for white, can gather together into its extension instances of white that differ in their color qualities, provided "we mean that our word *shall* inalterably signify" a color common to them. "The impossibility of isolating and fixing this quality physically is irrelevant, so long as we can isolate and fix it mentally, and decide that whenever we say 'white,' that identical quality, whether applied rightly or wrongly, is what we shall be held to *mean*. Our meanings can be the same as often as we intend to have them so" (*SPP* 57). James uses "we" in this passage in the distributive sense, since each one of us must adhere to his own private intention always to call things "white" that have the same color as the specimen he has mentally isolated and officially dubbed as the standard of white-

---

[6] According to Alfred Schuetz, James's principle that the mind can intend to refer to the same again is the same as Husserl's "synthesis of identification" (JSC 443).

[7] It also is seen in his remark in *The Meaning of Truth* that a feeling must "be held fast in that first intention, before any knowledge about it can be attained" (19).

ness. James does allow for the possibility of the speaker "rightly or wrongly" applying "white," but only the speaker is able to determine whether he is correctly adhering to his own private rule. The reason is that his paradigm of whiteness, which is a mental image private to himself, is not in principle accessible to anyone else. It is Wittgenstein's beetle in the matchbox that is observable only by the matchbox's owner. Therefore no one else can check up on the speaker to determine whether he is consistently adhering to his rule always to call things white that have the same color as his mental paradigm of whiteness.

It is this commitment to an in-principle private language that earned James the distinction of being the major whipping boy of the later Wittgenstein. One gets the feeling that Wittgenstein wrote his *Philosophical Investigations* with an open copy of *The Principles of Psychology* before him, especially the chapter on "The Stream of Thought." But it was not just Wittgenstein who was troubled by James's account of linguistic meaning in terms of the speaker's intention to follow a private rule. Several James commentators have pointed out the unfortunate subjectivistic upshot of James's theory of meaning.[8] H. S. Thayer, in his introduction to *The Meaning of Truth*, points out that, regretfully, "The very suggestive theory of meaning as a social activity within a community of interpretation (which was close to ideas of Peirce) seems to have had little interest for James" (xxii). James's neglect of the social group in his theory of meaning is part and parcel of his general neglect of the social, one example of which, as will be seen in Chapter 8, is his treatment of the self from an exclusively first-person perspective. John J. McDermott is quite right when he wrote that "James failed to focus on the fact that my own self-consciousness comes into being inseparable from how I am consciously 'had' by others.... He neglected ... the formative power of the social situation, which, despite our Promethean protestations, conditions all of our visions of what we are doing" (*SE* 53). Max Otto had said that James, "like Emerson ... was captivated by the ideal of absolutely unentangled and unfettered individuality" (*CB* 189). Other commentators who have criticized James for his failure to

---

[8] There are, however, some notable exceptions. Hilary Putnam claimed that "According to the pragmatists ... when one human being in isolation tries to interpret even the best maxims for himself and does not allow others to criticize the way in which he or she interprets those maxims, or the way in which he or she applies them, then the kind of 'certainty' that results is always fatally tainted with subjectivity" (*WL* 172). This generalization is highly anachronistic, fitting Peirce, Mead, and Dewey, but definitely not James. Henry Samuel Levinson, in his otherwise admirable book, *The Religious Investigations of William James*, radically overemphasizes, in general, the role of the social in James's philosophy. Eugene Fontinell, another excellent James commentator, tends to agree with his socializing interpretation (see especially *SGI* 157). That James was highly gregarious and loved his fellow creatures should not hide from us the fact that he wallowed in subjectivism in his theory of meaning, as well as his theory of truth, as was shown in the previous chapter.

give sufficient importance to the social are Charles Morris (*PM* 143 and 151) and Israel Scheffler (*FP* 124 and 145–6).

II. Singular Concepts

Singular concepts or ideas have a special philosophical importance because it is through them that our thought and language are hooked onto reality. In order for us to say something true or false about the world we must ultimately employ some singular concept that refers to a real-life individual, even if it be just a place or a time. It was for this reason, no doubt, that James implicitly reduced questions about truth to ones about knowledge, and the latter, in turn, to questions about singular reference (see, for example, *ERE* 28, 31–3, *MT* 128–30, and *ERE* 152). James begins by asking a question about the conditions under which a belief is true but immediately replaces it by a question about how the belief can be known, which he then replaces by the question about how we can refer to or be acquainted with the real-life individual(s) that the belief is about.

James presents his account of singular reference as a way of escaping from Royce's ingenious reference-based argument, in his 1885 *The Religious Aspect of Philosophy*, for the thesis that everything is a part of a single Absolute Mind. James portrays the importance that this argument had for his own philosophical development in a way that is reminiscent of Kant's praising Hume for awakening him from his dogmatic slumber by his treatment of relations, especially that of causation: "But for the teachings of my colleague, Dr. Josiah Royce, I should neither have grasped its [the problem of reference's] full force nor made my own practical and psychological point of view as clear to myself as it is" (*MT* 23).[9]

[9] I think there is considerable hyperbole and exaggeration in the importance that James attributed to this argument. In 1884, one year before Royce's book appeared, James published an essay, "The Function of Cognition," that contained an alternative to Royce's theory of reference, based on a sequence of experiences that leads from the referring idea to the referent, and that avoids commitment to a single Absolute Mind. But when this essay was later included as the opening chapter of the 1909 *The Meaning of Truth*, he added a footnote in which he said of Royce's argument that "At the time [1885] I could not refute this transcendentalist opinion. Later, largely through the influence of Professor D. S. Miller (see his essay 'The Meaning of Truth and Error,' in the Philosophical Review for 1893, vol. 2, p. 403), I came to see that any definitely experienceable workings would serve as intermediaries quite as well as the absolute mind's intentions would" (*MT* 23). A letter of 1887 contains more of the same: "I have vainly tried to escape from it [Royce's argument]. I still suspect it of inconclusiveness, but I frankly confess that I am *unable* to overthrow it" (*LWJ* 1: 265). James's doctrine of reference as leading or guiding the referrer to the referent through a connecting sequence of experiences also is found in the 1890 *The Principle of Psychology*: "All that a state of mind need do, in order to take cognizance of a reality, intend it, or be 'about' it, is to lead to a remoter state of mind which either acts upon the reality or resembles it" (445). Although the solution to Royce's argument was available to James as early as

Royce's argument begins with Descartes's method of systematic doubt, in which everything that is the slightest bit dubitable is to be put aside, bracketed, done without. Royce escapes from this slippery slope of doubt by holding that a proposition cannot be false unless it is false of some real-life individual; and, thus, in doubting a proposition it cannot be doubted that it at least succeeds in referring to some existent reality. Furthermore, we know for sure that we believe or doubt some proposition and thus can be equally certain that we successfully secure reference to some real-life reality, even if it be only a region of space-time at which the event reported by the proposition fails to occur. But how is such reference to be explained? Royce's argument amounts to a transcendental deduction of the this-or-no-way form according to which reference is possible only if the referring term and its referents are the contents of a single Absolute Mind.

The argument proceeds by rejecting the representative realist or, in James's terminology, intellectualist, view of reference that has a mental image mysteriously jump out of its own skin and hit some transcendent target. A person's image of the Empire State Building, or its name, in some unexplained way manages to reach out and grab hold of the Empire State Building itself. Royce finds this account unacceptable because the reference relation is a nonmediated, primitive relation that is empirically vacuous, being an instance of James's reviled nonempirical saltatory relation. It is incapable of explaining how the finite mind is able to aim at and hit its Empire State Building target. As James put it in his exposition of Royce, "If thought be one thing and reality another, by what pincers, from out of all the realities, does the thought pick out the special one it intends to know?" (*ECR* 386) So far James is in complete agreement with Royce.

Having disposed of the representative realist or intellectualist account of reference, Royce goes on to contend that the only possible way in which reference can succeed is if the referring idea in the finite mind, along with its real-life referent, are parts of a single mind, the Absolute, that brings it about via its intention that the former refers to the latter. This results in an idealism in which everything, along with our finite minds and their contents, is an idea in the Absolute Mind.

1884, his theory of reference had not yet been sufficiently developed and refined, as it later was to be in *Essays in Radical Empiricism, Pragmatism*, and *The Meaning of Truth*, so that he could have sufficient confidence in it. As Sprigge has properly pointed out, "Although when he first wrote the [1884] article he doubted the adequacy of its psychological and practical solution as an alternative to Royce's more mystical one, he eventually thought it only required a more thorough working out to provide an adequate philosophical riposte thereto" (*JB* 31). James, as was his wont, also vastly exaggerated his debt to Miller's 1893 essay. In fact, it was Miller who owed a debt to James, as his essay is a rehash of James's 1884 article. For an insightful account of James's reaction to Royce's argument, see Kuklick, *RAP* 176–9 and his *JR* 25–37 for a detailed explanation of the argument itself.

James, of course, rejects Royce's argument that reference can be secured only in this way. But at exactly what station does James get off the Royce Express? He agrees with Royce that there is nothing problematic about how a mind is acquainted with or refers to one of its own ideas. Following Grote, he dubs it "knowledge as acquaintance" (*MT* 18–9). To be conscious of a content or a that ipso facto is to know or refer to it. It was seen in James's account of general concepts that there is nothing problematic about a mind's identifying and reidentifying one of its ideas, this serving as the basis for his in-principle private language. James further agrees with Royce that there is nothing problematic about how a mind uses one of its ideas to refer to another of its ideas. For here the referent aimed at is an empirical content of the mind of the referer, unlike representative realism, in which it is transcendent. In response to James's challenge to explain how it is possible for the representative realist to know what is the target of his purported reference, John Russell responded, "When I think, I know what I am thinking about, just as I know what mark I am aiming at when I am engaged in target-shooting" (*ERE* 152–3). But this analogy misfires because, for the representative realist, the referential target is a transcendent one and thereby cannot be aimed at. If the target itself were a content of the mind of the referer there would be no such problem, for it would know what target was aimed at by its referential thought. And, moreover, it could bring it about via its own intending that this thought referred to this target.

James agrees with all this, so how does he escape from Royce's argument? In his summary of Royce's argument, James writes that it assumes "that we *could* make anything in our own mind refer to anything else *there*, – provided, of course, the two things were objects of a single act of thought" (*ECR* 386). Although James agrees that the mind has this power to intend that one of its ideas refer to another one of its ideas, he rejects the requirement that the relata in this referential relation be copresent in "a single act of thought." An earlier idea can refer to a later idea in the same mind via an ambulatory relation that *guides* or *leads* the thinker through a connecting sequence of intermediary experiences. For example, a person located at Thirty-seventh Street and Fifth Avenue at time t_1 entertains an image of the Empire State Building or its name that guides or leads him, quite literally, through a sequence of intervening steps to Thirty-fourth Street and Fifth Avenue at the later time t_4, at which time he has a vivid percept of the building. If the initiating idea at t_1 involved the use of the name "Empire State Building," it would not resemble the terminating percept. When the 1884 "The Function of Cognition" was reprinted in the 1909 *The Meaning of Truth*, James added a note saying that it gave "undue prominence . . .

to resembling, which altho a fundamental function in knowing truly, is so often dispensed with" (*MT* 32).

James's alternative analysis of reference, at least on its face, seems to be as idealistic as Royce's, for the referential relation is between *ideas in a single mind*, albeit successive rather than simultaneous ones. James claims that "Experiences are all" (*ECR* 552) and that "experience and reality come to the same thing" (*MT* 64). He boasts that his pragmatism converts the "empty notion of a static relation of 'correspondence' [reference] . . . between our minds and reality, into that of a rich and active commerce . . . between particular thoughts of ours, *and the great universe of other experiences in which they play their parts and have their uses*" (*P* 39; my italics). "The only function that one experience can perform is to lead into another experience; and the only fulfillment we can speak of is the reaching of a certain experienced end" (65). It would be a mistake, however, to jump from surface appearances to the conclusion that James was an idealist, for it will be seen in Chapter 7 that James rejected, at least for the period of time between 1904 and 1906, the view of experience as intrinsically mental or subjective and held instead that an experience is neither mental nor physical *simpliciter*, but becomes one or the other only when taken as functioning in a certain manner. This doctrine of "pure experience" or, as Russell called it, "neutral monism," involves a rejection of the Cartesian mental–physical dualism. It will be seen in Chapter 10 that James ultimately rejected his doctrine of pure experience and espoused a type of panpsychism or idealism as his final philosophy.

James says over and over again that the earlier thought *leads* or *guides* the thinker to the later one through a sequence of connected experiences, but exactly how does it do this? James's account of the manner in which the earlier referring thought leads to the later referent thought through a connecting sequence of experiences contains the same clash between the normative and nonnormative causal accounts as was found to infect his account of the connection between a general idea and its associated behavioral disposition. On the one hand, James says that the singular referential idea is an "impulse" (*MT* 80) that "instigates"(*P* 97), "inspires" (*P* 99), or "tends to call" (*MT* 96) the sequence of steps that "follows on" it (*MT* 34). These are nonnormative causal notions, as is his talk about the successive steps "obeying their [the ideas'] tendencies" (*MT* 29), with the referent being "whatever terminates" the sequence (*MT* 64). This does not make any room for a distinction between a right and a wrong referent for the original, initiating idea.

For the most part, however, James describes the connection between the initial and final ideas in normative terms. Herein he speaks of the initial idea's "intent" (*MT* 129) or what it "had in mind" (*ERE* 31), and its "fulfilled intention" (*ERE* 29) when the terminating idea has a "sense of fulfillment" (*ERE* 43). The process of locating an idea's referent requires "looking in its direction" (*ERE* 43). "Whatever terminates" the sequence, pace the purely causal account, need not be the referent of the initial idea, as it might not fulfill its intent. Not only must there be something that the referer initially has in mind, but each of the steps in the sequence must be anticipated and the referer must be "conscious of [their] continuing each other" (*ERE* 23) as each "passes into another" (*ERE* 25). There are "felt transitions" between the successive stages in the leading or guiding (*ERE* 29), a "feeling of continuously growing fulfillment" (*MT* 63).

The conscious intent of the initial idea, involving anticipation of the subsequent steps, is called its "penumbra," "halo," and "fringe."[10] These are not distinct sensible ideas, such as anticipatory images, but, rather, vague feelings of tendencies. They involve anticipations of the kinaesthetic sensations that the referer will experience as he walks along Fifth Avenue toward the Empire State Building and of what he will experience when he finally gets there. This requires that the content of the referer's mind at the initial moment, t_1, be enriched so as to accommodate the halo of felt anticipations. The content of his halo will change with each step he takes. It is by the halo of felt expectations and resolutions that the initiating idea at t_1 can intend the terminating idea at t_4. Furthermore, the uncontested occupation of the referer's mind with the thought of his subsequent walk down Fifth Avenue to Thirty-fourth Street constitutes an intention, or willing to so act, for James.

Is James's account of singular concepts as mired in subjectivism as his account of general concepts was found to be? One way in which it is has to do with his including in the criteria for a successful terminating experience that the referer finds it "worth while to have been led to" this experience (*P* 98). "Agreement thus turns out to be essentially an affair of leading – leading that is useful because it is into quarters that contain objects that are important" (*P* 103). To count as the referent of the initial idea the terminating experience "must yield satisfaction" (*P* 104). As was pointed out in the discussion of the "house along the cow-path" in Chapter 5, persons can differ in the satisfaction they experience upon coming upon the house (remember that it might contain a hungry wicked witch). Similarly, the Empire State Building might contain a crazed Palestinian mass murderer, which could result in one person being pleased to wind up there because he wants his life to end but cannot bring himself to commit suicide whereas another person, who wants to go on living, is displeased with the outcome. It was de-

---

[10] For a valuable account of these concepts see William J. Gavin's *WJ*.

cided to do James a favor and eliminate conative and emotional states from his web, thus making it a web of belief rather than a web of mentation. The same move is to be made here.

But eliminating personal satisfactions as being, at least in part, determinative of what constitutes the referent of a singular thought does not eliminate all of the subjectivistic worries occasioned by James's account. A singular concept, for James, really is a type of causal recipe that intentionally guides the referer through a succession of experientially vouchsafed steps that terminates in grabbing the referent by the lapels, that is, having a direct perception of it or what goes proxy for it, as is the case with the mental states of others and theoretical entities. The problem is that persons will have different causal recipes for getting hold of a given object because of their different spatial positions. For example, a person who is at Thirty-first Street and Fifth Avenue at t_1 will have a different causal recipe for reaching the Empire State Building than does a person located at that time at Thirty-seventh Street and Fifth Avenue. The former recipe involves vague anticipations of what will be experienced as he journeys north up Fifth Avenue from Thirty-first Street; the latter, of what will be experienced as he journeys south down Fifth Avenue from Thirty-seventh Street. Does this variation in causal recipes across differently positioned referers constitute an objectionable type of subjectivism?

There is available to James an easy way of dispelling any worries about subjectivism because of this variation in the meaning of singular concepts. He could avail himself of a variant of Frege's sense-reference distinction or Mill's connotation-denotation one. Because Jones and Smith attach different meanings to the singular concept of the Empire State Building in the sense that they have different causal recipes for guiding them there, it does not follow that these respective recipes cannot guide them to one and the same building. Furthermore, James has an account for their terminating percepts being of one and the same object based on a coincidence between their indexical references, a touching of their index fingers as they point to the building. Whether one is pleased and the other displeased in coming upon the building is irrelevant, in my amended account of James, to whether they are co-referers.

It is via overt acts of ostension that they ultimately are able to hook their referring terms onto the world and, moreover, know that they are co-referers. In his "Syllabus of Philosophy 3" for 1902–3, James wrote: " 'Two can't have the same object, because each has its object inside of itself.' Pragmatic answer: How can I tell *where* your object is except by your acts? To show where, you point to *my* object with your hand which I see" (*ML* 269). When the index fingers of two referers actually touch each other it establishes that their respective referents are spatially coincident and thus one and the same.[11] James speaks of "that spot wherein our hands meet, and where each of us begins to work if he wishes to make the hall [our common referent] change before the other's eye" (*ERE* 41). It is not just the spatial coincidence of different acts of ostension that establishes co-reference but also the coordinated manner in which the co-referers act upon their common referent that does. "Your hand lays hold of one end of a rope and my hand lays hold of the other end. We pull against each other. Can our two hands be mutual objects in their experience, and the rope not be mutual also? What is true of the rope is true of any other percept" (*ERE* 38). Although persons who indexically co-refer to the Empire State Building at a given time cannot together lift or push the building, they can jointly act on it in various ways; imagine that they are realizing the pipe dream of every tin man and are jointly aluminum siding the building. It is through such shared activity that Berkeley's "congeries of solipsisms" is escaped (*ERE* 38–9). This emphasis on the need for shared activity for two people to be co-referers is in the spirit of the Mead–Dewey requirement that there be a social community of people engaged in cooperative pursuits for there to be linguistic communication. James would have to apply the same communitarian requirements to general concepts if he were to escape the radical subjectivism of his in-principle private-language account of them; however, it would be beyond the scope of this book to attempt this on his behalf.

Even if James's theory of singular reference can avoid the problem of subjectivism, it still faces what Lovejoy aptly called "the paradox of the alleged futurity of yesterday."[12] The paradox arises from James's theory of meaning, along with those of Peirce and Dewey, being completely future oriented. Recall that James, following Peirce, said that

to develop a thought's meaning we need only determine what conduct it is *fitted to produce*: that conduct is for us its *sole* significance. . . . To attain perfect clearness in our thoughts of an object, then, we need only consider what conceivable effect of a practical kind the object may involve – what sensations we are to *expect* from it, and what reactions we must *prepare*. Our conception of these *effects*, whether immediate or remote, is then for us the *whole* of our conception of the object, so far as that conception has positive significance at all. (*P* 28–9; my italics)

That the pragmatic theory of meaning was exclusively future oriented is made manifest in the following remark by Peirce.

But of the myriads of forms into which a proposition may be translated, what is that one which is to be called its *very meaning*? It is, according to the pragmati-

[11] Andrew Reck perceptively pointed out that, for James, "The varying percepts are related to a single object when they are focused on a common location in space" (*WJ* 65).
[12] For a full account of this paradox, see my essay "Dewey and the Problem of the Alleged Futurity of Yesterday," *Philosophy and Phenomenological Research* (1962), 501–11.

cist, that form in which the proposition becomes applicable to human conduct, not in these or those special circumstances, nor when one entertains this or that special design, but that form which is most directly applicable to self-control under every situation, and to every purpose. *This is why he locates the meaning in future time; for future conduct is the only conduct that is subject to self-control.* (*CP* vol. 5, para. 425; my italics)

It was just seen that for James the meaning of a singular concept is a causal recipe for grabbing the referent by the lapels in the *future*. This is in accord with the underlying Promethean spirit of his philosophy in which our whole way of conceiving the world is geared to furthering our quest to gain control and mastery over objects so that we can use them to maximize desire-satisfaction. Toward this end we must be able to concoct recipes that will lead us to these objects so that we can effectively use them. This exclusively future-oriented causal theory of reference stands in stark contrast with the past-oriented causal or historical theories of singular reference, championed in recent times by Kripke, Donnellan, Putnam, and Burge, in which the causal chain begins in the past with a baptismal-type bestowal of a proper name that then gets continuously passed on from one referer to a subsequent one in an ongoing linguistic community and terminates in a present use of the name. Whereas this theory of reference fails to do justice to the pragmatic aspect of reference, James's theory seems to make it impossible to refer to a past object.

When confronted with this paradox James would respond by appeal to the way in which we ordinarily indirectly verify statements about the past. In regard to the problem of referring to the past person Julius Caesar, James wrote: "Caesar had, and my statement has, effects; and if these effects in any way run together, a concrete medium and bottom is provided for the determinate, cognitive relation, which, as a pure *actio in distans*, seemed to float too vaguely and unintelligibly" (*MT* 121). He also said that "All human thinking gets discursified; we exchange ideas; we lend and borrow verifications, get them from one another by means of social intercourse," which seems to bring in the ongoing linguistic community of the historical theory of reference of Kripke et al. (*P* 102). But James fails to realize that, according to his exclusively future-oriented pragmatic or operationalist theory of meaning, his claim that "Caesar *had* effects" or that "we lend and borrow verifications" has as its *whole* meaning a set of conditionalized predictions that report what experiences we will have in the future if we perform certain operations. The apparently retrospective meanings get converted into exclusively future-directed ones.

That it is impossible to refer to a past individual creates the following problem for reference to individuals in the future, which I owe to Henry Jackman. Imagine that I have a cap I have continuously owned since I purchased it in the K-Mart seven years ago, before it went high-class. I left it on a table in the next room and now entertain a thought of it. According to James, the meaning of this thought for me is a recipe that will guide me step by experiential step from where I am now to the cap on the table in the next room so that I can grab it by the "lapels." I follow this recipe and reach a cap that exactly resembles my initiating thought of it, even down to having a dark spot on its bill where the dog had an accident, but, unbeknownst to me, some practical joker, out to give a counterexample to James, has replaced it with an exact duplicate. I take the cap to be the referent of my initiating thought because it not only resembles my original cap but also satisfies all the pragmatic functions of the original cap, such as discouraging panhandlers from approaching me for money. But it is not my cap, and there seemingly is no way to explain why it is not without tracing the past history of this cap against that of my original cap in order to show that it is not spatio-temporally continuous with the original cap. Thus, unless it is possible to refer to a past object qua past object, it is not possible to determine that a present object is the referent of a past act of reference.

James has available to him the resources to escape from the problem of how reference can be made to an individual, as well as the more general paradox of the alleged futurity of yesterday. It was shown that he shuttled back and forth between an operationalist and content version of empiricism. What he needs to do is explicitly to recognize content empiricism as an additional species of empirical meaning in addition to that of operationalism. Thus, the meaning of my thought that Caesar crossed the Rubicon need not be exhausted by statements predicting what experiences I will have if I read certain books and the like but also involves a subjunctive conditional statement describing what experiences someone *would* have had if he *were* to have directly observed the crossing. The latter, of course, can be contrary to fact. In the case of my cap that is now in the next room, my causal recipe for getting my hands on it must be supplemented by a description of the cap's past history, its continuous history since I purchased it seven years ago in the K-Mart – that is, a description of the experiences that would have been had if an observer had continuously observed it over this seven-year interval.

What is the textual support for this way of interpreting, or should I say reinterpreting, James? Although for the most part James identified an idea's whole meaning with its operationalist meaning, especially when he was explicitly presenting his pragmatic theory of meaning, there are several crucial passages in which he countenanced content empiricism as another species of meaning. We have already seen his content empiricist manner of handling the man-circling-the-squirrel example and his distinction between the "function" of an idea and its "substantive content," with the latter being an idea's content empirical meaning (*SPP* 38). James introduced this distinction in a casual manner, failing to alert the reader that it undercuts his previous official commitment to a univocalist operationalist theory of meaning. A similar sort of sudden and casual qualification of the latter occurs in a footnote (!) in *The Varieties of Religious Experience* regarding the "objective truth" of religious experiences: "The word 'truth' is here taken to mean something additional to bare value for life, although the natural propensity of man is to believe that whatever has great value for life is thereby certified as true" (*VRE* 401). This crucial qualification of his former pragmatic theory of truth deserved to be put up in bright lights rather than to be buried in a footnote.

A begrudging and buried recognition of content empiricism is also found in James's much discussed treatment of whether an idea can have a meaning if there literally is no future, therefore denying a belief any pragmatic consequences. His discussion works with the examples of theism and atheism, misleadingly called "materialism" by James, but it is intended to have full generality. They differ in virtue of making different predictions about the *future* course of history, theism predicting that good will everlastingly win out over evil if we collectively exert our best moral efforts against evil, and materialism that all will end in death and destruction because the lower forces are ultimately in control. Notice that James interprets the future in question to be *quoad* our now asserting the theist or materialist proposition, not *quoad* the time of the event reported by the proposition asserted. From this he seems to infer the absurd consequence that, if there were to be no future, these seemingly opposing theories would have the same meaning – namely none at all.

He [the pragmatist] asks us to imagine how the pragmatic test can be applied if there is no future. Concepts for him are things to come back into experience with, things to make us look for differences. But by hypothesis there is to be no more experience and no possible differences can now be looked for. Both theories have shown all their consequences and, by the hypothesis we are adopting, these are identical. The pragmatist must consequently say that the two theories, in spite of their different-sounding names, mean exactly the same thing, and that the dispute is purely verbal. (*P* 50–1)

James also says that "It makes not a single jot of difference so far as the *past* of the world goes, whether we deem it to have been the work of matter or whether we think a divine spirit its author" (*P* 50). "Thus if no future detail of experience or conduct is to be deduced from our hypothesis, the debate between materialism and theism becomes quite idle and insignificant" (*EP* 127).

What are we to make of these highly counterintuitive claims? First, there is a minor problem of internal consistency. Elsewhere he says that

theism guarantees that "an ideal order . . . shall be permanently preserved" (*EP* 130). That the world comes to end, according to this rendering of theism, would settle the issue decisively against theism, *pace*
what James says. Let us not worry about this, for there are even more
serious difficulties.

Because "the debate between materialism and theism becomes quite
idle and insignificant" without a future, as lacking in emotional interest, does not entail that these theories are completely devoid of meaning. James is only expressing his personal dislike for such debates. This
becomes clear when he says that "in every *genuine* metaphysical debate
some practical issue . . . is involved," the "genuine" qualification being
a tip-off that an evaluatively based, disguised linguistic innovation is in
the offing (*P* 52; my italics). James adds that such debates are of
"purely intellectual" interest and urges his reader to avoid them (*EP*
126).[13] But such a debate, no matter how unworthy of a Promethean
subject's attention, must have some meaningful content since it has at
least an "intellectual" interest. By his use of "intellectual" and "idle
and insignificant," James is begrudgingly recognizing an additional species of meaning to that of operationalism or pragmatism. In the case of
the theism–materialism debate, this additional meaning is the content
empirical meaning of statements describing the past states of the universe.

A similar conclusion is to be drawn from his remark that "When a
play is once over, and the curtain down, you really make it no better by
claiming an illustrious genius for its author, just as you make it no worse
by calling him a common hack" (*EP* 127). The proper response to this
is that although your passing judgment on the worth of the author in
no way alters the aesthetic value of the completed play, the intrinsic
qualities of the play themselves serve as evidence for whether it has an
author at all, and, if so, how good a one. Thus, the choice between the
author–no author hypotheses or the good author–hack author hypotheses is decidable even if the world comes to an end when the curtain
comes down. But this requires that these hypotheses have genuine *past*
empirical content, as is required by content empiricism. Otherwise, the
paradox of the alleged futurity of yesterday arises.

Another flaw in James's discussion is his claim that, if there is no
future, then "no future detail of experience or conduct is to be deduced from our hypothesis" of theism (*P* 52). Whether there be a

---

[13] This disguised normative claim is of a piece with Dewey's responding to the charge that
his exclusively future-oriented theory of meaning is committed to the paradox of the
alleged futurity of yesterday by saying that "To isolate the past, dwelling upon it for its
own sake and giving it the eulogistic name of knowledge, is to substitute the reminis-
cence of old-age for effective intelligence" (MW, 10: 10).

future or not does not make any difference in respect to what predictions a hypothesis logically entails, only in respect to the truth of these predictions, it being assumed by James that all predictions are false if there be no future. If having predictive consequences is necessary for a hypothesis to be meaningful, then a hypothesis can possess such pragmatic meaning even when there is no future.

Maybe the most decisive refutation of James's claim that there is no difference in meaning between atheism and theism in the no-future case is that it winds up violating the principle of the temporal homogeneity of *being evidence for* – namely, if E counts as evidence for or confirms proposition p at time T, then E counts as evidence for or confirms p at any time. *Being evidence for* must not be confounded with *being taken to be evidence for.* The former, in spite of being an epistemic relation, is existentially grounded in an objective relation between two worldly states of affairs, whereas the latter is relative to the epistemic state of a subject – what he knows and believes at a certain time. A certain type of rash is taken by a doctor, but not a layman, as evidence of a certain disease; but nevertheless the rash is evidence for both of them of this disease. Being evidence for is homogeneous not only among times but persons as well. James seems to violate the temporal homogeneity of *being evidence for* when he says that a benevolent course of events in the future would serve as evidence for, even be verificatory of, theism, but this very same course of events in the past would not be.

There are indications that James saw serious difficulties with his discussion of the theism–materialism debate in the no-future case in his 1898 ''Philosophical Conceptions and Practical Results''; for when he repeated it eight years later in *Pragmatism*, he added, ''I am supposing, of course, that the theories *have* been equally successful in their explanations of what is'' (*P* 51). Thus, James seems to be assuming, although he does not explicitly state it, that the past of the no-future world in his example is an ambiguous mixed bag of moral good and evil that does not speak clearly either for atheism or for theism. But, if he is to handpick his example in this manner, while he escapes the foregoing charge of relativizing *being evidence for* to a time, he cannot generalize from his example, as he plainly does; for immediately after completing his discussion of the no-future example, he draws this general conclusion: ''Accordingly, in *every* genuine metaphysical debate some practical issue, however conjectural and remote, is involved,'' in which the ''issue'' concerns what is future *quoad* now (*P* 522; my italics).

We do not have just to infer that James saw a difficulty in his 1898 address. In *The Meaning of Truth* he comes right out and tells us what it is: ''I had no sooner given the address than I perceived a flaw in that part of it; but I left the passage unaltered ever since, because the flaw did not spoil its illustrative value" (*MT* 103).[14] James not only mislocates the source of the difficulty, failing to see that it temporally relativizes *being evidence for* and makes meaning wholly prospective, but makes a concession to the content empiricist that undercuts his claim that an idea's pragmatic consequences exhaust its meaning. He finds the difficulty with his former identification of the whole meaning of theism with what is outwardly observable in the future to be analogous to what we find missing in a soulless "automatic sweetheart" whose outwardly observable behavior is "absolutely indistinguishable from a spiritually animated maiden, laughing, talking, blushing, nursing us, and performing all feminine offices as tactfully and sweetly as if a soul were in her" (*MT* 103). What we find woefully inadequate is its lack of inner conscious states, because its outward behavior "is valued mainly as an expression, as a manifestation of the accompanying consciousness believed in" (*MT* 103). James's worry about whether it is good for her too shows him to be a closet Cartesian, as does his use of the Cartesian argument from analogy for the existence of other minds (*MT* 24 and 30, and *ERE* 36 and 38). Analogously, what we sorely miss in his former rendering of theism in terms of the future triumph of goodness, provided we do our moral best, is the inner conscious states of God, for humans desire a being "who will inwardly recognize them and judge them sympathetically." Herein what is *outwardly* observable, whether future or not, cannot constitute the whole meaning. A wedge is being driven between the inner states of consciousness that constitute at least part of the statement about God or the real sweetheart and what is outwardly observable. These inner states would constitute part of the *content empirical* meaning of statements about the two individuals.

James's change in the way he interpreted the concept of God, in which his pragmatic view of God as only our ally in our efforts to make good win out over evil in the future gets supplemented with being the possessor of inner consciousness, mirrors a change in the way he conceived of the idealist's Absolute. In *Pragmatism*, James gave an outlandish reductive pragmatic analysis of the Absolute in terms of its licensing us to take an occasional moral holiday, as it assures the eventual tri-

---

[14] One cannot help but wonder why James did not go to the trouble of correcting this flaw when he reprinted this discussion in *Pragmatism*. The only explanation I can offer is that he had an incredibly low threshold of boredom and just couldn't get himself to chew over an earlier discussion. To be sure, James eagerly read proofs of his work, but only to improve its style, not its philosophical substance. Another example of James's block against making substantive revisions in what he had written is his letter to Abauzit, the French translator of *The Varieties of Religious Experience*, in which he tells him to go ahead with his translation in spite of his book having a flaw in it that Abauzit had brought to his attention (Appendix 6 of *VRE* 508). There is something to be said, after all, in favor of the Germans, about whose method of investigation in psychology James said: "taxes patience to the utmost, and could hardly have arisen in a country whose natives could be *bored*" (*PP* 192).

umph of good over evil no matter what we do. "The cash value when he [the Absolute] is pragmatically interpreted" is that men "may relax their anxieties occasionally, in which the don't-care mood is also right for men, and moral holidays in order" (*P* 41). In the "Preface" to *The Meaning of Truth*, James expresses mock surprise and disappointment at the rejection of his "conciliatory olive-branch" by his absolute idealist opponents.

Using the pragmatic test of the meaning of concepts, I had shown the concept of the absolute to *mean* nothing but the holiday giver, the banisher of cosmic fear. . . . Apparently my absolutist critics fail to see the workings of their own minds in any such picture, so all that I can do is to apologize, and take my offering back. The Absolute is true in *no* way then, and least of all, by the verdict of the critics, in the way which I assigned. (*MT* 5)

But this is not the end of the story, for subsequently, in *A Pluralistic Universe*, James supplements his reductive pragmatic analysis with a substantive content. "On the debit side of the account the absolute, *taken seriously, and not as a mere name for our right occasionally to drop the strenuous mood and take a moral holiday*, introduces all those tremendous irrationalities into the universe which a frankly pluralistic theism escapes" (*PU* 57; my italics). It is typical of James to make this major change in his theory of meaning in an offhand remark, without any indication that it involves a countenancing of another species of meaning in addition to his official pragmatic one. Supposedly, since the Absolute is a mind, it has the same sort of inner consciousness as does his theistic God and, hopefully, his sweetheart.

James had an even more liberal theory of meaning than has so far been depicted. In addition to countenancing an operationalist and content empirical species of meaning, both of which meet the requirements of the empirical postulate of his Radical Empiricism, he even found room for theoretical meaning. As will be seen in Chapter 11, most of the time James favored an instrumentalist theory of theoretical entities in science, according to which they are only convenient heuristic fictions that aid our ability to make inferences and calculations. But when it came to the Soul and God, James did not give such a reductive instrumentalist account. Although they had to play a role in explaining empirical phenomena, their nature is not reducible to the phenomena they explain.

James claimed that the substantive Soul, although devoid of explanatory power in psychology, did help to make sense of the moral life and certain extraordinary conscious states. That he is even willing to ask the question whether the theory of the Soul, understood as "both immaterial and simple," has "advantages as a theory over the simple phenomenal notion of a stream of thought accompanying a stream of cerebral activity, by a law yet unexplained," shows that he is countenancing another species of meaning in addition to the above two empirical species, since this sort of soul is accessible to neither external nor internal sense (*PP* 325). Although "The Soul-theory is, then, a superfluity, *so far as accounting for the actually verified facts of conscious experience*," it could have an explanatory value in metaphysics when understood as a transcendent "more" (*PP* 329; my italics). "For my own part I confess that the moment I become metaphysical and try to define the more, I find the notion of some sort of an *anima mundi* thinking in all of us to be a more promising hypothesis, in spite of all its difficulties, than that of a lot of absolutely individual souls" (*PP* 328). "The reader who finds comfort in the idea of the Soul, is, however, perfectly free to continue to believe in it; for our reasonings have not established the non-existence of the Soul; they have only proved its superfluity for scientific purposes" (*PP* 332).

James also puts the Soul theory to work in explaining and justifying our belief that we have free will, as was seen in Chapters 3 and 4. The question of whether the amount of effort we make to attend to an idea in a case of conflict is "spontaneous or unpredictable in advance" is "a purely speculatively one, for we have no means of objectively ascertaining whether our feelings react on our nerve-processes or not" (*PP* 424). He then asks whether the Soul might not be "an original psychic force" that we need to postulate for the purpose of leading the morally strenuous life, which question, we know from Chapter 4, he answered in the affirmative (*PP* 428). Clearly, James is treating the Soul, even in his non-Cartesian version that denies an endurance to it, as a theoretical entity whose nature is not reducible to the empirical phenomena that it is invoked to explain. It is no mere heuristic device.

Another example of James's countenancing a nonreducible theoretical type of meaning is his treatment of Cardinal Newman's scholastic theory of God's nature in terms of his essential "omni"-properties, as well as those of absolute simplicity and aseity. Initially, he recognizes some "emotional worth" in his theology, such as might be possessed by poetry (*VRE* 349). But he heaps rhetorical scorn on the divine attributes, at least the "metaphysical" ones, charging them with being "destitute of all intelligible *significance*" because they have no practical consequences for our lives (*VRE* 351; my italics). "Pray, what specific act can I perform in order to adapt myself the better to God's simplicity?" (*VRE* 352). But he then goes on begrudgingly to grant that "Men . . . involuntarily *intellectualize* their religious experience. They need formulas, just as they need fellowship in worship" (*VRE* 361; my italics). In the italicized portions of these quotations we see the same contrast between an idea's "significance" and its "intellectual" meaning or content that was found in James's discussion of the atheism–materialism debate when there is no future. Furthermore, even on his narrow operationalistic theory of meaning, Newman's theology counts as meaningful because it forms an elaborate deductive system, and thereby licenses certain "pencil and paper" operations. Herein is the poverty of operationalism.

Yet another example of James's attributing a theoretical meaning to a concept that cannot be cashed in pragmatically is his discussion of the Eucharist. "Since the accidents of the wafer don't change in the Lord's supper, and yet it has become the very body of Christ, it must be that the change is in the substance solely. The bread-substance must have been withdrawn, and the divine substance substituted miraculously without altering the immediate sensible properties" (P 46–7). This sounds like the description of an empirically vacuous change, but surprisingly James goes on to endorse the meaningfulness of the Eucharist doctrine by saying, herein "The substance-notion breaks into life . . . with tremendous effect, if once you allow that substances can separate from their accidents, and exchange these latter" (P 47). Plainly, James is willing to countenance as meaningful a concept that has a theoretical meaning that does not entail anything empirical.

So far it has been found that, in spite of James's official endorsement of the pragmatic theory of meaning as capturing the *whole* meaning of a concept, he also recognized a content empirical and theoretical sort of meaning. Thus, when all is said and done, James did not have a pragmatic theory of meaning but, as Suckiel has nicely put it, a theory of pragmatic meaning (Suckiel, PP 31 and 145). Giuffrida and Madden held that James recognized a "definitional" or cognitive" meaning in addition to a pragmatic one (JMS 27). Thayer, in basic agreement, called this extrapragmatic meaning "definitional meaning" and "antecedent cognitive meaning" (JT 3 and 4, and introduction to MT xxviiff). Suckiel also finds in James a recognition of an idea's "cognitive meaning or intelligible content" (PP 44) Basically, my account is an attempt to add further flesh to theirs by spelling out what James meant by "definitional" and "cognitive" meaning.

While it is reasonably clear from the text that James countenanced a content empirical species of meaning (as well as a theoretical one) in addition to his favored pragmatic one, it is not clear whether he thought that possessing a pragmatic meaning is necessary for an idea or belief to be meaningful. It was suggested that the belief that Caesar crossed the Rubicon, in addition to possessing an operationalist meaning in terms of how one would indirectly verify this belief in the future, also has a "substantive content," which I called its "content empirical" meaning, consisting in the experiences that would have been had were an observer to have been present. Without the latter sort of meaning James's theory of meaning is committed to the paradox of the alleged futurity of yesterday. But is having a pragmatic or operationalist meaning a necessary condition for a belief to be meaningful for James? I believe that it is, as seems to be attested to in James's final letter to John E. Russell.

> Dear Russell: We seem now to have laid bare our exact difference. According to me, 'meaning' a certain object and 'agreeing' with it are abstract notions of both of which definite concrete accounts can be given.
>
> According to you, they shine by their own inner light and no further account can be given. They may even 'obtain' (*in cases where human verification is impossible*) and make no empirical difference to us. To me, using the pragmatic method of testing concepts, this would mean that the word truth might on certain occasions have no meaning whatever. I still must hold to its having always a meaning, and continue to contend for that meaning being unfoldable and representable in experiential terms. (*ERE* 153; my italics)

What James is saying is that, without our being able in practice to verify a belief, which, it will be recalled, requires our being able to pin down the referents of its referring terms, the belief is meaningless. If we were completely causally cut off from the past Caesar, so that no future indirect verification is practically possible, the belief that Caesar crossed the Rubicon, in spite of having a content empirical meaning, would not be meaningful. James's point can be recast in terms of a distinction that was made by subsequent logical positivists. Schlick distinguished between a statement's actual and its logical verification, Carnap between its practical and its theoretical verifiability, and Ayer between its practical and its in-principle verifiability. The latter member of each of the three distinctions corresponds to James's content empirical meaning, since it concerns what an *ideal* observer who was suitably equipped and stationed in space and time would have observed. The former concerns how it is practically possible for a present person to verify a statement, this often involving indirect verification. James does not think that the mere "logical," "theoretical," or "in-principle" possibility of verification is enough for meaningfulness. There also must be the practical possibility of verification by a present person. This completes my account of James's theory of meaning, and it now can be asked what theory of truth falls out of it, on the assumption that a theory of meaning supplies truth-conditions for sentences.

The following argument attempts to show what theory of truth is entailed by James's pragmatic theory of meaning, if this assumption is accepted.

The Truth-Conditions Argument

  (i) A belief is true if and only if it corresponds with reality. [necessary truth in virtue of the definition of "true"]
 (ii) A belief is true if and only if its meaning corresponds with reality. [necessary truth (P 131)]
(iii) The meaning of a belief is a set of conditionalized predictions of

Unlike pure experience, the stuff of which reality is made is not onto-logically neutral.[11] Therefore, pure experience is not identical with but rather has been replaced by the conscious and spiritual realities of his final two books and *The Varieties of Religious Experience*, because pure experience is pure potentiality but these spirits are already partly deter-mined in virtue of having the monadic property of being conscious.[12]

This completes the exposition of the Promethean pragmatism of Wil-liam James. But James had a deep mystical streak that struggled against his Promethean pragmatism, and it is now its turn to occupy the spot-light. Herein the deep division within James's self is not between his scientific and moral-agent self but between all of the above and his mystical self.

---

[11] I am in complete agreement with Bruce Kuklick's claim that "neutral [pure] experience was now [subsequent to 1905] not neutral, but throbbing, alive, constantly coalescing and recoalescing. This conscious experience was not unitary but contained ever-widening spans of consciousness within some of which human consciousness might lie" (*RAP* 333).

[12] Henry Levinson, in what otherwise is a very sensitive and insightful interpretation of James, argues that the doctrine of pure experiences applies to the spiritual and mystical realities countenanced by *The Varieties of Religious Experience* on the ground that these beings qualify as physical, as they are causally efficacious (*RI* 183). To be sure, these spirits, such as God, are causally efficacious, but they are not so in a law-like manner. God's causally efficacious will, for example, does not work in accordance with any uni-versal causal law. What Levinson fails to realize is that, for James, a being qualifies as physical only if it is a member of a sequence whose members are connected by causal laws.

The Anti-Promethean Mystic

8

The Self

James's Promethean pragmatist, being a restless, indefatigable desire-satisfaction maximizer, was seen in Part 1 to be always on the make in his quest to have it all. Toward this end he had to adopt an externalized stance toward worldly objects, since his concern was with successfully manipulating them for his own purposes. His pragmatic theory of meaning and truth supplied him with recipes for successfully riding herd on them. In addition, they served as a univocal methodological reconciler or mediator between the projects and interests of his many different selves, but only a partial reconciler because conflicts still remained between the perspectives of these selves, especially those of the moral agent and the scientist with regard to the issue of determinism and free will as well as bifurcationism. The stronger medicine of a Poo-bahistic ontological relativism was needed, requiring him never to go anywhere or do anything without being armed with a "qua"-clause. Even the doctrine of Pure Experience, which turned out to be a failed though noble experiment, had a reconciling intent. Poo-bahism, however, will be seen in Chapter 10 to be in conflict with the mystical self's absolutistic outlook, creating the deepest unresolved aporia in James's philosophy, and it will be the task of Chapter 11 to explore ways of resolving it within a broadly Jamesian approach. All of these pragmatic theses about meaning, truth, freedom, and reality were suitable options for the will to believe, James's ultimate Promethean doctrine, as it licenses us to believe in matters metaphysical (and thereby epistemically undecidable) in a manner that will best enable us to have it all.

But the stance of the externalized Promethean pragmatist toward worldly objects, including other persons, did not satisfy James's deep mystical longings for a more intimate and personal relation to them, a relation so intimate that it would ultimately involve a union with them, yet one that stopped short of the numerical identity of monistic mysticism. To experience such union it was necessary to overcome his active Promethean self and learn to become passive so that he could penetrate to the inner consciousness of worldly objects through acts of conceptless sympathetic intuition. The promethean quest to have it all has given way to the mystical quest to spiritually penetrate all.

All references in this chapter are to *The Principles of Psychology*, unless otherwise noted.

This mystical quest for intimacy and union was both deeply rooted in William James the man and endemic to his era, which felt threatened by the seemingly meaningless, impersonal world that had become the professed official view of science since the rise of the "new physics" in the seventeenth century. It seems as if everyone in New England in the second half of the nineteenth century had been inoculated by the Concord bacilli of mystical transcendentalism as an immunization against this threat. Along with Peirce and Dewey, James made the overcoming of this pernicious bifurcation between man and nature the chief goal of his philosophy.

James accepts without question the bifurcationist upshot of science. "The essence of things for science is not to be what they seem, but to be atoms and molecules moving to and from each other according to strange laws" (*PP* 1230). What James means by this cryptic remark is that "Sensible phenomena are pure delusions for the mechanical philosophy" based on modern science (*PP* 1258). "Even today, secondary qualities themselves – heat, sound, light – have but a vague place in the scheme of understanding. In the common-sense meaning and for practical purposes, they are absolutely objective, absolutely physical. For the physicist, they are subjective. For him, only form, mass, and movement have an outer reality" (*ERE* 266).

This scientific image of the world challenges our deepest humanistic longings and aspirations. Some of the most eloquent and poignant passages in James attest to the sense of alienation and forlornness wrought by this bifurcation. Science holds that "all the things and qualities men love, *dulcissima mundi nomina,* are but illusions of our fancy attached to accidental clouds of dust which will be dissipated by the eternal cosmic weather as carelessly as they were formed" (*PP*1260). "The romantic spontaneity and courage are gone, the vision is materialistic and depressing. Ideals appear as inert by-products of physiology; what is higher is explained by what is lower and treated forever as a case of nothing but – nothing but something else of a quite inferior sort" (*P* 15). Our "personal" and "romantic" view of life is incompatible with the mechanistic and materialistic world view of science.

Science has come to be identified with a certain fixed general belief, the belief that the deeper order of Nature is mechanical exclusively, and that non-mechanical categories are irrational ways of conceiving and explaining even such a thing as human life. Now this mechanical rationalism, as one may call it, makes, if it becomes one's only way of thinking, a violent breach with the ways of thinking that have until our own time played the greatest part in human history. Religious thinking, ethical thinking, poetical thinking, teleological, emotional, sentimental thinking, what one might call the personal view of life to distinguish it from the impersonal and mechanical, and the romantic view of life to distinguish it from the rationalistic view, have been and even still are, outside of well-drilled scientific circles, the dominant forms of thought. But for mechanical rationalism, personality is an insubstantial illusion; the chronic belief of mankind that events may happen for the sake of their personal significance is an abomination; and the notions of our grandfathers about oracles and omens, divinations and apparitions, miraculous changes of heart and wonders worked by inspired persons, answers to prayer and providential leadings, are a fabric absolutely baseless, a mass of sheer *un*truth. (*EPR* 134–5; see also *PU* 16)

Not only does the mechanistic and materialistic worldview of science undermine our personal and romantic ways of thinking, it renders the world an unfit habitation for a moral agent, as it gives him no reason for wanting to take life seriously, and this is the worst defect in a philosophy because it does not give our active propensities any

object whatever to press against. A philosophy whose principle is so incommensurate with our most intimate powers as to deny them all relevancy in universal affairs, as to annihilate their motives at one blow, will be even more unpopular than pessimism. . . . This is why materialism will always fail of universal adoption. . . . For materialism denies reality to the objects of almost all the impulses which we most cherish. . . . We demand in it [the universe] a *character* for which our emotions and active propensities shall be a match. (*PP* 940–1)

Any philosophy that presents a view of the world that is devoid of human significance is unacceptable. ''Nothing could be more absurd than to hope for the definitive triumph of any philosophy which should refuse to legitimate and to legitimate in an emphatic manner, the more powerful of our emotional and practical tendencies'' (*PP* 943). ''It surely is a merit in a philosophy to make the very life we lead seem real and earnest'' (*PU* 28).[1] Herein James is speaking both as a man and as a sociologist of philosophy.

James's panacea for the evils of scientifically based bifurcationism is to follow the way of inwardness, something that was later to be advocated by the existentialists and contemporary Continental philosophers.

The only form of thing that we directly encounter . . . is our own personal life. The only complete category of our thinking . . . is the category of personality, every other category being one of the abstract elements of that. And this systematic denial on Science's part of personality as a condition of events, this rigorous belief that in its own essential and innermost nature our world is a strictly impersonal world, may . . . be the very defect that our descendants will be most surprised at in our own boasted Science. (*EPR* 136–6)

This passage reveals the most fundamental assumption of James's philosophy – that the true nature of reality is to be ascertained not through the employment of symbols or concepts but rather through personal

[1] Given James's abhorrence of the dehumanizing effect of the bifurcation between man and nature that was wrought in the name of modern science, it is a mystery to me how Stuart Hampshire could say that ''Science was for him [James] a symbol of health and metaphysics a relapse'' (*MW* 102).

experience. "So long as we deal with the cosmic and the general [as does Science], we deal only with the symbols of reality, but *as soon as we deal with private and personal phenomena as such, we deal with realities in the completest sense of the term*" (*VRE* 393). "Individuality is founded in feeling; and the recesses of feeling, the darker, blinder strata of character, are the only places in the world in which we catch real fact in the making, and directly perceive how events happen, and how work is actually done" (*VRE* 395).

James's advocacy of the inner approach to understanding reality develops an important theme expressed by Emerson, who wrote in his *Diary* for 1833: "There is a correspondence between the human soul and everything that exists in the world; more properly, everything that is known to man. Instead of studying things without, the principles of them all may be penetrated into within him. . . . The purpose of life seems to be to acquaint man with himself. . . . The highest revelation is that God is in every man." Through looking into our own souls – that is, introspecting our own minds – we discover the way things really are, and, not surprisingly, they will turn out to be of a like kind to ourselves. Thus, by giving pride of place to introspection, James assures that our view of the universe will be a personal, romantic one. Gerald Myers showed great insight when he wrote that "in intent, technique, and effect [introspection] is preeminently *personal*" (in R. Putnam, *CC* 20). As will be seen in the next chapter, it will enable each of us to address our universe as a "Thou."

In recommending that we follow the way of inwardness or subjectivism, James, in effect, is giving pride of place to introspection over the way of objective analysis in terms of cause and effect. In *The Principles of Psychology* James held these approaches in a precarious dynamic equilibrium, ultimately siding with the introspective approach. Not only did he say that "Introspective Observation is what we have to rely on first and foremost and always," but he let it have the final say when he dealt with humanistically valuable concepts, such as the self and its free will.

The story to be told in Part 2 of this book is how James ultimately came to rely on the inner approach of introspection to ascertain the nature of reality, projecting onto reality at large what he discovered from introspecting his own consciousness; not surprisingly, he ended by espousing consciousness to be the stuff of everything, the subject of experience partially merging with what he experienced in the same way different phases of a conscious process melt into each other. The story will begin in this chapter with an account of James's theory of the self and how he relied solely on the revelations of introspection to reveal its nature.

James's analysis is guided by the underlying leitmotiv of his whole pragmatic philosophy – that the essence of consciousness is to be selectively attentive on the basis of what is interesting or important. This issues in the distinctively Promethean theme that we create a world out of the big blooming, buzzing confusion of the perceptually given by attending selectively to those perceptions that are of interest to us and, moreover, within them, selecting those which are to be constitutive of the essence of the objects perceived. The famous chapter on "The Stream of Thought" in *The Principles of Psychology* immediately precedes that on "The Consciousness of the Self" and beautifully segues into it. Just after arguing that consciousness is interested in some parts of the given "to the exclusion of others, and welcomes or rejects – *chooses* from among them, in a word – all the while," it concludes with the observation that for each person there is an ultimate, across-the-board selective partitioning of the world into that which he takes to be "mine" and all the rest (220).

> One great splitting of the whole universe into two halves is made by each of us; and for each of us almost all of the interest attaches to one of the halves; but we all draw the line of division between them in a different place. . . . The altogether unique kind of interest which each human mind feels in those parts of creation which it can call *me* or *mine* may be a moral riddle, but it is a fundamental psychological fact. (*PP* 278)

This theme is immediately taken up at the beginning of "The Consciousness of the Self," where it is advanced as the basis of James's account of the Empirical Self, which comprises the Material Self (one's body and possessions), Social Self (how one is recognized by others), and Spiritual Self (one's mental dispositions and stream of consciousness).[2]

> The Empirical Self of each of us is all that he is tempted to call by the name of *me*. But it is clear that between what a man calls *me* and what he simply calls *mine* the line is difficult to draw. We feel and act about certain things that are ours very much as we feel and act about ourselves. (*PP* 279)

James contends that the commonsense distinction between *me* and *mine* is without grounds, one of his famous differences that make no difference, as a person directs the same attitudes, feelings, and actions toward what he calls *mine* as he does to what he calls *me*.

> *In its widest possible sense,* however *a man's Self is the sum total of all that* he CAN *call his,* not only his body and his psychic powers, but his clothes and his house, his wife and children, his ancestors and friends, his reputation and work, his lands and horses, and yacht and bank-account. All these things give him the same emotions. (*PP* 279)[3]

---

[2] The pure ego, whether in the form of a Cartesian soul substance or a Kantian transcendental ego, is charged by James with being explanatorily vacuous and therefore is not taken into account in his positive analysis of self-identity. Like Locke, but unlike Hume, he does not go so far as to accuse the concept of such an ego of being meaningless.

[3] It is interesting to note that James will offer an analysis of identity over time only for the Spiritual Self. No doubt he would have accepted a spatio-temporal continuity–type anal-

It would not be wildly anachronistic to see this attempt to analyze
Self identity in terms of distinctive sort of emotions, attitudes, and actions that give importance to Self identity as a forerunner of Derek
Parfit's account. Both men attempt to pare off from the bare numerical
identity of common sense those importance-bestowing features that are
its almost invariable but contingent accompaniments and replace the
former by the latter, thereby bringing about a number of departures
from common sense. For example, being identical with, pace common
sense, now will admit of degrees because being important does. Another revisionary consequence is to assimilate numerical to qualitative
identity. When a person, upon undergoing a psychological upheaval
that results in a radical difference in the way in which he remembers
and evaluates the importance of things, says, "I am no longer the same
person," it is not to be parsed in its ordinary manner of "I am numerically one and the same person throughout but have just changed in
my psychological traits." Rather, that person bears little if any numerical identity to the past person. James says, in regard to our Material
Self, that when we lose a loved one "a part of our very selves is gone"
(280), and, in regard to the person who has suffered a radical disrup-
ture in psychological continuity that he rightfully "disowns his former
me, gives himself a new name, identifies his present life with nothing
from out of the older time" (319; see also 351, especially his endorsement of the quotation in its n. 40).

The most startling departure from common sense is the jettisoning
of its transitivity requirement. While James's analysis of the identity of
the Spiritual Self, as will be seen, implausibly attempts to retain transitivity, plainly his analysis of the material self does not. For example, if

ysis of the identity of the Material Self when confined to one's own body. If other parts
of the Material Self were included, such as one's possessions, one's history would involve
an absurd array of disconnected world-lines similar to the mass Goodmanian cat whose
parts are all the individual cats there are. For example, you go wherever your jockey
shorts go, so right now you are taking a spin in the dryer, but you also go wherever your
coat goes, so right now you are also at the cleaner's being mangled, thereby suffering
from a severe case of spatial gappiness and disconnectedness. Further, we have no idea
of how a question of identity over time could be raised for your Social Self, other than
to make the answer parasitic upon the identity over time of one of your other selves.
That your Social and Material Self, other than your body, does not have a "real" identity
over time should make us suspicious of James's including them in the Empirical Self.
Maybe there is more to the me-mine distinction than he recognizes. I cannot resist using
this discussion of the Material Self as a pretext for quoting my favorite sentence among
the countless memorable sentences within his corpus: People who lose their possessions
"are all at once assimilated to the tramps and poor devils whom we so despise, and at
the same time removed farther than ever away from the happy sons of earth who lord it
over land and sea and men in the full-blown lustihood that wealth and power can give,
and before whom, stiffen ourselves as we will by appealing to anti-snobbish first principles, we cannot escape an emotion, open or sneaking, of respect and dread" (281). How
can someone write a sentence like that?

you and I co-own a desk beloved by both of us, it turns out, if transitivity is retained, that I am identical with you in virtue of each of us being able to call the desk "mine" and therefore, on this revisionary analysis, "me." As not even James would accept something as outré this, he must give up the transitivity requirement. (All three of these revisions, by the way, are to be found in the Parfit analysis.) While James had a whole-some respect for common sense, he avoided making it an Idol of the Tribe, and, as was seen in Part 1, made radical departures from it in his analyses of matter, mind, and truth. As he made clear in his chapter on "Pragmatism and Common Sense" in his *Pragmatism*, its tenets and categories are subject to revision and often are repositories for past metaphysical theories.

The crucial challenge to any revisionary analysis is to justify its depar-ture from common sense. Parfit's is that, by accepting his revisionary analysis and thereby potentially having a larger Self than is ordinarily allowed, we will be more altruistic and less subject to harmful regrets and fears about the gnawing tooth of time, but it is left obscure why this is so. James's justification, on the other hand, is based in part on his pragmatic theory of meaning requiring that every difference make some practical difference in terms of what experiences we are to expect or how we should act. As there is no experiential or behavioral differ-ence between the case of bare numerical identity and one in which the importance-bestowing relations obtain, there is no difference. Common sense mistakenly takes there to be a difference because of its acceptance of the pragmatically vacuous Cartesian soul substance theory, a good example of common sense being metaphysically biased in the way just alluded to by James (15). Another justificatory reason for preferring an importance-based analysis is that it supports his humanistic Promethean thesis of man as creator: We make things what they are by taking them in a way that is based on our feelings of what is important or interesting. James saw such a humanism as having morally desirable consequences by encouraging us to live the morally strenuous life of creators of value and meaning.

With these preliminary issues about orientation and motivation out of the way, we can now zero in on James's analysis of the Spiritual Self. In accordance with a time-honored philosophical slogan that there is no entity without identity, he attempts to uncover its nature through an analysis of its identity conditions, especially its identity over time. It is a difficult task for an expositor to say just what James's analysis is an analysis of, for running throughout much of *The Principles of Psychology* is a distinction between two radically different ways in which a psychol-ogist can investigate a psychic state. "There are, as we know, two ways of studying every psychic state. First, the way of analysis: What does it consist in? What is its inner nature? Of what sort of mind-stuff is it composed? Second, the way of history: What are its conditions of production, and its connection with other facts?'' (913).

The ''analysis'' is a phenomenological one based on introspection of an ''inner'' psychic state of consciousness, while the ''historical'' way is in terms of those publicly observable events that cause the psychic state. Given these dichotomous approaches, the particular psychic state of ''consciousness of personal sameness'' can be treated ''as a subjective phenomenon or as an objective deliverance, as a feeling, or as a truth. We may explain how one bit of thought can come to judge other bits to belong to the same Ego with itself; or we may criticise its judgment and decide how far it may tally with the nature of things'' (314). The analysis of Self identity as a ''subjective phenomenon'' is exclusively in terms of what I will call ''first-person criteria,'' these being states of consciousness that are introspectively available to the subject and reportable by propositions of the form ''I am now conscious in such-and-such a way.''

James makes several cryptic allusions to ''third-person criteria'' (in my terminology) based on publicly observable events for Self identity as an ''objective deliverance.''

The psychologist, looking on and playing the critic, might prove the thought [of Self identity] wrong, and show there was no real identity, there might have been no yesterday, or, at any rate, no self of yesterday; or, if there were, the sameness predicated might not obtain, or might be predicated on insufficient grounds. In either case, the personal identity would not exist as a *fact*; but it would exist as a *feeling* all the same; the consciousness of it by the thought would be there, and the psychologist would still have to analyze that, and show where its illusoriness lay. (*PP* 315–16)

At another place James seems to anticipate the controversial contemporary ''best candidate'' or ''only candidate'' requirement for Self identity over time. ''The way in which the present Thought [one's momentary total state of consciousness] appropriates the past is a real way, so long as no other owner appropriates it in a more real way, and so long as the Thought has no grounds for repudiating it stronger than those which lead to its appropriation'' (341). James gives an early indication of what these objective defeaters or overriders could be when he says that ''The experiences of the body are thus one of the conditions of the faculty of memory being what it is'' (17). This seems to imply that neurophysiological facts about brain processes and states could defeat a personal identity claim based on apparent memory by showing that the right sort of causal process was not in operation within the body. The later chapter on ''Memory'' in *The Principles of Psychology* will be seen to give some support to this interpretation.

James says nothing more about the nature of these third-person defeaters and their relation to first-person criteria. In a later section of this chapter, an attempt will be made to follow through on his behalf, but this will have to await the unearthing and attempted resolutions of various aporias concerning first- versus third-person criteria. Until this is done it will remain uncertain whether James's analysis is of personal identity over time as such or only the introspective experiences that lead us to reidentify our selves. For the time being, we will assume the simple but, it will turn out, simple-minded, view that it is concerned only with the latter, that is, with a phenomenological analysis of first-person criteria, thereby leaving the issue completely open as to connection between first- and third-person criteria.

James's analysis is an amalgam of the bundle analyses of Locke and Hume according to which the enduring self (or, in Hume's case, what we ordinarily but mistakenly call such) is reduced to a succession of conscious stages. A strong verificationist sentiment, which requires eschewing any nonempirical entity, such as a Cartesian soul substance or Kantian transcendental ego of apperception, recommends this analysis to James. He praises his Associationist predecessors by saying that they "have taken so much of the meaning of personal identity out of the clouds and made of the Self an empirical and verifiable thing" and claims that his own analysis, in terms of "resemblance among the parts of a continuum of feelings . . . constitutes the real and verifiable '*personal identity*' which we feel" (319; see also 328 and 341)[4] The aim of James's reductive analysis, accordingly, is to eliminate all references to or quantification over the Self in favor of references to conscious stages and descriptions of their interconnections.

A bundle theory of the Self must answer two questions. Exactly what are the elements or relata in the bundle? And, what is the relation(s) between them that renders them parts of the history of a single Self? James's answer to the first question shows a departure from the psychological atomism of Locke and Hume. Whereas they took a stage or state of consciousness to be compounded out of phenomenologically discriminated atomic components, James argued that it is a phenomenologically "indecomposable unity" that constitutes the total way in which a person is conscious at a given time (350). The taste of lemonade is not decomposable into separate sensations of tartness and sweetness, although its external cause is decomposable. It would be an instance of James's "Psychological Fallacy" to read back into the *experiencing* of the lemonade's taste features of the cause of this experience. This differ-

---

[4]In his entry on "Person and Personality" for the 1895 *Johnson's Universal Cyclopedia*, James claims that "The importance of Locke's doctrine lay in this, that he eliminated 'substantial' identity as transcendental and unimportant, and made of 'personal' identity (the only practically important sort) a directly verifiable empirical phenomenon" (*EPS* 318).

ence with his predecessors is not very important, because James was able, five years after the publication of *The Principles of Psychology*, in "The Knowing of Things Together," to change his view about this without having to change any other feature of his analysis. He called such a momentary total state of consciousness a "Thought" and attempted to reduce the endurance of the Self to a succession of momentary pulses of such Thoughts. There is a lingering atomism, however, in James's employment of a succession of numerically distinct momentary pulses of Thought. The "specious present" of *The Principles of Psychology*, as will be seen in Chapter 10, failed to avoid such atomism, for not only is there a succession of discrete specious presents but within each there is a discrimination between successive contents that differ in their degree of liveliness. It remained for him to offer a more radical Bergsonian solution in his *A Pluralistic Universe* and *Some Problems of Philosophy*, according to which the law of noncontradiction does not apply to our experience of change – a solution that did not thrill everybody.

All of the psychological states, processes, and dispositions that were formerly predicable of the person or Self now are to be predicated of a momentary Thought. Thus, it is a present Thought that knows, remembers, believes, wills, and the like. Herein is yet another respect in which James's analysis, like any bundle analysis, departs from common sense or ordinary usage, but this, as already seen, would not crush James. There is, however, the lingering suspicion that the Jamesian Thought, in virtue of being the common bearer and therefore unifier of all these psychological attributes, is a traditional substance of the sort he hoped to exorcise. Since they perform similar functions, they are the same on the basis of his principle that a difference that makes no difference is no difference. James's response could be that there is some difference, though not as great as he had believed – namely, that his Thought, unlike a traditional soul substance, does not ground the identity of the Self over time. But this does not allay the suspicion that James is sleeping with the enemy by countenancing something nonempirical, even if it is only a momentary nonempirical something.

James's answer to the second question, concerning the bundling relation, resembles the accounts of Locke and Hume, but with two important exceptions: he holds it to exist in *de rerum natura*, thereby rendering the bundle a *real* unity and, furthermore, sees it as man-made, in accordance with his Promethean humanism.[5] To discover the rela-

[5] Locke, at one point in his *Essays Concerning Human Understanding* (Bk. II, chap. 27, sec. 26) comes close to espousing this Promethean view when he writes: "This personality extends itself beyond present existence to what is past only by consciousness whereby it becomes concerned and accountable, owns and imputes to itself past actions, just upon the same ground, and for the same reason, that it does the present. . . . And therefore whatever past actions it cannot reconcile or appropriate to that present self by consciousness, it can no more be concerned in, than if they had never been done. . . ."

tion, James follows Locke's strategy of basing it on the relation that obtains between a Self and its present Thought (or idea, for Locke).[6] The reasons a Self (really a Thought) has for self-ascribing a present Thought will be the same as those it has for self-ascribing a past Thought. The issue, then, comes down to the phenomenal grounds on which a Self self-ascribes a present Thought.

It is important to bear in mind that, for James, it is not a conceptual truth that every Thought is had by one and only one Self, something that was seen in the discussion of Pure Experience in the last chapter. When he said, in listing the five characters in Thought, "Every thought tends to be part of a personal consciousness," he meant the "tends" qualification seriously. He argued that the then current work on multiple personality in abnormal psychology and on mediumship and automatic writing in paranormal psychology provided counterexamples to this. In fact, he even claimed to have had an experience in 1906 of a dream that seemed to him to be someone else's (*EP* 163–4). This caused great dread, as he feared that he was disintegrating into one of Janet's split personalities. Thus, it is a real problem for James how a Self identifies some Thought as its own, since it could have access to the Thoughts of others, or even Thoughts that were no one's – free-floating bits of consciousness in Fechner's surrounding mother-sea of consciousness.

James's answer is that it does so on the basis of the warmth and intimacy of the apprehended Thought (*PP* 314 and 316). Since what has warmth and intimacy is what is of interest, this is to say that a Thought is self-ascribed on the basis of interest, which fits the underlying leitmotiv of his analysis based on the interest-based selectivity of consciousness. A past Thought is self-ascribed by a present one – taken to be copersonal with it – when it is recaptured in memory with the same warmth and intimacy it had when present, thereby agreeing with Locke that the grounds for self-ascribing a present Thought are the same as for self-ascribing a past one.

There are several ways in which James describes this recapturing of the original warmth and intimacy of a past Thought by a present one. Most often, it is said that the latter "appropriates" or "adopts" the former. The present Thought is said also to "own" the past one. Each Thought, other than the first or last in a personal history, is "born an owner, and dies owned, transmitting whatever it realized as its Self to

---

[6] Herein James is speaking with the vulgar by referring to the Self, and, if he is to think with the learned, he must eliminate such reference in favor of reference to Thoughts. In the initial stages of his analysis, James speaks with the vulgar when he says: "For, whatever the thought we are criticising may think about its present *self*, that *self* comes to its acquaintance, or is actually felt, with warmth and intimacy" (*PP* 316; my italics). To think with the learned he must speak of how a present Thought identifies itself. As his discussion progresses, he exorcises such verboten references to the nonempirical Self.

its own later proprietor" (322). At another place James uses the simile of the passing on of "the 'title' of a collective self" from one Thought to another (322). You might say that every Thought goes from Champ to Chump in a brief moment rather than in the fifteen minutes envisioned by Andy Warhol. This comparison with the successive holders of a title misfires, because they are not copersonal, whereas the successive appropriators are.

The attentive reader will have noticed a seeming inconsistency in James's account of the conditions for a present Thought to be copersonal with a past one. It appears as if James says that it is both made and discovered, which presents the second major aporia for later discussion. The appropriating and adopting accounts of it speak to its being made, as these are intentional acts that the present Thought performs at will, on purpose, and so on. But the warmth and intimacy account speaks to it being discovered, since we cannot, be it for conceptual or causal reasons (I am not sure which), take something at will or voluntarily to have these qualities or be interesting, any more than we can love at will.

But before we wrestle with this aporia more must be said about James's bundling relation, in particular whether it is transitive – that is, if Thought T_1 appropriates T_2, and T_2 appropriates T_3, does T_1 appropriate T_3, and the nature of its phenomenal qualities of warmth and intimacy. For the time being, we will avoid the problem posed by the possibility of a split in psychological continuity, such as might occur through a brain bisection followed by a successful implanting of each hemisphere in a different body, or simply through two contemporaneous Thoughts appropriating the same past Thought, which must qualify as a distinct possibility for James, one he made use of in his doctrine of Pure Experience.

In answer to the first question, a distinction must be drawn between "propositional-memory" – remembering that p, in which p is some proposition – and "image-memory," representation of a former experience of one's own through an affective or phenomenal reenactment of it. Whatever might be the case regarding the transitivity of propositional-memory (if I remember that I remembered that I went to the circus, do I remember that I went to the circus?), it is dubious that image-memory is; and from what James says in support of the transitivity of appropriation, it is clear that he is concerned exclusively with image-memory. Initially he supports its transitivity by claiming that "Who owns the last self owns the self before the last, for what possesses the possessor possesses the possessed" (322). But this reliance on the metaphor of ownership is not sufficiently probative; for, even if there were a positive legal code according to which a slaveowner owns everything that his slave owns, it would have no relevance to James's copersonality sense of ownership. More to the point is his diagram (324) to illustrate the manner in which a Thought appropriates every Thought appropriated by any Thought it appropriates. It consists in a series of Chinese boxes with their bottom halves cut away. Each box represents a single Thought, with its phenomenal content included within the box. The initial (present) Thought-box in the series includes within itself, its phenomenal content, the phenomenal content included within each Thought-box included within it. As a consequence, the visual image content of a Thought contains the visual image content of any Thought it appropriates, just as a painting of a scene including a painting contains the represented painting in miniature.

The worry is that there is a finite bound to the number of possible successive appropriators and thus a rupture in transitivity, due to a limiting threshold on the smallness of the images we can be conscious of, just as there is a limiting threshold on how many contained paintings there can be in a painting that contains a miniature version of itself, in this case due to limitations imposed by materials and skills, as well as on our power of making visual discriminations. Furthermore, usually when I affectively recapture a past Thought through image-memory I do not have an image of every one of its phenomenal contents. I affectively recall my agonizing over this chapter yesterday evening, but I do not have a phenomenal awareness of every content of my total state of consciousness at that time, such as my itching from a mosquito bite. This, incidentally, should make us suspicious of James's claim that a total state of consciousness is not phenomenally decomposable, for how could I have an image-memory of a proper phenomenal part of such a state unless it contained as proper parts distinct phenomenal contents.

Given the function that James assigns to his bundling relation, there is no need for him to fight in the last ditch for its having an image-memory-based transitivity. This function is to secure sufficient qualitative similarity between successive phases of the stream of thought so that they can qualify as copersonal. His image-memory is only a device, as it was for Hume, for securing the kind of qualitative continuity that is necessary for the identity over time of any enduring individual or continuant.

The sense of our own personal identity, then, is exactly like any one of our other perceptions of sameness among phenomena. It is a conclusion grounded either on the resemblance in a fundamental respect, or on the continuity before the mind, of the phenomena compared. (PP 318)

James follows Locke in holding that the temporal phases of a continuing individual can vary qualitatively, provided that they do so in a gradual and continuous manner.

If James grants, as he should, that image-memory, for the reasons just given, is not transitive, he will have to complicate his account so as to handle cases in which transitivity fails to hold. He could avail himself of the grandfather relation to image-memory and say that successive Thoughts are copersonal just in case either one of them has an image-memory of the other or they are connected by an unbroken succession of image-memories. This, of course, will not meet the problem posed by the logical possibility of the same Thought being image-remembered by different simultaneous Thoughts. James would not worry about such mere *logical* possibilities, since his analysis had the modest aim of describing how things *actually* are. In general, as has been pointed out in the discussion of truth in Chapter 5, James never claimed that his analyses or accounts gave logically or conceptually sufficient and necessary conditions.

Another aspect of the appropriation relation requiring further consideration is the role played by the qualities of warmth and intimacy upon which it is based. The charming example by which James attempts to illustrate this is fraught with difficulties: "Peter, awakening in the same bed with Paul, and recalling what both had in mind before they went to sleep, reidentifies and appropriates the 'warm' ideas as his, and is never tempted to confuse them with those cold and pale-appearing ones which he ascribes to Paul" (317). This fails as a phenomenological analysis of the grounds on which a person self-ascribes an idea. Imagine that Peter's own ideas prior to falling asleep were quite "cold and pale-appearing" compared with the ideas of Paul that were then related to him. Peter was thinking about a boring departmental meeting he had just attended in which five hours were given over to discussing whether a graduate student representative should be allowed to vote on junior faculty appointments at the very time Paul was relating to him the exciting details of his evening with some lady. Peter is not under any temptation, either at that time or when he reconsiders these ideas upon waking, to take Paul's ideas as his own, in spite of their greater warmth and interest.

A similar objection applies to James's phenomenological account of how we identify our own body. Our bodies "too are percepts in our objective field – they are simply the most interesting percepts there" (304). The hunchback of Notre Dame, no doubt, finds the body of his beloved far more interesting than his own without thereby taking it to be his. James also errs in making "liveliness, or sensible pungency" (928) one of the important phenomenological characteristics on the basis of which we take a sensation's object to be real. "Whilst absorbed in the novel, we turn our backs on all other worlds, and, for the time, the Ivanhoe-world remains our absolute reality" (922). Again, this is belied by the phenomenological facts, for, not only are our dreams usually more lively and vivid than our run-of-the-mill waking sense experiences without thereby being taken to be of a reality that supplants or stands alongside of the ordinary sensible world, but one fails to read a novel as a novel if the actions it depicts are taken to be real-life.

What response to these objections to his basing of copersonality on warmth and intimacy might be available to James? These objections employed a generic version of these qualities. But such qualities cannot be individuative for persons, for every Thought, except possibly a free-floating one in the mother-sea, has warmth and intimacy for someone. Thus, a Thought's being warm and intimate does not discriminate among selves. My Thoughts, for example, do not just have warmth and intimacy, for that would not distinguish them from other people's Thoughts. Rather, they have warmth and intimacy *for me*. What is needed are more esoteric, personally individuating versions of these qualities such that each person experiences one, and only one, of them.

James's simile of the herd owner who rounds up his cattle on the basis of their unique brand mark suggests that he might have intended this esoteric, "existential" sort of warmth and intimacy.

The 'owner' symbolizes here that 'section' of consciousness, or pulse of thought, which we have all along represented as the vehicle of the judgment of identity; and the 'brand' symbolizes the characters of warmth and continuity, by reason of which the judgment is made. There is found a *self* brand, just as there is found a herd-brand. Each brand, so far, is the mark, or cause of our knowing, that certain things belong together. (*PP* 319–20)

It would be fully in the spirit of James's philosophy of language in *A Pluralistic Universe*, and especially *Some Problems of Philosophy* (with which *PP* 40 is in complete agreement), which insists on the privacy of meanings and the impossibility of fully communicating them in language as well as the strong existential emphasis of many of the essays in *The Will to Believe*, to understand this "*self* brand" type of warmth and intimacy in terms of personal indexical senses of restricted accessibility. The basic idea is that a different Fregean sense or property will be expressed by each person's use of "my warmth and intimacy," which can be grasped only by that person, just as successive utterances of "now" express different senses that are accessible only to persons existing at the time of utterance. To put it simply, only you know what it is like to be you. As a consequence, the tokening of "the Thought of the department meeting has my warmth and intimacy about it" by different persons will express different Fregean *de dicto* propositions, just as successive tokenings of "It is now raining" do.[7] These personal indexical senses or properties of warmth and intimacy do not perfectly fit the

---

[7] For a full account of *de dicto* and *de re* indexical propositions, see my book *On the Nature and Existence of God* (Cambridge: Cambridge University Press, 1991), 75–82.

simile, for whereas a unique *self* brand is experientially accessible to people other than the owner of the herd, the sense of property which each person expresses by using "my feeling of warmth and intimacy" is entertainable only by the user.

These *de dicto* indexical senses or propositions are not everyone's cup of tea, as is indicated by the legion of contemporary philosophers of language who have attempted to deny their reality and replace them with *de re* indexical propositions, but plainly James would have looked with favor upon them, given his penchant for wallowing in the subjective and ineffable. One minor change, however, will have to be made in *The Principles of Psychology* if James is to be able consistently to accept them. James claimed that a Thought cannot refer to or appropriate itself – "the Thought never is an object in its own hand" (323). The use of the indexical phrase "my feeling of warmth and intimacy," however, refers to the person (momentary Thought for James) who uses it. By jettisoning this claim we not only save James from commitment to a patently false doctrine but also eliminate an inconsistency in his text, for some of the things he says elsewhere imply its falsity. For example, he says that "we shall assimilate them [Thoughts] to each other and to the warm and intimate self we now feel within us as we think," but it is hard to see how this could be done if we cannot refer to our present Self or Thought (317). He imagines a "subtle reader" objecting to his denial of the possibility of reflexive self-reference by saying that "the Thought cannot call any part of its Object 'I' and knit other parts on to it, without first knitting that part on to *Itself*, and that it cannot knit it on to Itself without knowing itself" (323). James's answer, that "The words *I* and *me* signify nothing mysterious and unexampled – they are at bottom only names of *emphasis*," is really a nonanswer that gives in to the objection (324). For in calling them "names" he grants that they refer, his only point being the anti-Cartesian one that they refer to an object with good empirical credentials – the present Thought.

This completes our overview of James's phenomenological analysis of the identity of the Self over time, and a more in-depth probe is now required if we are to resolve its *making versus discovering* and *first- versus third-person criteria* aporias.

I. The Making versus Discovering Aporia

A good way to broach this aporia is through the herd simile. James initially says that "There is found a *self* brand, just as there is found a herd brand," which, by its use of "found," plainly supports the discovering thesis. If the making theorist should object that the herdsman had initially to brand loose, unowned cattle, James imagines the response that "They are not his because they are branded; they are branded because they are his" (320). (The respondent must never have heard of cattle thieves, or even settlers.) He mounts an objection to his dispensing with an enduring soul based on the analogous fact that The Thought does not capture or appropriate its own Thoughts, "but as soon as it comes into existence it finds them already its own," to which his response again is the anti-Cartesian one that the present Thought can perform all the functions that a soul substance does (321). What he fails to realize is that this fact counts against his claim that the present Thought makes the unity by its appropriative act. It renders this act otiose by requiring it to unify that which already is unified, thereby resulting in the contradiction that the unity of the Self over time is both made and discovered.

It was pointed out in Chapter 7 that the same aporia infects James's account of existence or reality. According to his phenomenological analysis, we take as real *"whatever things we select and emphasize and turn to* WITH A WILL. . . . The world of living realities as contrasted with unrealities is thus anchored in the Ego, considered as an active and emotional term" (926). But these claims in favor of the making thesis of reality were seen to clash with his claims that we take a sensation's object to be real primarily when it has "Coerciveness over attention, or the power to possess consciousness," and, secondarily, on the basis of "Liveliness, or sensible pungency, especially in the way of exciting pleasure or pain" (928). These two sets of claims clash, because we do not make something lively or interesting, no less coercive, by an act of will. The order of explanation goes from something's being interesting to its being attended to, rather than vice versa. A similar aporia also runs throughout James's general account of belief. On the one hand, his sentiment of rationality doctrine stresses that our beliefs are determined by our emotions and passions, which renders them nonintentional. On the other hand, his Promethean will-to-believe doctrine requires that we be able to choose our beliefs at will, something we accomplish by making the intentional effort to concentrate our attention in a certain way, as was shown in Chapter 2. James would like to believe that each of us is a *causa sui*, totally responsible for everything we are and do, but he is too good a psychologist to go down the line with this Promethean doctrine, with the result that an aporia arises.

But the herd simile can also be put to use in service of the making thesis. James now imagines that "wild cattle were lassoed by a newly-created settler and then owned for the first time" (321). We can further imagine that upon lassoing them, the herder imprints his unique self brand on them, thereby making them his, this being analogous to the present Thought appropriating a Thought, be it present or past, as its own. The herd simile, since it permits both the discovering and the making interpretations, limps on all four hoofs and should be permanently retired to Gabby Hayes's Wild West Museum in Canton, Ohio. A new start is needed.

James's account of the self-ascription of a Thought, be it present or past, begins with the phenomenal fact that some Thought is given to a present Thought with the qualities of warmth and intimacy of a special sort. "Our own past states of mind . . . appear to us endowed with a sort of warmth and intimacy that makes the perception of them seem more like a process of sensation than like a thought" (218). So far there is no intentional act, only passiveness, as one cannot choose to make something warm or interesting. The Thought simply discovers via passive sensation its copersonality with other Thoughts, which fits squarely with his passionate insistence that "The knowledge the present feeling has of the past ones is a real tie between them" (340). The relation of copersonality, like all relations, pace Hume and Mill, are experientially given and inhere in the real world.

The problem is what work is left over for the intentional act of appropriation or adoption to do. James says that when Peter awakens from sleep he "reidentifies and appropriates the 'warm' ideas as his" (317), and that this act "collects . . . some of the past facts which it surveys, and disowns the rest . . . and so makes a unity that is actualized and anchored and does not merely float in the blue air of possibility" (321). Although James repeatedly uses "appropriates," at one place even within what look like scare quotation marks (326), he never says just what it involves and candidly admits at the end of his account that "The only point that is obscure is the *act of appropriation* itself" (323). I will consider three different ways of expanding what it is.

On the basis of what James says, an appropriative act, whatever else it may be, is an act of self-ascription that involves selective emphasis. Such a self-ascription necessarily requires that the present Self or Thought refer to itself by the use of a first-person indexical expression, such as "I" or "me." But they, along with every other indexical expression, according to James, "are at bottom only names of *emphasis*" (324). Herein we find the sought-for intentional act of selective attention, as "the distinction between *I* and *you*, like that between *this* and *that*, *here* and *there*, *now* and *then* . . . is the result of our laying the same selective emphasis on parts of place and time" (273). Furthermore, we can think of the appropriative act as influenced, but not determined, by what appears warm and intimate, thereby finding some role for these feelings to perform in the account of copersonality.

Unfortunately, this way of finding something for the appropriative act to do in determining copersonality between Thoughts rests on a radically mistaken view of how first-person indexical words work, wrongly assimilating them to selective indexical terms such as "this."[8] A use of "this" is indeed selective among objects, since if the user had chosen on that very occasion of use to point in a different direction than he had in fact pointed, he would have pointed to a different object than he in fact did. Because a use of "I" cannot refer to anyone other than the user, it is not selective in this counterfactual manner. Similarly, a use of "now," pace James and Russell, does not select or choose some time from out of a group of other times that could have been denoted instead *on that very occasion*.

A second, and more promising, way of finding useful employment for the appropriative act is supplied by Gerald E. Myers. Myers rightly sees James as holding that "the present self or act of thinking both finds and fashions *the unity* that causes us to think that we are the same person throughout successive experiences," and attempts a resolution of this seeming contradiction (*WJ* 349; my italics). It should be obvious that any resolution must equivocate on "unity." Myers does not disappoint us.

James used *appropriation* as the name for the act by which the present self recognizes its continuity with its former selves, and what he said about appropriation seems both to find and to fashion unity. The present self appropriates what it literally finds as warm and belonging to itself, yet since it has the unifying feature of any act of thought (collecting various items into a single act of attention or consciousness), it actively contributes to the judgment in terms of which the recognition of the continuity between past and present self is expressed. (*WJ* 349)

Myers's solution to the aporia involves a distinction between two types of "unity" – the *copersonality unity* of successive Thoughts that are connected by the relation of *being warm and intimate to* (or its grandfather relation) and the *unity of the judgment* formed by the present Thought that there is the former type of unity. The appropriative act creates the unity of the judgment but only discovers the warmth and intimacy based unity of successive Thoughts upon which the judgment is based. Furthermore, given James's lifelong rejection of abstract propositions, it could be added onto Myers's account that the appropriative act also creates, in addition to the judging, the proposition judged.

[8] Bertrand Russell, whose account of "emphatic or egocentric particulars" closely follows James, committed this very error when he stated: "I think it is extremely difficult, if you get rid of consciousness altogether, to explain what you mean by such a word as 'this,' what it is that makes the absence of impartiality. You would say that in a purely physical world there would be a complete impartiality. All parts of time and all regions of space would seem equally emphatic. But what really happens is that we *pick out* certain facts, past and future and all that sort of thing; they all radiate out from 'this' " (PLA 55–6; my italics). For a full discussion and critique of this, see my book *The Language of Time* (London: Routledge & Kegan Paul, 1968), 200.

Although Myers's resolution of the aporia has some textual support, it trivializes the making role of the appropriative act. There is a third way of interpreting this act that accords well with James's making thesis in other areas of his philosophy and assigns it the far more exciting task of creating the copersonality unity itself, and not just the unity of the judgment or proposition judged. Taking seriously the oft-made remark that "It was all there, at least in germ, in *The Principles of Psychology*," an attempt will be made to understand the cryptic claim that the Thought "makes a unity that is *actualized* and anchored and does not merely float in the blue air of *possibility*" (*PP* 321; my italics) by relating it to this attempt to resolve a making–discovering aporia nineteen years later, in *The Meaning of Truth*:

A fact [of there being seven stars in the Big Dipper constellation] virtually preexists when every condition of its realization save one is already there. In this case the condition lacking is the act of the counting and comparing mind. But the stars (once the mind considers them) themselves dictate the result. . . . We have here a quasi-paradox. Undeniably something comes by the counting that was not there before. And yet that something was *always true*. In one sense you create it, and in another sense you *find* it. You have to treat your count as being true beforehand, the moment you come to treat the matter at all. (*MT* 56)

James's account bears a startling resemblance to Aristotle's claim in his *Physics* (Book 4, Chapter 10) that the act of measuring the duration of a succession of events makes time actual. Just as a succession of events is only potentially time and becomes so in actuality only when a mind counts or measures their duration, it is just potentially a fact or true that the Big Dipper constellation contains seven stars and becomes so in actuality only when a mind counts them. It can similarly be said, given James's claim in the quotation from *The Principles of Psychology*, that the copersonal unity is "actualized," ceasing to be a mere "possibility," only upon the making of the judgment by the present Thought, that a succession of Thoughts connected by the *being warm and intimate to* relation is only potentially a copersonal unity of successive Thoughts, and becomes so in actuality only when a present Thought judges that they are a copersonal unity.

Aristotle's account misfires because there could not be a succession of events (what he calls "the Before and After") unless there actually were time, and the worry is that James's parallel account of the making actual of a copersonal unity by the appropriative act of judgment fails for a similar reason. James, however, says some things in passing that could be marshaled to show that it at least is not a complete nonstarter.

These remarks concern the forensic aspect of Self identity over time, an aspect that James for the most part rightfully neglects, given that his analysis is a phenomenological one. He agrees with what he takes to be the dictates of the law and "common sense" (Locke!) that a man should not be punished for what he no longer remembers, because "he is not the same person forensically now which he was then" (352). It would be very much in the spirit of this (benighted) sentiment to hold that image-memory alone is not sufficient for forensic responsibility, the reason being that a person could have an image-memory of the Thought that accompanied his past transgression but not know, because he fails to judge or believe, that he is copersonal with the person who had that Thought. It is not enough that the present Self be potentially copersonal with the wrong-doing past Self, which is all that image-memory can achieve, it must actually be, and this requires it to judge or believe that it is. But this propositional-memory is nothing but James's appropriative act.

It could be objected that even if propositional-memory is required for actual copersonality, it does not require that the propositional judgment or belief of copersonality be an appropriative *act*, meaning something done intentionally or at will. This raises the basic problem with the will-to-believe doctrine's assumption that we can voluntarily control our beliefs. At the end of the chapter on "The Perception of Reality," James admits that we cannot voluntarily choose to have certain beliefs and gives a causal recipe for indirectly inducing them based on acting as if you believe them. What he does not realize is that it is only in rare cases that one can believe something at will. As a consequence of the rarity of appropriative acts, there rarely are, for James, cases of Self identity over time, certainly a reductio ad absurdum of his analysis.

II. The First- versus Third-Person Criteria Aporia

The problem, it will be recalled, was whether James's avowedly phenomenological analysis based solely on first-person criteria is intended as an analysis of what Self identity over time really is, and, if it is, how third-person criteria are relevant. The simplest answer is that he did not intend his analysis to be revelatory of what such identity is, as he was quite explicit that it was an exclusively introspective analysis that excluded third-person criteria and gave the title of "The Sense of Personal Identity" to the section in which he developed it, thereby indicating that he had no concern with how third-person criteria were relevant (314).[9] The truth of the matter, however, is not this simple, for there are several good reasons to think that James took his analysis to be of Self identity over time as such and simply failed to follow through and come to grips with the way in which third-person criteria are relevant.

The "inner" approach to understanding the nature of persons contrasts with the "outer" or objective approach that treats persons as what

[9]This is the answer given by Graham Bird (WJ 86–7).

I will call, in a somewhat extended sense of the term, a "natural kind," meaning a type of object whose nature is to be determined through natural science. These contrasting approaches are at the foundation of the split in twentieth-century philosophy between so-called Continental and analytical approaches. They also form the real basis of James's contrast between the tough- and tender-minded given in *Pragmatism*, in spite of their not appearing explicitly in his account. The traits listed under "The Tender-Minded," for the most part, are those which assure an unbifurcated world and are vouchsafed through the inner approach, as contrasted with those listed under "The Tough-Minded," which represent the natural scientist's temper of mind, with its natural-kinds approach to understanding persons and their world.

In the first place, there are several cases in which James took an introspective analysis of a given concept to be an analysis of the concept as such. In these cases he makes an inference from what we experience X to be – the experiential reason for calling something "X" – to both what we mean by "X" and what X really is. Five prominent examples of this derivation of semantic and metaphysical conclusions from an introspective analysis are his analyses of good, truth, matter, negation, and reality. In Chapter 1, James's attempt to define *good* in terms of the experiential conditions under which we take something to be good, namely when it satisfies a desire or demand, was expounded. His claims in *Pragmatism* that "The reasons why we call things true is the reason why they *are* true" (37), and in *The Meaning of Truth* that truth is "what truth [is] *known-as*" (48), give further evidence of his proclivity to determine the nature of something on the basis of how we experience it, as does his oft-repeated endorsement of Berkeley's reductive analysis of material objects in terms of our experiential grounds for believing that they exist.

These four cases, however, are not sufficiently probative in showing that James thought Self identity over time could be analyzed in terms of first-person criteria alone, since third-person criteria, having to do with things like the endurance of a body, also are experientially accessible, though not in as direct and immediate a way as are our own conscious states. Even so, these experiences of bodies would not be the whole or even a significant part of what we experience as our own personal identity and thereby our reasons for taking ourselves to endure over time.

Of more moment are James's analyses of negation and reality. From the analysis of the psychological grounds for a negative belief – "we never disbelieve something except for the reason that we believe something else which contradicts the first thing" – he draws a conclusion concerning the nature of the logical concept of negation – "Compare this [just mentioned] psychological fact with the corresponding logical truth that all negation rests on covert assertion of something else than the thing denied" (*PP* 914). The most telling example is that of reality. He begins with the psychological question "*Under what circumstances do we think things real?* (*PP* 917), to which his answer is that we do so when they "appear both *interesting* and *important*" (*PP* 924). But from this psychological analysis he draws the semantic conclusion that "*reality means simply relation to our emotional and active life*" and that "this is the only sense which the word ever has in the mouths of practical men" (*PP* 924). For further details the reader is referred back to Section 2 of Chapter 7.

James's account of Self identity over time shows a similar inference of semantic and metaphysical conclusions from a psychological or introspective analysis. To start with, he asks "what the consciousness may mean when it calls the present self the *same* with one of the past selves which it has in mind" (316). He boasts that the introspective analyses given by himself and his Associationist predecessors, "have taken so much of the *meaning* of personal identity out of the clouds and made of the Self an empirical and verifiable thing" (319; my italics). And a few pages later he makes the strong statement that "It is impossible to discover any *verifiable* features in personal identity which this sketch does not contain," which seems to render third-person criteria otiose, given that his "sketch" is exclusively in terms of first-person criteria (322). These quotations still are not decisive, as it could be argued that his use of "mean" is short for "psychologically mean," because it occurs within the scope of the sectional title, "The Sense of Personal Identity."

What really cinches my case are the unrestricted endorsements of an exclusively introspective analysis given in publications subsequent to *The Principles of Psychology*, thereby escaping this scope problem. In the 1902 *The Varieties of Religious Experience* James praises Locke for analyzing "personal identity" in terms of "its cash-value," meaning what it is "*known as*" (*VRE* 350). In his series of articles on Pure Experience published during 1904–5 James argued that no experiential datum is conscious or physical *simpliciter* but only in a relational manner. Placed in one kind of network of relationships to other experiential data it qualifies as physical, but in a different kind of network as conscious. The latter kind of network is said to be that of the history of a single Self over time, which he explained as follows:

In the chapter on 'The Self,' in my *Principles of Psychology*, I explained the continuous identity of each personal consciousness as a name for the practical fact that new experiences come which look back on the old ones, find them 'warm,' and greet and appropriate them as 'mine.' (*ERE* 64; see also 39 and 270)

Herein he is asserting without qualification or restriction what constitutes the identity of the Self over time.

I take it that some good reasons have just been advanced for taking James's analyses based exclusively on first-person criteria as an analysis of Self identity over time as such. But, it will be objected, this cannot be the whole story. To be sure, James's introspective approach to understanding Self identity supports his antibifurcationism, since it gives an account of the Self in terms of what has *importance* for our emotions and active propensities, which, it will be recalled, formed the underlying leitmotiv of his analysis. The dramatic portrayal of personal endurance it presents secures a central place for our values and aspirations, thus helping to prevent our world from becoming a bifurcated one devoid of human meaning. James, however, is not exclusively an "inside man," for he wrote *The Principles of Psychology* primarily for the purpose of establishing psychology as a *natural* science and, toward that end, gave prominence to the "outside"-based work (actually it was done indoors in a laboratory) of his German friends and colleagues, about whose exact scientific method he said that "it could hardly have arisen in a country whose natives could be *bored*" (192). A tension runs throughout the book between the outer and inner methodological approaches, or between his functional psychology and phenomenological psychology.[10] But, as has been already shown, there unquestionably are places in *The Principles of Psychology* where one of the approaches becomes dominant and is appealed to as being revelatory of the true nature of the phenomenon under investigation, and some good reasons have been advanced to show that James gave priority to the inner approach for revealing the true nature of personal identity.

A more serious objection is that there are strong materialistic undercurrents in *The Principles of Psychology*, in particular its reductive phenomenological analysis of our prized, active inner Self, that Self of all the other Selves, which is the source of will and effort, to a collection of bodily sensations, primarily movements in the head (287–8). Herein James seems to come close to Dewey's natural-kinds view of a person, which speaks against his having exclusively first-person criteria for Self identity over time. But surface appearances deceive here. First, James's reductive analysis is explicitly restricted, Poo-bah style, to phenomenal appearances, and, when he waxes metaphysical and moral in the chapters on "Attention" and "Will," this active Self turns into something nonmaterial that defies description and explanation by natural science,

[10] In one of the least helpful remarks ever made by any commentator, William R. Woodward, in his introduction to James's *Essays in Psychology*, says that "James's ability to hold the two approaches in a 'productive paradox' was a better paradigm for the significant study of psychology than either would be alone" (*EPS* xiii). This gives us no help in resolving the first- versus third-person criteria aporia.

as was shown in Chapter 3 (424 and 1179–82). It must be remembered that James is an arch relativist who always speaks qua some human perspective or interest. The apparent contradiction between his claim in *The Principles of Psychology* that "there is no neurosis without psychosis" (133; see also 18) and his account of the independence of consciousness from matter (his filtration theory of the brain) in his later writings, especially the lecture on *Human Immortality: Two Supposed Objections*, *The Varieties of Religious Experience*, and *A Pluralistic Universe*, vanishes once it is realized that the former claim is restricted to our perspective as natural scientists. Similar considerations hold for his comments about determinism. Qua scientist, we assume determinism, but, qua moral beings, we must reject it. This is in accord with his Poobahism, as seen in the previous chapter.

What has been primarily overlooked by those, like Dewey, who have attributed a naturalistic or materialistic view of persons to James on the basis of his phenomenological reduction of the inner Self to a collection of bodily movements is that James nowhere bases Self identity over time on the body or even some core part thereof, such as the brain, that is causally responsible, according to science, for what is most important and distinctive about persons. He does not hold it to be even a necessary condition for such identity, as is attested to by his claim that "The same brain may subserve many conscious selves, either alternate or coexisting . . ." (379). If a person were identical with a living human body or brain, then they should have the same criteria of identity, but plainly they do not for James, otherwise he would have said so somewhere.

But, it could still be objected, we must take seriously the quotations earlier in this chapter in which James alluded to the possibility of defeating an introspectively based claim of Self identity over time by appeal to third-person criteria. He does not explicitly tell us what they are, but if we dig deeply enough we might find them, and they might very well involve a requirement of some sort of spatio-temporal continuity of a body, thereby showing that his phenomenological analysis is not the whole story about personal identity over time.

The most likely place to look for these defeaters is in the "Memory" chapter, the reason being that James's introspective analysis based on the state of seeming to remember – that is, judging a past Thought which appears warm and intimate to be yours – inevitably leads to the question of when such an apparent memory is veridical, and thus the apparent identity a real one. The hope is that we shall find in this chapter some causal requirement for an apparent memory to be veridical that could serve as the sought-for third-person criteria by which a claim of personal endurance based on apparent memory could be challenged or defeated. That this chapter is placed six chapters after that on "The Consciousness of Self" does not preclude its containing these defeaters, as James had some reason for placing it where he did in *The Principles of Psychology*, namely, he might have wanted to contrast the account of immediate memory given in the chapter that immediately precedes it on "The Perception of Time" with its account of secondary memory of what has lapsed from consciousness. Nevertheless, that there is such a wide separation between the chapters should give us some pause.

The plot of the "Memory" chapter is the familiar one in which an introspective analysis is given initially and then followed by a historical or causal one. The phenomenological analysis merely repeats the one given in the "The Consciousness of Self." For me to remember a past event I must have "directly experienced its occurrence. It must have that 'warmth and intimacy' which were so often spoken of in the chapter on the Self, as characterizing all experiences 'appropriated' by the thinker as his own" (612). The historical analysis of the causes of memory, in contrast, is a straightforward neurophysiological one.

Whatever accidental cue may turn this tendency [to recall] into an actuality, the permanent *ground* of the tendency itself lies in the organized neural paths by which the cue calls up the experience . . . the condition which makes it possible at all . . . is . . . the brain-paths which *associate* the experience with the occasion and cue of recall. (616)

Retention "is no mysterious storing up of an 'idea' in an unconscious state." It is "a morphological feature, the presence of these 'paths' . . . in the finest recesses of the brain's tissue" (617).

The big question, which James makes no attempt to answer, is how the phenomenological and causal accounts of memory are connected, this being just a special instance of his general failure to connect together the "inner" and "outer" approaches of *The Principles of Psychology*, which is one of the big unresolved aporias in his philosophy. James now has before him everything that is needed for placing a causal requirement on memory. *But he doesn't.* Were he to opt for making the neurophysiological causes of memory necessary for memory, his memory theory of personal endurance would in effect be treating persons as natural kinds in the manner of contemporary memory theorists such as Shoemaker and Perry, the reason being that he would be giving natural science the prerogative of determining the identity conditions and thereby the nature of persons. *But he doesn't!*

Based on what James both says and fails to say when the opportunity presents itself, his criteria for memory are, as they are for Locke and Quinton, of a coherentist sort, subject to the lone defeater requiring that there be no other equally good or better claimant under these coherentist criteria, which is my construal of his remark that the present Thought veridically appropriates a past one "so long as no other owner appropriates it in a more real way" (341). The role of this defeater is to save the transitivity of identity in the case in which coexistent persons are equally good claimants under these criteria for having memories of the same past Thought. The mayor of Queensbury's apparent memories of the Thoughts of Socrates are veridical, and thereby he is identical with Socrates, just in case his apparent memory corresponds with the past and properly coheres with a sufficiently rich set of other historically accurate apparent memories he has of Socrates' past, and there does not exist at that time anyone who qualifies at least as well under this memory-coherence account to have memories of Socrates.[11] James, with his lifelong passion for investigating paranormal phenomena, is the last person to balk at the possibility of such a case of reincarnation.

It might be asked whether James can find some role, however diminished, for a defeater based on the causal requirement supplied by the neurophysiological analysis of memory. Hopefully, it has been made clear why James could not accept this caused-in-the-right-way criterion as either sufficient or necessary for personal endurance, and thus for the veridicality of the sort of phenomenal or apparent memories that he takes to be both sufficient and necessary for such endurance. What he could say is that it is a very weak defeater, in that an apparent memory's failure to satisfy it merely lessens the probability that it is veridical, though not necessarily so that it is less than one-half. James never told us what he believed about this matter, and, given that he is dead, if we are to find out, we shall have to do so by coming upon him or one of his free-floating "Thoughts" in the mother-sea of consciousness that envelops our ordinary finite minds. Which is my way of saying that we'll never find out.

[11] It might be objected by the likes of Williams and Parfit that the best-candidate requirement violates the underlying leitmotiv of James's analysis enjoining us to analyze personal identity in terms of what is important, for, according to their intuitions, it should not matter to the mayor whether an equally good claimant exists. I happen not to share their intuitions, not even when it is added that he is ignorant of the latter's existence, for the fact that something is important to a person does not entail that she is conscious of it.

9

The I–Thou Quest for Intimacy
and Religious Mysticism

The preceding chapter described the first lap of William James's quest for intimacy, in which he adopted the insider's approach to understanding the nature of his own Self through an introspective analysis of its conditions of identity over time. The next lap in his journey is his attempt to achieve a deep intimacy, ultimately a union, with the inner life of other persons, both natural and supernatural, even with the world at large.

I. The I–Thou Experience

James begins with a special inward manner in which one person experiences another as a "Thou" rather than an "It" and then extends this to the experience of the world at large, resulting in panpsychism. His analysis of the I–Thou experience bears a striking resemblance to that offered by Martin Buber some thirty years later. Buber starts with the "It" mode of experience.

> The life of a human being does not exist merely in the sphere of goal-directed verbs. It does not consist merely of activities that have something for their object. I perceive something. I feel something. I want something. I sense something. The life of a human being does not consist merely of all this and its like. All this and its like is the basis of the realm of It. But the realm of Thou has another basis. (*IT* 54)[1]

Buber's I–It experience is James's pragmatic mode of experiencing worldly individuals in terms of how we can ride herd on them and use them for the achievement of our goals. Toward this end we conceptualize them in a way that enables us effectively to use them.

Unlike the experience of It, the experience of a Thou, Buber tells us, does not have *something* for its object in the sense of one object among others that border on it and delimit it, because "Thou has no borders. Whoever says Thou does not have something; he has nothing. But he stands in relation" (*IT* 55) The relata in an I–It relation are external and separate from each other, but in the I–Thou relation they exist within the *relation* in the sense of entering into each other. "The world

---

[1] I have retained the "Thou" of the original translation rather than the "You" that Walter Kaufmann, the translator, uses in the 1970 edition at the urging of Buber himself.

as experience belongs to the basic word I–It. The basic word I–Thou establishes the world of relation" (*IT* 56). Through a fusing of their originally separate consciousnesses they enter into, what Buber terms, "relational processes and states" in which they partially fuse or mush together (*IT* 70).

The best place to begin the exposition of James's version of the I–Thou experience is with his great account of the lovers Jack and Jill. To a disinterested, objective observer they might look completely uninteresting, just another ordinary boy and girl, except maybe for the fact that they have a penchant for falling down hills and breaking their crowns. Both of them, however, because they have a deep empathetic awareness of the other's inner consciousness, experience the other as something wondrously unique. Through this reciprocal merging of psyches each expands his/her own consciousness and gains a deeper knowledge of the other than could be obtained from an objective, scientific account. James's description of their reciprocal I–Thou-ing of each other, though he doesn't yet use this language, reserving it for the religious person's experience of nature at large, warrants full quotation.

Every Jack sees in his own particular Jill charms and perfections to the enchantment of which we stolid onlookers are stone-cold. And which has the superior view of the absolute truth, he or we? Which has the more vital insight into the nature of Jill's existence, as a fact? Is he in excess, being in this matter a maniac? or are we in defect, being victims of a pathological anaesthesia as regards Jill's magical importance? Surely the latter; surely to Jack are the profounder truths revealed; surely poor Jill's palpitating little life-throbs *are* among the wonders of creation, *are* worthy of this sympathetic interest; and it is to our shame that the rest of us cannot feel like Jack. For Jack realizes Jill concretely, and we do not. He struggles towards a union with her inner life, divining her feelings, anticipating her desires, understanding her limits as manfully as he can, and yet inadequately, too; for he also is afflicted with some blindness, even here. Whilst we, dead clods that we are, do not even seek after these things, but are contented that that portion of eternal fact named Jill should be for us as if it were not. Jill, who knows her inner life, knows that Jack's way of taking it – so importantly – is the true and serious way; and she responds to the truth in him by taking him truly and seriously, too. May the ancient blindness never wrap its clouds about either of them again! Where would any of *us* be, were there no one willing to know us as we really are or ready to repay us for *our* insight by making recognizant return? We ought, all of us, to realize each other in this intense, pathetic [doesn't James mean empathetic or sympathetic!], and important way. (*TT* 150–1)

This might be the most profound passage in James – hardly, as James feared, "the mere piece of sentimentalism which it may seem to some readers" (*TT* 4). It requires considerable fleshing out, though. The passage might be read by some as imputing to the lovers a special mode of access to each other's minds that renders their judgments about each other incorrigible. This, however, would fly in the face of James's deep commitment to fallibilism, even to the extent of denying in *The Principles of Psychology* that introspective reports could not be mistaken. James's point, rather, is that there are features of another person's consciousness that can be known in the full-blooded existential sense only through an act of sympathetic intuition. To know what-it-is-like-to-be-Jill, which is the really important fact about Jill for James, one must enter into her inner life and experience the world the way she does. This is what is meant by James's claim that "Jack realizes Jill concretely." Because he does, he has a "truer" grasp of Jill than does the detached observer: "The truer side is the side that feels the more and not the side that feels the less" (*TT* 133). This has the consequence that you can *really* know someone only if you love her.

James's romanticism comes to the fore in his ecstatic descriptions of the marvelous ponderousness of the inner life that one grasps through the I–Thou experience. He speaks of its "vital secrets," "zest," "tingle," "excitement," "mysterious inwards," and "mysterious sensorial life" (*TT* 132, 135, 137, 149), along with its "acutest internality" and "violent thrills of life" (*ERM* 99). To miss the joy of this inner consciousness in another person is to miss all, for it is this that makes her life significant, provided it is coupled with the requisite strength of character to see to it that it gets properly expressed in her overt behavior. James prizes this inner life so highly that he holds that "In every being that is real there is something external to, and sacred from, the grasp of every other" (*WB* 111).

James deduces different normative conclusions from this "sacredness" of an individual's inner life, some benevolent and others less so. Among the benevolent consequences is his principle of democracy, requiring us to respect other persons, even nations, and to adopt a live-and-let-live hands-off policy. He calls this "respect for the sacredness of individuality . . . the outward tolerance of whatever is not itself intolerant."[2] It served as the basis of his opposition to what he saw as American imperialism in the Philippines (*TT* 4). He even goes so far as to deploy this democratic principle to oppose the "Aristocratic" or snob objection to immortality – namely, that if there were immortality, heaven would become overcrowded with a bunch of undesirable riffraff. He charges this objection with displaying a blindness to other creatures due to a failure properly to I–Thou them.

You take these swarms of alien kinsmen as they are for you: an external picture painted on your retina, representing a crowd oppressive by its vastness and confusion. . . . But all the while, beyond this externality which is your way of realizing them, they realize themselves with the acutest internality, with the most violent thrills of life. 'Tis you who are dead, stone-dead and blind and

---

[2] Here is yet another of James's deontological normative pronouncements that cannot be accommodated by his official desire-maximizing ethical theory.

senseless, in your way of looking on. You open your eyes upon a scene of which you miss the whole significance. Each of these grotesque or even repulsive aliens is animated by an inner joy of living as hot or hotter than that which you feel beating in your private breast. (*ERM* 99)

And, for good measure, he adds that "The heart of being can have no exclusions akin to those which our poor little hearts set. The inner significance of other lives exceeds all our power of sympathy and insight" (*ERM* 101). To deny immortality to these "poor little hearts" on the grounds of their worthlessness would be a case of "letting blindness lay down the law to sight" (*ERM* 101).

There were, however, less benevolent uses that James made of the sacredness of the inner life. At times it led him to indulge in overly romantic sentimental glorification of the inner life to the exclusion of the social and economic conditions that are necessary for such inner flourishing. Max Otto was quite right to criticize James for being blind "to the character-forming significance of the economic conditions under which men live and work." Like Emerson, he adds, James "was captivated by the ideal of absolutely unentangled and unfettered individuality" (*CB* 189). For James, in sharp distinction from Dewey, "man is *in*, but not *of*, the environment." James's socialism was one of the spirit divorced from economic realities. His glorification of the stoic person who manages to cultivate and keep alive a rich inner life regardless of how unfortunate her external circumstances is its result. James admitted that "society has . . . got to pass towards some newer and better equilibrium, and the distribution of wealth has doubtless slowly got to change," but he immediately adds that such changes will not make "any genuine vital difference . . . to the lives of our descendants. . . . The solid meaning of life is always the same eternal thing – the marriage . . . of some unhabitual ideal, however special, with some fidelity, courage, and endurance; with some man's or woman's pains. – And whatever or wherever life may be, there will always be the chance for that marriage to take place" (*TT* 166). And "no outward changes of condition in life can keep the nightingale of its eternal meaning from singing in all sorts of different men's hearts" (*TT* 167). He naively thinks that the conflicts between rich and poor, workers and owners, result largely from the fact that "Each . . . ignores the fact that happiness and unhappiness and significance are a vital mystery; each pins them absolutely on some ridiculous feature of the external situation; and everybody remains outside of everybody else's sight" (*TT* 166). Romantic sentimentalism does have its price.

James's reactionary use of his romanticism about the inner life also underlies his account of habit.

Habit is thus the enormous fly-wheel of society, its most precious conservative agent. It alone is what keeps us all within bounds of ordinance, and saves the children of fortune from the envious uprisings of the poor. It alone prevents the hardest and most repulsive walks of life from being deserted by those brought up to treat therein. . . . It is well for the world that in most of us, by the age of thirty, the character has set like plaster, and will never soften again. (*PP* 125–6)

In a letter to his sister Alice in 1865 from the Amazon he expresses the same conservative sentiment. "The boy has acted so far as cabin boy. His blue black hair falls over his eye brows, but he is a real willing young savage & we hope, by keeping him low & weak to make an excellent servant of him for all the time we are on the Amazons" (*CWJ* 4:114).

The same reactionary spirit runs throughout James's *Talks to Teachers on Psychology*. Instead of making his pragmatism the basis of his theory of education, as Dewey did, he leans heavily on Associationist psychology and its rote methods of training, because the purpose of education is to inculcate in students the right set of habits so that they will fit into a preexisting society. Education "consists in the organizing of resources in the human being which shall fit him to his social and physical world" (*TT* 27). This conservative emphasis is especially prominent in "The Will" chapter of the book, in which it is said: "Thus are your pupils to be saved: first, by the stock of ideas with which you furnish them; second, by the amount of voluntary attention that they can exert in holding to the right ones, however unpalatable; and third, by the several habits of acting definitely on these latter to which they have been successfully trained" (*TT* 110). Whereas Dewey wanted to use the educational system radically to reconstruct society, his only difference from Plato being that Plato cultivated Dionysius of Syracuse and Dewey the teacher's union, James wanted to use the educational system to propagate a society with which he basically was quite content. His numerous letters to the established members of Boston society attest to this, as does the good-old-boy mentality that is expressed in his numerous derogatory references to Jews, blacks, Italians, and others in his letters (see: *LWJ* 1:51, 56, 94, 112, 114, 121, 172, 233, 275, and 2:60–1, 148, 196, 199, 223, 228, 245). No harm was meant by his use of pejoratives like "niggers," "boys," "darkies," "dagoes," "a faithless Israelite," "a Shylock," "old clothes men," "ambitious young Jews," since in real life he was totally without prejudice and, in fact, was exceedingly kind and helpful to minority individuals. It was just James's way of being affable by letting his correspondents know that he was a member of their club.

To return to the I–Thou experience, what requires further elucidation is James's all too brief description of how Jack "struggles toward a union with [Jill's] inner life."[3] He is supposed to achieve this through

[3] Given that James thought it possible for persons to enter intimately into each other's consciousness through an I–Thou experience, it is odd that Horace Kallen would write that James held that "An impregnable, a never-to-be-stormed aliency cuts off each indi-

an act of sympathetic or empathetic intuition, but just what is that? James, of course, cannot give a straightforward literal answer. Since the inner life that is the object of this intuition is said to be mysterious and ineffable, so is the act that intuits it. Indirect communication, of the sort practiced by mystics, is needed. Buber followed this path in his account of the I–Thou experience in the preceding quotations, which is why many readers, no doubt, were mystified. Maybe the best that can be done is to write a novel or play or, better yet, a typical Tin Pan Alley song. Jack takes one look at Jill and "Whammo! Zing Went the Strings of His Heart." As he peers deeply into her eyes he feels he has known her all his life. His focus of orientation has radically altered so that now he perceives the whole world through her. He locks in on her inner joy and tingles, which is what bestows meaning and value on her life. Jack's I–Thou-ing of Jill is reciprocated by Jill, thus bringing about a mutual partial merging of their consciousnesses.

It is interesting to compare James's sympathetic intuition with Sartre's experience of the "glance" in *Being and Nothingness*. Both involve a mysterious sort of direct awareness of one conscious being by another that renders otiose a need to employ a Cartesian argument from analogy for the existence of other minds. But here is where they part company. For Sartre, the other person is a threat, being, if not a member of the Gestapo, then at least a collaborator. Through his judgmental perception he makes you into an object on public display and thereby subject to being judged by him in ways that you cannot control, resulting in a restriction on your freedom to control your world through your own subjectivity. Whereas hell is other people for Sartre, as depicted in his play *No Exit*, they are heaven for James, as he sees them as presenting him with the occasion for expanding his consciousness through merging with theirs. In short, James likes people and Sartre doesn't. Buber certainly is squarely on James's side in this matter, being one of the biggest I–Thou-ers of all time, if the scurrilous rumors are to be trusted.

James did not stop with I–Thou-ing his fellow humans. He even wanted to I–Thou the beasts and fishes, as well as nature. He writes in a letter of 1873: "Sight of elephants and tigers at Barnum's menagerie whose existence, so individual and peculiar, yet stands there, so intensely and vividly real, as much as one's own, so that one feels again poignantly the unfathomableness of ontology, supposing ontology to be at all" (*LWJ* 1:224). Not to slight the fishes, in a letter of 1899 to his wife, he wrote: "four cuttle-fish in the Aquarium. I wish we had one of them for a child – such flexible intensity of life in a form so inacces-

---

vidual from every other, keeps each in ultimate oppugnance to every other, forces them to try conclusions upon each other in the struggle to survive" (*ML* 46). This is Kallen, not James.

sible to our sympathy" (quoted from Allen, *WJ* 309). Maybe James would have had more luck I–Thou-ing a cat, as did Buber.

James wanted to go all the way and I–Thou the entire universe, as nature mystics have traditionally done. Clearly, he is personalizing the universe when he writes: "The Universe is no longer a mere *It* to us, but a *Thou*, if we are religious; and any relation that may be possible from person to person might be possible here" (*WB* 31). Taking a religious stance to the world "changes the dead blank *it* of the world into a living *thou*, with whom the whole man may have dealings" (*WB* 101). "Infra-theistic ways of looking on the world leave it in the third person, a mere *it* . . . [but] theism turns the *it* into a *thou*" (*WB* 106).

James's I–Thou-ing of nature is within the tradition of cosmic consciousness or nature mysticism. He endorses the following lines of Wordsworth's poem, *The Prelude*:

> To every natural form, rock, fruit or flower,
> Even the loose stones that cover the high-way,
> I gave a moral life: I saw them feel,
> Or linked them to some feeling: the great mass
> Lay bedded in a quickening soul, and all
> That I beheld respired with inward meaning.
> (quoted in *TT* 139)

Wordsworth's "strange inner joy" resulted from his responsiveness "to the secret life of Nature roundabout him" (*TT* 140). It is clear that James accepts the panpsychic upshot of this sort of nature mysticism experience. Herein panpsychism enters in, not as it did in the last chapter, as an intellectual device for saving the doctrine of Pure Experience from the challenge posed by unperceived events, but as something experientially vouchsafed by I–Thou experiences of nature.[4] In the next chapter it will be seen how this experientially based panpsychism turns into a form of spiritualism or idealism in his final two books, this time with intellectual considerations working hand in glove with experiential ones.

Another part of James's account of the I–Thou relation that needs further elaboration is just how unified a person becomes with her Thou, be it another person or nature. There are monistic mystics who take the unification to be one of complete numerical identity, but James, being squarely ensconced within the Western theistic mystical tradition, takes it to be something less than that, a case of what he liked

---

[4] James reports having had a Wordsworthian type of mystical experience on a night in 1898. "I spent a good deal of it in the woods, where the streaming moonlight lit up things in a magical checkered play, and it seemed as if the Gods of all the nature-mythologies were holding an indescribable meeting in my breast with the moral Gods of the inner life. . . . The intense significance of some sort, of the whole scene, if one could only *tell* the significance; the intense inhuman remoteness of its inner life, and yet the intense *appeal* of it" (quoted from Perry *TC* 364).

to call, using Blood's marvelous phrase, "ever not quite" (*EP* 189). Throughout his career he was a self-proclaimed "pluralistic mystic." Buber was not as unequivocally committed as was James to a dualistic interpretation of the I–Thou experience, for he reports in *Between Man and Man* that he once had a mystical experience in which it appeared as if he became one and the same as God, but upon subsequent reflection (i.e., he remembered that he was Jewish), came to realize that it stopped short of strict numerical identity. This is reminiscent of Meister Eckhardt's "little point" that God gives men so that they can rotate around it and find their way back to their creaturehood, and thereby realize that they are distinct from God the Creator. In the next chapter, James's other type of mystical experience, the Bergsonian conceptless intuition of the mushing together of spatio-temporal neighbors, will also be seen to fit the format of James's pluralistic mysticism . Furthermore, in both types of mystical experience, the individuals, whether persons or contiguous events, enter into relations with each other in which they lose their distinct identities. These are the "relational processes and states" of Buber (*IT* 70). Our concern in this chapter, however, is only with the I–Thou experience and, in particular, the role it plays in the sort of "religious" mysticism that James wound up embracing in his classic work on *The Varieties of Religious Experience.* It will be seen to form the basis of this type of mysticism.

II. Religious Mystical Experiences

The major thesis of this book, and one I think is successfully maintained to James's everlasting credit, is that the basis of religion, including its institutional structure, theology, and personal religious feelings and beliefs, is rooted in religious experiences of a mystical sort in which the individual has an apparent direct, nonsensory perception of a "More," an "Unseen" supernatural or purely spiritual reality into which she is to some extent absorbed and from which spiritual energy flows into her. This "perception" of the "More" can be viewed as a very heightened and intense form of the I–Thou experience. Through these I–Thou experiences of the More the subject receives "an assurance of safety and a temper of peace, and, in relations to others, a preponderance of loving affection" (*VRE* 383). In the Introduction it was shown that it was this sort of assurance that James's "sick" or "morbid" self needed in order to face the evils of the world, especially the sort that occasioned an experience of existential angst. James's mystical self is the other side of the coin of his healthy-minded Promethean self, the one itching to engage in a Texas death match with evil without any assurance of who will emerge victorious.

Surprisingly, James claims not to have had any mystical experiences himself – "my own constitution shuts me out from their enjoyment almost entirely, and I can speak of them only at second hand" (*VRE* 301). If this is so, is not the underlying thesis of this book, that James had a mystical self that clashed with his Promethean pragmatic self, especially in regard to the challenges posed by evil, wrong? How can one be a mystic, or even be so sympathetically inclined to mystical experiences as to accept their cognitivity, as James will be seen to have done, without having mystical experiences? I have two replies.

My first response is that even if it were true that James did not have any mystical experiences, at least of the more developed type, it could be the case that he had a deep sensitivity to and appreciation of them and what they seemingly reveal, just as someone who lacks the musical genius to compose an *Eroica* Symphony can resonate to it aesthetically. As Walter Stace, a virgin to mystical experience who nevertheless was one of the greatest expositors and defenders of mysticism, was fond of pointing out, people are possessed of varying degrees of mystical sensitivity and talent. James's claim that "we all have at least the germ of mysticism in us" can be seen as making this point (*P* 76).

Second, James is not leveling with his audience. Mystical experiences for him cover a broad spectrum of cases, ranging from the relatively undeveloped experiences of a heightened sense of reality, an intensification of feeling and insight such as occurs under the influence of alcohol, drugs, nitrous oxide, art, and even the raptures of nature, to the fully developed monistic experience of an undifferentiated unity in which all distinctions are obliterated. James never had an experience of the latter kind, but he did have more than his share of the less developed ones, given his penchant to experiment on himself with nitrous oxide and mescal.[5] He was no stranger to alcohol either and gives glowing descriptions of its effects, along with impassioned sermons on its evils (*VRE* 307). Footnote 4 to this chapter reports a fairly developed nature mysticism experience that James had in the Adirondacks in 1898, shortly before he caused irreparable damage to his heart, from which he eventually died, by overtaxing himself on a trek. James reports four mystical experiences he had in 1906 in his 1910 "A Suggestion about Mysticism," in which he apparently became aware of experiences

---

[5] Dimitri Tymoczko, in an article in *The Atlantic Monthly* of 1996 titled "The Nitrous Oxide Philosopher," vastly exaggerates the importance of the experiences these occasioned in the development of James's mystical philosophy, saying that "For James, these alternate forms of consciousness [i.e., mystical ones] were accessible only by way of artificial intoxicants" (94). This overlooks James's non-drug-induced nature mysticism experiences, such as that of 1898, and his I–Thou experiences, as well as his Bergsonian backyard mystical experiences, which Chapter 10 will explore. The author portrays James as a forerunner of the flower children of the sixties, not doubt to enlist James as an ally in his quest to have drugs legalized.

not his own. Whether these experiences should be called "mystical" will be broached later.

What was said in Chapter 3 about the reason for James's misrepresenting his exceedingly tender-minded view of the will and its freedom in his presidential address to the "brethren of the American Psychological Association" applies here. He was very sensitive to the suspicions that his tough-minded scientific colleagues had of his interests in disreputable types of psychic and mystical experiences and went to considerable pains to appear as tough-minded as they, rather than as some sentimental apologist for the wild claims made in behalf of these experiences. His deepest fear was to wind up like his father, an eccentric whose writings everybody safely neglected. This was evident in his patronizing Willy Loman "farewell" letter to his father and the great pain he experienced over the abysmal sales for *The Literary Remains of the Late Henry James*, as witnessed in the quotations given in Chapter 3 from his letters to his brother Henry.

Another example of his misrepresenting himself so as to disarm the suspicions of the tough-minded in his audience is his 1898 lecture, "Human Immortality: Two Supposed Objections to the Doctrine." He begins by saying that he cannot understand why the Ingersoll Committee chose him to give this lecture, as he is no friend of the doctrine of human immortality and has little personal concern for it, something that was shown in the Introduction not to be the case. He then goes on to neutralize the two major objections to immortality, mount an inference to the best explanation argument in support of it, about which more will be said, and end with a will-to-believe justification for believing in it!

Granted that James had every right to be a sympathetic expositor and defender of mysticism, we can now consider the specifics of his account. The first question concerns whether our apprehension of the supersensible reality is conceptual or via some direct presentation. Throughout *The Varieties of Religious Experience* James works with a perceptual model of mystical experiences, likening them to ordinary sense perceptions in that both involve a direct acquaintance with an object, although only the latter has a sensory content. "Mystical experiences are . . . direct perceptions . . . absolutely sensational . . . face to face presentations of what seems to exist" (*VRE* 336). A perception is "direct," I assume, if the existential claims made by the subject on the basis of her experience are noninferential. Another important, and highly controversial, assumption James makes in his likening mystical experiences to sense perceptions is that mystical experiences, like sensory ones, are intentional, in the sense that they have an apparent accusative that exists independently of the subject when the experience is veridical. In this respect, they are unlike a feeling of pain, which takes only a cognate or internal accusative, since feeling a pain is nothing but paining or feeling painfully.

James tries to take a neutral stance on whether mystical experiences support a monistic or a pluralistic view of the More or Unseen reality, in spite of his own strong emotional commitment to the pluralistic version. At one place he seems to come down on the side of the modern-day mystical ecumenicalists, Suzuki, Stace, and Merton, who contend that there is a common phenomenological *monistic* core to all unitive mystical experiences which then gets interpreted by the mystic so as to accord with the underlying culture of her society, as for example Buber's imposition of a dualistic interpretation on his apparently monistic mystical experience. "In mystic states we both become one with the Absolute and we become aware of our oneness. *This is the everlasting and triumphant mystical tradition, hardly altered by differences of clime or creed*" (*VRE* 332; my italics). Some of James's major contentions in *The Varieties of Religious Experience*, however, require a dualistic experience of the sort called "theistic" by R. C. Zaehner in his *Concordant Discord*. For example, James says that prayer is "the very soul and essence of religion" and then describes prayer as involving two-way interaction between two subjects (For someone who takes such a strong antiessentialist stance in Lecture II, James managed to say a lot of things about the essence of religion.) James's strong Protestant leanings caused him, for the most part, to give a dualistic interpretation of mystical experiences.

One of the features of mystical experiences, as well as conversion experiences in general, that James stresses, so much so that it is used as one of the four defining conditions of a mystical experience, is that the subject is passive in respect to them. Although persons can take steps, such as following the mystical way, to help induce the experience, its coming is viewed by religious mystics as the free bestowal of a gift upon them by the grace of God. Through the experience the subject feels that her conscious will is held in abeyance as she finds absorption in a higher unity. "The mystic feels as if his own will were grasped and held by a superior power" (*VRE* 303). In both cases there must be a canceling out of the finite so as to open ourselves to the infinite. This resignation and abandonment of the finite self and its conscious will is found in the mystical and conversion experiences of both the once- and twice-born, or the healthy- and morbid-minded.[6]

---

[6] James used this pair of distinctions as if they were interchangeable, but actually they sit askew of each other. The former is an *etymologically* based distinction that concerns whether or not one undergoes a rebirth along the way to salvation; the latter, a *doctrinally* based distinction concerning the status that is accorded to evil in one's worldview. Were

James, no doubt with his sick soul's experiences of existential angst in mind, stresses how such mystically based resignation cannot "fail to steady the nerves, to cool the fever, and appease the fret, if one be conscious that, no matter what one's difficulties for the moment may appear to be, one's life as a whole is in the keeping of a power whom one can absolutely trust" (*VRE* 230). The mystical experiences that such submission of the conscious will helps to foster are "reconciling and unifying states" that "tell of the supremacy of the ideal, of vastness, of union, of safety, and of rest" (*VRE* 330 and 339). In such mystical union there is a "life not correlated with death, a health not liable to illness, a kind of good that will not perish, a good in fact that flies beyond the Goods of nature" (*VRE* 119). This is just what the Promethean self's beloved religion of meliorism cannot deliver; it cannot help him make it through the dark nights of his soul, nor face the hideous catatonic epileptic youth described in the Introduction. A theme that runs throughout *The Varieties of Religious Experience* is the insufficiency of meliorism. It is condemned as being "the very consecration of forgetfulness and superficiality" (*VRE* 118–19).

Herein we see the first of several dramatic clashes between James's Promethean and mystical selves. First there is the clash between the active self of the Promethean moral agent and the passive self of the mystic. The Promethean self *is* the active will, which, James says, is "the substantive thing which we *are*" (*PP* 1181). But for the mystic the true self, that "self of all the other selves," no longer is identified with the active aspect of a person, her free conscious will. Quite the contrary, it is that very self, along with its Promethean will to believe and the meliorism it favors, that must be surrendered. The true or higher self is that aspect of us, identified by James with the subconscious or transmarginal self, that is able to enter into a complete or partial union with a supersensible reality, which is a "More" of the same kind as it.

The mystical self displaces the active will by "a willingness to close our mouths and be as nothing in the floods and waterspouts of God" (*VRE* 46). "To give up one's conceit of being good, is the only door to the Universe's deeper reaches" (*ERM* 128). By meeting despair with religious resignation, we uncover "resources in us that naturalism, with its literal virtue, never recks of, possibilities that take our breath away, and show a world wider than either physics or Philistine ethics can

the distinctions identified, it would result in cross-classification, since some healthy-minded persons are twice-born in that their eventual upbeat worldview concerning evil has resulted from a rebirth or conversion experience. The French translator of *The Varieties of Religious Experience*, Abauzit, wrote to James about this difficulty, but James, with his typical abhorrence of rewriting except when it concerned only stylistic matters, wrote back to proceed with the book in spite of this flaw, giving the lame excuse that we should "Beware of logic in natural history" (Appendix 6 of *VRE* 508).

imagine. Here is a world in which all is well, *in spite* of certain forms of death, indeed *because* of certain forms of death, death of hope, death of strength, death of responsibility, of fear and worry" (*ERM* 128). The death of strength and responsibility is the death of the Promethean moral agent, along with its melioristic religion. "Sincerely to give up one's conceit or hope of being good in one's own right is the only door to the universe's deeper reaches" (*PU* 138). The overcoming of our active self does not assure that we will achieve some kind of experiential union with God, but it is a necessary first step along the way to such mystical illumination.

It would be a mistake to think that the clash between James's Prometheanism and his mysticism is a clash between the early and the late James. Some commentators, such as Bennett Ramsey and Paul Croce, have depicted James as relinquishing by the end of his career the assertive self in favor of a religious acceptance of forces beyond its control. This cannot be right, because James closes his final two books with a reaffirmation of his most Promethean of all doctrines – the will to believe. Furthermore, there are several earlier publications in which mystical doctrines are espoused, most notably the 1902 *The Varieties of Religious Experience*, as well as some articles of the late 1890s, even at one place in the 1890 *Principles of Psychology* (*PP* 328). The clashes between James's Promethean and mystical selves, therefore, cannot be explained away as diachronic ones, since he was a highly divided self throughout his life. The clashes, rather, are synchronic. At every moment in his career James was of several minds about everything, and that is why his philosophical writings are like a philosophical wheel of fortune. Whatever doctrine it stopped on and temporarily illuminated reaped a rich payoff, for every one of his many philosophies was espoused with incredible brilliance and passion. Whether James would defend pragmatism or mysticism on any given day depended on his mood, whether he was in a healthy- or a sick-minded one.

James can neutralize the clash between his morally strenuous Promethean self and the passivity and quietism of his mystical self by playing Poo-bah and suitably "qua"-clausing the claims made by these selves, thereby allowing them to take turns in being his dominant interest; for example, he could be a Promethean moral agent on the weekdays and a mystic on the weekends. This is the Promethean "solution," but it has the unattractive upshot of making him into a temporalized schizophrenic. Chapter 11 will explore ways in which James might have moved beyond this and become a truly unified self.

Another significant clash between James's pragmatic and mystical selves is the one between their respective reality-claims. In the first place, there is an apparent clash in the content of these claims, the Promethean pragmatist asserting the existence of a multiplicity of dis-

tinct objects changing in space and time and the acosmic mystic denying the reality of this multiplicity. This contentful clash can be neutralized by Poo-bah-izing the respective reality-claims by restricting them to
a given person's interests at a certain time. A far more serious conflict
concerns *how* the respective reality claims are made rather than *what*
they claim. In the first place, mystical claims, unlike those made by the
Promethean pragmatist, are not advanced in the spirit of fallibilism, as
hypotheses to be tested by future experiences and thus subject to revision or withdrawal. They are, instead, claims to absolute certainty, without which there would not accrue the feeling of peace and safety so
needed by James's morbid self. Second, and most important, they are
advanced as noetic claims that are revelatory of an ultimate or absolute
reality – the really real in comparison with which everything is a mere
illusion or emanation of some sort. They are nonrelativized reality-
claims and therefore are incompatible with Prometheanism's doctrine
of Ontological Relativism, which played such a key role in enabling us
to have it all by requiring that all reality claims be relativized to the
interests of a person at a time. The mystic definitely is not saying that,
qua the mystical point of view, reality is some kind of a unity or oneness,
but rather that it is so *simpliciter.* To restrict mystical reality-claims to the
mystical perspective would, in effect, be awarding an ontological status
to the mystic's reality that is on all fours with Ivanhoe and Pegasus,
certainly a booby prize. In the next chapter it will be found that James's
Bergsonian-type mystical claims also are advanced in an absolutistic,
nonrelativized manner, as revelations of the true nature or essence of
reality, which phrases are anathema to the Promethean pragmatist.
This clash is far more serious than one of content, since it cannot be
met by playing Poo-bah; instead, it is the Ontological Relativism of Poo-
bah-ism that is being challenged. This is one of the most serious aporia
in all of James's philosophy and must await Chapter 11's attempted
resolution.

It is not surprising that Ontological Relativism is largely subdued in
The Varieties of Religious Experience, as well as the final two books in which
James promotes his version of Bergsonian mysticism, which I call
"Backyard Mysticism." It is interesting to note that Ontological Relativ-
ism does make its way into one of the drafts for Lecture II.

What . . . determines our living attitudes has *reality* for us in so far forth. In fact,
if you open some of the books on psychology, you will find them saying that the
way in which the feeling of the thing grasps us and decides our living attitudes
is all that we *mean* by its reality. What thus grasps us is by that very fact believed
in, is real. That is all that the word real signifies, – you hear these psychologist
insist. (*VRE* 483–4, Appendix 2)

Why did James omit from his final draft the Poo-bah-istic account of
reality of *The Principles of Psychology?* Probably, it was because he realized

that it conflicts with the absolutistic reality-claims that he endorsed in the book. Some commentators would like to believe that James gave up his Ontological Relativism because he realized that it was, in general, fallacious to derive semantic and ontological conclusions from a genetic analysis of how we come to acquire a given concept, something which he has been seen to do with the concepts of good, truth, negation, self-identity, and material objects. Owen Flanagan dogmatically claims that it is a mistake to think that "*ontology recapitulates ontogeny*"[7] and tries to interpret James so that he does not commit this fallacy, in spite of the fact that over and over again James infers what we mean by *X*, as well as what it is to be *X*, from a genetic analysis of how we experientially acquire the concept of *X* (*CP* 44–5). It is too harsh to brand this a fallacy. Rather, it is a time-honored way of doing philosophy, which ran rampant among James's British empiricist predecessors, that happens not to be favored by Flanagan. There is no evidence that James ever came to doubt this method of doing philosophy. All that his dropping Ontological Relativism from the final draft of *The Varieties of Religious Experience* is evidence for is that he saw that it is not applicable to mystical claims; however, he continued to apply it to reality-claims made from the Promethean perspective of his pragmatic selves, such as the moral agent and the scientist.

Mysticism also challenges James's pragmatic theory of meaning and truth. The pragmatic theory of meaning, as contrasted with the theory of pragmatic meaning, was interpreted in Chapter 6 as holding that the meaning of *X* is a set of conditionalized predictions of what experiences we shall have upon performing certain operations, with a belief in the reality of *X* becoming "true" when these predictions are verified. The reason for the scare quotation marks around "true" is that it means "epistemically warranted," true beliefs being, for James, those which maximize desire-satisfaction for their believers, so he was interpreted by me. But the mystic's conception of the Absolute, the undifferentiated unity, the eternal one, God, is not based on how we can ride herd on it, for there is nothing that we do to or with this mystical reality, or ways in which it is expected to behave if we perform certain operations. It does not dissolve in aqua regia. It simply *is*, and is just what it *appears* to be in the immediate experience of the mystic. A door-to-door salesman of mystical reality, therefore, would be stymied when asked, "But what does it do?" or "What can I do with it?" Herein the content of the

---

[7] I must confess that I am among those who dogmatically charged James with committing this fallacy: "Since James was fond of devising names for the 'fallacies' committed by his adversaries, it is only fitting that a name be created for James's penchant to semanticize and ontologize his explanations of the psychological causes of . . . [concept acquisition]– 'The James Fallacy.' " "Pragmatism versus Mysticism: The Divided Self of William James," *Philosophical Perspectives* 5 (1991): 245.

proposition that this reality exists is not reducible to any set of prag-matic conditionalized predictions. The star performer finally gets into the act, unlike the case of the pragmatically favored melioristic religion, which reduced "God exists" to the conditionalized prediction that good will win out over evil in the long run, if we collectively exert our best moral effort. The reason James chose meliorism as his example of a religion in the final lecture of *Pragmatism* is that it can be shown to employ the same pragmatic theory of meaning and truth as does sci-ence, which fits his program of reconciliation through methodological univocalism.

In order to account for the meaning of mystical reality-claims, James will have to resort to content empiricism, which was found in Chapter 6 to be his alternate species of empiricism to that of pragmatism. Since the meaningful content of the mystic's reality-claim is based on the manner in which she is phenomenologically appeared to in an of-God-type experience, the truth of the claim will depend on whether her experience is objective or cognitive. The spiritual and moral benefits that the experience occasions, as will be seen, become relevant, but only as a means of indirect verification, there now being, as there was not for meliorism, a distinction between direct and indirect verification, with an assertion's meaning being identified primarily with the former, that being the apparent object, the intentional accusative, of the mysti-cal experience. James seems to recognize this when he says that "the word 'truth' is here taken to mean something additional to bare value for life" (*VRE* 401). Accordingly, James makes the issue of the cognitiv-ity or objectivity of mystical experience a central issue in *The Varieties of Religious Experience.* Concerning them, he asks about their "metaphysi-cal significance" (308), "cognitivity" (324), "authoritativeness" (335), "objective truth" (304), "value for knowledge" (327), "truth" (329), and whether they "furnish any *warrant for the truth* of the . . . superna-turality and pantheism which they favor" (335), or are "to be taken as *evidence* . . . for the actual existence of a higher world with which our world is in relation" (384). James is quite explicit that the answer to the "objectivity" question is independent of the biological and psycho-logical benefits that accrue from mystical experiences.

James concludes that there is a generic content of the many different types of mystical experiences that "is literally and objectively true" (*VRE* 405.) His arguments for this are not made sufficiently explicit, so much so that it has led some commentators to claim that James gave no arguments at all.[8] With a little sympathetic imagination and anach-

---

[8] Even so sensitive and sympathetic a critic as John Wild has claimed that James's accep-tance of the objectivity of mystical experiences "is not based on theoretical argument, nor on causal inference of any kind" (*RE* 325), though he later inconsistently says that, on the basis of the similarity between mystical and sense experience, "James *concludes*

ronistic hindsight, I believe that two arguments can be detected in the text: the argument from analogy with sense experience and the argument from an inference to the best explanation. The former is far more important and will be considered first.

This argument has been very ably defended in recent years by William Wainwright, Richard Swinburne, Gary Gutting, and especially William Alston, whose book *Perceiving God* should become a classic. First, an overview will be given of a generic brand version of their arguments, and then an attempt will be made to locate it, or at least the germ of it, in James, hopefully without being anachronistic to the point of developing a private history of philosophy. It is an argument from analogy that goes as follows. Mystical and sense experiences are analogous in cognitively relevant respects; and, since the latter are granted to be cognitive, so should be the former, in which a cognitive type of experience is one that counts, in virtue of some a priori presumptive inference rule, as evidence or warrant for believing that the apparent object of the experience, its intentional accusative, objectively exists and is as it appears to be in the experience.[9] For sense experience, the presumptive inference rule is that if it perceptually appears to be the case that X exists, then it probably is the case that X does exist, unless there are defeating conditions. These defeating conditions consist in tests and checks for the veridicality of the experience that get flunked on this occasion. Prominent among these tests are: agreement among relevant observers, law-like coherence between the experience's content and the content of earlier and later experiences, and being caused in the right way. The presumptive inference rule is said to be a priori, because it cannot be justified by appeal to sense experience without vicious circularity.

If mystical experiences are to be subject to an analogous a priori presumptive inference rule, they must be analogous to sense experiences in having defeating conditions – checks and tests that can get flunked. All of the contemporary defenders of the cognitivity of mystical experiences argue that the great religious mystical traditions employ a fairly elaborate network of tests for veridicality of mystical experiences, usually including that the subject, as well as her community,

that this [the intentional accusative of a mystical experience] is real" (328; my italics). If there are no arguments, then there are no conclusions. A. J. Ayer, in his introduction to the joint edition of *Pragmatism* and *The Meaning of Truth*, also fails to find any arguments in James, though he says that "There is a suggestion in *The Varieties of Religious Experience* that he is willing to count religious experiences as evidence" for the existence of a supersensible reality (xx). This will be seen to be a radically misleading understatement.
[9] The idea of objective existence is that of existence independent of being perceived or thought of. Thus, an object that has objective existence could exist even if there were to be no conscious beings. That the object of an experience exists independently of that experience does not assure objective existence, since, as Berkeley argued, this does not entail that it can exist without being experienced by anyone.

display favorable moral and/or spiritual development as a result of the experience, and that what her experience reveals accords with her religion's holy scriptures and the mystical experiences of past saints and notables, to name two of the more important tests of most of the great religious mystical traditions.

These tests are admittedly not exactly analogous to those which inform the sense experience doxastic practice[10] in that, most notably, they do not contain any requirements for being caused in the right way or having nomic connections between the content of the experience and those of earlier and later experiences. An attempt is made to explain away these disanalogies by showing that they can be accounted for in terms of a categorical difference between the intentional accusatives of the two types of experience, these being material objects for sense experiences and God (the eternal one, etc.) for mystical experiences. Whereas material objects, for the most part, behave according to scientific laws, and thus permit predictions to be made of future experiences and a distinction to be drawn between a right and a wrong way for a sense experience to be caused, God, being an absolutely free supernatural being, precludes our being able to predict how he will behave and, in particular, when and to whom he will choose to reveal himself directly, as well as our being able to distinguish between a right and a wrong way for an of-God type of experience to occur.[11] Given that God supernaturally causes a mystical experience by his efficacious will, there is no causal chain of events linking God with a mystical experience in the way in which there is such a chain linking a material object with a veridical perception of it.

With a little imagination we can find most, but not all, of the elements of this analogical argument in *The Varieties of Religious Experience*; in fact, a good case can be made that James deserves to be credited with being the founding father of this argument. In the first place, James makes prominent use of a perceptual model of mystical experience, which is the analogical premise of the contemporary argument for cognitivity. He comes right out and says:

---

[10] A doxastic practice is a normative-rule-governed social practice that enables us to go from an experiential input of some kind to an existential belief output, that is, from an experience of it experientially seeming to be the case that X to the belief that X is objectively the case.

[11] I am doing my best to give a sympathetic exposition of the analogical argument for the cognitivity of mystical experiences in spite of the fact that I have been a very hostile critic of it in the following publications: Chapter 8 of *The Nature and Existence of God* (Cambridge: Cambridge University Press, 1991); "Why Alston's Mystical Doxastic Practice Is Subjective," *Philosophy and Phenomenological Research* 54 (1994); "The Overall Argument of Alston's *Perceiving God*," *Religious Studies* 30 (1994); "Swinburne on Religious Experience," in *Reason and the Christian Religion*, ed. Alan Padgett (Oxford: Oxford University Press, 1994); and a critical study of Keith Yandell's *The Epistemology of Religious Experience*, forthcoming in *Faith and Philosophy*.

Our own more 'rational' beliefs are based on evidence exactly similar in nature to that which mystics quote for theirs. Our senses, namely, have assured us of certain states of fact; but mystical experiences are as direct perceptions of fact for those who have them as any sensations ever were for us. The records show that even though the five senses be in abeyance in them, they are absolutely sensational in their epistemological quality. (*VRE* 336)

Furthermore, like the contemporary analogical arguers, James goes on to expand the analogy by showing that there are mystical analogues for some of the tests for the veridicality of sense experience. What is apparently revealed by mystical experiences "must be sifted and tested, and run the gauntlet of confrontation with the total context of experience just like what comes from the outer world of sense" (*VRE* 338). Mystical experiences are also likened to "windows through which the mind looks out upon a more extensive and inclusive world" than is revealed by our senses, and just as we have checks and tests for mediating between rival sensory-based claims there are analogous ones for mediating between rival mystically based claims. Because of these background defeating conditions, it will be possible for mysticism to have "its valid experiences and its counterfeit ones, just as our world has them. . . . We should have to use its experiences by selecting and subordinating and substituting just as is our custom in this ordinary naturalistic world; we should be liable to error just as we are now" (*VRE* 339). Further indication of just how close James is to the contemporary analogical arguers is his claim that mystical experiences "establish a presumption" in favor of the thing being as it appears to be in them (*VRE* 336), which sounds very much like their presumptive inference rule.

If James did accept such a presumptive inference rule, he would not be committing the howler of inferring that the apparent object of a mystical experience objectively exists from the mere fact that it appears to exist to its subject, as he seems to do in the following: "The theologian's contention that the religious man is moved by an external power is vindicated, for one of the peculiarities of invasions from the subconscious region is that they take on objective appearances, and suggest to the Subject an external control" (*VRE* 403; see also *PU* 139 for more of the same). James seemingly drops the intentional operator "take on" and "suggest" as he moves from the "seeming" premise to the "objectively is" conclusion. Given the presumptive inference rule, the inference becomes valid provided the conclusion is weakened to "*It probably is the case* that the apparent object of a mystical experience exists." In other words, a mystical experience, like a sensory one, bestows only a *prima facie warrant* to believe that the apparent object exists. The belief is defeasible because of the battery of background overriders or defeaters.

There is one very important respect in which James differs from contemporary analogical arguers that renders his argument less attractive than theirs, namely, he completely eschews any attempt to place the relevant background tests, which are the overriders or defeaters, within the shared practices of ongoing religious community. In general, James's failure to see the importance of religious institutions, with their shared beliefs and communal practices, is a significant limitation in the account that is given of religious experience in *The Varieties of Religious Experience*. This is yet another example of James's overglorification of the isolated individual. His mystic is a lone-gun mystic, cut off from any doxastic practice of a continuing religious community. Where his mystic gets her tests from and how they are enforced remains a mystery. Just as James was found in Chapter 6 to be committed to a private language in which the speaker follows rules that only she can determine are being followed correctly, so James's mystic, in virtue of being isolated from a community of fellow believers and practitioners, must follow her own private tests.

Contemporary analogical arguers are intent on justifying the various ongoing mystical doxastic practices as being reliable for the most part. James, on the other hand, works only on the *retail* level, his concern being exclusively with the justification for an individual mystic's taking one of her experiences to be veridical. He fails to see that this justification cannot be isolated from the *wholesale* justification of the shared social practice of basing objective existential claims on mystical experiences. James fails to realize that by eschewing the wholesale level, he significantly weakens the effectiveness of his will-to-believe justification for the lone mystic believing that one of her experiences is veridical. This is a very important application of the will to believe, as what she believes in this matter could have the most important consequences for her future moral and spiritual development, that is, for her quest for sanctification. Certainly, she will be aided in her attempt to get herself to believe on will-to-believe grounds that her mystical experience is veridical if she first believes that the general doxastic practice of basing existential claims on mystical experiences is a reliable one that yields true existential beliefs for the most part. This belief also must be based on will-to-believe grounds, since the mystical doxastic practice, like the sensory one, does not admit of any noncircular external justification. James's analogical argument, along with his will-to-believe justification for believing in the veridicality of an individual mystical experience, welcome supplementation by bringing in the doxastic practice in which his tests are embedded.

With this in mind, a survey can now be made of the different tests he recognized as relevant to determining the veridicality of a mystical experience. Like the contemporary analogical arguers, James recognizes a mystical analogue to the sensory agreement and prediction tests, though he adds a third one – the immediate luminosity test. Here, in brief, is how they work.

James makes a very broad application of the agreement test so that it concerns not only whether there is agreement among the mystics themselves but whether their reports agree with ordinary sensory-based ones. In regard to the former, he first says that there is a consensus among mystics, and that "it would be odd . . . if such a unanimous type of experience should prove to be altogether wrong" (*VRE* 336). However, he immediately counters that "the appeal to numbers has no logical force" and that there is considerable disagreement among the monistic and pluralistic mystics, not to mention their collective disagreement with demoniacal mysticism. Not only does the agreement test not support the objectivity of mystical experience when only mystical experiences are considered, it counts against this when the sensory-based experiences are brought in. Mystical experiences "do not come to everyone; and the rest of life makes either no connexion with them, or tends to contradict them more than it confirms them" (*VRE* 22). And, against the claims of monistic mystics, James says that the "eaches" of the pluralists "are at any rate real enough to have made themselves at least appear to everyone, whereas the absolute has as yet appeared immediately to only a few mystics, and indeed to them very ambiguously" (*PU* 62).

James, I believe, tries to soften this clash between mysticism and sense experience by giving a very understated conclusion concerning what mystical experiences ultimately proclaim.

As a rule, mystical states merely add a supersensuous meaning to the ordinary outward data of consciousness. They are excitements like the emotions of love or ambition, flights to our spirit by means of which facts already objectively before us fall into a new life. They do not contradict these facts as such, or deny anything that our senses have immediately seized. (*VRE* 338)

The same protective strategy seems operative in James's bizarre initial set of four defining characteristics of a mystical experience – being ineffable, noetic, transitory, and passive (*VRE* 302–3) – in which he fails to include being a unitive experience, their most important and distinctive feature but one that seems to conflict with the deliverances of ordinary sense experience, which presents us with a multiplicity of distinct objects in space and time. This aptly could be called the "comic book" theory of mystical experiences, since they are supposed to function as do the field of force lines that comic books place around an object that is perceived or thought in a specifically intense manner. This, at best, fits the experiences at the undeveloped end of the mystical spectrum, such as drunkenness, but not those unitive experiences at the developed end, which not only report new facts, James's higher dimensions of reality, but also sometimes seem to contradict our sensory-based beliefs concerning the reality of space, time, and multiplicity. James does not want us to have to serve on a jury and decide whether to believe the testimony of the mystics or that of the vast majority of mankind, but he does not map out any effective strategy for preventing the matter from going to trial. He wants to find some common denominator of all mystical experiences that is sufficiently watered down so as not to conflict with the deliverances of sense experience, but this fails to address the issue of whether the more developed mystical experiences are veridical.

Whereas the agreement test did not offer any support to the objectivity claim of mystics, quite to the contrary according to James, the prediction test does. Because of the passive and transitory nature of mystical experiences, we are not able to predict their occurrence, and, to this extent, the prediction test counts against their objectivity. But this is more than offset by the fact that so many mystics grow morally and/ or spiritually as a result of their experience. In attacking reductivistic causal explanations of mystical experiences James says that we must "inquire into their fruits for life," rather than their causes (*VRE* 327). This is an ongoing theme in *The Varieties of Religious Experience*, especially in Lectures I, XIV, and XV.

Unfortunately, James does not clearly distinguish between these good consequences being epistemologically confirmatory of the *proposition* believed and their pragmatically justifying, in the will-to-believe manner, our *believing* it. The following is a typical example of this unclarity. "*Believing* that a higher power will take care of us in certain ways better than we can take care of ourselves, if we only genuinely throw ourselves upon it and consent to use it, it finds *the belief*, not only not impugned, but corroborated by its observation [of good consequences]" (*VRE* 103; my italics). Belief is being used here in a way that is ambiguous between the psychological state or act of believing and the what-is-believed, the proposition. This opens James to the standard objection that he confused the psychological benefits of believing a proposition with the confirmation of the proposition believed. It is here that James is far outstripped by his contemporary analogical arguers, such as Alston, who makes it clear in his use of the prediction test that the good consequences for the mystic and her community are confirmatory of the objectivity of the mystical experience in virtue of a conceptual or categoreal link between these consequences and the nature of the apparent object of the experience. As God is essentially good, it is probable that those who have had an objective experience of him will benefit morally and spiritually. By the same reasoning, one should count the deleterious consequence of a mystical experience as evidence for it having been a veridical perception of a malevolent being like the devil.

Immediate luminosity, the subject's intense feeling of delight and reality, figures prominently in James's network of confirmatory tests, sometimes being accorded pride of place over good consequences (*VRE* 23) and at others taking second place to them (*VRE* 21–2). An interesting question is why James, unlike his contemporary analogical arguers, used this test. The answer might be that *The Principles of Psychology*'s interest-relative account of existence, although not explicitly endorsed in *The Varieties of Religious Experience*, still weighed heavily in James's thinking. This might account for his seeming relativization of *being evidence for* to persons in his first two conclusions regarding what mystical experiences establish.

1. Mystical states, when well developed, usually are, and have the right to be, absolutely authoritative over the individuals to whom they come.
2. No authority emanates from them which should make it a duty for those who stand outside of them to accept their revelations uncritically. (*VRE* 335)

This makes it look as if the occurrence of mystical states constitutes evidence for their objectivity for those who experience them but not for those who do not, which clearly violates the principle of universalizability of *being evidence for* among persons, as well as times, as argued in Chapter 6. If E is evidence for proposition p, then E is evidence for any person (or at any time) that p. As emphasized in Chapter 6, *being evidence for* is an existentially grounded relation and must not be confused with *being taken to be evidence for*, which is relative to a person's epistemic situation – what she knows and believes. What mystics know that many nonmystics do not is that mystical experiences occur and therefore that there exists certain evidence for the existence of God. Nonmystics can have only indirect knowledge through the testimony of mystics that such evidence obtains; and, as a consequence, they have less epistemic warrant for believing that mystical states occur than do the mystics themselves. This completes my rather hasty exposition of James's analogical argument for the cognitivity of mystical experiences and therefore the likelihood that their intentional object exists. It has not been my aim to evaluate the analogical argument critically, which is something I do at length in the publications listed in Footnote 10, only to show that James deserves great credit for laying the foundation for the contemporary version of this argument.

James's second argument for the cognitivity of mystical experience, based on an inference to the best explanation, is only hinted at in *The Varieties of Religious Experience* on pages 303, 304, and 381, being more fully developed in other works. Mystical states, like many other psychic or paranormal phenomena, among which James recognized telepathy and alternative or secondary personality, such as prophetic speech, automatic writing, hypnotic and mediumistic trances, all admit of explanation if we follow Frederic Myers and Gustav Fechner and posit "a continuum of cosmic consciousness, against which individuality builds accidental fences, and into which our several minds plunge as into a mother-sea or reservoir. . . . Not only psychic research, but metaphysical philosophy and speculative biology are led in their own ways to look with favor on some such 'panpsychic' view of the universe as this" (*EPR* 374). In certain exceptional states the ordinary threshold of consciousness is lowered so that we become aware of what is contained or going on in this surrounding mother-sea of consciousness, the supermind or minds, since there might be more than one mother-sea. James employed this mother-sea hypothesis to explain his 1906 mystical experience in which he seemingly became aware of mental states not his own – free-floating states within this surrounding consciousness. He distinguished his experiences from the full-blown mystical states he featured in *The Varieties of Religious Experience* by pointing out that, "in my case certain special directions only, in the field of reality, seemed to get suddenly uncovered, whereas in classical mystical experiences it appears rather as if the whole of reality were uncovered at once" (*EP* 160).[12]

There are some outstanding difficulties with this inference to the best explanation for the objectivity of mystical experiences. The subconscious is far too motley a crew of odd-ball states and actions to warrant an inference to the objectivity of any given subconscious state or experience. Some of them are plainly noncognitive, such as hysteria, which James also assigned to the subconscious, while others, such as hypnotism and a secondary self's perceptions, are explicable in terms of ordinary sensory ways of gaining, though not processing, information, there being no need to postulate a surrounding mother-sea of consciousness containing free-floating bits of consciousness.

James favors the pluralistic interpretation of the mother-sea-of-consciousness hypothesis, so that there is not a single all-encompassing surrounding sea of consciousness but more than one, with God merely being the most outstanding of them in terms of power, knowledge, and goodness, but still only finite. In a mystical experience, according to the surrounding mother-seas hypothesis, the subject becomes unified with one of these super consciousnesses in a way that falls short of becoming literally numerically one and the same with it but rather in the weaker sense of becoming cognizant that it is a *part* of this enveloping consciousness. This inclusion of one conscious self within another raises several problems, the least of which is the one that worried James concerning how one conscious state can be part of another.

---

[12] For other formulations of the mother-sea hypothesis for explaining the full gamut of paranormal phenomena, see *EPR* 98 and 195ff.; *PU* 134–5 and 140; and *ERM* 92–4.

To begin with, the idea of an individual being a proper part of an-other individual of the same kind is troublesome. Aristotle argued, suc-cessfully in my opinion, that no *substance*, in his special sense, could be a proper part of another substance of the same *natural kind*: A human organism, for example, cannot be a proper part of another human organism. Aristotle would not have felt challenged by our doggy door, which is a proper part of another functioning door, because a door is an *artifact* and therefore not a *substance* in his sense.

But what about a self or mind? Is it a substance and thereby subject to Aristotle's stricture? In the last chapter, James was expounded as holding that the self is not a natural kind, because he did not leave it up to science to determine its identity conditions and therefore its na-ture. Maybe it is possible, after all, for a Jamesian self, understood as a succession of mental states in which the later members remember the earlier ones, to be a proper part of another self. Be that as it may, there remains the question whether it is possible for a *person*, understood as a morally responsible agent – one who performs intentional actions for which she is morally praised or blamed – to be a proper part of another person. That such a person is not a natural kind does not settle the matter in the affirmative.

James, judging by the following rhetorical question in "The Miller-Bode Objection" notes, favored an affirmative answer: "Why can't I have another being own and use me, just as I am, for its purposes without knowing any of these purposes myself" (*MEN* 129). This goes along with his remark that "If we assume a wider thinker, it is evident that his purposes envelop mine. I am really lecturing *for* him" (*ERE* 89). Maybe James had in mind only a case in which one person is another person's lackey or gofer, rather than one that involves actual inclusion within this person, but the text does not favor this weak ren-dering of his inclusion doctrine.[13]

I believe that this doctrine is conceptually absurd for the following reason. A person, in virtue of being morally responsible for certain of her actions, must be an autonomous unit, it being the whole person, and only that person, who is held responsible for them. The reason for the "only that person" is that, according to James's Libertarianism, a morally responsible action is done freely, and it is done freely only if the agent is the sole cause of it, which rules out there being another person who is responsible for the action. But if one person were a proper part of another person, both persons would be morally respon-sible for an intentional action performed by one of them, which is absurd.[14]

---

[13] A helpful discussion of this doctrine is to be found in Marcus Peter Ford's *WJ* 43–4.

[14] Eugene Fontinell, an extremely sensitive and imaginative interpreter of James, seemed to be oblivious of this conceptual difficulty when he wrote that "we can retain our

A deeper understanding of this absurdity can be acquired by taking seriously the common occurrence in grade school when one child punches another and says, "I didn't do it, my hand did." Since the hand that delivered the punch is to be held morally responsible, it constitutes the *entire* body of the person who intentionally does the punching and does so even though it is a proper physical part of a human organism. The person whose body is entirely constituted by this human organism is supposed not to be morally responsible for delivering the punch. But if the person whose body is entirely constituted by the hand is a proper part of the person whose body is entirely constituted by the human organism, then both persons are morally responsible for the same act of delivering the punch. And this is the very absurdity in question, assuming that the act is free and we accept James's Libertarianism.

That one *person* cannot be part of another person undercuts the major attraction that pluralistic mysticism had over monistic mysticism for James. For it was in order to save the moral agency of the mystic that he felt compelled to reject all forms of monism, whether it be that of absolute idealism or monistic mysticism. But it is just this moral agency that must be sacrificed by his pluralistic mystic. Earlier in the chapter, another reason was seen for James's mystic having to give up being a moral agent, namely, that in order to have a mystical experience it is required that one overcome one's active self, which is the moral-agent self, and adopt a passive attitude toward the world. Complete or partial absorption in or unification with an enveloping supernatural consciousness is all right, but the price of admission is to cease being a person – a moral agent. This is a big price for James's Promethean self to pay, as what is most dear to its heart is its functioning as a morally responsible agent.

Before concluding this chapter on James's religious mysticism, I should point out that the surrounding mother-sea of consciousness, be it a single sea or a plurality of seas, as the monistic and pluralistic mystic respectively would have it, with which the mystic becomes wholly or partially absorbed, is a supernatural entity through and through, as James repeatedly states. It is an unseen order said to be "behind the veil" (*ERM* 76, 86, 87) to those of us "here below" (*ERM* 82, 87). It is a "transcendental world" (*ERM* 93, 96) that makes "influx" into a person's ordinary consciousness when the dam or threshold of receptiv-

individuality and *agency* even if we are encompassed by, or co-conscious and confluent with a larger consciousness" (*SGI* 122; my italics). That the included self is a morally responsible agent is further reinforced by his subsequently adding, "If there are other experiential grounds, however, for believing that these narrower fields [of consciousness], along with their ideals, purposes, striving and the like, are included with the purposes of the wider consciousness, then the substantive field-self as herein described presents no logical or experiential obstacles to the realization of such purposes" (131).

ity is lowered (*ERM* 93). Of primary importance is that in calling the
surrounding mother-sea(s) of consciousness "supernatural" James
means that science cannot describe and explain it. This has the consequence that the doctrine of Pure Experience cannot be applied to it,
even if the weakest version of its Tenet 3 from the previous chapter is
operative, the one that holds that for every individual there are possible
sequences of events such that it qualifies as mental in some of them
and physical in others. The reason for this is that a physical sequence
of events is a law-like one, but a supernatural being does not behave in
a law-like manner, thus the mother-sea(s) of consciousness is not ame-
nable to scientific explanation. In anticipation of this counterexample
to Pure Experience, I restricted the doctrine at the very beginning to
sensible individuals, thus ruling out the invisible individuals behind the
veil.

The clash between James's active Promethean self and his passive
mystical self, along with the conflict between the Ontological Relativism
favored by his Promethean self and the nonrelativized reality-claims
made by his mystical self, are the two deepest aporias that arise from
James's quest to have it all. Readers will have to wait until Chapter 11,
if they can stand the suspense, for an attempt to resolve these aporias.

10

The Humpty-Dumpty Intuition
and Panpsychism

The previous two chapters have followed the first two legs of James's journey to find a cozy personal world with which he could establish an intimate communion because it would answer back to his deepest inner feelings and emotions. It began with his attempt to be intimate with himself through an introspective analysis of what made him one and the same self from one time to another. Next, he attempted to be intimate with others – be it man, beast, nature, or God – through a special type of I–Thou experience that partially unified him with their inner conscious life. To achieve this sort of mystical intimacy James found it necessary to conquer his Promethean self, in the process creating a deep unresolved aporia.

This chapter will explore the third and final leg of his journey in which James cultivates a backyard mysticism based on the Bergsonian conceptless intuition of the temporal flux. Whereas his religious mysticism was based on an effort to I–Thou other selves, most importantly supernatural ones, backyard mysticism is directed at the most mundane sort of individuals – the contents of our ordinary sense experience of the temporal flux – but it sees them in a new, mystical way as mushing together in just the way that successive conscious states of a person do, which, it will be recalled, served as the basis for self-identity over time. Thus, what we find upon introspecting our own consciousness is the way in which things, in general, are in the world. This results not just in panpsychism but in spiritualism. These backyard individuals that are enmeshed in the perceptual flux are not merely imbued with but turn out to be nothing *but* consciousness, which results in about as cozy a world as one could wish for. Like the bluebird of happiness, mystical reality has been in our own backyard all along, but we have been blinded to it by our inveterate pragmatic bent of thought. What to do about the crabgrass? Are the coals hot enough to put on the burgers? As was the case with religious mysticism, we are required to overcome our active Promethean selves and learn to experience passively, without employing concepts. James's message is that salvation can be found even in our own backyards. An important issue that will be considered in the next chapter concerns the connection between James's religious and backyard mysticism.

In order to see how James arrived at this backyard mysticism, it is necessary to take an in-depth look at his accounts of our perception of time. There is, to put it euphemistically, a "tension" between James's accounts of our perception of time in the chapters on "The Perception of Time" and "The Stream of Thought" in his 1890 *The Principles of Psychology*. (All references in this chapter are to this book, unless otherwise noted.) The former presents the *specious present* account – that each pulse of perceptual experience has a content that comprises a succession of discrete events. The latter, on the other hand, liquefies or, better, cotton-candifies these successive events so that they melt and fuse together, thereby denying their discreteness. Subsequent to *The Principles of Psychology* and its abridged version (*PBC*) of 1892, which contains shortened versions of these two chapters, James never speaks of the specious present by name in any published work.[1] In his final two books, *A Pluralistic Universe* and *Some Problems of Philosophy*, he emerges as a full-fledged Bergsonian, although he does not explicitly disown his earlier specious present account.

That each of these accounts is supported by an appeal to what is introspectively or phenomenologically vouchsafed should raise one's suspicions. In each case the phenomenology is faked and gives a blatantly distorted account of our way of experiencing time. James, like so many phenomenologists, is a Jack Horner who is able to pull out of his phenomenological pie whatever is philosophically required.

The reason these conflicting accounts pull out different philosophical plums is that they address a different datum whose presumed existence must be shown to be possible. The specious present account is an attempt to answer the *psychological* question of how it is possible for us to have, as we certainly seem to, the conceptions of temporal precedence and the past, the answer being that temporally successive *discrete* events are the content of a single act of perception, thereby satisfying the concept empiricist's demand to give a concept an experiential birth certificate. The stream-of-thought account, on the other hand, begins with the undoubted reality of change and addresses the *metaphysical* question of how change is possible, the answer being that change must be a processual kind of cotton-candyish glop in which temporal neighbors do not possess a distinct identity but instead fuse and melt together. By faking their phenomenological credentials, both analyses cover over the fact that they really are transcendental deductions of the either-this-or-nothing variety. Since the specious present doctrine is the

---

[1] In 1908 he wrote, in his unpublished "Miller-Bode Objections" manuscript: "The relation of succession is a good one to begin illustrating by, for in the specious present the 'was' and the 'about-to-be' commingle. The logically distinct are not the ontologically separate" (*MEN* 120). Although he retains the term here, the description he gives plainly involves a rejection of the discreteness of *The Principles of Psychology*'s account of the specious present in favor of the Bergsonian stream-of-thought one.

one that eventually gets spurned, we will begin with it and then go on to consider why it had to be rejected on the basis of the fundamental philosophical intuitions that motivate the stream-of-thought account. The latter will then be subjected to a critical analysis.

I. The Specious Present

That the specious present doctrine purports to be introspectively based is made manifest in the opening sentence of the chapter when James says, "I shall deal with what is sometimes called internal perception, or the perception of *time*..." (570). Such "internal perception" is an instance of the first of James's two ways of studying a psychic phenomenon. "There are, as we know, two ways of studying every psychic state. First, the way of analysis: What does it consist in? What is its inner nature? Of what sort of mind-stuff is it composed? Second, the way of history: What are its conditions of production, and its connection with other facts?" (913). This inner approach seems to be identical with what he earlier calls "introspective observation," which is "the looking into our own minds and reporting what we there discover" (185). He gives pride of place to introspection over the causally based historical method: "*Introspective Observation is what we have to rely on first and foremost and always*" (185).

It also is made manifest that the motivation behind the account is to supply the required experiential credentials for our concepts of temporal succession and the past. In general, James's concept empiricism requires that "Every one of our conceptions is of something which our attention originally tore out of the continuum of felt experience, and provisionally isolated so as to make of it an individual topic of discourse" (439). All subject matters, even logical and mathematical ones, are "abstracted and generalized from long forgotten perceptual instances from which they have as it were flowered out" (*SPP* 34). "To understand a concept you must know what it *means*. It means always some *this*, or some abstract portion of a *this*, with which we first made acquaintance in the perceptual world, or else some grouping of such abstract portions" (*SPP* 46). When James asks, "What is the original of our experience of pastness, from whence we get the meaning of the term?" he is making a specific application of this generalization (570).

To have a relational concept it is required that the relata "be known in a single pulse of consciousness for which they form one complex 'object' . . . so that properly speaking there is before the mind at no time a plurality of *ideas*, properly so called" (383). Since "*there is no manifold of coexisting ideas, . . . Whatever things are thought in relation are thought from the outset in a unity, in a single pulse of subjectivity, a single psychosis, feeling, or state of mind*" (268; see also 267 and 573). "If we do not feel both past and present in one field of feeling, we feel them not at all" (128). As applied to the case of the relation of temporal succession, this has the consequence that "A succession of feelings, in and of itself, is not a feeling of succession" (591). This parallels a similar claim about our apprehension of spatial relations: "*If a number of sensible extents are to be perceived alongside of each other and in definite order they must appear as parts in a vaster sensible extent which can enter the mind simply and all at once*" (788).

The upshot of this is that to have the concept of temporal succession it is necessary that the conceiver have had a perception of a succession in which both the relata were presented together, and moreover as successive. Fortunately, every perception represents such a complex of successive objects.

Part of the complexity is the echo of the objects just past, and, in a less degree, perhaps, the foretaste of those just to arrive. Objects fade out of consciousness slowly. If the present thought is of A B C D E F G, the next one will be of B C D E F G H, and the one after that of C D E F G H I – the lingerings of the past dropping successively away, and the incomings of the future making up the loss. These lingerings of old objects, these incomings of new, are the germs of memory and expectation, the retrospective and the prospective sense of time. (571)[2]

James follows E. R. Clay in calling the temporal duration presented in each pulse of perceptual experience "the specious present," and con trasts it with the "strict present," which is the mathematically punctal one of the physicists (573). He even adds, inconsistently as we shall see, that "Reflection leads us to the conclusion that it [the strict present] *must* exist."

It would appear that the successive objects, A B C . . . , within a single specious present are discrete in the sense of being distinct from each other. Not only does this seem to be supported by his distinguishing between the successive objects A B C . . . and tracking them across successive specious presents, it plainly is maintained by authors whom James quotes with approval. Wundt's claim that when similar pendulum strokes follow each other at regular intervals in a consciousness other-

---

[2] There appears to be a vicious infinite regress lurking in this account of how we acquire our retrospective and prospective senses. It is required that we be aware of certain contents as lingering from one specious present to an immediately successive specious present. But, according to James's concept empiricism, this requires that we relate these specious presents together, and this can be done only if they are copresent to a single perception. Thus, there must be a second-order perception of these specious presents as successive; but since these successive specious presents are given together to this second-order perception, there is no experience of a lingering of contents from the earlier to the later one. This creates the need to bring in yet a third-order perception of a succession of second-order perceptions, and so on ad infinitum. This regress is vicious because at each stage in it we are left with the same problem that we originally set out to solve, namely to account for the perceptual basis of our sense of lingering.

wise void, "When the first one is over, an image of it remains in the fancy until the second succeeds" is endorsed by James (573), as are Hodgson's remarks that, "if I have consciousness at all, [it] is a sequence of different feelings" (572) and

In a succession of events, say of sense-impressions, A B C D E . . . the presence of B means the absence of A and of C, but the presentation of this succession involves the simultaneous presence, in some mode or other, of two or more of the presentations A B C D. In reality, past, present, and future are differences in time, but in presentation all that corresponds to these differences is in consciousness simultaneously. (593)

Maybe the strongest reason for taking the successive objects to be discrete is that, if they were not, we could not derive our idea of temporal succession from an experience of them; for, in general, it would seem that we can perceive a relational complex as a relational complex only if we perceive the relata in it as distinct from each other. The later doctrine of Radical Empiricism, which asserts, pace both Hume and Kant, that relations are perceptually given, also is committed to the numerical distinctness of the relata. The queerness of the disagreement between James and Hume over the perceptual givenness of relations should make us suspicious that each of them was practicing a Jack Horner type of phenomenology that was based on their own respective a priori criteria for what could be phenomenologically or introspectively given. Think in this connection of Berkeley's "good" Hylas's obviously bogus introspective search for an idea of a triangle in general and his feigned disappointment at his failure to find it. There was no need for such a "search," as it could have been deduced in advance from Berkeley's definition of an "idea" that no such idea would be an object of introspection.

Although this is the way that the text calls out to be read, there is a remark by James that speaks for the cotton-candifying of the successive objects. He begins by saying that "The experience is from the outset a synthetic datum, not a simple one," which speaks for the discreteness of the objects or elements within a specious present, but immediately adds that "to sensible perception its elements are inseparable although attention looking back may easily decompose the experience, and distinguish its beginning from its end" (574–5).[3] It might be objected that if these elements really are insepar*able*, they cannot later be decomposed and distinguished from each other, for the inseparable is that

---

[3] Another way in which James seems to Bergsonize the specious present is by his claim that "The specious present has . . . a vaguely vanishing backward and forward fringe . . ." (578). This seems to be of a piece with his endorsement of Hodgson's remark that the rearward and forward limits of the specious present are "ready to melt into other minima, proceeding from other stimuli" (572).

which cannot be decomposed. James might respond that they are ontologically inseparable but logically or conceptually distinguishable.[4]

Even if this surface inconsistency can be neutralized in this way, there remains the problem that if "time is always of something given as a unit, inside of which attention afterwards discriminates parts in relation to each other," the discriminator must already possess the concept of succession, otherwise how could a discrimination be made between these successive parts of the specious present. As a result, the concept of succession, pace James, would not be derived from the perception of a specious present. Thus, by cotton-candifying the contents of the specious present, James undercuts his attempt to show how our concept of succession is derived from the experience of a specious present. Before we delve into why the allure of Bergsonism was so strong – so strong that he could not prevent it from overlapping from the chapter on "The Stream of Thought" into the one on "The Perception of Time," thereby creating this aporia – more needs to be said about his specious present doctrine and what might have led him to abandon it.

James plainly would not accept my interpretation of his specious present doctrine as an a priori analysis that purports to give the only way in which it is possible for us to have the concept of succession, assuming the truth of concept empiricism, for he supports it by appeal to: (i) an introspective analysis of our experience of time; (ii) the neurophysiological causes of sensations; and (iii) experimental data that determine the duration of a specious present's content. Each of these apparently contingent reasons will be explored and found to be misinvoked.

(i) Exactly what is supposed to be revealed by an introspective analysis of a perception of a specious present? Are the successive A B C objects of a sensory nature – colors, sounds, and the like? And what about the relation of succession between them, is it sensory or not? The second, but not the first, question receives a clear answer. James is quite explicit that in general we do not have a sensory image or idea of any relation. While he so far agrees with Hume, he goes on to contend, in opposition to Hume's restriction of possible objects of introspection to sensory ideas, that we nevertheless are conscious of them (239ff.). We are said to have a "feeling" or "thought" of them, which are James's most generic terms for consciousness, of which the being aware of a sensory image is only one species (186). These feelings of relation are said to be a fringe, halo, wraith, or overtone that attaches to the relata in a relation (260).

The first question concerns whether the A B C relata in a relation of succession within a specious present are sensorial images. A straightfor-

---

[4] In fact, he seems to say just this in the 1908 remark, quoted in footnote 1, that "the logically distinct [elements within a specious present] are not ontologically separate."

ward reading of the text supports an affirmative answer and thus a sensory model of the specious present. After this model is thoroughly discredited, a more subtle reading of the text will show it to contain the germ of a "perceiving-as" model of the specious present that escapes these objections.

The major support for the sensory model interpretation comes from the actual language James uses to describe our perception of a specious present. The title of the section in which he presents the doctrine of the specious present is "The Sensible Present Has Duration" (573). The claim that *"the original paragon and prototype of all conceived times is the specious present, the short duration of which we are immediately and incessantly* **sensible**" continues this use of sensory terms (594; my boldface). In his summation at the end of the chapter he says that the specious present varies "in length from a few seconds to probably not more than a minute, and that this duration (with its content *perceived* as having one part earlier and the other part later) is the original intuition of time" (603; my italics). The perceptual nature of the specious present is repeated in the "Memory" chapter: "Within the few seconds which constitute the specious present there is an intuitive perception of the successive moments" (619). This dovetails with the claim in the opening sentence of "The Perception of Time" chapter that our experience of time involves "internal perception" (570). The use of "perception" is not decisive, however, for, as we shall shortly see, the perception could be interpreted as a perceiving-as.

More decisive support is found in his description of a strictly past and a future object within the specious present as, respectively, an "echo" and a "foretaste," since echoes and tastes are sensory in nature (571). This sensory unpacking of the content of a specious present dovetails with the analogies he draws between the perception of space and time. First, there is the claim that there is "a marked *difference between elementary sensations of duration and those of space*" in that "the former have a much narrower range; the time-sense may be called a myopic organ, in comparison with the eye, for example" (575). Yet another analogy is that "There is . . . a sort of *perspective projection* of past objects upon present consciousness, similar to that of wide landscapes upon a camera-screen" (593).

Further proof comes from the fact that the persons whom he quotes with approval plainly have a sensory model: Hodgson, for example, speaks of "the simultaneous perception . . . of a sequence" (572); Herbart, of successive elements being "present with equal clearness together"; and Wundt of an immediately past sound remaining as "an image in the fancy" (573).

The sensory model is based on Jack Horner fake phenomenology. Clay's claim, which James also implicitly endorses, that "All the notes

of a bar of a song seem to the listener to be contained in the present"
is the description of someone who hears a chord, the notes of which
vary in loudness according to most sensory models of the specious present, as earlier phases within a single specious present are supposed to
have, according to Broad and Ducasse, less vivacity or liveliness than
later ones. Mozart is quoted in behalf of our perceptual present being
able to encompass a succession of elements of quite some span. In
regard to a symphony he composed, he wrote that he "can see the
whole of it at a single glance in my mind, as if it were a beautiful
painting or a handsome human being; which way I do not hear it in my
imagination at all as a succession – the way it must come later – but all
at once, as it were" (247; notice the "as it were" qualification). If
Mozart had a 30-minute *auditory* specious present that contained the
succession of sounds within an entire symphony, he must have had
some terrible headaches. Wilfrid Sellars, in the appendix to his *Science
and Metaphysics*, neatly brought out the false phenomenology of the
sensory model of the specious present by showing that it had the consequence that, when I see your arm rise, I am also seeing all of the
earlier positions of it when I see it at its topmost position and thereby
see you as a Hindu god. To be sure, sometime when we hear a tolling
bell we are quite literally hearing past sounds in the form of after-
images; there is a ringing in our ears. But these are exceptional cases,
pace the sensory model of the specious present. Clay's claim, in support
of the sensory model that "All the changes of place of a meteor seem
to the beholder to be contained in the present" is beside the point,
because in such a case our present perception is not of the past positions of the meteor but of the present trail that it has left (574).

Not only is the sensory model at variance with the phenomenological
facts, if the content of the specious present really were sensory, it could
not be invoked to show how we acquire our concept of *temporal* succession. If I perceive a rising arm in the Hindu god–like fashion, as is
required by the perceptual model, then I am perceiving an order of
coexistent arms, not a temporal order of successive events. And similarly, when I hear the final notes of the melody I am not apprehending,
according to Clay, a succession of notes as successive but as coexistent
members in a chord (One wonders how I would be able to hear the
repetitions of a note in a melody.)

(ii) A possible explanation for James's failure to realize just how out
of whack his sensory model of the specious present was with the introspective facts is that he thought certain facts about the neurophysiological causes of sensations required the sensory model. At many, but by
no means all, places in *The Principles of Psychology*, James adopts the
working hypothesis of physiological psychology that there is "No psychosis without neurosis" (133). It is assumed that our sensations are

caused by these neuroses. Because "The phenomena of 'summation of stimuli' in the nervous system prove that each stimulus leaves some latent activity behind it which only gradually passes away" it follows that *"there is at every moment a cumulation of brain-processes overlapping each other, of which the fainter ones are dying phases of processes which but shortly previous were active in maximal degree"* (597–8). Since these overlapping brain-processes causally condition sensations, it follows that, since "the changes of neurosis are never absolutely discontinuous, so must the successive psychoses shade gradually into each other" (236). "If recently the brain tract *a* was vividly excited, and then *b*, and now vividly *c*, the total present consciousness is not produced simply by *c*'s excitement, but also by the dying vibrations of *a* and *b* as well" (235). These considerations have the consequence that a sensation has a specious present content: "All stimuli whose first nerve-vibrations have not yet ceased seem to be conditions of our getting this feeling of the specious present" (609).

Further neurophysiological support for the sensory model is found in James's claims that "the *echo* of the whence, the sense of the starting point of our thought, is probably due to the dying excitement of processes but a moment since vividly aroused" (248; my italics), and that, just as a note and its overtones "are not separately heard by the ear . . . so do the waxing and waning brain-processes at every moment blend with and suffuse and alter the psychic effect of the processes which are at their culminating point" (249). By appeal to the same sort of neurophysiological facts James includes a small portion of the future in the specious present. In many cases we have a "preperception" of a future impression due to our anticipating a perception in our imagination (415–16), also called "the foretaste of those [objects] just to arrive" (571). But this "foretaste of the terminus must be due to the waxing excitement of tracts or processes which, a moment hence, will be the cerebral correlatives of some thing which a moment hence will be vividly present to the thought" (248).

As we know that our sensations, for the most part, do not have a sensory specious present, either James's neurophysiological claims are contrary to fact or his assumption that there is a correlation between the waning and waxing of neural processes and sensory states of consciousness is unwarranted, being an instance of his own "Psychologist Fallacy," in which the psychologist confuses *"his own standpoint with that of the mental fact* about which he is making his report" (195). Herein it takes the form of an unwarranted assumption that the features of the publicly observable cause of a conscious state must be something of which the conscious state is aware or which has a correlate in its content.

(iii) The experimental data that James appeals to in support of his sensory model of the specious present are of no more avail than were his appeals to introspection and neurophysiology. Wundt and his student Dietze attempted "to determine experimentally the *maximal extent of our immediate distinct consciousness for successive impressions*" (577). Toward this end, they would play for a subject a sequence of rhythmically arranged sounds to determine how much of it could "be remembered as a whole, and identified without error when repeated." They found that "the *maximum filled duration* of which we can be both distinctly and immediately aware" is about 12 seconds (577).

James immediately goes on to claim that "These figures may be roughly taken to stand for the most important part of what, with Mr. Clay, we called, a few pages back, the specious present" (578). It should be obvious to the reader that the experimental data radically underdetermine the theoretical construal James places on them. All the data show is the maximum duration of strokes that, as James himself says, can "be remembered as a whole, and identified without error when repeated." This in no way establishes that when the subject is hearing the final stroke of this duration, the earlier strokes that he is immediately conscious of also are *auditorily* apprehended. A skilled drummer like Max Roach very likely could identify or play back without error a very intricate rhythmic pattern lasting many minutes, whereas the layman might be good for only several seconds' worth. But this hardly shows that Max is having a Mozartian Excedrin Two–type headache when he hears the final sound, in virtue of his literally hearing at that time all of the earlier sounds.

With this we bid farewell to the doctrine of the *sensory* specious present, one of the all-time philosophical abortions, whose widespread acceptance is attributable to the mistaken belief that it was soundly supported by a triumvirate of introspection, experimental data, and neurophysiology. While there is ample textual grounds for imputing this benighted doctrine to James, other aspects of his text permit attribution of a nonsensory model to him, in particular a "perceiving-as" version, according to which the immediately past and future members of the specious present are not perceived but inferred.

The basis for this attribution is found in James's distinction between a *sensation*, which is an immediate sensory awareness of a color, odor, and so on, and a *perception*, which is a conceptualized sensation (653). Since perception involves the conceptualization of a given sensation and concepts are rules for inferring things not then given, every perception is a perceiving-as – a perceiving of something as being an instance of a certain concept. The sensation gives acquaintance with an object but the perceiving-as relates it to what is not then present. James's notion of perceiving something as having a fringe, halo, wraith, or overtone is the same as perceiving-as, for it is perceiving something as related to something else not then given. Remember that for James these relations are not sensorily presented but are felt or thought in his highly generic sense of being something of which we are consciously aware.

This perceiving-as account of perception is developed in "The Stream of Thought" chapter. When we hear thunder after silence, we hear the thunder *as* having been preceded by the silence. "Our feeling of the same objective thunder, coming . . . [after silence] is quite different from what it would be were the thunder a continuation of previous thunder" (234). Each word of a recited sentence that we understand is heard with a special "overtone, halo, or fringe," meaning that each word is not merely heard, but heard-as related to earlier and/or later words of the sentence that are not themselves then heard (271). This yields the basis for a nonsensory model of the specious present, according to which the span of perceptual awareness is determined by the inferential range of the concept that is applied. Some of James's own formulations of the specious present in "The Perception of Time" chapter employ the perceiving-as idiom, as for example when he says "that we are constantly conscious of a certain duration – the specious present – varying in length from a few seconds to probably not more than a minute, and that this duration (with its content *perceived as* having one part earlier and other part later) is the original intuition of time" (603; my italics). At another place he speaks of the successive elements in a specious present being "thought of together" and quotes with approval Volkmann's claim that successive elements are "represented *as occurring in succession*" (592).

It is not my contention that the perceiving-as model of the specious present works, only that it is not subject to the glaring difficulties of the sensory model. The challenge it faces is to give an adequate account of what it is to have a concept and apply it to a given sensation, but it is not clear that progress cannot be made in this endeavor. The discussion has at least been put back on track; a skein of absurdities and confusions has been replaced by a genuine problem. And that's progress.

Why did James give up the doctrine of the specious present after *The Principles of Psychology and* the abridged version? It is understandable why he gave up using the *term* "the specious present," since, given his later Radical Empiricism's identification of reality with the way things appear in experience, it has the shoe on the wrong foot. It is not the experiential present that is specious but rather that of the physicists; and, moreover, as will be seen, he thinks he has Zeno's support for his charge of speciousness against their mathematically punctal present. But why did he give up the *doctrine?* One would want to believe that it was because he eventually saw all of the above difficulties that have been pointed out, but there is no textual support for this. The most likely reason is that James saw that its commitment to *discrete* succession was unacceptable on metaphysical grounds, and that the concept of discrete succession, as a result, was bogus and thus not in need of experiential legitimation. The concept that does require experiential legitimation is that of *promiscuous* succession, in which the relata get into each other because they merge, fuse, or melt together. You cannot have a discrete promiscuous affair. It will now be seen how and why the stream-of-thought account attempted to legitimate this mushing together relation.

II. The Stream of Thought

The opening sentence of "The Stream of Thought" chapter makes manifest the introspective basis of the account to follow: "We now begin our study of the mind from within" (219).[5] Consciousness is metaphorically likened to a flowing river, because neither contains distinct, isolatable parts (233).

Every definite image in the mind is steeped and dyed in the free water that flows around it. With it goes the sense of its relations, near and remote, the dying echo of whence it came to us, the dawning sense of whither it is to lead. The significance, the value, of the image is all in this halo or penumbra that surrounds and escorts it – or rather that is fused into one with it and has become bone of its bone and flesh of its flesh. (246)

The discrete successive events of the specious present's content have now become cotton-candified, mushed together. When we successively hear the words of a sentence, "They melt into each other like dissolving views," thereby showing that in the thought no "parts can be found corresponding to the object's parts. Time-parts are not such parts" (269).

Herein James is making a contrast between the discrete successiveness of the objects perceived and the nondiscrete mushing together within the content of the perceptual experience.

The things are discrete and discontinuous; they do pass before us in a train or chain, making often explosive appearance and rending each other in twain. But their comings and goings and contrasts no more break the flow of the thought that thinks them than they break the time and the space in which they lie. (233)

This stream-of-thought account is reaffirmed in his final two books, but with one important difference: a priori arguments are presented

[5] A similar remark occurs at the beginning of the abridged version of this chapter in the Abridged Version: "We are now prepared to begin the introspective study of the adult consciousness itself" (*PBC* 139). The use of "consciousness" in place of *The Principles of Psychology*'s "thought" runs throughout the Abridged Version and is a concession he made to the criticism of the psychologist George Turnbull Ladd that *The Principles of Psychology* short-shrifted consciousness.

for the impossibility of a discrete succession, in fact for the impossibility of a discrete immediate relation of any kind. In arguing for this he winds up with spiritualism. Let us carefully dog his steps along the way to this startling conclusion.

The phenomenological analysis of the final two books is the same as that of the stream-of-thought account of *The Principles of Psychology*, differing only in the richness of its newly acquired Bergsonian descriptions of the mushing together relation. What our conceptualizing intellect falsely cuts asunder into discretely successive events really "compenetrates" and "telescopes" through a sort of "endosmosis" or "conflux" (*PU* 114): "In the real concrete sensible flux of life experiences compenetrate each other so that it is not easy to know just what is excluded and what not" (*PU* 113). This agrees with *Some Problem of Philosophy*'s claim that "Boundaries are things that intervene; but nothing intervenes save parts of the perceptual flux itself, and these are overflowed by what they separate, so that whatever we distinguish and isolate conceptually is found perceptually to telescope and compenetrate and diffuse into its neighbors" (*SPP* 32).

He further claims that in the mushing relation each relatum becomes its own other, in Hegel's sense:

Every individual morsel of the sensational stream takes up the adjacent morsels by coalescing with them. . . . [so] that no part absolutely excludes another, but that they compenetrate and are cohesive; that if you tear out one, its roots bring out more with them; that whatever is real is telescoped and diffused into other reals; that, in short, every minutest thing is already its Hegelian 'own other,' in the fullest sense of the term. (*PU* 121; see also 127)

James realizes that his mushing together relation defies the ordinary logic of identity, since it gives us an identity that is not really an identity because it is nontransitive. "For conceptual logic, the same is nothing but the same, and all sames with a third thing are the same with each other. Not so in concrete experience" (*PU* 114–15). Furthermore, James realizes that his counterlogical descriptions of our experience of change "will sound queer and dark" (97). But an "empirical look into the constitution of [reality shows] . . . that some of them are their own others, and indeed are so in the self-same sense in which the absolute is maintained to be so by Hegel." Spatial neighbors also behave like Playdoh. "What is true here of successive states must also be true of simultaneous characters. They also overlap each other with their being" (*PU* 130; see also *MEN* 123). James seems to be saying, if I may paraphrase the punch line to the old shaggy-dog joke, that these immediate neighbors are identical but not *that* identical. This is another form taken by James's pluralistic mysticism.

The commentators, with the exception of Marcus Peter Ford, fail to take seriously the mystical commitments of these passages from *A Plu-*

ralistic Universe and *Some Problems of Philosophy.*[6] Ford, however, takes them too seriously and winds up claiming that James's pluralistic mysticism is not a pluralism at all. "Indeed, if *two* things could be both separate from each other and, at the same time, not separate, in what sense are they actually separate at all? A philosophy based on the premise that what is true of successive events is also true of contemporary events is finally a form of metaphysical monism" (*WJ* 54). Herein Ford is claiming that James's mushing together relation between temporally and spatially adjoined individuals results in a real identity of the transitive sort rather than in James's nontransitive Hegelian sort. James would object that his brand of pluralistic mysticism, which is of the sort favored by Western theistic mystics, is a viable alternative to the monistic brand of the East.

A common strategy among the commentators who don't want to countenance James's mysticism, in either the pluralistic or the monistic form, is to give a Whiteheadian process gloss of his mushing together relation. Ford, for example, drops James's requirement that spatially adjoined individuals are connected by the *symmetric* Hegelian mushing together relation and reinterprets this relation between successive events as a Whiteheadian *asymmetric* relation of "prehension." "At any given moment there is absolute insulation and irreducible pluralism," but earlier actual occasions "are literally in each present actual occasion, though not vice-versa" (99). This interpretation builds on those of Victor Lowe and Andrew Reck. According to Lowe "you actually feel your experience of a moment ago growing into your present experience and compelling some conformation to it" (*WJ* 114). James's act of appropriation, by which the present Thought or experiences makes a past Thought copersonal with it, involves a past occasion "becoming itself present in the experience that is now ... what was outside came inside ... what is inside is felt as having come from outside" (116–17). In the same vein Reck writes that "James's explanation of how the 'I' as the passing Thought may serve as a principle of unified selfhood within the flux of experience anticipates Whitehead's later doctrine of prehension" (*PP* 310).[7] The manner in which the self gets unified over time by the asymmetric prehensive relation holds for all changing realities.

The key question is exactly in what sense does a past Thought or occasion "become present in the experience that is now." If it is pres-

---

[6] R. B. Perry wrote that in this volume there is "a definite turning away from ... mysticism" (*TC* 352). Richard Bernstein's introduction to *A Pluralistic Universe* conceals the underlying mystical message of this book. As will be seen, he falsely claims that "James is not playing off rationality against a nonrational or irrational intuition of the way things" (*PU* xv).

[7] For other Whiteheadian process interpretations of James's flow of thought, see Craig Eisendrath's *UM* and Eugene Fontinell's *SGI*, especially pp. 93 and 148.

ent only in the sense of being an intentional accusative of the present Thought or occasion, the account is far too watered down for what James was after in his dark Hegelian sayings. I will have to leave it to Whitehead scholars to determine whether the prehension relation is something more mystical than thinking of or being an effect of.

Is James's claim that we *ordinarily* experience change in the mushing together manner phenomenologically vouchsafed? (The importance of this qualification will become clear later.) Plainly not! I no more see the immediately adjoined temporal phases of a moving arm's trajectory as mushing together than I see it in the Hindu god–like manner. Maybe James did see them as having "a sort of later suffusion from one thing into another, like a gas, or warmth, or light. The *places* involved are fixed, but what fills one place radiates and suffuses into the other by lateral movement, 'endosmosis' " (*MEN* 91–2). If he did, he must have been smoking some funny cigarettes, or the damage to his eyes from his 1865 bout with smallpox was more severe than he let on. Of course, if an arm moves very rapidly, I do see its trajectory in a blurry manner, but this is not so for the vast majority of movements. Furthermore, I do not see spatial neighbors engaging in "endosmosis" except in the rare cases in which they actually do engage in endosmosis or are abutting ice-cream cones in a hot sun. Maybe I'm too clean-minded, but I do not find that promiscuity runs rampant in my experience. Again, we find James playing Jack Horner and pulling what is philosophically needed out of his phenomenological pie.

But why is it needed? It is in answer to this question that the final two books go beyond *The Principles of Psychology*, which officially eschewed metaphysical speculation, although James could not withstand the temptation to defend his beloved contracausal theory of free will. Herein *a priori* arguments are advanced to show the conceptual impossibility of change being a discrete succession or, more generally, there being an immediate relation between discrete, that is, numerically distinct, concrete entities.[8] His motto could be "No relations without promiscuity." Since promiscuous relations are the only alternative to discrete relations that we can conceive of, his argument in effect is a transcendental deduction. He masks this when he says in regard to change that, although we have conceptual arguments against discrete succession, "The field is thus open for any other hypothesis; and the one which we shall adopt is simply that which the face of perceptual experience suggests" (*SPP* 85). It is patent, and must have been to James, that "the face of perceptual experience," *at least ordinary perceptual experience*, hardly suggests that successive events are promiscuous,

[8] This is not because all relations are internal in the sense of being required by the essences of the relata. James opposed the absolute idealist's doctrine of internal relations (*ML* 290).

and thus his claim really is that this is how it must be. It is either this or nothing. Thus, our ordinary way of experiencing the world must be defective, it being our pragmatic orientation to the world that causes it to distort reality.

Before we consider James's specific arguments for this motto, such as those based on the various paradoxes of Zeno and Bradley, the underlying assumption that drives these arguments for James must be brought to light. William James, along with his fellow pragmatists and their absolute idealist opponents, were overly impressed by the fate of poor Humpty-Dumpty: Once he fell off the wall and disintegrated into separate pieces, all the king's horses and all the king's men couldn't put him back together again. They had a "Humpty-Dumpty Intuition," for they believed that if we ever allow reality to fall apart into numerically distinct substances there is no way that all the king's philosophers can put them back together into relational complexes again. There are stronger and weaker versions of this intuition. James had a weak version of it, as he believed that a relation could obtain between numerically distinct concrete individuals provided they were connected by a chain of mushing together relations, whereas others, like Bradley, denied the possibility of any relation at all obtaining between them. Their Humpty-Dumptyism commits them to countenancing only one true substance.

James's Humpty-Dumpty Intuition applies across the board to all concrete relations, not just temporal ones. He enlists Bradley as an ally in this regard, because Bradley agrees that "immediate feeling possesses a native wholeness which conceptual treatment analyzes into a many, *but can't unite*" (*SPP* 52; my italics). Paradoxes of the Zenoian and Bradleyian sort "arise from the vain attempt to reconvert the manifold into which our conception has resolved things, back into the continuum out of which it came" (*SPP* 51). In the "The Miller-Bode Objections" manuscript, which is a most valuable document for helping us to see the gut intuitions that drove James's philosophy, he makes the same point, when he succinctly remarks, "You can't *confine* content" (*MEN* 84). We fall into these paradoxes because our conceptualizing intellect commits us to "No discrimination without separation; no separation without absolute 'independence' and thereupon impossibility of union" (*MEN* 113). Things that are "logically distinct nevertheless [do] diffuse . . . you can't pen reality in . . . its nature is to spread, and *affect*, and . . . this applies to relations as well as to terms, so that it is impossible to call them absolutely external to each other" (*MEN* 120–1).

The writings of the early Dewey present us with a clear case of the Humpty-Dumpty Intuition in action. His 1884 doctoral dissertation charged Kant with committing the cardinal sin of beginning with a dualism between the subject of experience and its numerically distinct object. But, having allowed Humpty-Dumpty, ab initio, to fall off the wall, there is no way that Kant can reassemble him so that the subject and object can stand in epistemic relations to each other, such as the subject's perceiving and knowing the object. "The relation of subject and object," he tells us, "is not a 'transcendent' one, but an 'immanent,' and is but the first form in which Reason manifests that it is both synthetic and analytic; that it separates itself from itself, that it may thereby reach higher unity with itself" (*EW* 1:41). There is an all-enveloping background Consciousness or Reason, which is Hegel's Absolute Idea, that "differentiates itself so as to give rise to the existence within, that is for, itself of subject and object." Therefore, "The relation of subject and object is one which exists within consciousness" (*EW* 1:130–1). This sounds a lot like the traditional mystical doctrine of emanations and could earn Dewey the sobriquet of "The Plotinus of Burlington." Under the influence of Darwinian psychology, especially as developed by James in *The Principles of Psychology*, Dewey *apparently* gave up this Hegelian account; but all he did was to pour old wine into new bottles by changing the name of the universal, all-inclusive "Consciousness" or "Reason" to that of "Experience," the subject and object, now called the "organism" and its "environment," emanating in some mystical manner out of the background unity of Experience. No wonder no one ever understood what Dewey meant by "experience." It was not due to his limitations as a writer but to its being a result of the mystical Humpty-Dumpty Intuition. A case could be made that Dewey is back with the Milesians, with Experience being his "water" just as it was for James's doctrine of pure experience.

The Humpty-Dumpty Intuition has a positive component in addition to its negative one prohibiting an immediate relation between numerically distinct individuals that endorses what is apparently vouchsafed by backyard mystical experiences, namely, that is of the very nature or essence of ordinary sensible things to mush together with their spatio temporal neighbors. James's description of the content of these backyard mystical experiences is rich in gaseous and watery metaphors of "melting, merging, fusing, and flowing together," "undergoing endosmosis," "compenetrating," as well as "telescoping and diffusing into each other." These experiences are not our ordinary ones, as they can be had only by a subject who has followed the proper mystical way and learned to perceive in a pure, conceptless way.

What exactly is the connection between the negative and positive component of the Humpty-Dumpty Intuition? It might be said that the positive component gives experiential support for the negative one. If so, it would not support the negative thesis that it is *impossible* for there to be an immediate relation between numerically distinct individuals. Furthermore, it would render it odd that James, as will be seen, should have gone on to give a priori arguments to support the negative thesis.

The explanation might be that the backyard mystical experiences that undergird the positive component are given to their subjects as revealing the true nature or essence of *reality*, and thus in comparison to them an immediate relation between relata that do not mush together is not a *real* relation. It could be argued, furthermore, that each of the a priori arguments has a premise itself vouchsafed by the backyard mystical experiences that support the positive thesis.

III. From Promiscuity to Panpsychism

With the Humpty-Dumpty intuition clearly in mind, we can see how James went from promiscuity to panpsychism and from that to spiritualism. The general schema of his argument for panpsychism from his Humpty-Dumpty Intuition is as follows.

1. A relation can immediately obtain between concrete relata only if they are nontransitorily identical with each, i.e., are identical but not *that* identical. [the Humpty-Dumpty Intuition]
2. Only in the wondrously mysterious medium of consciousness can there be such a relation of nontransitive identity – an identity that is not an identity. [some kind of truth]
3. Therefore, every concrete individual that is a relatum in an immediate relation, which would include every concrete thing, has an inner core of consciousness.

The argument for the Humpty-Dumpty Intuition on which Premise 1 rests is yet to be given, and the best that can be marshaled in support of Premise 2 is that we are unable to think of any other medium in which mushing together relations could occur. That we cannot imagine any alternative does not establish that there isn't any; but in philosophy we must ultimately settle for what we can make intelligible to ourselves after we have made the best effort we can.

It now will be shown how James filled in this general argument from promiscuity with the specific cases of change and causation. James seems to have been born with an innate fear of Zeno, for as early as *The Principles of Psychology* (237) he claims that Zeno's paradoxes show the impossibility of change through a succession of numerically distinct states, whether it be mathematically dense, continuous, or discrete. In the final two books he argues that the theory of the continuum in modern mathematics fails to neutralize Zeno's challenge, because there cannot be a succession of numerically distinct states even if their ordering is dense or mathematically continuous.[9] The problem is to explain

---

[9] It is for this reason, no doubt, that James never bothers to distinguish between those of Zeno's arguments directed against a dense succession (the racecourse and the Achilles-and-the-tortoise) and those directed against a discrete succession (the arrow and the stadium).

how there can be a transition from an earlier to a later state. Given the Humpty-Dumpty Intuition, there is no way to explain this if the states are discrete. Herein it is clear that the Humpty-Dumpty Intuition is appealed to in support of a key premise in the Zenoian a priori argument to prove the impossibility of change without immediate successors mushing together. The only way in which change can be understood is by introspecting what goes on when we intentionally move or change. Thus, he indicts the mathematical physicist's account of change because "it fails to connect us with the inner life of the flux, or with the real causes that govern its direction. Instead of being interpreters of reality, concepts negate the inwardness of reality altogether . . ." (*PU* 110). The physicist gives us a "knowledge *about* things, as distinguished from living contemplation or sympathetic acquaintance with them . . . [which] touches only the outer surface of reality" (*PU* 111). The only way to understand change or flux "is either to experience it directly by being a part of reality one's self, or to evoke it in imagination by sympathetically divining someone else's inner life" (*PU* 112). Only in this way can we penetrate to "the inner nature of reality" and understand "what really *makes it go*" (*PU* 112).

The demand to understand change from the "inside" by an act of "intuitive sympathy" is based on James's gut intuitions about what constitutes a rationally satisfying account of reality – a case in point of his own "the sentiment of rationality" doctrine, according to which philosophers attracted to radically opposed philosophies have different personal predilections about what will count as an adequate explanation. James has been depicted in the last two chapters as an inside man who wants to penetrate to the conscious inner core of everything, motion included. Thus, motion must be explained by introspecting what goes on in our consciousness when we intentionally move. Not surprisingly, it is found that our action guiding recipe is not, and conceptually could not be, that of the physicist's description of a traversal of a distance, since it fails to specify an initial and final doing, and thereby fails to satisfy a conceptual requirement for being a recipe. This is the point that James really is making when he asserts that the runner "perceives nothing, while running, of the mathematician's homogeneous time and space, of the infinitely numerous succession of cuts in both, or of their order" (*PU* 114). By placing yourself "at the point of view of the thing's interior doing . . . all these back-looking and conflicting conceptions lie harmoniously in your hand" (*PU* 117).The demand to understand change as an intentional action also informs his discussion of Zeno in *Some Problems of Philosophy*. He interprets Zeno's dichotomy paradox as demanding that the "number of points to be occupied . . . be *enumerated* in succession" (*SPP* 82; my italics). This converting of a motion into an intentional action clearly underlies James's claim that the "continuous process to be traversed . . . is a *task* – not only for our philosophic imagination, but for any real agent who might try physically to compass the entire performance" (*SPP* 88).

Given James's Humpty-Dumpy type sentiment of rationality, the only way to explain change is by promiscuous succession. James, however, avoids this transcendental form of argumentation and instead engages in some fake Jack Horner type phenomenology. When we introspect our mind we find that motion is a type of flowing sludge. The only case in which we are experientially acquainted with such change is in our own consciousness. It is not that our awareness of our own conscious-ness when we perform an action of moving gives us a paradigm case, or even a case that is seminal in the order of concept acquisition. It gives us the only case of motion that we can imagine, every case of motion having to be understood in these agency terms. And this is panpsych-ism!

James's argument is perspicuously rendered as a special case of the general from-promiscuity-to-panpsychism argument.

4. Change requires promiscuous succession. [Humpty-Dumpty Intui-tion]
5. Promiscuous succession can occur only in consciousness. [some kind of truth]
6. Therefore, all change involves an inner core of consciousness.

If change is a nonpromiscuous succession, Zeno wins. There is change, and the only way it is possible, given the impossibility of nonpromis-cuous succession, is by promiscuous succession.

The case of causation is yet another special instance of the general from-promiscuity-to-panpsychism argument. Because of the widespread acceptance of Hume's unjustified confinement of the possible objects of introspection to sensible ideas, it was widely believed that causation cannot be anything more than uniform association. While James agrees that we do not have a sensible idea of causation, or any relation for that matter, he claims that we have a *feeling* of causation from an introspec-tion of our own mind when we act so as to bring something about. This is the only way in which causation can be understood, just as the only way motion can be understood is by introspection of what goes on in our consciousness when we intentionally move. Other cases of causa-tion must be understood by projecting onto external objects what we find to go on in our consciousness when we act. And this is panpsych-ism!

Exactly what do we find through introspection in the cases in which we act?

In all these what we feel is that a previous field of 'consciousness,' containing (in the midst of its complexity) the idea of a *result*, develops [*sic*] gradually into another field in which that result either appears as accomplished, or else is prevented by obstacles against which we still feel ourselves to press. . . . It seems to me that in such a continuously developing experiential series our concrete perception of causality is found in operation. If the word have any meaning at all it must mean what there we live through. (*SPP* 106)

What we observe in these personal cases is "the essential process of creation" and "where we predicate activities elsewhere . . . we have a right to suppose aught different in kind from this" (*SPP* 108). Because we take our personal experiences "as the type of what actual causation is, we should have to ascribe to cases of causation outside of our own life, to physical cases also, an inwardly experiential nature" (*SPP* 109). And this is panpsychism!

The argument, when explicitly mounted, is an instance of the general argument from-promiscuity-to-panpsychism.

7. Causation requires a promiscuous relation between cause and effect. [Humpty-Dumpty Intuition]
8. A promiscuous relation between cause and effect can occur only in consciousness. [some kind of truth]
9. Therefore, all causation involves a conscious process.

IV. From Promiscuity to Ineffability

The a priori arguments of Zeno and Bradley for the impossibility of discrete concrete relations also show that reality is ineffable. Before presenting James's best argument for this, it is necessary, so as to avoid confusion, to set aside two very bad reasons James gives for reality being ineffable. The first is based on the impossibility of any description capturing the full richness and determinateness of reality. "Conceptual knowledge is forever inadequate to the fullness of the reality to be known" (*SPP* 45). The second is based on the failure of concepts to be qualitatively isomorphic with their instantiators. One version of this claim is the indictment against conceptual representations for failing to produce what they represent. Activity and causation, for example, are said to be incomprehensible, because "the conceptual scheme yields nothing like them" (*SPP* 48). The physicist's space–time diagram of a motion is deficient because it fails to "*reproduce* it" (*SPP* 47). It doesn't leap off the blackboard and run around the room.

Another version of the lack-of-qualitative-isomorphism objection is that, necessarily, concepts are discrete (there is no "coming and going" in the Platonic heaven) and the percepts or concrete individuals they represent mush together, and thus they fail to be qualitatively identical with these concreta. "The conceptual scheme, consisting as it does of discontinuous terms, can only cover the perceptual flux in spots and incompletely. The one is no full measure of the other, essential features of the flux escaping whenever we put concepts in its place" (*SPP* 46).[10] Plainly, this ground for the charge of ineffability rests on a self-predication howler that would have done Plato proud. It is required that concepts or words be autological (i.e., apply to themselves) if they are to be adequate representations of reality. Since concepts of a qualitatively continuous or mushing together reality are themselves discrete, they fail to meet this requirement. By this reasoning, it could be shown that the concepts of the morning star and the evening star fail to be coreferential because they are not identical with each other.

Furthermore, both of these ineffability claims are vacuous, because James fails to subject them to his pragmatic requirement that the success of concepts in representing reality is to be determined by how well they realize the purpose for which they are used. By abstracting from a context of human interests and purposes, James renders vacuous, by his own pragmatic principle, the question of whether descriptions are adequate representations of reality. When James is making mystically based claims about the true nature or essence of reality, he is abstracting from any context of human interest or use.

There is another, and far more interesting, argument to be found in James based on the discreteness of concepts and the Humpty-Dumpty-based intuition that concreta are nondiscrete because they must participate in promiscuous relations with their spatio-temporal neighbors. He begins by granting Hegel's premise that every concrete thing "must in some sort be its own other" and then adds that, "When conceptually . . . treated, they of course cannot be their own others" (*PU* 53). No element of our active life can "be treated as a . . . stable grammatical subject, but that whatever *is* has the *durcheinander* character, meaning by that that when you say it is anything, it obliges you also to say not only that it is more and other than that thing, but that it *is not* that thing, both the *is* and the *is not* implying at bottom only that our grammatical forms, condemned as they are to staticality and alternation, are inadequate, if we use them as literal substitutes for the reality" (*MEN* 123).

Promiscuous relations violate the law of identity, because each of the concrete relata in an immediate relation fails to be strictly identical with itself in virtue of being identical, but not *that* identical, with the other relatum. "To act on anything means to get into it somehow; but that would mean to get out of one's self and be one's other, which for intellectualism is self-contradictory" (*PU* 115).[11] The reason a concep-

---

[10] This argument is presented enthymemically in *The Principles of Psychology*. Concepts "form an essentially discontinuous system, and translate the process of our perceptual experience, which is naturally a flux, into a set of stagnant and petrified terms. The very conception of flux itself is an absolutely changeless meaning in the mind: it signifies just that one thing, flux, immovably" (442).

[11] Readers must be alerted that the "intellectualism" that James opposes keeps changing before their eyes. Sometimes it is adherence to a logic that obeys the laws of standard

tual system must satisfy the law of identity is that the purpose of a concept is to be discriminatory by partitioning the world up into those individuals that are and those that are not instances of it. This entails that any instance of a concept cannot enter into promiscuous relations, as then it would fall on both sides of the partitioning. The reason for this is that the concrete individual which is an instance of concept F would also fail to be an instance of F because it merges with one of its spatio-temporal neighbors that has a property incompatible with being F. But it is just this which is necessarily the case with concrete individuals. Therefore, it is conceptually impossible that concepts apply to them and thus they are absolutely ineffable.[12] This argument, when explicitly mounted, looks like this.

10. Necessarily, every concrete individual is promiscuously related to its others. [Humpty-Dumpty Intuition]
11. Necessarily, concepts can apply only to individuals that are not promiscuously related to their others. [law of identity]
12. Therefore, concepts do not apply to concrete individuals, i.e., they are ineffable.

This argument uses conceptually based reasons to show the limitations of concepts. "That concepts can neutralize other concepts is one of their great practical functions. This answers also the charge that it is self-contradictory to use concepts to undermine the credit of conception in general. The best way to show that a knife won't cut is to try to cut with it (SPP 60).[13] If we are to penetrate to the inner essence of reality we must learn "to think in non-conceptualized terms" (PU 131). James's task, like that of the traditional mystic, is to "deafen [us] to talk" (PU 131), and he accomplishes this, not by following the tradi-

---

[12] logic, such as that of identity and noncontradiction (PU 98, 46, 53, 67, 94). "Intellectualistic logic," sometimes called "conceptual logic" (PU 109), requires that identity be transitive (PU 98 and 115). At other places, intellectualism is the strawman doctrine that a name excludes "from the fact named what the name's definition fails positively to include," which James calls "vicious intellectualism" (PU 32; see also 53 and 99 and MT 149). Yet another version of it is that reality can be adequately captured through concepts (PU 98 and 130–1). At one place it is nothing but Platonic essentialism (PU 99 and SPP 48). Intellectualism also is said to be the view that "What can be distinguished . . . is separate; and what is separate is unrelated" (PU 134). To complete this confusing plethora of senses of "intellectualism" is the identification of it with "the belief that our mind comes upon a world complete in itself, and has the duty of ascertaining its contents; but has no power of re-determining its character, for that is already given" (PU 111). One can reject the spectator theory of knowledge (or essentialism) and still adhere to the laws of logic. The relevant sense of intellectualism for my purpose is the first one, involving acceptance of the traditional laws of logic.

[12] A vague concept also cannot apply to an individual that enters into a promiscuous relation. A vague concept permits there to be an instance that is neither clearly an instance of the concept nor clearly not an instance. Thus, this borderline individual would not fall on both sides of the divide, as would be the case with an individual in a promiscuous relation that is an instance of a nonvague concept.

[13] James, of course, means *energetically* cut, as was seen with the ginzu knives in Chapter 7.

tional mystical way of meditation and asceticism, but rather by contemplating the koans supplied by the arguments of Zeno, Green, Bradley, McTaggart, Taylor, and Royce to show the contradictory nature of our ordinary conceptual scheme.[14]

When we have learned the trick of jettisoning all concepts we shall be able to intuit sympathetically the mushing together of spatio-temporal neighbors. Will we have reverted, thereby, back to "baby's first sensation" of the big, blooming, buzzing confusion, which also is a conceptless sensing? And what is the connection between the mushing together experience and the experience of a widespread unification, such as is reported by pluralistic and monistic mystics? In answer to the first question, the backyard mystical experience of ordinary things as mushing together differs from baby's first sensation in that the former is a richer and more sophisticated experience in which the subject experiences ordinary individuals *as* mushing together, and thus appears not to be completely devoid of concepts. Only someone who had formerly applied concepts to these ordinary individuals could experience them *as* ceasing to satisfy these concepts in virtue of their entering into promiscuous relations. If I am right, there is the employment of a second-order concept in a backyard mystical experience, namely, the concept of an individual that formerly was conceptualized in a certain way no longer being conceptualizable in that way.

The answer to the second question is to be found by examining James's 1910 "A Suggestion about Mysticism." It begins with the mushing-together account of our perception of time. "The present field as a whole came continuously out of its predecessor and will melt into its successor as continuously again" (*EP* 158). The sort of mushing together relations that we grow aware of in backyard mystical experiences become vastly expanded in the more traditional type of mystical experiences. Herein the threshold of ordinary sensory awareness is lowered

---

[14] Numerous commentators have failed to realize that James's claim of ineffability is rooted in his mystical Humpty-Dumpty Intuition, which is just one way in which they ignore or downplay the centrality of mysticism in his metaphysics. Bernstein interprets James as saying that "concrete reality and experience are richer, more dynamic, and thicker than can possibly be expressed by our concepts." This is James's trivial sense of ineffability and completely overlooks his exciting Humpty-Dumpty-based sense. In a similarly distorted vein, Fontinell writes that "James's concern for the concrete and his recognition that 'life exceeds logic' should not be interpreted as a mode of irrationalism or antiintellectualism except insofar as rationalism and intellectualism are understood as confusing concepts or ideas with the full richness of experience and reality" (*SGI* 62). Yet another example is Peter Hare's claim that "James did not wish to discredit all conceptual thinking but only to encourage the development of more flexible thinking" (*SPP* xl). He warns us that "The romantic side of *Some Problems of Philosophy* should be kept in perspective and not allowed to obscure the fundamental features of the metaphysics James outlined so lucidly and persuasively" (xli). Pace Hare, the metaphysics of this book, as well as that of *A Pluralistic Universe*, is based on an appeal to his romantic Bergsonian conceptless intuition. Plainly, all three commentators ignore the mystical basis of James's ineffability claim in his Humpty-Dumpty Intuition.

and there is a "very sudden and incomprehensible enlargement of the conscious field" (*EP* 159). We become conscious of a unification of reality in which "the sense of *relation* will be greatly enhanced." It is not just that our ordinary field of consciousness is vastly expanded, for there is nothing especially mystical about a wide-angle lens view – a mystic isn't someone with especially good peripheral vision – but rather that we experience a richer complex of things as mushing together. The experience is more than just a unifying experience: It is an experience of unification, of the melting together of things that formerly were taken to be discrete (*EP* 159). Traditional mystical experiences of a widespread unification, therefore, differ from backyard mystical experiences only in regard to the extent of the unification. But the fusing and merging together never realizes, for James, that of complete union, and that is why the identity of a thing with its "other" is not transitive. Accordingly, James calls himself a "pluralistic mystic," and thereby aligns himself with the traditional theistic mystics who claimed to experience their becoming identical with God, but not *that* identical.

Is this account of our conceptless, or almost conceptless, experience of change based on Jack Horner phenomenology? I don't know. I'll have to leave it to those who have realized this special state of consciousness to decide. But one thing is certain. It is not an account "of the adult consciousness itself" as it purports to be at the outset of "The Stream of Consciousness" chapter in the abridged version (*PBC* 139). If it is an account of anything, it is of a highly unusual form of consciousness, such as might be had if we had learned the trick of ridding ourselves of all concepts and intuiting in a pure manner.

James employs the a priori arguments of rationalists against immediate relations between distinct individuals as koans that can help shock us out of our inveterate pragmatic state of consciousness so that we can perceive without concepts and thus come to an existential knowledge of the true essence of reality as a type of flowing sludge. Except for Zeno's paradoxes, whose acceptance was a constant in James's philosophy, he appears on the surface to make a 180-degree turnaround in his evaluation of the other a priori arguments against the possibility of multiplicity and change. In the 1905 "The Thing and Its Relations" he considers two of Bradley's most infamous arguments: (1) that a thing cannot enter into different relationships because its identity cannot survive the transition from one to the other in virtue of every one of its properties being essential to its existence; and (2) that relations are impossible in general because "relations *separate* terms, and need themselves to be hooked on *ad infinitum*" (*ERE* 58). (Bradley, obviously, never bothered to look at a chain, as Wittgenstein wryly pointed out in his remark, at 2.03 in the *Tractatus*, that in an atomic fact objects hang in each other like links in a chain.)

James is quick to dismiss these arguments on both logical and experiential grounds, adding that Bradley "abuses the privilege which society grants to all us philosophers, of being puzzle-headed" (*ERE* 59). Argument (1) is charged with a word–object or, in later terminology, a use–mention confusion: "All that I can catch in their talk is the substitution of what is true of certain words for what is true of what they signify" (*ERE* 51). Different words can be coreferring, such as "Tully" and "Cicero." James's experiential refutation of both arguments appeals to his Radical Empiricism doctrine of the immediate givenness of relations in experience. He uses the watery metaphors of *The Principles of Psychology*'s chapter on "The Stream of Thought" to describe the relations between spatio-temporal neighbors and the successive Thoughts of a single self, but he does not go all the way, as he does in his final two books, and "promiscuize" them so that each of their relata becomes its own Hegelian other.

Given how severe James is in his 1905 condemnation of these arguments, it should confound his interpreter to find him seemingly embracing them in the final two books, saying that "No real activities and indeed no real connexions of any kind can obtain if we follow the conceptual logic. . . . The work begun by Zeno, and continued by Hume, Kant, Herbart, Hegel, and Bradley, does not stop till sensible reality lies entirely disintegrated at the feet of 'reason' " (*PU* 110). Concepts not only do not completely capture the nature of reality – one of his trivial senses of ineffability – "they falsify . . . and make the flux impossible to understand" (*SPP* 45). James claims that Bradley and Bergson "have broken my confidence in concepts down" (*EP* 155). James even goes so far as to endorse the above Humpty-Dumpty-based argument of the early Dewey against any subject–object dualism. "*Knowledge is impossible*, for knower is one concept and known is another. Discrete, separated by a chasm, they are mutually 'transcendent' things, so that how an object can ever get into a subject, or a subject ever get at an object, has become the most unanswerable of philosophic riddles" (*SPP* 49). How is James's apparent capitulation to his absolute idealist opponent to be explained? Is he making a pact with the devil so as to advance the cause of his beloved Humpty-Dumpty Intuition?

My highly speculative explanation for this apparent defection is that in the interim between the 1905 essay and the final two books, the Humpty-Dumpty Intuition came to occupy a position of dominance in James's thinking, and he thereby looked with favor on these previously discredited a priori arguments because they gave additional argumentative support to his Humpty-Dumpty Intuition that concepts cannot in principle be true of reality. A concept, in virtue of its segregating role, cannot be instantiated by an individual that also is an instance of another concept that is incompatible with it. But, according to the Humpty-Dumpty Intuition, such a distinct individual cannot enter into immediate relations with another distinct individual, such as that of exerting a causal influence over or knowing it. "To act on anything means to get into it somehow; but that would mean to get out of one's self and be one's other, which for intellectualism is self-contradictory" (*PU* 115). The watery and gaseous metaphors for describing the temporal flux from the 1905 article and its earlier *The Principles of Psychology* have now become Humpty-Dumpty-fied. James agrees with Bradley that it is impossible that numerically distinct individuals be immediately related to each other and that concepts, in virtue of their segregating role, require that this be the case, thus showing the inapplicability of concepts to reality.

Where, then, does James part company with Bradley? It is not over the nature of what is immediately given in sense experience, for they both accept the positive tenet of the Humpty-Dumpty Intuition that sees "the minimum of feeling as an immediately intuited much-at-once" – that is, neighborly individuals as promiscuously related. James, unlike Bradley, is willing to believe that this backyard type of mystical experience is revelatory of reality, that the bluebird of happiness is in his own experiential backyard; but Bradley, being of a rationalistic bent of mind, cannot trust the deliverances of sense experience and thus must satisfy his hunger for unity by seeking for his bluebird of happiness beyond both the sensible and the conceptual orders of being. In support of his own sentiment of rationality, James claims that

When the alternative lies between knowing life in its full thickness and activity, as one acquainted with its *me's* and *thee's* and *now's* and *here's*, on the one hand, and knowing a transconceptual evaporation life like the absolute, on the other, it seems to me that to choose the latter knowledge merely because it has been named 'philosophy' is to be superstitiously loyal to a name . . . I sincerely believe that nothing but inveterate anti-empiricist prejudice accounts for Mr. Bradley's choice. (*EP* 155)

V. From Panpsychism to Spiritualism

In the previous section arguments were given to show that the Humpty-Dumpty Intuition entails *panpsychism* – that every concrete individual has an inner consciousness and thus has some properties of a conscious sort. It now will be shown that the conjunction of panpsychism with the rationalist's a priori arguments against the possibility of a nonpromiscuous immediate relation entails *spiritualism* or *idealism* – that every concrete individual is nothing but consciousness, has only properties of a conscious sort. This is demonstrated by the following from-panpsychism-to-spiritualism argument.

10. A concrete individual can have a property of a physical sort only if it stands in certain immediate nomic relations to other concrete individuals. [James's doctrine of Pure Experience]
11. It is impossible for a concrete individual to stand in an immediate

relation to another individual that it doesn't promiscuously mush together with. [from the a priori arguments of the rationalists]

2. Only in the wondrously mysterious medium of consciousness can there be such a promiscuous mushing together relation. [some kind of truth]

12. Every property of a concrete individual is of either a physical or conscious sort. [some kind of truth]

13. The only properties possessed by a concrete individual are conscious ones. [from 10, 11, 2, and 12]

3. Every concrete individual has an inner core of consciousness and thus has some properties of a conscious sort. [stylistic variation of the conclusion of the from-promiscuity-to-panpsychism argument]

14. Every concrete individual has properties of a conscious sort. [from 3]

15. Every concrete individual has properties of a conscious sort and only such properties. [from 13 and 14]

Although the scholastic look of this argument would horrify James, all of its premises are ones that James accepts or is committed to accepting. Premise 10 rests on the first tenet of James's doctrine of Pure Experience, which was expounded in Chapter 7, according to which no piece of pure experience, no concrete individual in other words, counts as mental or physical *simpliciter* but only as it is related to earlier and later events. Some of these relations, of course, will be nonmediated. It will count as physical when its relations to these temporally surrounding events obey causal laws of science. I am not sure how to argue for Premise 12, and it is the only premise that cannot be traced directly to something that James wrote.

VI. A Big Aporia

There is a big aporia that my exposition of how James's doctrine of the specious present became superseded by the Humpty-Dumpty Intuition has so far conveniently overlooked. It is due to his oft-repeated claim that our experience of change is pulsational, and must be if we are to escape the clutches of Zeno. This creates a big aporia, as there is a seeming contradiction between the pulsational and the Humpty-Dumpty accounts of our experience of change. An effort will be made to neutralize this aporia by Poo-bah-izing James's apparently inconsistent claims.

That our experience of time's flow is pulsational is maintained in *PP*. "... we tell it off in pulses. We say 'now! now! now!' or we count 'more! more! more!' as we feel it bud. This composition out of units of duration is called the law of time's discrete flow" (585; see also *PU* 129 and *SPP* 88 for more of the same).

That "Time itself comes in drops" (*PU* 104) is not only purported to be phenomenologically vouchsafed but also supported by neurophysiological facts concerning the thresholds for perceptual awareness (*PU* 104). Furthermore, only if change is pulsational can we escape Zeno's paradoxes.

> Either we must stomach logical contradiction, therefore, or we must admit that the limit is reached in these successive cases by finite and perceptible units of approach – drops, buds, steps, or whatever we please to term them, of change, coming wholly when they do come, or coming not at all. (*SPP* 93–4)

We should be suspicious of any phenomenological support for a claim that also is supported by a priori arguments, for the phenomenology invariably turns out to be of the faked Jack Horner variety. Our expectations are not disappointed in this case. James's phenomenologically based claim that "Sensibly, motion comes in drops, waves or pulses" (*PU* 107) flies in the face of ordinary experience. I do not see the rising arm as a discrete succession of droplet-type things, as I might if I were watching a motion picture of the rising on an out-of-whack projector. Pace James, we need not, and usually do not, experience a bottle emptying drop by drop (*PU* 103–4). It is not uncommon to see a bottle of Chivas Regal decanting in this manner, but not when it is a bottle of Bankers Club vodka. It just pours out! James is right that our experience is pulsational when we count or reiterate the word *now*, but this hardly is typical of our ordinary experiences of change.

How is the aporia to be resolved? One obvious way, which even has some textual support, is to make a distinction between the *act* of experiencing and the *content* of the experience and hold the former alone to be pulsational, the latter being of the mushing-together sort. Immediately after formulating the "law of time's *discrete flow*," James adds that "The discreteness is, however, merely due to the fact that our successive acts of *recognition* or *apperception* of *what* it is are discrete. The sensation is as continuous as any sensation can be" (*PP* 585). This act–content distinction seems to inform his claims that, whereas "things are discrete and discontinuous . . . their comings and goings and contrasts no more break the flow of the thought that thinks them than they break the time and space in which they lie" (*PU* 233), and there cannot be found "in the thought any parts . . . corresponding to the object's parts. Time parts are not such parts" (*PU* 269). If James means to be making this act–content distinction, we must understand his ambiguous claim that our "acquaintance with reality grows literally by buds or drops of perception" (*SPP* 80) as applying only to the perceptual acts, not to their phenomenological contents. Via this distinction we can

escape having to countenance James's Jack Horner pulsational phenomenological account. This way of interpreting James's pulsational
theory of passage makes him an anticipator of Whitehead's doctrine
that there is a becoming of continuity, but not a continuity of becoming
in which what becomes is some content.

Unfortunately, James cannot consistently accept this way of applying
the act–content distinction to the passage of time, because it has the
pulsational manner in which our acts of perception pass constitute the
real nature of temporal passage rather than their phenomenological
contents, which supposedly reveal a promiscuous type of passage. The
most holy of holy philosophical truths for James is that reality is just
what it experientially appears to be. " 'The insuperability of sensation'
would be a short expression of my thesis" (*SPP* 45). It was because
James awarded the ontological laureate to the revelations of gross sense
experience that he stopped using the term "the specious present," with
its commitment to the physicist's mathematically punctal present as the
real present.

The act–content distinction left us with a *succession of numerically distinct* acts of perception, but this clashes with James's Humpty-Dumpty
Intuition, buttressed with the a priori arguments of the rationalists, that
there cannot be such a succession. It would appear that we have the
following choice: We can agree with James that only a pulsational succession of distinct events can avoid Zeno's paradoxes and thereby abandon the Humpty-Dumpty Intuition, or we can hold onto to this intuition and reject James's demand that change is to be understood in
terms of a pulsational succession. Given how central the Humpty-
Dumpty intuition is to James's overall philosophy, he would do better
to withdraw his pulsational account of change.

The apparent inconsistency between James's pulsational and
Humpty-Dumpty accounts of change can be eliminated if we Poo-bah-
ize them with suitable "qua"-clause restrictions. Qua Promethean
agent, change is pulsational, the reason being that an agent requires an
action-guiding recipe that presents him with a discrete succession of
actions having a first and last member. But, qua backyard mystic, his
response to Zeno is to "promiscuize" change. Thus, Zeno's paradoxes
challenge both the Promethean agent and the backyard mystic, and
each has his own separate response. The unresolved problem with this
Ontological Relativism solution to the aporia is that it raises an even
bigger aporia – the really big aporia – that James's Ontological Relativism clashes with the absolute, nonrelativized reality-claims made by
both the religious and the backyard mystic, which is to be an important
topic of the next chapter.

11

Attempts at a One-World
Interpretation of James

As this book has progressed a number of aporias have been shown to arise out of James's text, and promissory notes were issued for their resolutions, this being the chapter in which they are to be paid in full. If I do not make good on them, as well I might not, I could be accused of being a philosophical tease for letting the tension build with the promise of relief in this chapter, and now, when it gets time to deliver, nothing happens. No one wants to be called a "tease," philosophical or otherwise.

Before I undertake this most difficult constructive task, it will be helpful to give a brief summary of these aporias. The biggest, of which the others are special cases, is to find a way to unify James's many selves and the many worlds toward which their interests are directed. James's deep need to find a philosophy that he could live by precludes any self-unification that is not rooted in a metaphysical unification of the many worlds. This need is especially pressing for James, as there were apparent clashes between the things that he said from the perspectives of these different selves, especially the mystical and Promethean selves, the latter comprising both the scientist and the moral agent. These are the deepest and most seemingly intractable aporias. In order to bring them into clear relief, a brief recap will be given of the account of James's mysticism in the previous two chapters.

James's "religious mysticism," based on the I–Thou experience, in volved a partial union with the inner consciousness of other beings, starting with his fellow human beings and extending all the way to a supernatural but finite God, with some stopoffs to I–Thou the beasts and fishes. Even nature itself was fair game for the I–Thou experience, if one could only learn to adopt the personal stance toward it of the theist. The upshot of this nature mysticism is panpsychism. Like nature mysticism, James's "backyard mysticism" is directed at nature and manages to see it in a radically different way than Promethean man does; the individuals that the latter sharply separates by applying concepts to them are perceived as mushing together into promiscuous relations, though not to the extent that they cease to have any identity of their own. The upshot of this brand of mysticism was not just panpsychism, since only in consciousness could such promiscuous mushing occur, but spiritualism, when the rationalist's a priori arguments against the possibility of discrete relations were included.

There are striking similarities between James's religious and backyard mysticism. Both involve conceptless, and thereby ineffable, experiences of unification that are obtainable only by a passive self. This requires that one's Promethean self be held in abeyance and thus occasions the first of the clashes between James's Promethean and mystical selves. Far more troublesome is the fact that each type of mystical experience is taken by its subjects to be a cognitive revelation of the true nature of reality. The absolute, nonrelativized reality-claims based on these experiences clash with the *universal* doctrine of Ontological Relativism. Furthermore, Promethean concept-involving reality-claims hold there to be discrete relations between neighbors, but the reality-claims based on backyard and nature mysticism promiscuize these relations. Both reality-claims cannot be true, unless they are Poo-bah-ized, but this is exactly what the nonrelativized reality-claims of the mystics will not allow. The mystic would charge any attempt to neutralize the contentful clash between mystical and Promethean reality-claims by applying restrictive "qua"-clauses to them as begging the question.

There are, however, two apparent differences between James's religious and backyard mysticism. First, unlike the case of an I–Thou experience, there is no talk about the subject of a backyard mystical experience becoming unified with what it experiences, only of a unification among the contents of the experience. Second, whereas the I–Thou experience makes personality central, since one person relates to another person *as* a person, backyard mystical experiences seem devoid of personality. I am not sure how deep these differences are.

To be sure, the description of the apparent object of an I–Thou experience makes it appear to be a person, but it is a very odd, truncated sort of "person," because it is claimed by James to have another person as one of its proper parts; and, as was argued in the last chapter, it is not possible that an *agent* (someone who deliberates and makes choices that are intentionally carried out), have another agent as one of its proper parts. That the "persons" involved in an I–Thou experience are nothing but consciousnesses undercuts the major attraction of pluralistic over monistic mysticism for James, which was that only the former makes room for agency and real evils that are to be conquered. That the absorbing and absorbed consciousness is a non-Promethean type of consciousness brings the I–Thou experience closer to the backyard mystical experience.

The apparent object of a backyard mystical experience, on the other hand, seems not to be completely impersonal, thus bringing the two types of mystical experience even closer together. As C. I. Lewis insightfully said about the role of these experiences in the philosophies of

Bergson and James: "Life has a meaning forever hid from the coldly logical mind, its secret lies open only to those, who, discarding reason, face the mystery with instinctive or intuitive insight. . . . One understands [it] as one would understand a friend – that is, by intuitively identifying one's self with the friend, and thus grasping the true import of the friend's inner life" (*CP* 47). Thus, a backyard mystical experience of the mushing together of ordinary things bestows on them a sort of personality, although, again, one that stops short of agency. I am not sure that this attempt to assimilate backyard to I–Thou mystical experiences is correct. It might be that they are fundamentally different in a way similar to that in which theistic mystical experiences differ from monistic ones, in that the former alone have a personal content. Basically, I have been making use of Thomas Merton's counter to the charges of R. C. Zaehner that Eastern mystical experiences are devoid of personality. Regardless of what subtle differences there might be between James's two types of mystical experience, they agree in their rejection of the practical world of the Promethean self, along with its active, Poo-bah-izing self.

Before considering how to unify James's Promethean and mystical selves, along with their separate worlds, the more general problem of unifying his many worlds and selves will be considered. Initially, only quests for unification that can be directly located in James's text will be considered. They will be found to be inadequate, both individually and collectively. This will be followed by attempts to find a unification that is Jamesian in spirit though it goes well beyond the text, having only a tenuous or even ambiguous relation to it. Herein, interpretation fades into what-James-ought-to-have-said-but-really-didn't.

I. James's Quests for Unification

James's Ontological Relativism was central to his Promethean philosophy, for it held that what is real (actual, existent) is relative to the passing interests of an agent. For each of James's many selves there is a world toward which its distinctive desires and interests are directed. As a person's interests change so will the world that is taken to be actual. Immediately after introducing this plethora of worlds ontologically on all fours with each other, James raises the question of what unifies them into a universe, it being up to the philosopher to find an answer. He never gives any explicit answer, so it is left to the interpreter to draw one out of the text and thereby complete what James himself described as the "incomplete arch" in his philosophy.

Chapter 7 presented a Promethean solution to the unification problem that consisted in each of the many worlds being a possible target for a Promethean agent's interest, thereby gaining unification by their common relation to this agent. This enables James's many selves to achieve a first-I'm-this-and-then-I'm-that sort of unification but leaves him a Poo-bah-type schizophrenic. It appears as if James's quest to have it all cannot have the one thing that James most wants – to be a truly unified self. There is a quote from Emerson that beautifully expresses the agony wrought by this taking-turns solution as it applies to the mystical and Promethean selves, termed the "soul" and "understanding," respectively.

> The worst feature of this double consciousness is, that the two lives, of the understanding and of the soul, which we lead, really show very little relation to each other; never meet and measure each other; one prevails now, all buzz and din; and the other prevails then, all infinitude and paradise; and, with the progress of life, the two discover no greater disposition to reconcile themselves. (quoted from Matthiessen, *AR* 3)

Lowell epitomized Emerson as "a Plotinus-Montaigne." James, certainly, hoped to do better than Emerson in this regard. Unfortunately, his Ontological Relativism failed to unify his many selves because it had no way of resolving the clashes between his Promethean and mystical selves in regard to whether reality is relative to the interests of an agent and whether concepts should be employed, which really comprise the question of whether one should take an active or a passive stance toward the world.

As James matured as a philosopher he sought a deeper type of unification than the very tenuous one supplied by his Poo-bah-istic Ontological Relativism. One indication of this is a subtle shift in terminology. Whereas he formerly spoke of different worlds in *The Principles of Psychology*, twelve years later he spoke, in *The Varieties of Religious Experiences*, of "other dimensions of existence from the sensible" one (*VRE* 406). We are said, furthermore, to "enter into wider cosmic relations" when we have mystical experiences, rather than experiencing a different world (*VRE* 407). Mystical experiences "open out the possibility of other orders of truth" (*VRE* 335) and are "windows through which the mind looks out upon a more extensive and inclusive world" (*VRE* 339). These quotations support Henry S. Levinson's claim that mystical experiences reveal, for James, "not so much *another* world as . . . a *wider* world than the ones that most naturalists, positivists, moralists, and materialists affirmed" (*RI* 99). This shift in terminology from "worlds" to a "wider world" and different "dimensions" of a single world does not in itself achieve any unification, for it leaves it undetermined just how these different dimensions, such as those revealed through sense and mystical experiences, are related. In fact, it is misleading to use "dimensional" talk at all, because whatever has a position in any one dimension of an ordinary dimensional or coordinate system has a position in every other dimension of the system, but it is unclear how a mystical or supernatural reality or entity could have a position in every dimension, including those of space and time, of some higher-order dimensional coordinate system.

Fortunately, James's quest for unification went deeper than a mere shift in terminology, and an obscurantist one at that. It took many different forms, with no one of them achieving a complete unification of all of the worlds, thus raising the question of whether in conjunction they do the trick. Some of the forms it took were: (1) instrumentalism; (2) working hypotheses; (3) concept empiricism; and (4) transworld causation. Solutions (1) and (3) both attempt to show there is a world that is seminal or basic in some sense, all the other worlds being dependent upon it in this respect. The orders of dependency might be the familiar ones from the history of philosophy consisting of existence or knowledge, what Aristotle called the orders of nature and experience.

(1) James's Ontological Relativism was quite content to countenance a sharp clash between the commonsense world of sensible objects and the world of theoretical entities of science, between what Wilfrid Sellars was later to call the manifest and scientific images, due to the latter being devoid of all of the secondary and tertiary properties manifested in the former. The following quotations give expression to this clash. "Sensible phenomena are pure delusions for the mechanical philosophy" (*PP* 1258). "The essence of things for science is not to be what they seem, but to be atoms and molecules moving to and from each other according to strange laws" (*PP* 1230). For example, "There is no such thing as 'water' for 'science'; that is only a handy name for H_2 and O when they have got into the position H-O-H, and then affect our senses in a novel way" (*PP* 1250). The most serious aspect of the clash between the scientific and commonsense worlds is that the former is "a purposeless universe, in which all the things and qualities that give meaning to life, *dulcissima mundi nomina*, are but illusions of our fancy attached to accidental clouds of dust which will be dissipated by the eternal cosmic weather as carelessly as they were formed" (*PP* 1260).

James no longer is willing to meet the threat of bifurcationism by applying his Ontological Relativism to the commonsense and scientific worlds. Instead, he finds a way of unifying them through an instrumentalistic reduction of the latter to the former. An extreme, activistic form of his instrumentalism, similar to Dewey's, is that "physics is the science of the ways of taking hold of bodies and pushing them" (*P* 30). Scientific theories are not to be interpreted realistically as offering a "transcript of reality . . . [but] are only a man-made language, a conceptual shorthand . . . in which we write our reports of nature; and languages . . . tolerate much choice of expression and many dialects" (*P* 33). Scientific entities "should not be held for literally true. It is *as if* they existed; but in reality they are like co-ordinates or logarithms, only artificial short-cuts for taking us from one part to another of experience's flux" (*P* 92). "The term 'energy' doesn't even pretend to stand for anything 'objective.' It is only a way of measuring the surface of phenomena so as to string their changes on a simple formula" (*P* 103). "Aether and molecules may be like co-ordinates and averages, only so many crutches by the help of which we practically perform the operation of getting about among our sensible experiences" (*PU* 123). By instrumentalizing theoretical entities, James goes quite a way toward neutralizing the bifurcation between man and nature as science depicts it.

That the commonsense world of sensible objects is more basic in the order of being than that of the theoretical entities of science in that the latter are reducible to the former, being only instrumental constructs out of them, does not show that the ontological contents of *all* worlds are thus reducible to sensible objects. Worlds comprised of abstract entities immediately come to mind. It will be up to concept empiricism to complete the task begun by scientific instrumentalism by showing that the ontological contents of all these other worlds are also in some way instrumental constructs out of ordinary empirical objects.

(2) There is, however, another respect in which (1) does not go far enough in its unifying efforts. Its exclusive concern with ontological reduction of theoretical to empirical objects leaves untouched the apparent clash between the scientist and the moral agent over the status of determinism, as well as epiphenomenalism. It is here that James can press into service his weak, working-hypothesis version of the will to believe. For scientists to ply their trade successfully they need not actually believe that determinism (or epiphenomenalism) is true; they need only to adopt determinism (or epiphenomenalism) as a working hypothesis, and they have ample will-to-believe-type justification for doing so, as there is extensive evidence from the history of science that doing so aids the progress of science. Promethean moral agents, on the other hand, must have sweating-with-conviction belief that they have contracausal freedom of the will. In Chapter 4, it was seen how James applied his will-to-believe doctrine in its strong sense, the one that involves actually believing, to justify their believing this; for their success as moral agents requires that they do so, assuming that their psychology is such that they are not going to make the requisite moral effort unless they believe their wills are free in the Libertarian sense, which was the basis of James's Dilemma of Determinism argument in Chapter 3 that a belief in determinism leads one into pessimistic despair.

Maybe this application of the believing and working-hypothesis versions of the will-to-believe doctrine succeeds in neutralizing the apparent clash in beliefs between the scientist and the moral agent over determinism (and epiphenomenalism), but it could not work for the apparent clash in beliefs between the mystic and the moral agent over the nature of reality, especially whether it even has an intrinsic nature. Moral agents must make use of concepts if they are to get around in the world successfully, but in doing so they must take reality to be made up of numerically distinct objects that stand in discrete immediate relations to their spatio-temporal neighbors. But this is just what James's mystic, whether a religious or a backyard one, denies: Reality cannot be captured by concepts because concepts are segregating.

But, plainly, it won't work to have either one of these mystics replace her belief with the adoption of a working hypothesis. What would it even mean for the mystics to treat their belief in a promiscuously mushed-together world as a working hypothesis? What end would they promote by doing so? Scientists adopt a proposition as a working hypothesis for the purpose of programming experiments that will enable them to put it to the test and discover new laws, but God or the Eternal One is not a deterministic being that is subject to experimental verification. Furthermore, the value of a mystical experience depends upon the experiencer *believing* it to be a gnostic revelation of the true essence of reality. The salvific consequences of this mystically based belief could not be served by merely adopting the proposition in question as a working hypothesis. Neither can moral agents accept a working hypothesis of their belief in a world that really is the way they take it to be on the basis of the concepts they wield. As James never tires of stressing, we would have no incentive to live the morally strenuous life of the moral agent unless we took the world to have a constitution that answers back to our deepest feelings and needs. Thus, moral agents need to have a real sweating-with-conviction belief, not just a working hypothesis, that the world has a structure corresponding to the concepts that they apply to it in their efforts to gain a Promethean mastery over it. The reality-beliefs of the extreme monistic mystic, with their acosmic denials of space, time, and multiplicity, present the most severe challenge to the reality-beliefs of the moral agent, which, of course, are committed to their reality. Why should one take the sensible world seriously if it is a mere illusion?

There is an even more decisive reason why Ontological Relativism cannot be reconciled with the absolutism of mystics by having mystical reality-claim downgraded to mere working hypotheses. Only a proposition, something that expresses a complete thought and thereby is either true or false, can be adopted as a working hypothesis. But, according to Ontological Relativism, a mystical reality-claim fails to express a proposition and therefore is not adoptable as a working hypothesis. The reason is that, according to Ontological Relativism, a reality-claim must specify a person at a time, in relation to whose interests the object or state of affairs is real or existent, just as a description of a brotherhood relation must refer to each of the brothers. The sentence "Jones is the brother of _____ ," fails to express a proposition, being called by logicians a "propositional function." Only when the blank space is filled with a personal constant or designation of a person does the sentence express a proposition, something true or false. According to Ontological Relativism, the mystical reality-claim "Reality in itself or essentially is an affair of promiscuous relations" really is the propositional function "Promiscuous relations are of special interest to person _____ at time _____ ." Only when the blank spaces are suitably filled in with the name of a person and a time does a proposition get expressed. And until a proposition is presented there is nothing that is adoptable as a working hypothesis. The same reasoning would also show that a mystical reality-claim cannot be believed on a will-to-believe basis, since one can have a will-to-believe option to believe only a proposition. Thus, no proposition, no will-to-believe option, and no adoption as a working hypothesis either.

(3) It was seen that (1)'s scientific instrumentalism did not go far enough, for it did not show how worlds other than that composed of the theoretical entities of science could be reduced to the world of sensible objects. James's concept empiricism generalizes the instrumentalistic account of scientific concepts as devices for leading us from one experience to another to all concepts.

Different universes of thought thus arise, with specific sorts of relation among their ingredients. The world of common-sense 'things'; the world of material tasks to be done; the mathematical world of pure forms; the world of ethical propositions; the worlds of logic, of music, etc. – all abstracted and generalized from long-forgotten perceptual instances from which they have as it were flowered out – return and merge themselves again in the particulars of our present and future perception. By those *whats* we apperceive all our *thises*. Percepts and concepts interpenetrate and melt together, impregnate and fertilize each other. Neither, taken alone, knows reality in its completeness. We need them both, as we need both our legs to walk with. (*SPP* 33–4)

This is a form of concept empiricism, because it requires that all concepts be analyzable in terms of the percepts from which they arise and in which they ultimately terminate. The foundational role of sense experiences informs his claim that

Philosophy must thus recognize many realms of reality which mutually interpenetrate. The conceptual systems of our mathematics, logic, aesthetics, ethics, are such realms, each strung upon some peculiar form of relation, and each different from perceptual reality in that in no one of them is history or happening displayed. Perceptual reality involves and contains all these ideal systems, and vastly more besides. (*SPP* 56)

This concept empiricism achieves at best only an epistemological sort of unification of the worlds. That we must form concepts in such a way that they flow out of and ultimately back again into percepts, thereby giving a centrality to the commonsense sensible world, hardly shows anything about the ontology of the different worlds. In fact, James himself seemed to balk at drawing ontological conclusions from his concept empiricism in respect to both scientific objects and Platonic abstracta. Scattered throughout his writings are remarks that seem to endow them with a self-subsisting existence. In regard to Ostwald's reduction of the "hypersensible entities, the corpuscles and vibrations" of science to our sensations, he says that "It seems too economical to be all-sufficient. Profusion, not economy, may after all be reality's key-note" (*P* 93). More generally, he held that "the existence of the object, whenever the idea asserts it 'truly,' is the only reason, in innumerable cases, why the idea does work successfully, if it work at all" (*MT* 8). This realistic intuition should apply to scientific objects as well as to ordinary ones. That James did so apply it is be borne out by his lumping together of ether waves and psychological states such as anger. "Ether-waves and your anger . . . are things in which my thoughts will never *perceptually* terminate, but my concepts of them lead me to their brink, to the chromatic fringes and to the hurtful words and deeds which are their really next effects" (*ERE* 36).

There also are unmistakable commitments to Platonism. Immediately after giving his conceptual empiricist reduction of Platonic abstracta to percepts, he goes on to balance the books by adding that "physical realities are constituted by the various concept-stuffs of which they 'partake' " (*SPP* 58). That James was happy to accept the realist commitment of this talk about participation in the forms is clear from his claim that the

absolute determinability of our mind by abstractions is one of the cardinal facts in our human constitution. Polarizing and magnetizing us as they do, we turn towards them and from them, we seek them, hold them, hate them, bless them, just as if they were so many concrete beings. *And beings they are, beings as real in the realm which they inhabit as the changing things of sense are in the realm of space.* (*VRE* 54; my italics)

Thus, with both scientific objects and abstract concepts, James seems to leave us with ontologically, although not epistemologically, disparate worlds. The fourth form of unification attempts to find a more ontological type of unification between some but not all of the many worlds.

(4) In *The Varieties of Religious Experience* James enriches his Ontological Relativism with the notion of interworld causation. The world consists "of many interpenetrating spheres of reality, which we can thus approach in alternation by using different conceptions and assuming different attitudes, just as mathematicians handle the same numerical and spatial facts by geometry, by analytical geometry, by algebra, by the calculus, or by quaternions, and each time come out right" (*VRE* 105).

The specific form that the interpenetration takes is between the commonsense world and the mystical or supernatural worlds. In religious experiences "spiritual energy flows in and produces effects, either psychological or material, within the phenomenal world" (*VRE* 382). James suggested that during moments of prayer and religious experience these higher spiritual forces enter us through our subconscious or subliminal self. "The conscious person is continuous with a wider self through which saving experiences come . . ." (*VRE* 405). James made sure to emphasize that the causal influence also went from the lower selves to the higher supernatural self: God is affected by man's actions.

There are two essays in which James emphasizes the importance of the mystical self being in the service of the Promethean one. In "What Makes a Life Significant," he insists on a union between one's inner ideal and virtuous overt behavior if one's life is to have significance. Your inner ideal is the ineffable feeling of joy and excitement, which can become the object of another's mystical I–Thou experience of you. Just as one's inner ideal must causally lead one to the right sort of Promethean actions, so a mystical experience, in general, must do likewise for its subject. Because of his concern with the moral upshot of mystical experiences, James favors, in "Reflex Actions and Theism," dualistic over monistic mystical experiences of God. He says that this experience, which is one "of self-surrender, of absolute *practical* union between one's self and the divine object of one's contemplation, is a totally different thing from any sort of substantial identity" (*WB* 106; my italics). His emphasis on the *practical* expresses his insistence on mystical experiences bearing fruit for life. What James is doing is pressing mystical experiences into the service of his melioristic religion, whose creed is now expanded so as to include a personal God, as well as the conditionalized prediction that good will win out over evil if we collectively exert our best moral efforts.

The aporia due to the clash between the active and passive selves has been made to appear more formidable than it really is. Even Promethean selves must be permitted to sleep, for they won't amount to much as Promethean agents if they don't. Similarly, they shouldn't be denied some mystical R and R if it enables them to return to the war zone better equipped to do battle with the forces of evil. Andrew Reck put it nicely: "Refueled by relating to the divine, the individual is, in James's account, readied to cope once again with the arduous moral tasks of human existence" (*WJ* 44). For James, mystical emotions and beliefs are valuable and should be cultivated, not just for their own sake, but also for their instrumental value in inducing morally desirable behavior. James even claimed that for a mystical experience to be veridical or objective its "fruits must be good for Life" (*VRE* 318). In general, the authenticity or worth of any experience or emotion depends on its

having a beneficial upshot in the workaday world of the moral agent –
thus the reason for his intense condemnation of the overly sentimental
Russian lady crying her eyes out at the theater while her footman was
freezing outside, mentioned in Chapter 4.

The R-and-R way of reconciling the Promethean and mystical selves
fails, however, to neutralize the clash between the reality-claims made
by these selves, with respect both to what they say and to how they say
it. There is no contentful clash between an I–Thou-based claim that
God, or some other supernatural spirit, exists and ordinary sensory-
based reality-claims; but there is one between the latter and the reality-
claims based on backyard and nature mysticism, as well as the more
extreme monistic mystical experiences that hold reality to be *nothing
but* an Eternal One or Undifferentiated Unity. But in all cases there
is a clash over the status of Ontological Relativism, since all mystical
reality-claims are nonrelativized.

This completes my attempt to find a solution to the unification problem that can be traced directly to James's text. Each of the attempted
solutions (1)–(4) to the unification problem achieved some unification,
provided that one is willing to grant (1)'s instrumentalism and (3)'s
concept empiricism, issues about which James was of two minds. But
each attempted solution alone failed to bring us all the way to the
promised land; and even when combined they fail to do so, because
they are helpless before two aporias that arise from a clash between
James's mystical and Promethean selves.

First, mystical reality-claims, because they are nonrelativized, clash
with the Promethean doctrine of Ontological Relativism. It is worth
reminding the reader of the absolutistic nature of these claims through
some choice quotations so as to emphasize just how severe the aporia
is. The backyard mystic, for example, insists that concepts "fail to connect us with the inner life of the flux. . . . Instead of being interpreters
of reality, concepts negate the inwardness of reality altogether" (*PU*
110). "The essence of life is its continuously changing character" (*PU*
113). This is discovered through a conceptless intuition of what goes
on in our own consciousness when we experience change and intentionally act. It is through such introspective awareness that we become
"acquainted with the essential nature of reality" (*PU* 96). Herein it is
discovered that "reality's true shape" does not accord with the transitivity requirement of the ordinary logic of identity (*PU* 127). "The real
nature of being is to be entire or continuous" in the sense that immediate spatial and temporal neighbors are identical with each other but
not *that* identical, since it is a nontransitive sort of "identity." James's
talk about "the essential nature of reality," the "interpreters of reality,"
"the essence of life," and "the nature of real being," makes it clear

that he is making absolute, non-world-relativized reality claims. But this clashes with his Ontological Relativism, which requires all reality claims to be relativized to a person at a time.

Second, the content of some, but not all, mystical reality-claims clashes with the content of Promethean reality-claims, whether based on the perspective of the scientist or of the moral agent, assuming, as was argued, that these respective claims cannot be Poo-bah-ized. It is not just the acosmic claims made by monistic mystics that do; even those made by the backyard mystic of James's final two books do. Concepts, which are the stock and trade of the Promethean self, take reality to be an affair of numerically distinct individuals that stand in discrete relations to their immediate spatio-temporal neighbors. This is what James called "intellectualist logic" and comprised the brunt of the rationalist's a priori arguments.

Before attempting to devise possible solutions to these aporia, as well as to the general unification problem, that are Jamesian in spirit, it should be asked why James could not adopt a radically Promethean solution: reject the law of noncontradiction and learn to live with these aporias – cheerfully, I might add, because he knows that thereby he is getting it all. If it should be pointed out to him that he is irrational, he could flash his button "I've given up noncontradiction and I love it!"

But would he really be happy with such an irrational, discombobulated life? James's career-long acceptance of the law of noncontradiction forbids him to accept such irrationalism. He says, in regard to a person's web of past opinions, that whenever "in a reflective moment he discovers that they contradict each other; or he hears of facts with which they are incompatible . . . he seeks to escape by modifying his previous mass of opinions," using the conservative strategy of saving "as much as he can" of his past opinions so as to create "a minimum of disturbance" (*PP* 34–5). In his very early essay, "The Sentiment of Rationality," James speculates that the reason why we cannot abide a contradiction is "as natural and invincible as that which makes us exchange a hard high stool for an arm-chair or prefer traveling by railroad to riding in a springless cart" (*EP* 33).

Maybe James was too timid in showing such excessive obeisance to the law of noncontradiction and not going all the way with his Promethean humanism, which holds that "Our nouns and adjectives are all humanized heirlooms, and in the theories we build them into, the inner order and arrangement is wholly dictated by human considerations, *intellectual consistency being one of them*" (*P* 122; my italics). It was argued in Chapter 5 that the law of noncontradiction really functions as an instrumental rule in James's theory of belief-acceptance, admitting of an exception when desire-satisfaction can be maximized by believing a contradiction. If it be asked why believe one contradiction rather than

any other, the reply of the rule-instrumental pragmatist is that the pragmatic benefits of such beliefs in regard to maximizing desire-satisfaction
varies with the contradiction. Thus, it might be pragmatically desirable
to believe the conjunction of Ontological Relativism and the absolute
reality claims of mystics but not to believe that the Chrysler Building is
taller than itself. The last of Prometheus's worries should be having to
countenance a contradiction. Better that than being forever bound to
the rocky peak on Caucasus or, in James's case, keeping the doors and
windows shut against the full richness of experience.[1]

Things could be done to make it easier to live with the radical Promethean solution. Certainly, we would not want actively or occurrently
to believe incompatible propositions at one and the same time. We
could create a pill that would keep us from actively remembering one
of our former beliefs, allowing it to remain dormant in the purely dispositional state. When we are in our mystical moods and are actively or
occurrently believing that reality in itself is just the way we are experiencing it to be, we could pop a pill that would prevent us from actively
recalling that in our earlier Promethean phases we believed in Ontological Relativism.

Even if we were up to performing such an elaborate juggling act with
our beliefs, there are, in my opinion, as well as James's, fatal flaws in
the radical Promethean solution. First, James thought that a person's
philosophy should be something that she lives by, something that actively guides her in her quest for self-realization. A metaethical theory,
for example, should serve as a guide for a person in making first-order
ethical choices. This desideratum would be violated by a utilitarian who,
on the one hand, promulgated a metaethical theory requiring us always
to act so as to maximize utility, and, on the other hand, required us to
make our first-order ethical choices on the basis of what principles of
virtue or justice require, since by doing so we maximize utility in the
long run. Analogously, James's universal thesis of Ontological Relativism should guide us in making first-order reality-claims so that we build
into them the required "qua"-clause restriction. But in the radical Promethean solution, one is supposed to believe Ontological Relativism yet
not make use of it when making their first-order mystically based reality-
claims.

---

[1] Hilary Putnam has asked, rhetorically, "If the fundamental aim of science is prediction,
might that aim not be more efficiently reached if we allowed a plurality of theories, each
consistent and successful in its own domain, even if their conjunction were not consistent?" (WJ 24). Analogously, if all we demand from a philosophy is that it aid us in
maximizing desire-satisfaction, might there not be a circumstance in which this would
best be achieved by having an inconsistent philosophy? James, of course, demanded
more of science than mere predictive power, as Putnam rightly points out. He demanded
coherence as well. Similarly, he demanded more of a philosophy than that it aid us in
our quest to maximize desire-satisfaction.

Second, James commitment to intellectual integrity would not have permitted him to be a pill popper, no matter how much it would maximize desire-satisfaction. There is an intrinsic value to being an intellectually integrated self who does not engage in self-deception. Here is yet another instance in which he has deep deontological intuitions that clash with his official casuistic rule requiring us always to act so as to maximize desire-satisfaction over desire-dissatisfaction. It is now time to try my own hand at finding a Jamesian-style solution to the unification problem, one that James himself could live with happily, because he now is wearing a button that says "I'm an integrated self and I love it!"

II. Some Jamesian-Style Solutions

To find a Jamesian-style solution to the unification problem, especially as it pertains to the clash between mysticism and Prometheanism, we must follow the lead of the Hollywood serials. At the end of last week's episode we saw the Lone Ranger hurtling off a 2,000-foot cliff in a burning wagon, but now we see that, thank God, it was only Tonto. Those dirty dogs spliced over the film! "Splicing the film" in James's case requires altering his text, in particular his Ontological Relativism and/or his mysticism, so that the outcome will be more pleasing to the contradiction-hating audience – it wasn't James but only Royce, thank God, who was tied hand and foot and thrown into the giant garbage compactor. The aim is to give a one-world interpretation of James that will be textually motivated and Jamesian in spirit, in spite of the need for some "splicing." In a one-world interpretation there will be no need to relativize different types of claims, especially reality-claims, to an agent at a time so as to avoid contradiction. There is only one world and all claims are unrestrictedly made *quoad* this world – that is, all the propositions that we want to assert are true in the actual world. Thus, the type of claims made from the perspectives of common sense, the moral agent, the scientist, and the mystic will be mutually compatible.

The first order of business is to neutralize the logical clash between Ontological Relativism and the nonrelativized mystical reality-claims. One of the two claims must be spliced out so that it will not have been James who was thrown into the giant garbage compactor. We could secure consistency by eliminating both, but this would violate James's conservative principle for belief revision and would render his philosophy completely unrecognizable. Each alternative shall be considered in turn, beginning with the splicing out of the nonrelativized reality-claims of the mystics, the less attractive of the alternatives in that it is the least Jamesian in spirit.

There are four ways in which we might try to revise the absolute reality-claims of mystics so as to bring them in line with the doctrine of

Ontological Relativism: (i) make them into working hypotheses or (ii) targets of a will-to-believe option; (iii) deny the cognitivity of the mystical experiences upon which they are based; and (iv) Poo-bah-ize them. It quickly can be shown that (i)–(iii) are nonstarters, leaving us with (iv), which, unfortunately, is completely at odds with the underlying spirit of James's philosophy.

It has already been shown why (i) and (ii) are not viable options. It is inconsistent to accept both the doctrine of Ontological Relativism and that the nonrelativized reality-claims of the mystics are either adoptable as working hypothesis or targets for a will-to-believe option, the reason being that the reality-claims fail to express propositions according to Ontological Relativism and only a proposition can be a working hypothesis or believed on a will to believe basis. Even if (iii) were right in its contention that mystical experiences are not cognitive in the sense that they do not afford evidence for the existence of their apparent accusatives, which is what I argue for in my publications listed in note 11 to Chapter 9, it would fail to make mystical reality-claims consistent with Ontological Relativism. The clash does not result from the mystics' claim that they know or have good evidence for their nonrelativized reality-claims but instead from the fact that their claims are nonrelativized, thereby violating Ontological Relativism.

Solution (iv) requires that a mystical reality-claim be relativized to the interests of a person at a time. Accordingly, what a mystic means by her claim that reality in itself consists of promiscuous mushing together relations is that, relative to her present predominantly mystical interests, promiscuous mushing together relations are real, or qua her present mystical perspective reality in itself consists of promiscuous mushing together relations. No mystic would want to say this, and thus the Promethean ''solution'' to the unification problem violates the heart and soul of James's philosophy because it does not provide a suitable habitat for the mystical James. There are two more objections to (iv).

First, it fails to unify James's many selves since it does nothing toward metaphysically unifying their many worlds. He winds up a schizophrenic Poo-bah of the first-I'm-this-and-then-I'm-that sort. This is almost as bad as the radical Promethean solution of accepting a contradiction by embracing both Ontological Relativism and nonrelativized mystical reality-claims, with or without the memory-masking pill.

Second, solution (iv) undermines James's passionate quest for intimacy and ultimate union with his world and all of its denizens, which is as strong a motivating force behind his philosophy as is the quest to have it all. One thing is certain: Any philosophy that did not enable him to achieve intimacy with the world would badly fail him in his quest to have it all. The preceding three chapters have detailed this quest for intimacy and why it requires the sweating-with-conviction belief that the true nature or essence of reality is as it appears to be in those special experiences of intimacy – the I–Thou experience in all its many forms and backyard mysticism. You cannot I–Thou someone unless you firmly believe that she exists. To Poo-bah-ize reality-claims based on these experiences would reduce the mystic to the level of a Promethean agent out to gain control over, rather than intimacy and union with, reality. The lover and the mystic do not put the objects of their passion on a par ontologically with every other possible object of their passing interest and fancy. It is special because it is the way things really are.

This brings us to the second way of splicing the text to achieve consistency, in which James's Ontological Relativism is to be given up or modified. This can be accomplished in three ways: by making out a textually based case that Ontological Relativism (v) was intended to be only a genetic account of the experiential conditions under which we acquire and use the concept of reality; or (vi) was given up after the 1890 *The Principles of Psychology*; or (vii) is to be Poo-bah-ized by being restricted to Promethean-type worlds. It will turn out that (vii) is not only the best alternative among this set of alternatives but also among the wider set that includes (i)–(iv) as well.

According to (v), when James pointed out, in *The Principles of Psychology*'s chapter on "The Perception of Reality," that what a person takes to be real at a given time is determined by what her dominant interest is at that time he did not intended it as a semantic account of what it means to be real, nor as an ontological account of what it is to be real, which is the way in which James was interpreted in Chapter 7. When a person now believes that X is real, it does not *mean* that X is now of primary interest to her; thus there is no clash between Ontological Relativism, understood as a purely psychology doctrine, and the non-relativized reality-claims of the mystics.

The textual support for this interpretation is identical with that which led in Chapter 6 to interpreting James as, occasionally and inconsistently, accepting a "content empiricist" theory of meaning in addition to his official pragmatic theory of meaning based on what an idea experientially portends for the future, this being the only way that he could escape from the objection that his exclusively future-oriented pragmatic theory of meaning is subject to "the paradox of the alleged futurity of yesterday." He seemed to distinguish between these two species of empirical meaning when he suddenly remarked that "In obeying this [pragmatic] rule we neglect the substantive content of the concept, and follow its function only" (*SPP* 38), and that "The word 'truth' is here taken to mean something additional to bare value for life, although the natural propensity of man is to believe that whatever has great value for life is thereby certified as true" (*VRE* 401), as well as his concessionary qualification, "the absolute, taken seriously, and not as a mere name for our right occasionally to drop the strenuous mood and take a moral holiday . . ." (*PU* 57). In these rare moments James goes back on his functionalist approach to meaning based on the slogan that the reason why we call something *X* is what it means to be *X* as well as what it is to be *X*. Just as James's content empiricism does not have the *entire* meaning of a belief consist in what future experiences are to be expected upon the performance of certain actions, it would not have it consist in the genetic factors that lead one to have this belief.

While there is rather slight textual basis for interpreting Ontological Relativism as only a genetic psychological analysis, there is far greater textual grounds for taking it to constitute a semantic and ontological analysis as well. This evidence is of a global nature and has already been presented in the earlier chapters of this book. First, there is James's official and widespread commitment to a pragmatic theory of meaning rather than a theory of pragmatic meaning, which recognizes pragmatic meaning as only one species of meaning. That James intended his genetic analysis of what leads us to believe that something is real to be a semantic and ontological analysis as well gains very strong support from the fact that, as was argued in earlier chapters, he certainly seemed to draw semantic and ontological conclusions from his genetic psychological analyses of truth, matter, negation, and the identity of the self over time. The text, however, is not decisive, and I fear that my "argument" may fall prey to some vicious circularity and begging of the question. Among my reasons for taking James's analysis of reality to be a semantic one is that his genetic analyses of certain other concepts are semantic analyses, thereby establishing a certain pattern in his philosophy. But my argument for why these latter analyses are semantic as well as genetic rests in part on my claim that his analysis of reality is both semantic and genetic, which looks viciously circular. And, if I avoid closing the circle by stopping with my claim that his analyses of these additional concepts are both semantic and genetic, my opponent can accuse me of begging the question. Although I think I have the text on my side, my major reason for favoring my interpretation is that I believe, as I will shortly try to establish, that it fits in with an overall interpretation that is both Jamesian in spirit and yields the most attractive philosophy in its own right, especially in regard to escaping the aporiamatic clash between Ontological Relativism and the nonrelativized reality-claims of the mystics.

Solution (vi) can concede that James really did accept Ontological Relativism in the 1890 *The Principles of Psychology* on the basis of his genetic analysis, as I have argued, because its contention is that the doctrine does not enter into any of his subsequent published writings. Thus, if he did hold it in 1890, he later gave it up. There is some textual evidence, mainly of a negative sort, that he did not ascribe to it subsequently. Nothing can be inferred from the fact that the chapter on "The Perception of Reality" does not in appear in the 1892 abridged version, since he made a conscious decision to shorten the book by eliminating metaphysical digressions, of which this chapter is the prime example. Of more moment is that there is a terminological shift in his later writings. Whereas he formerly spoke of different worlds, he now speaks of different dimensions of a single world. Furthermore, in Chapter 9, it was seen that Ontological Relativism is affirmed in its 1890 form in one of the drafts for Lecture II of *The Varieties of Religious Experience* but was dropped from the final draft. One might speculate that James decided to omit this reaffirmation of Ontological Relativism from his final draft because he had abandoned the doctrine, possibly because he came to realize that it clashed with the absolutistic reality-claims made by the mystics whose experiences he gave primacy to in *The Varieties of Religious Experience.*

Another indication in *The Varieties of Religious Experience* that James had abandoned Ontological Relativism can be seen in the following passage.

If you open the chapter on Association, of any treatise on Psychology, you will read that a man's ideas, aims, and objects form diverse internal groups and systems, relatively independent of one another. Each 'aim' which he follows awakens a certain specific kind of interested excitement, and gathers a certain group of ideas together in subordination to it as its associates; and if the aims and excitements are distinct in kind, their groups of ideas may have little in common. When one group is present and engrosses the interest, all the ideas connected with other groups may be excluded from the mental field. The President of the United States when, with paddle, gun, and fishing-rod, he goes camping in the wilderness for a vacation, changes his system of ideas from top to bottom. The presidential anxieties have lapsed into the background entirely; the official habits are replaced by the habits of a son of nature, and those who knew the man only as the strenuous magistrate would not 'know him for the same person' if they saw him as the camper. (*VRE* 160)

The significance of this paragraph consists in what it does not say, namely, that as old Teddy's interests change so does what he takes to be the real world. This, of course, does not constitute very weighty evidence that James had abandoned Ontological Relativism by the time he wrote *The Varieties of Religious Experience,* but it is some evidence nevertheless.

This textual evidence for (vi) is quite slight and is swamped by overwhelming textual evidence that James continued to adhere to Ontological Relativism in all of his books subsequent to 1892. Even in *The Varieties of Religious Experience* there is a reaffirmation of the doctrine near the very end of the book:

The whole drift of my education goes to persuade me that the world of our present consciousness is only one out of many worlds of consciousness that exist, and that those other worlds must contain experiences which have a meaning for our life also; and that although in the main their experiences and those of this world are discrete, yet the two become continuous at certain points, and higher energies filter in. (*VRE* 408; see also 54)

In a 1904 lecture, "Does 'Consciousness' Exist?" subsequently included in *Essays in Radical Empiricism,* James wrote that "Were there no perceptual world . . . [that is] 'stronger' and more genuinely 'outer' (so that the whole merely thought-of world seems weak and inner in comparison), our world of thought would be the only world, and would enjoy complete reality in our belief" (*ERE* 12). Ontological Relativism is reaffirmed in both *Pragmatism* (14 and 94) and *The Meaning of Truth* (25), as well as in his final two books (*PU* 55 and *SPP* 33–4 and 56). James certainly did not abandon Ontological Relativism after 1892, although he had a tendency to soft-peddle it somewhat.

Solution (vii), which was suggested to me by Nick Rescher, is the one that I will now argue should be adopted. The basic idea is to downgrade Ontological Relativism, so that it ceases to be a universal proposition that tells us for every possible world what it means and is to be real in that world but instead says only what it means and is to be real in the practical or Promethean worlds. This permits mystics to claim with impunity that what they seem to experience is real *simpliciter*, the really real, without qualification or relativization. There is no need for them to pop a pill, as they can consistently say, in one and the same breath, "Reality, *simpliciter,* is a promiscuous type of unity, but in Promethean worlds something is real only in relation to an agent at a given time." Since mystics are informing us only about what it is to be real in the actual world – the world in which their mystical experiences occur – they are leaving it open for reality to be otherwise in other possible worlds. If they were to have said instead that it is *necessary* that reality be a promiscuous mushing together, *simpliciter,* then they could not consistently say that reality is otherwise in other possible worlds; for what is necessary is true in every possible world. But this requires that they do not make use of the a priori arguments of the rationalists, for these arguments purport to prove the *impossibility* of there being discrete immediate relations, which entails that it is impossible for there to be any Promethean world and therefore any world in which to be real is to be relative to an agent at a time. The Jamesian mystic should not feel bad about having to give up these arguments, as they are quite bogus. There is no reason why a mystic has to be a muddlehead. One can believe in the unreality of time, for example, without giving a fallacious argument for its unreality à la McTaggart.

The following familiar dialectic can be followed to get Ontological Relativists to agree to restrict their doctrine to Promethean worlds. The first move in this dialectic is the oft-used self-refutation objection, in which the *universal* doctrine of Ontological Relativism is turned against itself. It makes a reality-claim of sorts, a second-order one, namely, that all reality-claims are world-relative; yet it is a universal doctrine that is not relativized to any world since supposedly true for every world. But this renders it self-refuting. To escape such self-refutation, it is necessary to Poo-bah-ize Poo-bah-ism by restricting it to a certain world(s). And what worlds might they be? Obviously, Promethean worlds, that is, worlds in which we conceptualize reality in a way that will enable us to succeed in realizing our goals. This will include the world of the moral agent, the world of the scientist, as well as the world of our practical activities. It will not include mystical worlds, as concepts are not employed in them; mystics are not engaged in any type of Promethean quest, but instead have learned the knack of overcoming the active self. Notice that when the doctrine of Ontological Relativism has built into it a restriction to these pragmatic worlds, it is universally true, even being true in mystical worlds in which reality is not taken to be world-relative. Even though Socrates, who is snub-nosed in the actual world, call it "*a*," is not snub-nosed in every possible world in which he exists (his mother might have taken some drug during pregnancy that would have produced a different shaped nose than the one he in fact had), the proposition that Socrates is snub-nosed in *a* is true in every possible world, including those in which he is not snub-nosed. More generally, if a proposition *p* is true in a possible world *W*, then the proposition that *p* is true in *W* is true in every possible world. Similarly, assuming that reality is world-relative in Promethean worlds, the proposition that reality is world-relative in Promethean worlds is true in every possible world, including those in which reality is not world-relative. By asserting nonrelativized reality-claims, the mystic is committed to reality not being world-relative in the actual world, but this is consistent with her admitting that reality is world relative in certain other possible worlds, namely Promethean ones.

What is the textual support for this world-restricted interpretation of Ontological Relativism? Just after James claims that reality is relative to a person at a time, in the chapter on "The Perception of Reality," he adds that "This is the only sense which the word ever has in the mouths of *practical* men" (*PP* 924; my italics). Herein there is an apparent restriction of Ontological Relativism to the world or perspective of the practical person or moral agent. It should be noticed, furthermore, that when James attempts to neutralize the apparent clashes between the perspectives of "common sense, common science, ultra-critical science and critical philosophy" by saying that "all our theories [of which all of these are instances] are *instrumental*, are mental modes of *adaptation* to reality, rather than revelations or gnostic answers to some divinely instituted world-enigma" (*P* 94), he has rather conspicuously omitted mysticism from the list. Thus, James's Ontological Relativism is the proposition that Ontological Relativism is true in the world of the practical person – the world in which all theories are nothing more than instrumental devices for helping us to get around more effectively in the world. Ontological Relativism is an expression of the practical self or moral agent bent on maximizing desire-satisfaction. The moral agent is aided in this endeavor by believing Ontological Relativism, since it enables her to give primary importance to different worlds or perspectives as her interests and desires change, thereby facilitating her endeavor to maximize desire-satisfaction. Plainly, the mystic's world is not one of these practical worlds.

There is a worry that the conjunction of the version of Ontological Relativism that is restricted to practical worlds with the acceptance of the nonrestricted reality-claims of mystics will undercut the seriousness with which Promethean agents pursue their quest to have it all. What effect will it have on Promethean agents to realize that their worlds, the ones that they are up to their neck in via their practical activities, are real only in relation to their passing interests but that the world of the mystic is real *simpliciter*? Might they feel that their practical reality is an ontological booby prize and thus not worth taking seriously, thereby undermining their effectiveness in their quest to have it all?

There is no simple answer to these questions as human psychology is highly variable in these matters. Some people get depressed more easily than others. The challenge to the Promethean moral agent posed by the conjunction of Ontological Relativism and mysticism certainly is far less than that posed by either determinism or bifurcationism, as was previously seen in Chapters 3 and 8 respectively. Many would be inclined to agree with James that their acceptance of determinism or bifurcationism would undermine their incentive to lead the morally strenuous life, but far fewer would find that acceptance of the conjunction of nonrelativized mystical reality-claims and the restricted version of Ontological Relativism does. There are many mystics of all different persuasions, from pluralistic to monistic, who accept the unreality or illusoriness of the sensible world within which the moral agent operates but nevertheless are uncompromising in their dedication to the cause of fighting worldly evils. No moral holidays for them. I am not sure what more to say about this murky issue, especially since James never addressed it.

Solution (vii), at best, solves only the single aporia that arose from the clash of Ontological Relativism in its unrestricted form with the nonrelativized reality-claims of the mystics. Although (vii) goes some way toward a one-world interpretation of James, making it possible to assert everything we want to *quoad* the actual world, it gives rise to two aporias. First, by endorsing the nonrelativized reality-claims of the mystics, (vii) endorses too much, for it runs up against the problem of religious diversity resulting from the seeming incompatibilities between reality-claims made by mystics within different religious traditions. Second, (vii) does not solve the general problem of unification, as it does not find a way of metaphysically unifying the many worlds, thereby leaving James and those of like psychological complexity as schizophrenic Poo-bahs. Some more editing of the film is required if our hero is to be saved from the ignominious fate of the cliff or the garbage compactor.

The problem of diversity among the reality-claims of mystics is the less serious of the two, though still serious in its own right. It shall be taken up first. James's brilliant survey of the autobiographical literature on mysticism includes both the dualistic experiences of Western theists and the monistic experiences of Eastern mystics. The major difference between these two types of mystical experiences is that the former but not the latter experiences have a subject–object structure, the subject of the experience being conscious of an intentional accusative that is taken to be numerically distinct from herself in spite of her achieving some unification with it. As a result of this difference, monistic mystical experiences, unlike theistic or dualistic ones, will support acosmic reality-claims that deny the reality of multiplicity, there being no distinction between the subject and the object of the experience or between different times and places.

James quotes several monistic mystics who make such acosmic claims on the basis of their experience. For example, he quotes Symonds's experience of the "obliteration of space, time, sensation, and the multitudinous factors of experience," which leaves Symonds wondering "which is the unreality?" (*VRE* 306), along with the Sufi who claims that "there is no being save only One" (333). James even goes so far as to claim that this type of monism "is the everlasting and triumphant mystical tradition, hardly altered by differences of clime or creed," thereby siding with those, like Walter Stace, Thomas Merton, and Daisetsu Suzuki, who find monism to be the common core of all mystical experiences.

Furthermore, James is well aware of the apparent conflict between the reality-claims based on these two types of mystical experience over the extent of the union achieved and the reality of the ordinary sensible world of space, time, and multiplicity. "It is when they treat of the experience of 'union' with it that their speculative differences appear most clearly. Over this point pantheism and theism . . . carry on inveterate disputes" (*VRE* 401–2). Nonmystics "must stand outside of them [rival mystical reality-claims] altogether and . . . decide that, since they corroborate incompatible theological doctrines, they neutralize one another and leave no fixed result" (*VRE* 404).

The problem is that James does not stand outside of the rival reality-claims made by dualistic and monistic mystics but instead *seems* to endorse *all* of them. As was seen in Chapter 9, his long discussion of mystical experiences ends with the conclusion that they are cognitive, that is, that they supply their subjects with evidence, analogous to that supplied by ordinary sense experience for the reality of physical objects, that reality is as it appears to be in their experiences (*VRE* 335–6). This conclusion makes no discrimination between dualistic and monistic mystical experiences and apparently is supposed to apply to all of the mystical experiences he had previously surveyed, which included both types. Plainly, James's breadth of sympathy and appreciation, termed his "philosophical satyrism" in the Introduction, is getting him in trouble, for he seems to be endorsing rival reality-claims as epistemically warranted. The following considers some of the options available to James to attempt to escape this problem.

The first strategy is the "no new facts" one. It will be recalled from Chapter 9 that James's summation of what mystical experiences ultimately proclaim is very watered down.

> As a rule, mystical states merely add a supersensuous meaning to the ordinary outward data of consciousness. They are excitements like the emotions of love or ambition, gifts to our spirit by means of which facts already objectively before us fall into a new expressiveness and make a new connexion with our active life. They do not contradict these facts as such, or deny anything that our senses have immediately seized. (*VRE* 338)

A similar watering-down strategy is seen in James's bizarre set of defining characteristics of mystical experiences in which he fails to include their being a unitive experience; this is a convenient omission, since it is this the feature that clashes with sensory-based reality-claims (*VRE* 302–3). To omit this unitive feature is to perform *Hamlet* without the Prince of Denmark. This was called the "comic book" theory of mystical experiences, as they are supposed to function as do the field of force lines that comic books place around an object that is perceived or thought of in a specially intense manner. This at best fits the experiences at the undeveloped end of the mystical spectrum, such as drunkenness. James's backyard mystical experiences of a processual glop in which temporal neighbors become their own Hegelian opposite, in spite of its having as its object the very same sensible reality that our pragmatic self perceives and conceptually breaks up into discrete objects, presents us with new facts about this sensible reality. The no-new-facts account plainly does not fit those unitive experiences at the developed end, which not only report new facts – for instance, the existence of James's higher dimensions of reality – but also sometimes seem to contradict our sensory-based beliefs concerning the reality of space, time, and multiplicity. In Lecture XX, "Conclusions," James in effect abandons his "no new facts" reconciling strategy from the earlier chapter on "Mysticism," when he writes that "Religion . . . is not a mere illumination of facts already given elsewhere, not a mere passion, like love, which views things in a rosier light. But it is something more, namely, a postulator of new *facts* as well" (*VRE* 407–8).

A second strategy is to agree that mystical reality-claims report facts above and beyond those that are attested to by sense experience but deny that there is any clash either among themselves or with the reality-claims based on ordinary sense experience. The reason is that each of these reality-claims is warranted relative to the criteria for epistemic warrant or acceptability built into the special doxastic practice or language-game within which it occurs. This way of neutralizing conflicts between reality-claims made within different religious traditions, and also between those made in any one of these traditions and those made on the basis of ordinary sense experience, was later to be called "language-game fideism." These different language-games or doxastic practices are incommensurable in that they have different criteria or rules for determining when an experientially based belief is epistemically warranted, thereby precluding external challenges to the reality-claims made in any one language-game by appeal to the claims made in another language-game. For example, each of the great mystical religious traditions has its own criteria for determining when a mystical experience is veridical, and thereby the reality-claim based on it warranted: They have different holy scriptures with which the content of the experience must agree, different religious authorities and paradigmatic mystical experiences, and different criteria for what constitutes desirable moral and/or spiritual development in the subject of the experience. There is no clash between the reality-claims made within these different mystical traditions, because each claim is implicitly relativized to and can be evaluated and challenged only in relation to the criteria of epistemic acceptability of its own doxastic practice. This also would solve the aporia that arises from the apparent clashes between mystically and sensorily based reality-claims, since the practice of basing existential claims on sensory experience is another doxastic practice.

Language-game fideism is nothing but Ontological Relativism dressed up in fashionable new Wittgensteinian clothing. Instead of talking about all reality-claims being relativized to one of James's worlds or selves, we now say that it is relativized to a language-game, that is, a normatively rule-governed human practice for using language. All claims still get "qua"-claused, only now it is not a "qua this world or self" restriction but a "qua this language-game" restriction. In both cases the result is Poo-bah-istic schizophrenia of the first-I-adopt-this-worldly-perspective-or-play-this-language-game-and-then-I-adopt-or-play-that-one. Whereas ordinary games are isolated, self-contained units of activity – "Tennis anyone?" – language-games are not: There is only one big language-game, and that is life itself, of which each language-game is an interconnected part. In addition to not solving – if anything, exacerbating – the general unification problem, language-game fideism also goes against James's career-long commitment to methodological univocalism, which was seen in Chapter 7 to be one of his major ways of reconciling the tough-minded perspective of the scientist with the tender-minded perspective of the moral agent and melioristic theist.[2] Furthermore, the epistemic undecidability requirement built into his will-to-believe option assumes a univocal account of epistemic decidability.

The third strategy for finding a way to reconcile the apparently conflicting reality-claims of dualistic and monistic mystics, which is the one that James actually defends, holds that there is a common phenomenological core to dualistic and monistic mystical experiences that gets interpreted differently by mystics within different religious traditions. The theoretical constructions or, as James would say, "over beliefs," placed upon their common phenomenological content are the cause of the clashes between the reality-claims made by mystics within different traditions. James's endorsement of the cognitivity of mystical experiences and the prima facie epistemic warrant they provide for believing that reality is as it appears to be in them must be confined to their common phenomenological content. The a priori presumptive inference rule of Chapter 9, "If it perceptually appears to be the case that X exists, then probably it is the case that X exists, unless there are defeating conditions," must restrict X to the phenomenological content of the perceptual experience.

I believe that this third strategy can be located in the text. James begins with the question whether it is regrettable that there are "so many religious types and sects and creeds," to which he replies that "The divine can mean no single quality, it must mean a group of qualities, by being champions of which in alternation, different men may all find worthy missions" (VRE 384). This attempt at an ecumenical solution to religious diversity, which has been championed in recent times by Hick and Swinburne, is fine as far as it goes, but it does not address the issue of incompatibility between different creeds. Showing why people in different cultural circumstances will experience and conceive of God differently does not neutralize the incompatibilities between their different ways of doing so; it shows only how it is possible

---

[2] The only textual support for his being a language-game fideist is his bizarre account of fiction. James claims that "Whilst absorbed in the novel, we turn our backs on all other worlds, and, for the time, the Ivanhoe-world remains our absolute reality (PP 922). Anyone who took the Ivanhoe-world to be the real one would not be reading the novel as a work of fiction.

for their different views to complement each other in cases in which their respective views of God, although different, are not incompatible. To solve the incompatibility problem James must do something more.

The something more that he does is to extract a common denominator from their apparently conflicting creeds. "I am expressly trying to reduce religion to its lowest admissible terms, to that minimum, free from individualistic excrescences, which all religions contain as their nucleus, and on which it may be hoped that all religious persons may agree" (*VRE* 397). "Under all the discrepancies of the creeds, a common nucleus" is to be found, namely, the religious person "*becomes conscious that this higher part* [of himself] *is conterminous and continuous with a* more *of the same quality, which is operative in the universe outside of him, and which he can keep in working touch with, and in a fashion get on board of and save himself when all his lower being has gone to pieces in the wreck.*" All of the religious experiences that he has surveyed in the course of *The Varieties of Religious Experience* "express the appearance of exteriority of the helping power and yet account for our sense of union with it" (*VRE* 400–1).

James applies this common nucleus approach to religious and mystical experiences when he says that "There is probably no autobiographic document, among all those which I have quoted, to which the description will not well apply. One need only add such specific details as will adapt it to various theologies and various personal temperaments, and one will then have the various experiences reconstructed in their individual forms" (*VRE* 401). This entails that there is a common denominator, a shared phenomenological content, to dualistic and monistic mystical experiences, since these experiences are among those which enter into the autobiographic documents he quotes in the book.

There are three serious difficulties with this way of resolving the conflict between reality-claims based on dualistic and monistic mystical experiences. First, showing that the disputants agree about something does not resolve their dispute. If two persons point to the same place and one says that it contains a Scotch terrier and the other a collie, their disagreement is not resolved by pointing out that they agree that there is a dog there. James is naively assuming that others share his large-mindedness and desire to find an ecumenical solution to religious diversity that will help to secure the brotherhood of mankind, and thus the defenders of rival creeds will be willing to pare down their creeds to some common denominator. The points of disagreement will be written off as theoretical excrescences that are of little moment, idle philosophical speculations. What counts are feeling and conduct, not thought. "We find a great variety in the thoughts that have prevailed [among different religions] . . . ; but the feelings . . . and the conduct . . . are almost always the same. . . . The theories which Religion generates, being thus variable, are secondary; and if you wish to grasp her essence, you must look to the feelings and the conduct as being the most constant element" (*VRE* 397). Most constant, yes, but more important than thought? – that will be challenged by many religious persons.

Assuming that dualistic and monistic mystics do share James's desire for reaching an ecumenical resolution of their dispute and thereby assign a low value to thought, how are they to isolate the common phenomenological core of their respective mystical experiences so that they may then pare off the added thoughts or theological constructions that divide them? James assumes that there is a common phenomenological given that they then conceptualize in different ways in accordance with their various religious traditions. James, however, does not speak with a single voice about the possibility of separating a phenomenological given from the manner in which it gets conceptualized. Quotations can be assembled to show that he came down on both sides of this issue. In his "G. Papini and the Pragmatist Movement in Italy," he first claims that we cannot separate the subjective from the objective factors in the development of truth, but then goes on to say that by studying this development in the past we can see how subjective factors were involved, thereby implying that we *can* separate the subjective contribution that is made by conceptualization from the objectively or phenomenologically given (*EP* 148). But, on the other hand, he says that "what we grasp is always some substitute for it [an independent reality] which previous human thinking has peptonized and cooked for our consumption . . . wherever we find it, it has already been faked" (*P* 119–20); but he then attempts to illustrate this through the use of presented figures, such as star configurations and geometrical shapes, that can be grouped together or interpreted in more than one way, saying that "in all these cases we humanly make an addition to some sensible reality" (*P* 121), which seems to imply that we can distinguish between the objective and subjective factors.

I believe that James's considered position on separating the phenomenologically given from its conceptualization is that, on theoretical grounds, we must postulate such a given – "baby's first sensation" – for otherwise our epistemological wheels would spin idly in a frictionless void, but that in practice we cannot make any absolute discrimination between the two, only a context-relative one. Our assignment of stars to different constellations involves a distinction between a perceptual given, the stars, and our contribution in organizing them into constellations through the use of concepts. But, in another context, that something qualifies as a star will involve an act of selection and construction on our part (which, I assume, is what the lecherous producer had in mind when he promised to make her a star), in ways analogous to that in which we construct different axiomatic systems in mathematics. Thus, within any given context there is a distinction between the phenomenological given and how we conceptualize it, but it is not an absolute distinction. Furthermore, it is very difficult to make this distinction, even within a given context. If this is James's considered position, it entails that in principle we are not able to separate, independently of a given context, what is phenomenologically given in a mystical experience from how the mystic conceptualizes it. But this raises the problem of what context is to be chosen. Is it to be that of the dualistic or monistic mystic or even that of a mystical ecumenicalist like Daisetsu Suzuki, Walter Stace, or Thomas Merton, as opposed to that of a Steven Katz or an R. C. Zaehner? There is no more difficult problem in philosophy than that of separating the phenomenologically given from the way it is conceptualized, and until it is adequately addressed, James's "common denominator" strategy will not amount to much.

Even if it were possible to separate in some non-question-begging way the phenomenological given from the conceptualization or interpretation of it, is it true, as James contends, that there is a common phenomenological content to dualistic and monistic mystical experiences? There are good grounds for doubting that James successfully located such a common phenomenological content. A strong indication that he has it wrong is his claim "that all the phenomena [religious experiences] . . . express the appearance of *exteriority* of the helping power" (*VRE* 400; my italics). The monistic mystic denies that her experience has any subject–object structure and thus that it has an *exterior* accusative. James adds that "The part of the content [of the religious experience] concerning which the question of truth most pertinently arises is the 'MORE of the same quality' with which our own higher self appears in the experience to come into harmonious working relation. Is such a 'more' merely our own notion, or does it really exist?" (*VRE* 401). Again, James is assuming that all mystical experiences, including monistic ones, have a subject–object structure, with the "more" being the intentional accusative. It would seem that James's quest for a common phenomenological core makes a hasty generalization from dualistic mystical experiences but plainly does not fit monistic ones. James's attempt to develop an empirical science of religion that "might sift out from the midst of their [different religions'] discrepancies a common body of doctrine which she might also formulate in terms to which physical science need not object" also shows a complete neglect of monistic mystical experiences and the religions based on them, since it is obvious that the acosmic claims sanctioned by these experiences – that space, time, and multiplicity are unreal – are ones to which science will object (*VRE* 402).

It is fair to conclude that solution (vii) does not adequately neutralize the problem posed by the seemingly incompatible reality-claims of dualistic and monistic mystics. An even more troublesome difficulty with solution (vii) is that it completely fails to solve the general unification problem, leaving James a temporalized schizophrenic Poo-bah: On weekends I'm a mystic and the rest of the time a Promethean pragmatic agent. To unify James's many selves requires metaphysically unifying the many worlds toward which their interests are directed, in particular the mystical world and the practical worlds comprised of a multiplicity of numerically distinct empirical objects in space and time. The practical self is puzzled by the reality-claims of mystics, and not just the extreme acosmic ones that deny in toto the reality of the sensible world. Even those of the backyard mystics that deny the applicability of concepts, any concepts, to reality are perplexing; for, if reality is not as we conceptualize it in our Promethean phases, why is it that our concepts do such a good job in helping us to succeed in our worldly endeavors. This is analogous to the acosmic mystic having to explain why the allegedly illusory sensible world appears so substantial and real. There is the story of the Indian *rashi* who, after completing a lecture on the unreality of the sensible world, is on his way home and has to climb a tree to escape a raging elephant; and, when asked why he did so, as the elephant is unreal, replied that it was only his unreal self escaping from an unreal elephant.

The intelligent reader should have realized all along that I have been playing the tease throughout this book in issuing promissory notes to find a way, on James's behalf, to unify his many worlds and selves, especially the Promethean and mystical ones. I certainly am not going to succeed where all of the great mystical traditions and mystically influenced metaphysicians have miserably failed, for they have been forced to leave it an ultimate mystery as to why there should be any world other than the mystical one. Metaphorical talk about emanations out of the Eternal One, or its overflowing like a fountain to yield a multiplicity of changing objects, is no help. James was in the same basic fix as were these past mystics and mystically inclined metaphysicians. One of our many selves, the mystical one, craves unity, self-containment, and the safety and peace that come from abiding in the present. But our Promethean self is always running ahead of itself into the future, living on the dangerous edge of things, risking failure, and facing its inevitable death. What James's quest to have it all most desires is to be both of these selves *at the same time*. What we really want is to be both a Sartrian *In-Itself* that self-sufficingly abides in its total completeness within the present and a *For-Itself* that is always racing ahead of itself into the future so as to complete itself. In other words, we want to be God. Not surprisingly, this is forever beyond our grasp. To be human is to accept the unresolvable tension between wanting to be both at the same time. The best we can hope for is a taking-turns solution of the first-I'm-this-and-then-I'm-that sort. One does not solve this problem. One can only bear witness to it. And no one has done so with more passion, honesty, and brilliance than William James. No one sang the blues with more soul than did James, with his "Divided-Self Blues" as his perennial chart topper.

Appendix

John Dewey's Naturalization
of William James

In the Introduction it was pointed out that all of the major philosophical movements of the twentieth century had their roots in James's philosophy, a tribute to the richness and originality of his ideas. Many devotees of these various movements, however, could not resist the temptation to coopt James for their own cause by giving anachronistic interpretations of his philosophy that made him look like a card-carrying member of their own pet movement. Most prominent of these self-serving portrayals of James were the naturalistic interpretations, in which all the mystical and spiritual aspects of James's philosophy, which it has been the purpose of this book to bring into bold relief, were neglected. The original and by far most influential of these distorting naturalistic interpreters was John Dewey. This appendix will attempt to counter the naturalistic interpretations of James by attacking them at their source in Dewey's accounts of James's philosophy.

It will come as a shock to many to be told that Dewey gave such self-serving anachronistic interpretations of William James, for if Dewey didn't get James right, who did. After all, he was both James's friend and fellow pragmatist, helping him to man the ramparts against the assaults of those "foreigners" who claimed that anyone who required that ideas have "cash value" was either a pimp, a captain of industry, or both. Furthermore, William James was John Dewey's philosophical hero, because his "biological psychology" of the 1890 *The Principles of Psychology* had led Dewey out of his bondage in the dark land of Hegel and into the sunshine of the wonderful land of naturalism. Dewey attempted to repay his debt by passionately expounding and defending James's philosophy over a period of fifty-one years, extending from 1897 to 1948. While not calling into question the philosophical brilliance of these essays, it will be shown that they gave a blatantly distorted, self-serving account of James's philosophy, the basic aims of which were to despookify and depersonalize it so that it would agree with Dewey's naturalism and socialization of all things distinctively human. Because the intent of my "exposé" of this act of hero worship turned philosophical usurpation is to counter naturalistic interpretations of James, only the former issue will be considered.

"Naturalism" has meant very different things to different philosophers. As my claim is that Dewey attempted to make James into "a good naturalist like himself," it is Dewey's sense that is relevant here. His naturalism comprises two components. First, there is no ontological dualism between the mental and the physical, be it in the form of an irreducible mental/physical substance or a mental/physical event dualism, psychological states and processes being reducible to certain distinctive ways in which an organism interacts with its natural environment. This is called "biological behaviorism" by Dewey and is invidiously contrasted with a "physiological behaviorism" that understands mental phenomena exclusively in terms of physical processes and states *within* the organism. Second, the sciences alone give us knowledge of reality, and they accomplish this by use of an objective common pattern of inquiry. Thus, every kind of individual is a "natural kind" in the sense that its nature is to be determined through scientific inquiry. Although Dewey would abhor this terminology, this in fact is what his scientism is committed to, minus, of course, any kind of fixity of species or nonfallibilist claims to certainty. Each of these two components will now be discussed in turn.

Ontological Naturalism

Dewey's attempt to transform James into an ontological naturalist occurs primarily in his 1940 "The Vanishing Subject in the Psychology of James." Because this essay shifts back and forth between an italicized and unitalicized use of "Psychology," its thesis is ambiguous between the self, and consciousness in general, disappearing from the book *Psychology* (Dewey's abbreviation for *The Principles of Psychology*) and its disappearing from the psychology developed therein (Notice the unitalicized "Psychology" in the essay's title but the italicized use of "Psychology" on pages 156 and 166 of *LW*, vol. 14. All references to Dewey are to this volume, unless noted otherwise.) This distinction is important because numerous metaphysical and epistemological excursions are interspersed with psychology throughout the book, in spite of James's repeated resolutions to the contrary. That Dewey argues for the stronger disappearance-within-the-book thesis, and thus for the self's disappearance from James's philosophy in general, becomes apparent when Dewey appeals for support to James's 1904–5 doctrine of pure experience, which is the centerpiece of James's metaphysics and epistemology. Pace Dewey, it will be argued that the self disappears neither from James's psychology nor from his book *The Principles of Psychology*, nor from his philosophy in general.

Throughout *The Principles of Psychology*, James strictly adheres to the commonsense dualism between conscious experiences and the physical objects and events that are perceived and referred to by these experiences. Dewey claims that James's acceptance of this dualism is merely verbal, a concession that he made for tactical purposes to his opponents – the associationists, rationalists, and automatists – all of whom accepted this dualism. This is not unreasonable, as James's major purpose in *The Principles of Psychology* was to draw together all of the recent work in psychology for the purpose of helping it to attain the status of a legitimate science. To challenge the almost universally accepted mental–physical dualism would have alienated his audience and thus been a self-defeating distraction.

Dewey advances a number of considerations in support of this thesis. First, there is James's subsequent claim in his 1904 "Does 'Consciousness' Exist?" that "For twenty years past I have mistrusted 'consciousness' as an entity." James is referring back to his 1884 "The Function of Cognition," in which the "epistemological gulf" is eliminated "so that the whole truth-relation falls inside of the continuities of concrete experience, and is constituted of particular processes, varying with every object and subject, and susceptible of being described in detail." While there is no explicit denial of the ontological dualism between the mental and the physical, there is a hint at one place of his later doctrine of pure experience when he says that "we believe that we all know and think about and talk about the same world, because *we believe our PERCEPTS are possessed by us in common.*" Herein there is no duplication in consciousness of the outer objects perceived, otherwise two minds could not share one and the same percept. Dewey speculates that if James were to have rewritten *The Principles of Psychology* after 1904, he would have completely dispensed with consciousness as a special sort of entity, be it of a substantial or an eventful sort, and replaced it with a full-blown biological behaviorism.

If Dewey's disappearance thesis were based only on this speculation about how James would have rewritten *The Principles of Psychology*, it would not show that within the book or the psychology developed within it there is any such disappearance, or even doubts about the mental–physical dualism. According to Dewey, the doubts about consciousness were expressed not just subsequently to the book but in the book itself. James had whittled the Self down to the passing Thought – a momentary total stage of consciousness – and, supposedly, he then went on "to express a doubt about the existence of even a separate 'thought' or mental state of any kind as the knower, saying that it might be held that 'the existence of this thinker would be given to us rather as logical postulate than as that direct inner perception of spiritual activity which we naturally believe ourselves to have' " (157). Immediately upon expressing this "doubt," James refers to an "important article" by Souriau in which the existence of consciousness as some sort of aboriginal stuff is denied, which anticipates James's doctrine of pure experience.

Pace Dewey's account, James does not express any doubts of *his own* in *The Principles of Psychology* about the existence of consciousness but merely alludes to a theory that is eliminative of consciousness. Immediately upon his brief exposition of this theory he adds that "Speculations like this traverse common-sense" and he "will therefore treat the last few pages as a parenthetical digression, and from now to the end of the volume revert to the path of common-sense again" (*PP* 291). This is hardly an expression of doubt on James's part. Far from expressing any doubts about consciousness in *The Principles of Psychology*, James, as will be seen, availed himself of every opportunity in the book to take the spooky route.

Fortunately, Dewey has stronger things to say in favor of his disappearance thesis than the false claim that James expressed doubts about consciousness in the book and counterfactual speculations about how James would have rewritten his psychology subsequent to 1904. Of more weight is Dewey's appeal to the overall orientation and tenor of the book, along with the biological-behavioristic approach to certain topics, most notably the Self.

As for general orientation, there is a concerted attempt, no doubt due to James's medical background, to give a biological grounding to psychology that "If it had been consistently developed . . . it would have resulted in a biological behavioristic account of psychological phenomena" (158). Dewey also enlists in support of his behavioral interpretation James's claim that "pursuance of future ends and choice of means for their attainment are the mark and criterion of mentality in a phenomenon" (21). But, as Dewey correctly points out, since this is said to be only "the mark and criterion by which to circumscribe the subject-matter of this work *as far as action enters in*," it allows for psychic phenomena that do not admit of a behavioral analysis (158–9).

The strongest support for the disappearance thesis comes from the way in which James handles specific topics. An important case in point is his account of habits in terms of neural pathways in the brain established by past experiences that allow for subsequent reflex arc type behavior. Discrimination, in turn, is based on habit, a point that James did not sufficiently emphasize. And what is true of discrimination will also hold for attention (as well as the will and belief, since each, for James, is a way of attending). Dewey also cites James's account of interest – the linchpin of his psychology and the basis of his later pragmatism. "Officially he assumes interest to be mentalistic. What he actually says about it is most readily understood in terms of the selection by motor factors in behavior" (160).

James did not treat sensations or impressions as physiological processes, but he should have, as he allowed for them to occur unnoticed (159). (Herein Dewey overlooks James's introduction of secondary selves to whom these sensations are consciously present.) An indication of just how desperate Dewey was to show that sensations really were physiological for James is that he offered on page 160 two allegedly corroborating quotations from *The Principles of Psychology* that in fact do no such thing.

Dewey also appealed to James's example of "Baby's first sensation" in which there is no distinction between the mental and the physical, it being the entire world to the baby, as containing the germ of James's later theory of neutral entities.

> The direct empirical meaning of *neutral* in this connection would seem to be that of indifference to the distinction between subjective and objective, this distinction arising when the proper guidance of behavior requires that we be able to tell whether a given sound or color is a sign of an environing object or of some process within the organism. Unfortunately his later writings seem at times to give the impression that these entities are a kind of stuff out of which both the subjective and objective are made – instead of the distinction being a question of the kind of an object to which a quality is referred. (164)

Herein Dewey is amplifying on his 1907 "The Postulate of Immediate Experience," in which he gave his variant of James's 1904–5 doctrine of pure experience. It is interesting to note that Dewey's denial therein that immediate experience is "any aboriginal stuff out of which things are evolved" is an almost direct quotation from James's claim in "Does Consciousness Exist?" that "I have now to say that there is no *general* stuff of which experience at large is made" (*ERE* 14). James's denial seemingly contradicts his claims in the very same essay that "My thesis is that if we start with the supposition that there is only one primal stuff or material in the world, a stuff of which everything is composed, and if we call that stuff 'pure experience,' then knowing can easily be explained as a particular sort of relation towards one another into which portions of pure experience may enter" (*ERE* 4) and "But thoughts in the concrete are made of the same stuff as things are" (*ERE* 19), as well as his identification of pure experience with "*materia prima*" in "The Place of Affectional Facts in a World of Pure Experience" (*ERE* 69; see also 13 and 46). This characterization of pure experience as a kind of prime matter, no doubt, is what Dewey had in mind when he mockingly said, in a letter to Bentley, that "at times he [James] seems to mix his neutrals with a kind of jelly-like cosmic world-stuff of pure experience" (*PC* 115).

In Chapter 7 it was argued at length that the best the way to neutralize this surface inconsistency, which James himself saw but did not attempt to resolve, is to distinguish between metaphysical and empirical (or scientific) constituents. His prime matter is meant to be a metaphysical constituent of everything, which is consistent with his denial that there are any empirical or scientific entities, such as atoms, of which everything is composed. Running throughout *The Principles of Psychology* is a kind of phenomenological materialism that reduces many psychic phenomena to physical sensations within the body. There is his famed theory of emotions as physiological sensations, and, most noteworthy for Dewey, his phenomenological reduction of the spiritual self, that inner active self from whom fiats and efforts seem to originate, to a collection of intracephalic sensations, and "What is further said about personal identity is consistent with this behavioral interpretation. The appropriations of the passing thought are 'less to itself than to the most intimately felt part of its present Object, the body, and the central adjustments, which accompany the act of thinking, in the head.' " (165–6). But, as T. L. S. Sprigge has perceptively pointed out: "James's phenomenological materialism does not imply that the consciousness of these physical processes is itself a physical process in any ordinary sense. It claims rather that our mode of 'being in the world' is through and through a physical one" (*JB* 76).

It now will be shown that Dewey's attempted ontological naturalizing of James fails to address the overall spookiness of *The Principles of Psychology*, as well as the extreme spookiness of *The Varieties of Religious Experience* and *A Pluralistic Universe*, in regard to both its metaphysics and its treatment of important psychological topics, such as the self and paranormal phenomena. The major causes of this failure are due to a total overlooking of the spooky parts of James's metaphysics and psychology and a failure to appreciate the restrictions James placed upon his materialistic claims. Dewey's ignoring of this spookiness resembles a parent making it a point not to notice a child's unruly behavior, hoping thereby to make it go away. There is some excuse for such omissions in essays that deal with some limited aspect of James's philosophy, such as the 1908 "What Pragmatism Means by Practical" and the 1922 "The Development of American Pragmatism," both of which focus primarily on his pragmatic theory of meaning and truth, but no excuse for the many articles that attempt a broad overview of his philosophy – most notably, the two death notices in 1910, the 1920 China lecture on James, and the two James centennial essays of 1942, "William James and the World Today" and "William James as Empiricist." More specifically, the following will be shown. (i) Far from adopting dualism in name only in *The Principles of Psychology*, he *argues* for its most virulent form, interactionism. (ii) A will-to-believe type of justification is given for believing in contracausal spiritual acts of effort or attention. (iii) Paranormal phenomena, wherein he thought the future of psychology lay, pace Dewey's speculations about how James would have subsequently rewritten his psychology, are given a spiritualistic explanation that laid the foundation for the subsequent enveloping world soul(s) ontology of *The Varieties of Religious Experience* and *A Pluralistic Universe*.

(i) For starters, James presents a protoversion of a conceptually based property-objection argument for the nonidentity of consciousness with any physical going-ons. "Everyone admits the entire incommensurability of feeling as such with material motion as such. 'A motion became a feeling!' – no phrase that our lips can frame is so devoid of apprehensible meaning" (*PP* 149). It looks like he is arguing for the nonidentity of the mental and physical on the basis of their necessarily not having all their properties in common, assuming, as would James, the Indiscernibility of Identicals.

Chapter V, attacking "The Automaton-Theory," is an extended metaphysical defense of an interactionist sort of dualism. The following is an argument for the causal efficaciousness of consciousness based on evolutionary success.

> The study *a posteriori* of the *distribution* of consciousness shows it to be exactly such as we might expect in an organ added for the sake of steering a nervous system grown too complex to regulate itself. The conclusion that it is useful is, after all this, quite justifiable. But, if it is useful, it must be so through its causal efficaciousness, and the automaton-theory must succumb to the theory of common-sense. (*PP* 147)

(ii) Throughout his adult life, James ardently believed in the Libertarian doctrine of free will, replete with its contracausal spiritual efforts. It was this belief that sustained him through his emotional crises by enabling him to lead the morally strenuous life. Dewey completely ignores James's passionate defenses of this doctrine in the chapters on "Attention" and "Will." Instead, he concentrates exclusively on James's phenomenological reduction of the active self to a collection of intracephalic sensations.[1] The cornerstone of his despookification of James is James's claim that

> the "*Self of selves*," when carefully examined, is found to consist mainly of the collection of these peculiar motions in the head or between the head and throat . . . it would follow that our entire feeling of spiritual activity, or what commonly passes by that name, is really a feeling of bodily activities whose exact nature is by most men overlooked. (*PP* 288)

What Dewey fails to realize is that James's identification of the active self with these physical sensations is restricted to phenomenological appearances. At the beginning of his analysis James makes this restriction manifest when he says "*Now*, let us try to settle for ourselves as definitely as we can, just how this central nucleus of the Self may feel,

---

[1] This oversight in his 1940 essay is especially surprising, as in his 1897 "The Psychology of Effort" Dewey recognized that James's account of the will is "spiritual" with respect to moral effort; but, even then, he tries to finesse James into the naturalist camp by pointing out that this ought not to be his considered position because it is inconsistent with James's claim that his sensationalizing of emotions did not detract from their spiritual significance (*EW*, 5:149).

no matter whether it be a spiritual substance or only a delusive word."
There are several other places in *The Principles of Psychology* where James
makes tough-minded claims but restricts them to a certain interest or
perspective (see *PP* 33 and 1179). In the chapter on "The Perception
of Reality," James develops a radically relativized account of reality according to which something is real only in relation to or qua someone's
interest in a certain "world," such as the world of commonsense objects, the theoretical entities of science, fictional realms, Platonic abstracta, and so on. In Chapter 7, James was shown to be a veritable Poo-
bah, the character in the *Mikado* who held all the offices of state and
always spoke qua this or that official, only for James it is qua this interest
or that. It is "qua"-clauses all the way on down until James gets to the
content of mystical experiences, for which unrestricted reality-claims
are made. The problem posed by the clash between Ontological Relativism and the nonrelativized reality-claims of mystics was a major topic
of the previous chapter.

Dewey deliberately overlooked certain passages in *The Principles of Psychology*, primarily in the interconnected chapters on "Attention" and
"Will." To summarize Chapter 2, volition is nothing but attention to
an idea. Belief, in turn, is a state in which an idea fills consciousness
without competitors, with the consequence that, in certain cases, we
can believe at will or voluntarily, as is required by his will-to-believe
doctrine, with its *option* to believe a proposition. For James, all actions
initially are involuntary. In some cases a sensory idea of the motion or
its immediate effects is formed. This creates a neural pathway from the
brain to the concerned motor organ so that now mere consciousness of
this idea causes the action. In the simplest cases, that of the "ideomotor" will, there is no fiat or effort. But human beings quickly become more complex, so that for many ideas they might entertain there
is a competing idea which blocks its motor discharge. Such a case of
conflict sets the stage for an occurrence of an effort to attend to one of
these competing ideas so that it alone will fill consciousness for a sufficient time with sufficient intensity and thereby lead to its motor discharge. This effort to attend is the voluntary will. "*The essential achievement of the will . . . when it is most 'voluntary,' is to ATTEND to a difficult
object and hold it fast before the mind. The so-doing is the fiat*; and it is a
mere physiological incident that when the object is thus attended to,
immediate motor consequences should ensue" (*PP* 1166).

James assumes that it is causally determined both which ideas enter
consciousness and whether an effort is made to attend to one of them
to the exclusion of its competitors. The question of all questions for
James is whether the *amount* of this effort to attend also is causally
determined, our answer determining "the very hinge on which our

picture of the world shall swing from materialism, fatalism, monism, towards spiritualism, freedom, pluralism, – or else the other way" (*PP* 424). The reason is that the amount of this effort, especially in cases in which we try to resist acting in the course of least resistance, can be the decisive factor in determining which idea emerges victorious and thus what action ensues, which, in turn, can have momentous consequences. It is only to "the *effort to attend,* not to the mere attending, that we are seriously tempted to ascribe spontaneous power. We think we can make more of it *if we will;* and the amount which we make does not seem a fixed function of the ideas themselves, as it would necessarily have to be if our effort were an effect and not a spiritual force" (*PP* 426–7).

James characterizes this spiritual force as an "original force" and the "star performer" (*PP* 428). To be an original force, for James, it must be an irreducibly conscious event that is not causally determined. After giving a very fair and forceful exposition of the "effect theory" of the amount of the effort to attend, according to which it is only a causally determined effect of physiological events, he expresses his personal preference for the "cause-theory." "The reader will please observe that I am saying all that can *possibly* be said in favor of the effect-theory, since, inclining as I do myself to the cause-theory, I do not want to undervalue the enemy" (*PP* 424–5). The basis of his preference is "ethical," since "the whole feeling of reality, the whole sting and excitement of our voluntary life, depends on our sense that in it things are *really being decided* from one moment to another, and that it is not the dull rattling off of a chain that was forged innumerable ages ago" (*PP* 429).

James's version of Libertarianism is far superior to that of others, from Aristotle down through Sartre and Chisholm, for he alone gives a detailed, closeup picture of just how free will works. What is distinctive about his version is that the immediate effect of a free volition, the amount of the effort to attend, is the sustaining and intensifying of an idea in consciousness rather than a bodily movement, as in Aristotle's example of the stick moves the stone, the hand moves the stick, and the man moves his hand. There is reason to think that this approach might have these two further advantages over its competitors, which, surprisingly, have not been mentioned by either James or his expositors. First, it avoids troublesome questions about backward causation, for when Aristotle's man freely moves his hand, he brings about *earlier* events along the efferent nerves linking his brain with his hand (By clenching my fist I ripple my forearm muscles.) Second, it gives some hope of escaping a violation of the conservation of angular momentum, since its immediate effect, being the strengthening of an idea in consciousness, does not involve an acceleration, as happens when the man moves his hand.

James sets up a will-to-believe option, as already developed in his 1878 "Some Reflections on the Subjective Method," to justify belief in the reality of such contracausal spiritual acts of attention. Roughly, but very roughly, as Chapter 4 argued, one has such a right or permission to believe when the proposition in question cannot be determined on intellectual or epistemic grounds, and by believing it one helps to bring about some morally or even prudentially desirable state of affairs.

That the amount of these efforts to attend against the course of least resistance, such as in a case of moral temptation, is causally undetermined cannot be epistemically determined, as we cannot make sufficiently fine-grained measurements of brain events to discover whether the effect-theory is true: "The feeling of effort certainly *may* be an inert accompaniment and not the active element which it seems. No measurements are as yet performed (it is safe to say none ever will be performed) which can show that it contributes energy to the result" (*PP* 428). Thus, "The last word of psychology here is ignorance, for the 'forces' engaged are certainly too delicate and numerous to be followed in detail" (*PP* 429).

James writes with great passion about the good that is realized by someone of a similar psychological constitution as himself believing in the cause-theory of the will. Our very sense of our own self-worth as persons and our ability to function as moral agents depend on this belief, since "the effort seems to belong to an altogether different realm, as if it were the substantive thing which we *are*, and those ["our strength and our intelligence, our wealth and even our good luck"] were but externals which we *carry*" (*PP* 1181). James extols the stoical hero who, regardless of external deterrents, can still find life meaningful "by pure inward willingness to take the world with those deterrent objects there" (*PP* 1181): "The world thus finds in the heroic man its worthy match and mate; and the effort which he is able to put forth to hold himself erect and keep his heart unshaken is the direct measure of his worth and function in the game of human life" (*PP* 1181). This sets the stage for the eloquent concluding paragraph of the section on free will.

Thus not only our morality but our religion, so far as the latter is deliberate, depend on the effort which we can make. "*Will you or won't you have it so?*" is the most probing question we are ever asked; we are asked it every hour of the day, and about the largest as well as the smallest, the most theoretical as well as the most practical, things. We answer by *consents or non-consents* and not by words. What wonder that these dumb responses should seem our deepest organ of communication with the nature of things! What wonder if the effort demanded by them be the measure of our worth as men! What wonder if the amount which we accord of it be the one strictly underived and original contribution which we make to the world! (*PP* 1182)

Here is the passionate, existential James, and it is a source of amazement how Dewey could have completely overlooked it in all his many expositions of James's philosophy, and in particular when he claimed that *The Principles of Psychology* was dualistic only in terminology. Whereas the active, inner self, qua phenomenological object, is nothing but cephalic sensations, as Dewey was right to point out, qua metaphysical entity required for being a morally responsible agent, it is a "spiritual force" that is the "substantive thing which we *are*" (*PP* 1181). And which perspective we adopt is to be decided in terms of the moral benefits that accrue.

(iii) Paranormal phenomena consisting of insane delusions, alternating selves, and mediumship are given prominence in *The Principles of Psychology*. In his later works James developed a spiritualistic metaphysical theory to explain these phenomena, along with mystical and conversion experiences. It really is a unifying inference to the best explanation that postulates a mother-sea of consciousness, of which there might be more than one, that is revealed in these exceptional experiences. In the 1898 lecture on "Human Immortality," it is said that, in veridical mediumship, contact is made with conscious states in a

transcendental world, and all that is needed is an abnormal lowering of the brain-threshold to let them through. In cases of conversion, in providential leadings, sudden mental healings, etc., it seems to the subjects themselves of the experience as if a power from without, quite different from the ordinary action of senses or of the sense-led mind, came into their life, as if the latter suddenly opened into that greater life in which it has its source. . . . All such experiences, quite paradoxical and meaningless on the production-theory [according to which consciousness is causally dependent upon brain events], fall very naturally into place on the other theory [that the brain merely is a filter through which consciousness passes and gets focused]. We need only suppose the continuity of our consciousness with a mother-sea, to allow for exceptional waves occasionally pouring over the dam. (*ERP* 93–4)

This mother-sea of consciousness theory becomes dominant in James's most mature work, wherein it is given a panpsychical twist. In the "Conclusions" to *A Pluralistic Universe* he writes:

The drift of all the evidence we have seems to me to sweep us very strongly towards the belief in some form of superhuman life with which we may, unknown to ourselves, be co-conscious. . . . The analogies with ordinary psychology, with certain facts of pathology, with those of psychical research . . . and with those of religious experience establish, when taken together, a decidedly *formidable* probability in favor of a general view of the world almost identical with Fechner's. (*PU* 140)

The same Fechnerian mother-sea(s) theory informs the 1909 "Confidence of a 'Psychical Researcher.' "

We with our lives are like islands in the sea . . . there is a continuum of cosmic consciousness, against which our individuality builds but accidental fences, and into which our several minds plunge as into a mother-sea or reservoir. Our 'normal' consciousness is circumscribed for adaptation to our external earthly environment, but the fence is weak in spots, and fitful influences from beyond leak in, showing the otherwise unverifiable common connexion. Not only psychic research, but metaphysical philosophy and speculative biology are led in their own ways to look with favor on some such 'panpsychic' view of the universe as this. (*EPR* 374)

The Varieties of Religious Experience also appeals to this theory to explain what is revealed by mystical and conversion experiences. James develops a perceptual model of mystical experience according to which, when they are veridical, they are direct apprehensions of this surrounding sea of consciousness. They are "windows through which the mind looks out upon a more extensive and inclusive world" (*VRE* 339). In conversion experiences this subliminal or transmarginal consciousness is a medium through which the divine consciousness in this more extensive and inclusive world salvifically flows into the subject. In general, the religious life shows "That the visible world is part of a more spiritual universe from which it draws its chief significance" (*VRE* 382). It supports

Fechner's theory of successively larger enveloping spheres of conscious life. . . . the tenderer parts of his personal life are continuous with a *more* of the same quality which is operative in the universe outside of him and which he can keep in working touch with, and in a fashion get on board of and save himself. . . . we inhabit an invisible spiritual environment from which help comes, our soul being mysteriously one with a larger soul whose instruments we are. (*PU* 139)

It is very difficult, to the point of being impossible, to treat the mother-sea of consciousness and our variegated experiences of it as neutral experiences – as neither physical nor mental *simpliciter,* counting as one or the other only when placed in a series of surrounding experiences, a mental series, unlike a physical one, being one in which the content of the successive experiences are not nomically connectable. It is for this reason that Dewey's beloved neutrals of James's 1904–5 essays have become the spiritual denizens of a panpsychical pluralistic universe. Even in these essays there are hints of panpsychism, as for example, when he deals with the problem posed by unperceived future events. His way out of the difficulty seems to go the panpsychic route, because he says of them that "If not a future experience of our own or a present one of our neighbor, it must be . . . an experience *for* itself," thereby imputing an inner consciousness to every physical event (*ERE* 43). Viewed in its historical setting, the phenomenological neutrals of 1904–5, although apparently materialism-friendly, really are a Trojan horse gift, for, unbeknownst to Dewey and his cohorts, it is only veridical *sense* perceptions that qualify as ontologically neutral, and not the motley crew of religious and paranormal experiences that James, in his extreme radical empiricism, also counted as cognitive. This was argued for at length in Chapters 7, 9, and 10.

Not only does Dewey overlook all of the spookiness of the post-1890 writings, he even overlooks their presence in *The Principles of Psychology* itself. Everything within the James corpus makes an appearance in this book, even the theories of the mother-sea of consciousness and the brain as a filter through which this flows. James asks what "more" the soul is than just a succession of Thoughts. His reply: "For my own part I confess that the moment I become metaphysical and try to define the more, I find the notion of some sort of an *anima mundi* thinking in all of us to be a more promising hypothesis, in spite of all its difficulties, than that of a lot of absolutely individual souls" (*PP* 328). This "anima mundi," which becomes Fechner's mother-sea of consciousness in his later writings, is implicitly appealed to when he says that "The perfect object of belief would be a God or 'Soul of the World,' represented both optimistically and moralistically . . . and withal so definitely conceived as to show why our phenomenal experiences should be sent to us by Him in just the very way in which they come" (*PP* 944–5). The filtration theory is hinted at by his remarks that

The brain is an instrument of possibilities, but of no certainties. But the consciousness, with its own ends present to it, and knowing also well which possibilities lead thereto and which away, will, if endowed with causal efficacy, reinforce the favorable possibilities and repress the unfavorable or indifferent ones. The nerve-currents, coursing through the cells and fibres, must in this case be supposed strengthened by the fact of their awakening one consciousness and dampened by awakening another. (*PP* 144–5)

Methodological Naturalism. Throughout *The Principles of Psychology,* James employs a dual method for investigating a psychic phenomenon: one based on a introspective "analysis" of what it is like to experience it; the other, the "historical" method, a third-person-based description of its publicly observable causes.

There are, as we know, two ways of studying every psychic state. First, the way of analysis. What does it consist in? What is its inner nature? Of what sort of mind-stuff is it composed? Second, the way of history. What are its conditions of production, and its connection with other facts? (*PP* 913)

Although Dewey praises James's introspective analyses as an advancement beyond those given by the rationalists and empiricists because it alone recognizes relations as given, he downplays its centrality and wishes that James would completely jettison it in favor of the "outer" causal approach, as is required by Dewey's methodological naturalism.

An example of Dewey's underestimating the importance of introspection to James is the remark in his 1920 China lecture on Bergson, that whereas Bergson assigned a major role to introspection, James did not (*MW* 12:221). Another example is Dewey's claim that "The work of James replaces a dialectic analysis of experience with one based upon scientific knowledge," which omits mention of James's reliance on introspection. One of the tricks Dewey used to downplay James's reliance on introspection was to convert his introspective analyses into something else, a good example of which is Dewey's construal of James's analysis of connections in the 1942 "William James and the World Today." When Dewey wrote this he was preoccupied with the challenge to democracy posed by totalitarianism to show how a society can be both unified and yet contain genuine individuals. Dewey found a solution in James's "each-form" analysis in *A Pluralistic Universe* – that immediately conjoined neighbors, be it in space or time, interpenetrate and melt into each other, but without losing their own identity, as is seen by the fact that this melting or fusing relation is not transitive. (If you don't understand this, then you understand it, as it is a mystical doctrine.) These "confluence" relations can unify a society, because even if two persons are not directly connected by such a relation they are indirectly connected by a chain of such relations (*LW* 15:5–6). Dewey's deployment of James's each-form analysis, though brilliant in its own right, fails to note that James's analysis, in spite of his use of the metaphor of a "federal republic" for his pluralistic world (*PU* 145), was not a political but a phenomenological one. It is an attempt to improve on *The Principles of Psychology*'s specious present phenomenological description of our experience of change, according to which each pulse of sensory experience has a temporally extended content of *distinct* successive events, with a Bergsonian analysis that fuses them into a cotton-candyish glop.

Because Dewey held that philosophical theories ultimately were sociopolitical in origin and intent, he might have believed that he was well within his rights to politicize James's phenomenological description of the flow of experience. In his 1904 graduation address at the University of Vermont, he said:

> It is today generally recognized that systems of philosophy however abstract in conception and technical exposition lie, after all, much nearer the heart of social, and of national, life than superficially appears. . . . philosophy is a language in which the deepest social problems and aspirations of a given time and a given people are expressed in intellectual and impersonal symbols. (*MW* 3: 73)

Dewey's metaphilosophical thesis faces a counterexample in James's Bergsonian account of change. Dewey, after correctly pointing out that Bergson's "intuition" of the "durée" is a form of mysticism, accounts for this mystical strain in terms of Bergson being a Jew from Alexandria, a crossroads for mystical cultures (*MW* 12:227). But James's description of change is, according to James himself, identical with Bergson's, and thus every bit as mystical. Are we to infer that James was Jewish and reared in an area that is a fleshpot of mysticism! James's rival sentiment-of-rationality metaphilosophical thesis, that one's philosophy is an expression of psychological predilections, seems far more in agreement with the empirical facts. The mystical mind-set knows no sociopolitical boundaries.

Rather than being a fifth wheel, introspection is accorded pride of place in James's existentially oriented philosophy. Even before James came out explicitly for panpsychism in his final years, there was a desperate effort, such as is found in many of the essays in the 1897 *The Will to Believe,* and especially in "On a Certain Blindness in Human Beings," to penetrate to the inner life of everything. This was expounded upon at length in Chapter 9. Whereas Dewey viewed the other person primarily as a coworker in a cooperative venture to realize some shared goal, James wanted to "I–Thou" this person, in fact the universe at large. In *A Pluralistic Universe* he even speaks of penetrating by an act of "intuitive sympathy" (*PU* 117) to "the inner life of the flux" (*PU* 110), to "the inner nature of reality" – "what really *makes it go*" (*PU* 112). This book is a plea for a philosophy of "intimacy" according to which "The inner life of things must be substantially akin anyhow to the tenderer parts of man's nature . . ." (*PU* 19).

How does this quest to penetrate to the inner life of things pertain to James's attachment to introspection? The use of it does not per se commit one to a mental–physical dualism, no less to panpsychism; recall James's phenomenological materialism about the active self and the emotions in this regard. However, if one already believed that everything had an inner conscious life that gave value and meaning to its existence, as did James, then precedence would be given to the introspective method. For through its use we can discover in our own case what it is like to enjoy or be some quality or thing, which then can be projected onto others via an act of "intuitive sympathy," sometimes buttressed, as it was for James, by a Cartesian type of analogical argument. The great attraction of introspective analysis for James was that it afforded him a way of preventing the bifurcation of man and nature, his ultimate enemy because it strips the world of any human meaning or value, as was shown in Chapter 8.

These existential themes clearly emerge in James's treatment of the identity of the self over time, another part of James that Dewey totally ignores. His analysis, as seen in Chapter 8, is exclusively introspective, thereby assuring that our concept of what we are will have the required intimacy, given that what we are, our nature, is tied to our identity conditions. It is given exclusively in terms of first-person criteria – states of consciousness that are introspectively available to the subject. This approach fits his antibifurcationist demand because it is based on what is important to us as emotional and active beings. It is just such considerations of importance that form the underlying leitmotiv of James's analysis of the Self.

This "inner" approach to understanding the identity of persons contrasts with the "outer" objective approach that treats persons as what could be called, in a somewhat extended sense of the term, a "natural kind," meaning a type of object whose nature is to be determined through natural science. It was suggested that Dewey's scientism places him squarely within the natural-kind camp. These contrasting approaches are at the foundation of the split in twentieth-century philosophy between so-called Continental and analytic philosophy. They also form the basis of James's contrast between the tough- and the tender-minded presented in *Pragmatism* (13). The traits listed under "The Tender-Minded," for the most part, are those which assure an unbifurcated world and are vouchsafed through the inner approach, as contrasted with those listed under "The Tough-Minded," which represent the natural scientist's temper of mind, with its scientisitic natural-kind approach to understanding the nature of persons and their world.

James's analysis is patterned after Locke's and holds that successive Thoughts are copersonal, just in case the later one "appropriates," that is, judges, the former to be its own on the basis of its having a special sort of warmth and intimacy. While James alludes in a couple of places to third-person criteria that could challenge or defeat a judgment of self-identity over time based on these sorts of apparent memories, the only defeater he seems to recognize is the existence of a better or equally good claimant, someone else whose apparent memories are more or just as rich and coherent and also match some real-life person's past. James's version of a memory theory of personal endurance treats persons as non-natural kinds, since it includes no causal requirement for memory. "The same brain may subserve many conscious selves, either alternate or coexisting" (*PP* 379), thus permitting persons to switch bodies à la Locke's prince and cobbler. This is the single most important feature of his analysis and sharply distinguishes it from natural-kind memory theories that treat memory as a causal process ultimately to be understood by natural science.

James's chapter on "Memory" is placed six chapters later than the one in which he gives an introspective analysis of personal endurance. He follows his usual pattern of first giving an introspective analysis, followed by a historical or causal one. After repeating his introspective analysis from the earlier chapter, he goes on to present a straightforward neurophysiological analysis of the causes of memory.

Whatever accidental cue may turn this tendency [to recall] into an actuality, the permanent *ground* of the tendency itself lies in the organized neural paths by which the cue calls up the experience . . . the condition which makes it possible at all . . . is . . . the brain-paths which *associate* the experience with the occasion and cue of recall. (*PP* 616)

One would think that this physicalist, natural-kind account of memory would supply third-person criteria for defeating introspectively based memory claims and the claims of personal endurance they carry. Such claims could be defeated by showing that the right sort of physical process does not connect the apparent memory with the past event. But James never places any causal requirement on memory. The turkey is on the table and all carved. All he has to do is sit down and eat. But he doesn't, thus following the non-natural-kind approach to the nature of the Self.

Concluding Thought. It is reported that in 1905 James and Dewey sat over a Ouija board together.[2] If the general thesis of this discussion is correct – that Dewey's philosophy is naturalistic all the way on down and James's spooky all the way on up – then Dewey must have had a big smirk on his face while the sweat of earnest conviction was pouring off James's.

[2] Mary V. Dearborn (*LPL* 95).

Bibliography of Works Cited

Works by James

All works by James, except for his letters, are contained in *The Works of William James*, edited by Frederick H. Burkhardt, Fredson Bowers, and Ignas Skrupskelis (Cambridge, MA: Harvard University Press, 1975–88). The original publication date appears in parentheses. These volumes will be referred to in the text and footnotes by the abbreviations listed below. Quotations are unaltered unless otherwise noted.

PP: The Principles of Psychology, 1981 (1890)
PBC: Psychology: Briefer Course, 1984 (1892)
WB: The Will to Believe and Other Popular Essays in Philosophy, 1979 (1897)
TT: Talks to Teachers on Psychology, and to Students on Some of Life's Ideals, 1983 (1899)
VRE: The Varieties of Religious Experience, 1985 (1902)
P: Pragmatism 1975 (1907)
MT: The Meaning of Truth, 1975 (1909)
PU: A Pluralistic Universe, 1977 (1909)
SPP: Some Problems of Philosophy, 1979 (1911)
ERE: Essays in Radical Empiricism, 1976 (1912)
EP: Essays in Philosophy, 1978
ERM: Essays in Religion and Morality, 1982
EPS: Essays in Psychology, 1983
EPR: Essays in Psychical Research, 1986
ECR: Essays, Comments, and Reviews, 1987
MEN: Manuscript Essays and Notes, 1988
ML: Manuscript Lectures, 1988
CWJ: The Correspondence of William James, Vols. 1–4. Edited by Ignas Skrupskelis and Elizabeth Berkeley. Charlottesville: University Press of Virginia, 1992
LWJ: The Letters of William James. Edited by Henry James. 2 vols. Boston: Atlantic Monthly Press, 1920

Works by Others

In text and footnotes, works are referred to by abbreviations in parentheses.

Aiken, Henry D. "American Pragmatism Reconsidered: II. William James." *Commentary* 34 (April 1962): 238–46 (APR).

Allen, Gay Wilson. *William James* (*WJ*). New York: Viking Press, 1967.

Ayer, Alfred J. *The Origins of Pragmatism* (*OP*). San Francisco: Cooper & Co., 1968.

Barrett, William. *The Illusion of Technique* (*IT*). Garden City, NY: Anchor Press, 1978.

Barzun, Jacques. *A Stroll with William James* (*SWJ*). New York: Harper & Row, Publishers, 1983.

Bird, Graham. *William James* (*WJ*). London: Routledge & Kegan Paul, 1986.

Bjork, Daniel W. *The Compromised Scientist: William James in the Development of American Psychology* (*CS*). New York: Columbia University Press, 1983.

Brent, Joseph. *Charles Sanders Peirce: A Life* (*CSP*). Bloomington: Indiana University Press, 1993.

Buber, Martin. *I and Thou* (*I&T*). Translated by Walter Kaufmann. New York: Charles Scribner's Sons, 1970.

Bush, Wendell T. "William James and Panpsychism." In *Studies in the History of Ideas*, vol. 2. New York: Columbia University Press, 1925. (WJ)

Clifford, William K. "The Ethics of Belief." In *Lectures and Essays*, vol. 2. London: Macmillan, 1879. (*LE*)

Conant, James. "The James/Royce Dispute and the Development of James's 'Solution.'" In *The Cambridge Companion to William James*, edited by Ruth Anna Putnam. Cambridge: Cambridge University Press, 1997. (*JR*)

Cotkin, George. *William James, Public Philosopher* (*WJ*). Baltimore: The Johns Hopkins University Press, 1990.

Coughlan, Neil. *Young John Dewey* (*YD*). Chicago: University of Chicago Press, 1973.

Davis, Stephen T. "Wishful Thinking and 'The Will to Believe.'" *Transactions of the Charles Sanders Peirce Society* 8 (1972): 230–45. (WT)

Dearborn, Mary V. *Love in the Promised Land* (*LPL*). New York: Free Press, 1988.

Dewey, John. *The Early Works of John Dewey* (*EW*). Edited by Jo Ann Boydston. 5 vols. Carbondale: Southern Illinois University Press, 1969–72.

The Middle Works of John Dewey (*MW*). Edited by Jo Ann Boydston. 15 vols. Carbondale: Southern Illinois University Press, 1976–83.

The Later Works of John Dewey (*LW*). Edited by Jo Ann Boydston. 17 vols. Carbondale: Southern Illinois University Press, 1981–90. [*EW*, *MW*, and *LW* will abbreviate, respectively, Early, Middle, and Later Works and will be followed by the volume and page number.]

Dewey, John, and Bentley, Arthur F. *A Philosophical Correspondence, 1932–1951* (*PC*). Edited by Sidney Ratner and Jules Altman. New Brunswick, NJ: Rutgers University Press, 1964.

Dore, G. L. "William James and the Ethics of Belief," *Philosophy* 58 (1983): 353–64. (EB)

Edie, James M. *William James and Phenomenology* (*WJP*). Bloomington: Indiana University Press, 1987.

Eisendrath, Craig. *The Unifying Moment: The Psychological Philosophy of William James and Alfred North Whitehead* (*UM*). Cambridge, MA: Harvard University Press, 1971.

Feinstein, Howard M. *Becoming William James* (*BWJ*). Ithaca, NY: Cornell University Press, 1984.

Flanagan, Owen. "Consciousness as a Pragmatist Views It." In *The Cambridge Companion to William James*, edited by Ruth Anna Putnam. Cambridge: Cambridge University Press, 1997. (CP)

Flower, Elizabeth, and Murphey, Murray G. *A History of American Philosophy.* 2 vols. (*AP*). New York: G. P. Putnam's Sons, 1977.

Fontinell, Eugene. *Self, God, and Immortality: A Jamesian Investigation* (*SGI*). Philadelphia: Temple University Press, 1986.

Ford, Peter Marcus. *William James's Philosophy: A New Perspective* (*WJ*). Amherst: The University of Massachusetts Press, 1982.

Gardner, Martin. *The Why of a Philosophical Scrivener* (*PS*). New York: Quilly, 1983.

"William James and Mrs. Piper." *Free Inquiry*, spring/summer 1992. (JP)

Gavin, William Joseph. *William James and the Reinstatement of the Vague* (*WJ*). Philadelphia: Temple University Press, 1992.

Giuffrida, Robert, and Madden, Edward H. "James on Meaning and Significance." *Transactions of the Charles Sanders Peirce Society* 11 (1975). 18–36. (JMS)

Gurwitsch, Aron. "William James's Theory of 'Transitive Parts' of the Stream of Consciousness." *Philosophy and Phenomenological Research* 3 (1942–3): 449–74. (WJ)

Hampshire, Stuart N. *Modern Writers and Other Essays* (*MW*). New York: Knopf, 1970.

Hare, Peter H., and Madden, Edward H. *Causing, Perceiving and Believing* (*CPB*). Dordrecht: D. Reidel Publishing Co., 1975.

Kallen, Horace M. *The Philosophy of William James* (*ML*). New York: The Modern Library, 1925.

Kuklick, Bruce. *The Rise of American Philosophy* (*RAP*). New Haven, CT: Yale University Press, 1977.

Josiah Royce: An Intellectual Biography (*JR*). Indianapolis: Hackett Publishing Co., 1985.

Levinson, Henry S. *The Religious Investigations of William James* (*RI*). Chapel Hill: The University of North Carolina Press, 1981.

Lewis, Clarence I. *Collected Papers of Clarence Irving Lewis* (*CP*). Edited by John Goheen and John Mothershead, Jr. Stanford, CA: Stanford University Press, 1970.

Lovejoy, Arthur O. *The Thirteen Pragmatisms and Other Essays* (*TP*). Baltimore: The Johns Hopkins Press, 1963.

Lowe, Victor. "William James and Whitehead's Doctrine of Prehensions." *Journal of Philosophy* 38 (1941): 113–26. (WJ)

Matthiessen, F. O. *The James Family* (*JF*). New York: Knopf, 1947.
    American Renaissance (*AR*). London: Oxford University Press, 1941.

McDermott, John J. *Streams of Experience: Reflections on the History and Philosophy of American Culture* (*SE*). Amherst: The University of Massachusetts Press, 1986.

Miller, Dickenson. *Philosophical Analysis and Human Welfare* (*PA*). Dordrecht: D. Reidel Publishing Co., 1975.

Moore, Asher. "The Promised Land." *Monist* 57 (1973): 176–90. (PL)

Moore, G. E. "Professor James' 'Pragmatism.' " *Proceedings of the Aristotelian Society*, n.s. 8 (1907–8): 33–77. (PJ)

Morris, Charles. *The Pragmatic Movement in American Philosophy* (*PM*). New York: George Braziller, 1970.

Murphy, Arthur E. "Pragmatism and the Context of Rationality, Parts I and II." *Transactions of the Charles Sanders Peirce Society* 29, nos. 2 and 3, respectively. (PCR)

Muyskens, James L. "James's Defense of a Believing Attitude in Religion." *Transactions of the Charles Sanders Peirce Society* 10, no. 1 (1974): 44–54. (JD)

Myers, Gerald E. *William James: His Thought and Life* (*WJ*). New Haven, CT: Yale University Press, 1986.

O'Connell, Robert J. *William James on the Courage to Believe* (*WJ*). New York: Fordham University Press, 1984.

Otto, Max. "On a Certain Blindness in William James." *Ethics* 53 (1943): 184–91. (CB)

Peirce, Charles Sanders. *Collected Papers of Charles Sanders Peirce* (*CP*). 6 vols. Cambridge: The Belknap Press of Harvard University Press, 1934. [References will give the volume number first and then the paragraph number within that volume.]

Perkins, Moreland. "Notes on the Pragmatic Theory of Truth." *Journal of Philosophy* 49 (1952): 573–87. (NP)

Perry, Ralph Barton. "Conceptions and Misconceptions of Consciousness." *Psychological Review* 11 (1904): 282–96. (CMC)
    The Thought and Character of William James: Briefer Version. (*TC*). Cambridge, MA: Harvard University Press, 1948.

Putnam, Hilary. "The Permanence of William James." *Bulletin of the American Academy of Arts and Sciences* 46, no. 3 (1992): 17–31. (WJ)

Words and Life (*WL*). Edited by James Conant. Cambridge, MA: Harvard University Press, 1994.

Putnam, Ruth Anna. "Some of Life's Ideals." In *The Cambridge Companion to William James*, edited by Ruth Anna Putnam. Cambridge: Cambridge University Press, 1997. (LI)

—— ed. *The Cambridge Companion to William James* (*CC*). Cambridge: Cambridge University Press, 1997.

Reck, Andrew J. *William James* (*WJ*). Bloomington: Indiana University Press, 1967.

—— "The Philosophical Psychology of William James." *Southern Journal of Philosophy* 9 (1971). (PP)

Rorty, Richard. *Consequences of Pragmatism* (*CP*). Minneapolis: University of Minnesota Press, 1982.

—— *Objectivity, Relativism, and Truth* (*ORT*). Cambridge: Cambridge University Press, 1991.

—— "Religious Faith, Intellectual Responsibility, and Romance." In *The Cambridge Companion to William James*, edited by Ruth Anna Putnam. Cambridge: Cambridge University Press, 1997. (RF)

Roth, John K. *Freedom and the Moral Life: The Ethics of William James* (*EJ*). Philadelphia: Westminster Press, 1969.

Russell, Bertrand. "Transatlantic 'Truth.' " *Albany Review* 2 (1908): 393–410. (TT). Reprinted in *William James' Pragmatism in Focus*, edited by Doris Olin. London: Routledge, 1992. [References are to this volume.]

—— "The Philosophy of Logical Atomism." *Monist* 28–9 (1918–9). (PLA)

—— "Professor Dewey's 'Essays in Experimental Logic.' " *Journal of Philosophy, Psychology, and Scientific Method* 16 (1919): 5–26. (PD).

—— *Mysticism and Logic* (*ML*). Garden City, NY: Doubleday Anchor Books, 1957.

Santayana, George. *Persons and Places* (*PP*). Cambridge, MA: MIT Press, 1986.

Scheffler, Israel. *Four Pragmatists* (*FP*). New York: Humanities Press, 1974.

Schneider, Herbert W. *A History of American Philosophy*. 2nd ed. (*AP*). New York: Columbia University Press, 1963.

Schuetz, Alfred. "William James's Concept of the Stream of Consciousness." *Philosophy and Phenomenological Research* 1 (1940–1): 442–52. (JSC)

Seigfried, Charlene Haddock. *Chaos and Context* (*CC*). Athens: Ohio University Press, 1978.

—— *William James's Radical Reconstruction of Philosophy* (*WJ*). Albany: State University of New York Press, 1990.

Simon, Linda, ed. *William James Remembered* (*JR*). Lincoln: University of Nebraska Press, 1996.

Skrupskelis, Ignas K. "James's Conception of Psychology as a Natural Science." *History of the Human Sciences* 8 (1995): 73–89. (J)

Sprigge, T. L. S. *James and Bradley: American Truth and British Reality* (*JB*). Chicago: Open Court, 1993.

Suckiel, Ellen Kappy. *The Pragmatic Philosophy of William James* (*PP*). Notre Dame, IN: University of Notre Dame Press, 1982.

    Heaven's Champion: William James's Philosophy of Religion (*HC*). Notre Dame, IN: University of Notre Dame Press, 1996.

Taylor, Eugene. *William James on Consciousness Beyond the Fringe* (*WJ*). Princeton, NJ: Princeton University Press, 1996.

Taylor, Eugene, and Wozniak, Robert H., eds. *Pure Experience: The Responses to William James* (*PE*). Bristol, Eng.: Thoemmes Press, 1996.

Thayer, H. S. "On William James on Truth." *Transactions of the Charles Sanders Peirce Society* 13 (1977): 3–19. (JT)

Townsend, Kim. *Manhood at Harvard: William James and Others* (*MH*). New York: W. W. Norton & Co., 1996.

Wernham, James C. S. "Did James Have an Ethics of Belief?" *Canadian Journal of Philosophy* 6 (1976): 287–97. (EB)

    James's Will-to-Believe Doctrine: A Heretical View (*WB*). Kingston and Montreal: McGill-Queen's University Press, 1987.

Wild, John. *The Radical Empiricism of William James* (*RE*). Garden City, NY: Doubleday, 1969.

Wittgenstein, Ludwig. *The Blue and Brown Books* (*BBB*). Oxford: Blackwell, 1958.

Index

Note

James's specific philosophical and psychological doctrines will be listed under the appropriate topical heading. Thus, his views on introspection, for example, will be listed under the heading of "introspection." "WJ" will abbreviate "William James."

conceptualism, 42
consciousness: filter theory of, 345; as
  nonphysical, 341
Cotkin, George, 1
Croce, Paul, 258

Darrow, Clarence, 158
Davidson, Thomas, 7
Davis, Nancy, 110
Davis, Stephen, 96
Darwin, Charles: biological psychology of,
  9–10, 32, 158, 289; evolutionary theory
  of, 9
deconstructionism, 20, 155; and the sociopolitical aim of philosophy, 348
Descartes, René, 36, 83, 85, 130, 133,
  167, 227
determinism, 74–5, 78–82, 196, 308; definition of, 78–80; implications of, 78–84;
  see also Libertarian theory of freedom,
  epistemic undecidability of
Dewey, John, 1, 21, 22, 26, 33, 127, 128,
  134, 135, 136, 138, 140, 155, 176,192,
  206, 220, 243, 250, 289, 307; and the
  naturalization of WJ, 28, 102, 165, 176,
  336–51
dilemma of determinism, 78–84, 189, 308;
  see also Libertarian theory of freedom
dispositions, 159; causal, 159–62, 169–70;
  normative, 159–62, 169–70
Donnellan, Keith, 173
Dore, G. L., 107
doxastic practices, 263, 265, 326
Ducasse, C. J., 99, 280
Duhem, Pierre, 145
Dummett, Michael,137

Eckhardt, Meister, 253
Eddington, Arthur, 79
Edie, James, 9
education: theory of, 250
Edwards, Paul, 80
Eisendrath, Craig, 15, 286
Eliot, Charles W., 17, 158
Emerson, Ralph Waldo, 40, 165, 222, 249,
  306
emotion, 340
empiricism, 153–4; WJ's commitment to,
  31, 131–3, 138, 144–5, 150, 152, 228,
  241
epiphenomenalism, 280–1, 309
Essays in Radical Empiricism, 200, 321
ethics, 51, 85, 96, 117, 119–20, 122, 150;
  causal theory of, 97, 111; deontological,
  10, 15, 18, 36–7, 39, 44–5, 48–9, 105,
  248, 345; and existentialism, 41–4; intu-
  itionist theory of, 26–8, 40–1, 43, 50;
  and the morally strenuous life, 40–1, 82;
  naturalistic basis of, 10, 32; and the

ought–is distinction, 30–2; Platonic theory of, 27–8, 31; utilitarian theory of,
  26, 32, 34–5, 37–8, 94, 97, 119, 136,
  315; WJ's maximizing theory of, 10, 25,
  27, 32–3, 35–41, 44–6, 48–9, 116–17,
  186, 197, 315
Eucharist, 181
evidence, 177, 268
evil, 80, 257; theodicy for, 82–4, 189; WJ's
  ambiguous attitude toward, 16–18, 80,
  257–8
experience, 54; identified with reality,
  169, 183; as subject to the act-content
  distinction, 302

fact, 138, 140
fallibilism, 145–6, 248, 259
Fechner, Gustav, 229, 269, 346, 347
Feinstein, Howard, 1
fictional entities, 197, 259, 327
first- and twice-born, 256, 257; see also
  healthy and sick soul
Flanagan, Owen, 207, 260
Flower, Elizabeth, 76–7, 103
Fontinell, Eugene, 7, 165, 270, 286
Ford, Marcus Peter, 99, 270, 285–6
Frege, Gottlob, 29, 233; on sense and ref-
  erence, 171
functionalism, 20, 242

Gardiner, Martin, 77, 127, 131
Gavin, William, 170, 207–8
genuine option, 98–100; see also will to be-
  lieve
Giuffrida, Robert, 156, 163, 181
Gizycki, Georg von, 196
gnosticism, 82–3, 136, 151, 185
God, 103, 160, 178, 189–90, 263, 269,
  303, 312, 313; as ideal social self, 41, 44;
  as infinite desirer, 36, 42; as omniscient,
  41–2, 143; omni-properties of, 180–1; as
  providential, 91–2; as unpredictable,
  215, 263, 267
Goodman, Nelson, 192, 224
Greek tradition, 151
Green, Thomas H., 33
Grote, John, 168
Gunn, Giles, 99
Gurwitsch, Aron, 204
Gutting, Gary, 262

habit, 159, 250, 338
Hampshire, Stuart, 221
Hand, Learned, 20
Hare, Peter, 214, 296
healthy and sick soul, 3, 17, 253, 257–9
Hebraic tradition, 151
Hegel, G. W. F., 3–4, 285, 286, 289, 294,
  298, 335